UNIVERSITY OF LONDON AND THE
WORLD OF LEARNING, 1836-1986

THE UNIVERSITY OF LONDON
AND THE WORLD OF LEARNING
1836-1986

EDITED BY

F.M.L. THOMPSON

THE HAMBLEDON PRESS
LONDON   AND   RONCEVERTE

Published by The Hambledon Press, 1990

102 Gloucester Avenue, London NW1 8HX (U.K.)

309 Greenbrier Avenue, Ronceverte WV 24970 (U.S.A.)

ISBN 1 85285 032 9

British Library Cataloguing in Publication Data

The University of London and the world of learning,
    1836-1986
    1. London, Universities: University of London, history
    I. Thompson, F.M.L. (Francis Michael Longstreth)
    378.421

Library of Congress Cataloging-in-Publication Data

The University of London and the world of learning 1836-1986/
    edited by F.M.L. Thompson
    Includes index.
    1. University of London – History.
    I. Thompson, F.M.L. (Francis Michael Longstreth)
    LF411.U55   1990
378.421′2 – dc20   90-47682
                                                                    CIP

This book is published with the assistance of grants from the
Twenty-Seven Foundation and the Isobel Thornley Bequest.

Printed on acid free-paper and bound in
Great Britain by Biddles Ltd., Guildford.

Contents

List of Illustrations

Between pages 4 and 5

1. William Wilkins, The London University: unfinished scheme (1827).

2. T. Roger Smith, University College: design for the completion of the Gower Street entrance (1895).

3. Sir William Chambers and Sir Robert Smirke, King's College, Somerset House river frontage (1829-35).

4. Sir James Penethorne, University Offices, Great Burlington Street (1867-70). Now the Museum of Mankind. Headquarters of London University, 1870-1900.

5. Charles Holden, The Senate House (1933-38).

6. C.C.T. Doll (?), design for a University of London on the present Senate House site (1912).

7. Sir Albert Richardson, scheme for extending Somerset House as a new University of London (1914).

8. Sir Albert Richardson, projected scheme for University of London, Bloomsbury (1926).

9. Sir Edwin Lutyens, project for a University of London, Bloomsbury (1914).

10. T.E. Colcutt, The Imperial Institute, South Kensington (1887-93; demolished, except for the tower). Headquarters of London University, 1900-36.

11. W.H. Crossland, The Royal Holloway College, Egham, Surrey (1879-87). Now Royal Holloway and Bedford New College.

12. Capt. G.S.C. Swinton (1859-1937). Lyon King of Arms; Chairman of the L.C.C.

13. Charles Holden (1875-1960), Architect of the Senate House.

14. Sir Ernest Graham-Little (1868-1950). M.P. for London University, 1924-50.

15. Sir William Beveridge, later Lord Beveridge (1879-1963). Vice-Chancellor, 1926-28.

Between pages 100-1

Introduction

F.M.L. Thompson

'Two figures have long haunted attempts to describe the University of London: the taxi-driver and the foreigner. The one can rarely identify where it is and the other can never understand what it is.' Negley Harte, *The University of London, 1836-1986: An Illustrated History* (1986), p. 12

Members of the University frequently have similar problems. It is only on grand ceremonial occasions, the graduation days and the conferments of honorary degrees, that the University is made visibly aware of its own existence; and the number actively participating in these rituals cannot be more than a tiny fraction of the whole body of teachers and students. For most of them their world of learning is bounded by their individual College or Institute, and the University remains a remote, unknown, nebulous, and vaguely threatening entity, little more than the source of red tape, mountains of largely incomprehensible paper, and unpleasant financial decrees. On the grandest ceremonial occasion in a lifetime, the commemoration of the sesquicentennial of the granting of the University of London's first Charter, the University came to life as a united community with an impressive if somewhat short-lived display of its identity as an outstanding and unique element in the intellectual life of the nation. That sense of identity rests on the common purposes shared by the many separate institutions and thousands of individuals who make up the federal University, and derives from the history which they have helped to make. A major part of this sesquicentennial era of good feelings in 'university consciousness' was expressed in Negley Harte's book. His history of the University explains how the various institutions have come to be what they are and where they are, and is thus, on top of its merits as a distinguished contribution to the history of universities, the ideal guide for bookish taxi-drivers and inquisitive foreigners.

At the time of the 1986 commemoration a different, and complementary, approach was made in a series of lectures, to explain to a wider public and to the University itself what the University does, and has done. In short an attempt was made to answer the question, what is the University of London for, by examining its contributions to learning, to scholarship, letters, science, and knowledge. These lectures used the faculty structure of the University to furnish the framework of a thematic appraisal of the contribution of London to the different branches of knowledge since 1836. The institutional setting for this academic activity was evoked in a lecture on the architecture of the University; and the strikingly pioneering role of London in the higher education of women was also given special attention. Revised and edited, but not revised to take into account the many changes in London and in the universities generally since 1986, these lectures form the basis of the collection of essays in this volume.

Many people, from philosophers to politicians, in many different times and countries, have reflected or pronounced on the purposes of a university. Their thoughts have ranged from the pursuit of knowledge, through the provision of a liberal education, to the creation of wealth through the production of skilled graduates. These essays seek to construct a statement about the purpose of the University of London not by abstract speculation or by derivation from any political theory or dogma, but by the sound empirical method of building up the record, block by block, of what has in fact been done in teaching and research since the foundation of the University. This might seem to define the purpose of the University by taking refuge in a tautology: the object of the exercise is to do whatever has been done in the past. That in itself is no mean or inconsiderable thing, for the preservation and transmission of so fragile and arduously accumulated a possession as the general body of knowledge, derived from the learning and understanding of earlier generations, is clearly one of the prime tasks of each succeeding generation of scholars. Each generation, however, in building upon the works of its forerunners redefines the subject matter, turns its curiosity in new directions, and changes the boundaries of knowledge.

The whole concept of human knowledge, its limits and its proper spheres, had been changing and expanding in Europe at least since the fifteenth century, and measured against that time scale the University of London arrived rather late on the stage: an after-thought of the Enlightenment, yet a forerunner of rational liberalism. Before the 1830s, however, most of the new developments had taken place outside the formal structure of universities, which had a powerful institutional conservatism that tended to give a bleak reception to intellectual innovations. Moreover, the really great explosions in scientific enquiry and discovery then still lay ahead, and London was to play a prominent part in the reorganisation of the branches of knowledge as they subdivided and multiplied, calling out for systematic classification and arrangement so that teaching could be well-ordered, and further advances in defined disciplines made possible. Since from 1836 to 1900 the University was purely an examining and degree-awarding body the main initiatives in mapping out new branches of knowledge necessarily happened in the separate teaching colleges. Nevertheless, the University controlled the examination system, and the examination syllabus was an important instrument for translating new knowledge into formal qualifications, and these in turn exerted a strong influence on the ways in which the colleges arranged their teaching.

This mechanism of a separation of powers between teaching and examining was to be a perennial source of friction between the colleges and the University, and at times, including the present, some colleges have doubted whether there is any need to have a University at all. Arguably the friction has been more a source of well-considered and constructive contributions to the framework of knowledge than a source of obfuscation, obstruction, and frustration of the forces of change. Teachers have frequently felt that their lack of control of syllabus and examination has frustrated innovation and stultified intellectual vitality by confining their courses in a rigid, traditional, and outmoded strait jacket of rules and regulations determined by a remote abstraction called 'the University'. Small groups of teachers, left to their own devices and unrestrained by any direct responsibility to a larger peer group, on the other hand, have an understandable tendency to cosy definitions of their subject in terms of what they happen to know and what happens to interest them, without such rigorous attention to the requirements of a balanced and sufficient academic diet as might satisfy a scholarly jury. The London solution to this problem of the tension between teachers, and what is to be taught and researched, has not been unchanging; nor has it been an unqualified success. That solution, in brief, has taken three forms: between 1836 and 1900 the University in the shape of a government-nominated Senate prescribed through examination syllabuses the necessary contents of its degrees; from 1900 to 1966 the teachers in effect took over this function, exercising subject-autonomy within a federal system by legislating for a single University degree in each subject through teacher-controlled Boards of Studies; since 1966 centralised control of the contents and standards of degrees has been relaxed, and largely abandoned, with each college enjoying the power to construct and administer its own degrees, although not formally to award them. In practice only a very few subjects have maintained their allegiance to the single federal degree, persuaded that it continues to provide the only structure capable of mobilising the potential of the great range of specialised expertise that is spread through the separate colleges of the University.

These arrangements have not been conducive to impetuous innovation or rash experiment. Yet the government-nominated Senate was far from old-fashioned when it prescribed, in the 1830s, what amounted to the first, and to date only, national curriculum for higher education. Classics, mathematics, and natural philosophy were, to be sure, tried and true staples of universities everywhere from time immemorial; but when the Senate added to those three a compulsory fourth degree paper in one of chemistry, botany, or zoology, it promoted to the status of subjects proper to a university education matters which were unheard of in Oxford and Cambridge and only just heard of in the Scottish universities which provided much of the initial inspiration for London. That London was setting the pace in university education in the country, in the range of subjects to be studied and the standards expected, may be inferred from the grumbles and complaints about the intolerable burden of novel and unreasonable demands which poured in to the Senate from various teaching institutions. That London began life as it meant to go on, with cautious innovation and not radical ventures into unknown academic territory, can be seen from the fact that Science did not figure as a separate Faculty in the trio with which London's degrees were launched.

The choice of the original three Faculties, Arts, Laws, and Medicine, was all the same distinctive, even radical, for its time. The omission of Theology (or Divinity) was as striking as it was inevitable, given the godless origins of University College London. Divinity was the mainspring and mainstay of scholastic life in the older universities, and it was intended that it should be so in the new University of Durham, created as an Anglican, collegiate, counterweight to London. The absence of divinity from the menu in London was a declaration of intellecutal independence and a signal that, even though religion might be studied and separately examined in an individual college such as King's, in London university education and university degrees were free to develop outside the clerical tradition. It was not simply that London was the university for Dissenters, although it was indeed that; it was much more that the way in which knowledge was defined, pursued, and communicated was detached from questions of faith and dogma, and left open to the interplay of reason and utility. These may not be better taskmasters, but they allowed greater scope for bringing the workings of human curiosity and the discoveries of the intellect within the ambit of the university. For the first twenty years of the University's life these developments had to be made to fit into the institutional framework of three respectably traditional Faculties. Arts was a catch-all designation for a great range of subjects, and the Faculty in which the great majority of students took their bachelor's degrees. Laws and Medicine were equally venerable as Faculties, and were present in the older universities from the high middle ages. That presence, however, was largely nominal and decorative. London could rightly claim to be 'the first University in this country which conferred degrees in Laws after and as a result of adequate examinations'.[1] The medical schools of Oxford and Cambridge, having shown some signs of vigour in the seventeenth century, sank into torpor

---

[1] Report of the University of London Commissioners, 1899, quoted by N. Harte, *The University of London, 1836-1986* (1986), p. 173.

and insignificance in the eighteenth, requiring no serious demonstration of medical knowledge or skill for the award of their degrees. The establishment of the Faculty in London, with its insistence on proper examinations, was therefore a fresh departure for medical education in England, and a critically important step towards giving London a medical school that could rival Edinburgh and eventually surpass it.

Advances in knowledge and the creation of new subjects for systematic enquiry and study were the work of individual thought, experiment, and discovery. Some advances led up intellectual blind alleys, and few would now maintain that craniology or phrenology, so fashionable and exciting to many Victorians, are fit subjects for university degrees. Other advances led towards a more permanent reorganisation and restructuring of knowledge. Much of the codification of these developments and the consolidation of new ideas and new methods into modes of thought and bodies of knowledge that were teachable, transmittable, and hence examinable, took place inside the Faculty framework and resulted in the multiplication and sub-division of discrete subjects or disciplines which are recounted in several of the chapters in this volume.

At the grandest level, the restructuring of knowledge was accompanied by a restructuring of the Faculty system itself. In this London set the pace. It remained reasonably abreast of the ideas of the best thinkers of the times, given an inevitable institutional and constitutional time-lag behind the most radical and innovative individual proposals, and ahead of other learned institutions. The decisive step was the creation of a separate Faculty of Science in 1858, in response to a memorial addressed to the University by the leading scientists of the day, and said to have been drafted by T.H. Huxley who was at the Government School of Mines at the time. 'The branches of human knowledge at present academically recognised are those of Arts, Theology, Law, and Medicine', the memorial stated, which was true of universities in general but not of London itself, which had no Theology. It went on to argue the case for a fifth branch of knowledge, which 'has gradually grown up, and being unrecognised as a whole, has become dismembered; some fragments consisting of mathematics and such branches of physics as are capable of mathematical treatment, attaching themselves to Arts; others, such as comparative anatomy, physiology, and botany, clinging to Medicine, amidst whose professors they took their rise'. The memorial showed that subjects such as electricity, magnetism, organic chemistry, geology, or palaeontology had been non-existent fifty or a hundred years previously, but had become central to endeavours to discover and understand the laws governing natural phenomena and to practical applications designed to improve material conditions. The conclusion that it was absurd to continue to insist on a tolerable acquaintance with classical literature before allowing a chemist or physicist to take a degree was accepted by the University in establishing the new degrees of Bachelor of Science and

Doctor of Science, which were first examined in 1860.[2]

This was the decisive step in turning the concept of a university from a community of scholars where everyone studied everything (for vocational subjects like law and medicine were not regarded as proper exceptions to this universality) into an institution where the whole range of human knowledge was on offer, but no individual attempted to master all of it. The gains in understanding, expertise, and new discoveries which flowed from increasing specialisation and the departmentalisation of knowledge undoubtedly outweighed the losses of collegiality, fraternity, and the all-round intelligence of the fully-educated person, but as academic disciplines went their separate ways the sense of belonging to a university migrated from the lecture room and examination hall to the sportsfield. With Science established as a separate degree specialisation led rapidly to the proliferation and definition of different sciences: biology, for example, was separated from chemistry in 1863, and in turn split into botany and zoology in 1866. London, in these developments, was leading the field in Britain, but was very largely itself following the example of academic structures pioneered in France and Germany. From the 1860s onwards London has had the flexibility, and the drive, to stay in the forefront in recognising and formalising new branches of science in the wake of the discovery and naming of new territories, such as those of genetics (the legitimate descendant of U.C.L.'s seductive and unreliable eugenics) or biochemistry in the early part of the twentieth century, and more recently crystallography or microbiology.

If London was the leading institution in Britain in drawing the academic map of the pure sciences, it was in a class of its own as the world leader in making engineering into a university subject. That was without benefit of a separate Faculty of Engineering, which was not established until after the 1898 Act which transformed the University from a purely examining body into a federal teaching institution. From the start U.C.L., with some interruptions, and King's, with greater continuity and distinction, had Chairs of Engineering, filled by eminent practitioners who pursued careers moving easily to and fro between spells of teaching and bouts of building railways or bridges. They were more than a generation ahead of Cambridge, which set up a chair of mechanism and engineering in 1875; Oxford lagged further behind still.[3] Moreover, the teaching of engineering required practical experience and the machines, equipment, and laboratories with which to acquire it. Engineering was thus the pioneer subject in introducing the apparatus and techniques of laboratory-based teaching into universities, an example quickly followed in London by the experimental sciences. This was an innovation of

[2] Quoted by Harte, *University of London*, pp. 109-10.
[3] Michael Sanderson, *The Universities and British Industry, 1850-1970* (1972), p. 43.

incalculable importance for the whole style, content, and effectiveness of university teaching, and it also served to bring advanced research out of private laboratories and workshops and into the university. Alas, some of the Victorian engineering equipment was so well-built and durable that it lasted far into the twentieth century, and thus bears some of the responsibility for the conservatism and technological backwardness of post-1945 British industry, to the extent that it was staffed with engineers trained literally in the Victorian mould.

It may be that the University as a whole, the teaching institutions as well as the examining and degree-giving centre, suffered from the disadvantages of an early start, and that what had initially been pioneering and exciting became uninspiring and deadening routine. Several of the chapters in this volume tell a tale of initial vitality followed by a period in the doldrums in the middle reaches of the century, with signs of renewed intellectual vitality from the 1890s. A pattern consisting of a springtime of high promise, half a century of patchy achievement, dissatisfaction, and internal wrangling, and then at last sustained growth in the twentieth century in quality, diversity, reputation, and numbers, would, after all, conform neatly with the constitutional history of the University. That is a history in which the years 1900, marking the establishment of the federal university, 1929 for the introduction of the structure of government that still survives beneath layers of later modifications, and 1981 when the University first acquired a full-time Vice-Chancellor and the process of restructuring, adminspeak for wholesale early retirements and amazing mergers of colleges, began, stand out as turning points and re-births just as prominently as 1836, the foundation year.

The neatness of such an interpretation is, however, illusory and derives from giving too much attention to the institutional arrangements, which were undoubtedly increasingly unsatisfactory during the second half of the nineteenth century as the friction between the teaching colleges and the examining University, whose examiners were all drawn from outside London, increased. For many contemporaries that was an irrelevance which did not affect the quality of the education which could be obtained in the colleges, nor detract from the fact that it was very good value for money in comparison with any university education on offer elsewhere in England (Scotland remaining at least as good and cheap). Thus in 1852 Charles Kingsley's advice for an eighteen-year old was

At King's College [London] he would get for forty pounds a year a far better education than he will have either at Oxford or Cambridge . . . I am convinced that *regular* education is the only thing to save a young genius from a thousand mistakes & buffets in the hard battle of life . . . Pray keep him from Australia – for ten years at least. Why is he to go & become a savage? When the gold fever is over & the land has reorganised itself, then let him, & everyone else who can, go & civilize the great young nation . . .[4]

Cardinal Newman was a witness of a different kind. He thoroughly disapproved of London University as a breeding ground of liberalism and irreligion, but when he told Cardinal Manning in 1873 that the University is 'a body which has been the beginning, and source, and symbol of all the Liberalism existing in the educated classes for the last forty years', he was, many would think, lavishing praise of a high order on the quality no less than the efficiency of the university education provided by London.[5]

To give London University sole credit for the dominant intellectual climate of the mid-Victorian decades was to exaggerate greatly its capacity to reach and influence the influential classes. Yet to make such a statement at all, even for polemical purposes, suggests that the University was a significant feature in the contemporary landscape of ideas, a force to be reckoned with in the formation of educated opinion, a much more active enterprise than the image of sloth implies. The activity which especially annoyed Newman was in the natural sciences, where biology, zoology, geology, and botany nurtured the evolutionary challenge to religious dogmas. The activities in these years before 1900 which made the most important contribution to society, however, were the theologically uncontroversial exploits of the several branches of engineering, where the innovations and practical utility of London's work probably exceeded the sum of all that was achieved in the great civic universities of Liverpool, Manchester, Leeds, Sheffield, and Birmingham which were established, with strong technical elements, at this period.[6] It was, indeed, largely in the Arts, in literature, history, languages, and philosophy, that London was feeble and anaemic during the fallow period before the 1900 reorganisation, registering a failure to live up to the initial promise of eminence in these fields chiefly because the prestige of Oxford and Cambridge, once they had abolished their religious tests, drew off the best of London's students who formed the habit of migrating to complete their degrees there.

This weakness, insofar as it also stemmed from the division between examining and teaching authorities in London, was not without compensating benefits. London degrees and London examinations were open to those who chose to enter, regardless of place of residence, and after 1858 candidates did not need to belong to insititutions specially recognised for this purpose. The Victorian civic universities, before they received charters in the 1880s giving them independent degree-giving

---

[4] Charles Kingsley to [Charles De la Pryne], 21 June 1852: Catalogue of MS Autograph letters, Michael Silverman, London, 1990.

[5] C.S. Dessain, ed., *Letters and Diaries of John Henry Newman*, XXVI (1974), p. 373.

[6] Sanderson, *Universities and British Industry*, pp. 106-18.

powers, took degrees of London University; smaller provincial colleges at Nottingham, Southampton, Reading, and Exeter continued to do so until well into the twentieth century. London regulations required all degree candidates to take some subjects in literature and classics, and hence all these non-metropolitan colleges were obliged to provide some teaching in the humanities, often reluctantly and against the inclinations of local leaders and benefactors. This, it has been argued, was a powerful factor in ensuring that these colleges grew into independent multidisciplinary universities and did not become technical high schools on the German model, or colleges of technology, separated from the mainstream of the British university system.[7] Maybe this was a mixed blessing. The hard school of philistine utilitarians regards the comparative absence of strong, single-purpose, schools of technology from the British higher education system as a source of economic weakness, and might wish to lay some of the blame for Britain's post-Victorian industrial decline at the door of London, for its part in diverting provincial institutions away from undivided concentration on practical skills by insisting on the retention of some traces, at least, of a classical and liberal education. Others would argue that British culture, society, and science were greatly enriched by the fact that a binary line dividing higher education into two spheres was not drawn in the 1880s or 1890s, when the university side would have been very small and the technology side would have become overwhelmingly large, but rather was only drawn in the 1960s, by which time a firm basis of multidisciplinary universities had been established throughout the country and the future of the university style of higher education, alongside other styles, seemed to be assured. The more farsighted of the businessmen who were putting up the funds for local colleges recognised that universities should be places where all subjects should be studied, and they did not expect or insist upon immediate practical returns for their money in the shape of useful discoveries or trained technicians. The dividends were sometimes taken in the form of civic pride and prestige, sometimes more philosophically in the form of satisfaction in the creation of scholarly communities which encouraged curiosity-driven research and the pursuit of knowledge; either way the availability of the London institutional and degree framework assisted the process.

Easily the most outstanding activity of the University during the second half of the nineteenth century, however, and the most constructive use of its examining and degree-giving powers, was in the service of higher education for women. Here, the lead given by London was at least as important to the whole of British society, and to the advancement of scholarship and the teaching profession, as the initial introduction of completely new academic subjects in the 1830s had been. It can be

[7] Ibid., pp. 105, 119.

maintained that the issue of proper secondary education for girls, let alone higher education for women, did not begin to attract serious attention from progressive circles until the 1840s and 1850s. Then, with the foundation of Queen's College in Harley Street (1848), the Ladies' College in Bedford Square (1849), and the North London Collegiate School (1850), all in London, and the Ladies' College in Cheltenham (1853), the early efforts were concentrated on providing decent secondary schooling for girls: for Bedford College, as it became, started out by catering for girls from the age of twelve, and did not move decisively into the university level until the 1870s. Within this timescale both the University and its colleges moved remarkably quickly in admitting women to full and equal participation in university education, including what seemed at the time the delicate and indecorous subject of medicine. During the 1860s and 1870s it seemed to the champions of women's education that the defenders of male privilege were using every trick in the book to frustrate them. The University deemed that its powers to confer degrees on 'all classes and denominations . . . without any distinction whatsoever' did not extend to females; in a famous case the Senate in 1862 decided by a single vote that Elizabeth Garrett was debarred by her sex from entering the London examinations, and she was forced to obtain her medical qualifications by the back door through the Society of Apothecaries; and in 1867 the University attempted to prolong segregation by instituting a separate but more or less equal matriculation and certificate of higher proficiency for women. Meanwhile University College was practising the same tactic of separate but more or less equal treatment in the teaching sphere, allowing women in literally by a special back door to separate lectures on English literature, physics, chemistry, and sound, from the late 1860s; gradually, subject by subject, these became mixed classes, starting with political economy and fine art in 1871, until by 1877 practically all the teaching was coeducational. King's, on the other hand, stuck to the separatist route with resolution, starting missionary lectures for the ladies of Richmond and Twickenham in 1871, and founding a separate 'Ladies' Department' in Kensington in 1885; not until 1915 were women welcomed inside the college itself in the Strand.[8]

Such delaying tactics were irritating. But when, in 1878, the University admitted women to all its examinations on equal terms, when the first four female graduates in Britain received their degrees in 1880, and when University College offered almost fully coeducational university teaching from 1878 (not entirely, since its Faculty of Medicine held out against women until 1917), London was pioneering a major reform and doing so after a much shorter period of debate, advocacy, and agitation than most other major reforms have required. The rest of the universities followed

---

[8] N.B. Harte, *The Admission of Women to University College London: A Centenary Lecture* (1979), esp. pp. 9-16, 20.

London's lead: Cambridge allowed women to take its examinations from 1881, Oxford from 1884, but women were not permitted to take the degrees themselves and become full members of the universities until 1920 in Oxford and 1948 in Cambridge. The separate women's colleges – Newnham and Girton in Cambridge (1871 and 1873), Somerville and Lady Margaret Hall in Oxford (both 1879), for example, as well as those in London, Bedford (1849), Westfield (1882), and Royal Holloway (1886) – are usually given pride of place in the history of higher education for women. Integrated, coeducational, university education, of the type pioneered in Britain by University College, was, however, the model eventually adopted by all British universities. Already in 1878 University College had nearly 300 women undergraduates, and in the 1890s around one-third of its total student body of 1,000 or so were women. At a time when student numbers at the women's colleges, both in Oxbridge and in London, were minute, this meant that University College was far and away the most important institution in the country providing higher education for women.[9]

It should be said that by the 1890s all the universities and young university colleges in Britain were broadly agreed on the character and contents of a university education and, to a somewhat lesser extent, on the importance of original research in the life and work of a professional scholar. The fellows of Oxford and Cambridge colleges on the whole took the view that their commitment did not extend beyond tutorial teaching, and that research was a matter for professors who were not permitted to teach undergraduates. But in the main, universities shared a common pattern of academic subjects, disciplinary organisation, degrees, and examinations, although there were obviously great differences in the means of delivering higher education, principally those between the residential collegiate and the non-residential unitary institutional forms, a spectrum in which London itself figured as a hybrid half-breed. The existence of this area of common ground, and its delineation, owed a great deal to the way in which London had acted as pioneer and pace-setter. That had been so not only over the admission of women, not only in the great restructuring of the academic map of knowledge in science and engineering, but also in the extraordinary innovations within the Faculty of Arts in the 1830s which, in the face of scepticism and derision from traditionalists elsewhere, staked out English literature and foreign languages and literatures, for the first time anywhere in Britain, as proper subjects for study at university. All this, by the 1890s, had become

[9] Harte, *Admission of Women*, p. 21; Negley Harte and John North, *The World of University College London, 1828-1978* (1978), p. 201. See also Janet Howarth and Mark Curthoys, 'The Political Economy of Women's Higher Education in Late Nineteenth and Early Twentieth-Century Britain,' *Historical Research*, 60 (1987), pp. 208-31, which finds little space for University College London.

incorporated into the common perception of the idea of a university, along with the newer idea of honours, or single-subject, degrees in which Oxford and Cambridge were making the running from the 1880s.

After the 1890s the scope for innovation on the grand scale, by London or by any other single university, was limited. When the University was reborn in 1900 as an institution combining, to a great extent, the functions of teaching and examining, its equipment with a full quiver of eight Faculties broke no new ground in general, although in terms of London's own history the acceptance of a Faculty of Theology was a momentous step in healing old controversies and in signalling that the radical institution had become part of the educational establishment. The earlier elevation of one of the eight, Music, to Faculty status in 1877 had not been particularly novel or controversial, although the London degree, with its requirement for general cultural education and not simply technical proficiency, was a good deal more demanding and rigorous than the easy-going and perfunctory degrees in Music available virtually on demand from Oxford and Cambridge. Besides Theology the other newcomers in 1900 were Engineering and Economics and Political Science. Both subjects had long been taught in the colleges before achieving this degree of independent academic identity, and indeed in mid-Victorian Britain political economy was only kept alive as a university subject by the professors at King's and University Colleges. From its foundation in 1895 the London School of Economics quickly rose to dominate the social sciences in London, and to national and international renown. It was L.S.E. students, under London's new 1900 structure, who became the first economics graduates in the country, a few years ahead of the first graduates in economics, and commerce, from Cambridge and Birmingham, the only other universities with comparable resources in the subject.

It is true that the Faculty structure of the University was not completed until Education acquired its independent status in 1966. This, however, was not so much a latter-day refinement in the organisation of knowledge into its component branches as a recognition of the importance of the transmission of knowledge, and of a national drive to enhance the professional status of teachers. London's concern with teacher-training and with providing diplomas or certificates of postgraduate qualifications in education dated back to the 1870s, and the London Day Training College, which evolved into the University's Institute of Education, had been established in 1902. The transition from certificates to degrees was made in response to professional rather than intellectual arguments: the movement to make teaching into an all-graduate profession, and the boost given by the Robbins Report in 1963 to the establishment of new B.Ed. degrees. London moved quickly to institute such degrees, and to invent the new Faculty which was needed to award them.

With that partial exception, twentieth-century academic developments have taken place within a settled Faculty framework. That framework was sometimes found irksome or obstructive in the multi-subject Faculties, Arts and Science, in which Faculty Boards attempted to promulgate general rules applicable to all subjects within their bailiwicks, until they were abolished in 1966. The other Faculties, being substantially single-subject or single-discipline operations, were denied such fruitful opportunities for constitutional conflict and struggles for academic power. In practice these institutional arrangements and bureaucratic difficulties made no noticeable difference to the ability of London to generate new subjects and remain in the lead in intellectual innovation. Thus, aeronautics was first launched as a subject of academic study in London, in the 1900s, as was biochemical engineering some fifty years later, and both of these were bred within the single-discpline Faculty of Engineering; but London's pioneering role in phonetics in the 1920s or linguistics a generation later was no less notable, and these were hatched within the multi-disciplinary Faculty of Arts. The decisive factor was the presence of outstanding and imaginative scholars, pressing on the frontiers of knowledge and able to mark out new fields of inquiry, not the fine detail of the institutional arrangements.

Where institutional arrangements did thrust London into a unique role in the spreading of higher education in the twentieth century they were those deriving from its origins as a purely examining body. The original Charter of 1836 established the general availablity of University of London degrees, subject to the requirement that candidates had to present a certificate of study at an approved institution (the infant University of Durham being the first, highly embarrassed, beneficiary of such approval). In 1858 this requirement was dropped, and London degrees became universally available, and were taken by students in Mauritius, Gibraltar, Canada, and Australia, as well as by those in the colleges in Liverpool and Manchester, in the 1860s; and by many who prepared themselves by individual study. After 1900 this accessibility was preserved by instituting the External Degree system, with syallabuses similar to but not always precisely the same as those of the Internal degrees taken by the colleges of the federal University. External degrees were much in demand by both private individuals and non-university institutions, and provided a route to degree qualifications which had no competitors until the 1960s. After the Second World War a refinement of the External degree system was devised, under which colleges that entered into 'special relationship' with London were able to take part in framing their own syllabuses and conducting their degree examinations while the University of London retained responsibility for standards. This arrangement steered many colonial university colleges through their apprentice years, before becoming independent universities; in Khartoum, the West Indies, Ibadan, Ghana, Makerere, Harare (Salisbury), Nairobi, and Dar-es-Salaam. The same special relationship was invoked by university colleges at home, which before 1946 would simply have entered their students for London External degrees: the future Universities of Southampton, Hull, Exeter, and Leicester in this way followed the path earlier marked out by the Victorian civic universities. The first English provincial university which did not start its life under the shade of the University of London was, indeed, the University College of North Staffordshire, founded in 1949, which became the University of Keele in 1962.

London's mission to help people England and the empire with university institutions came to an end in the 1960s with the decline of empire and the rise of a new breed of new universities at home, starting with Sussex, which were launched without any London connections. At much the same time the era that had started in 1858, during which London provided the sole chance for individuals to get degrees without attending any university, also came to an end, with the creation of the Council for National Academic Awards to validate degree courses outside the university sector, and the development of the Open University bringing distance learning into the home. The availability of these alternative routes to degrees caused London to think seriously, in the 1970s, of dismantling its External system altogether. In the event, although the system was run down for a while and overseas examination centres were closed, the surviving demand, especially from individuals who continue to prepare themselves by private study or who prefer the nature and standing of London degrees to other models on offer, has proved so substantial that External degrees are still provided in many subjects and External students still form nearly one-third of the total London student body on its widest definition.[10]

In these several ways the University of London has been the mother, or perhaps the midwife, of universities throughout the world, and has provided degrees of high standing for large numbers of people who have studied independently. Its children, it may be said, have inherited the academic and scholarly standards and habits of their mother, but not her institutional characteristics: the federal University has not bred a flock of federalists. The duties and responsibilities of midwifery are great, for life depends on the skill with which they are performed. Many University teachers and administrators devoted a great deal of time and thought to the successful running of these schemes, and although it may not have seemed that this use of their energies produced any immediate and direct results in the advancement of learning and knowledge, it is abundantly clear that it did make a major contribution to the dissemination of knowledge and the spread of higher education. It was, indeed, easily the largest contribution made at any time before the new universities of the late 1960s.

[10] *University of London Calendar, 1989-90* (1989), p. 263.

In the same way the scholars, from many different disciplines, who have contributed the chapters which follow have been diverted, for a while, from their own particular research interests. In doing so it may well be that they have not been engaged in advancing the frontiers of knowledge. But they have made a significant contribution to extending the body of work telling us what universities are for, what academics do, why the world of learning is arranged as it is, and how the University of London has influenced these things. In the course of its one hundred and fifty years the University has often been in turmoil, rarely in repose, its institutional structure has usually seemed bizarre, bewildering to insider and outsider alike, and it has appeared to lurch from crisis to crisis, punctuated by Royal Commissions and enquiries almost without number. As it speeds towards what some regard as the terminal crisis of the 1990s, it is well to be reminded that this, like its predecessors, is essentially an institutional problem, not a problem of academic quality or achievement. The record of intellectual achievement, scarcely more than sketched in this volume, is impressive by world standards, and it is a record of what has been done within the much criticised framework of the federal University, maybe in spite of it, maybe because of it, maybe because gifted individuals have got on with doing whatever they felt capable of doing. A goose which has laid such golden eggs is something to be treasured.

The University of London: An Outline Chronology

1826   Foundation of the 'University of London' [University College London] as a proprietory company

1828   'University of London' opened, in Gower Street

1829   Foundation of King's College, London, with a charter

1831   King's College, London opened, in the Strand

1836   University of London established by charter, with rooms in Somerset House. Separate charter granted to University College London
University organised in Faculties of Arts, Laws, and Medicine

1849   Opening of The Ladies' College in Bedford Square, the future Bedford College for Women

1850   University of London supplemental charter enabling institutions throughout British Empire to be recognised for purpose of entering candidates for London degrees

1853   University moved from Somerset House to rooms in Marlborough House

1856   University moved to rooms in Burlington House

1858   University of London's third charter, establishing Faculty of Science, and making London degrees open to all-comers without requiring institutional education

1867   University of London supplemental charter enabling Certificates of Higher Proficiency to be granted to women

1870   University moved into its own purpose-built premises in Burlington Gardens

1877   Creation of Faculty of Music

1878   University of London supplemental charter, enabling degrees to be granted to women

1880   First four female graduates awarded their degrees

1882   Foundation of Westfield College

1886   Opening of Royal Holloway College

1888   Royal Commission on the University of London (the Selborne Commission)

1892-3   Royal Commission on the University of London (the Cowper Commission)

1895   Foundation of the London School of Economics

1898   University of London Act, establishing a 'teaching university' of a federal character

1900   University moved from Burlington Gardens to the Imperial Institute, Kensington.
         Creation of Faculties of Economics, Engineering, and Theology

1900   The 'teaching university' started, with Internal degrees for the constituent Schools, and External degrees for those studying elsewhere. The original Schools were King's College, University College London, Bedford College, Royal Holloway College, the Royal College of Science, the South Eastern Agricultural College at Wye, the Central Technical College, the London School of Economics, and the ten metropolitan medical schools

1902   Westfield College became a School of the University

1905   The London School of Tropical Medicine became a School of the University

1907   The East London College (from 1934 Queen Mary College) became a School of the University

1907-8   Creation of Imperial College of Science and Technology, by amalgamation of the Royal School of Mines, the Royal College of Science, and the Central Technical College. Imperial College became a School of the University

1910   The London Day Training College (from 1932 the Institute of Education) became a School of the University, within the Faculty of Arts (Pedagogy only)

1909-13 Royal Commision on the University of London (the Haldane Commission)

1915   School of Slavonic Studies established in King's College. In 1932 it became the independent School of Slavonic and East European Studies

1917   School of Oriental Studies (later the School of Oriental and African Studies) established

1920   Birkbeck College became a School of the University

1921   Foundation of the Institute of Historical Research

1924-6   Departmental Committee on the University of London (the Hilton Young Committee)

1925   The School of Pharmacy (founded 1842) became a School of the

University

1926   University of London Act: commissioners appointed to make new statutes, which created the Court, with control of the University's property, funds, investments, and finances

1927   Bloomsbury site acquired from the Duke of Bedford

1932   Courtauld Institute of Art established

1936   Senate House building partly finished, central offices of the University moved from the Imperial Institute

1937   Institute of Archaeology founded

1944   Warburg Institute joined the University
        Royal Veterinary College became a School of the University

1945   The British Postgraduate Medical Federation became a School of the University

1947   Institute of Advanced Legal Studies founded

1949   Institute of Commonwealth Studies founded

1950   Institute of Germanic Studies founded

1953   Institute of Classical Studies founded

1963   Robbins Report on Higher Education, included call for University of London to reform itself or have reform imposed upon it

1965   Institutes of United States Studies, and Latin American Studies, founded

1966   Committee [of the University] on Academic Organization (the Saunders Committee); proposals enabled individual colleges to establish 'School-based' degree syllabuses
        Chelsea Polytechnic became Chelsea College and a School of the University
        Faculty of Education created

1972   Committee on the Governance of the University (the Murray Committee)

1978   University of London Act: creation of a full-time Vice-Chancellor and an enlarged Senate

1980   Flowers Report on the reorganisation of medical schools. Committee [external] on Academic Organization (the Swinnerton-Dyer Committee)

1985   Bedford College merged with Royal Holloway College, as Royal Holloway and Bedford New College
        Chelsea College and Queen Elizabeth College merged with King's College

1989   Westfield College merged with Queen Mary College, as Queen Mary and Westfield College

List of Contributors

Harold BILLETT. Emeritus Professor, University of London. Professor of Mechnical Engineering, University College London, 1965-80. Acting Provost of U.C.L., 1978-79. Hon. Fellow, Royal Corps of Naval Constructors.

Sir Hermann BONDI, K.C.B., F.R.S. Master of Churchill College, Cambridge, since 1983. Professor of Mathematics, King's College, London, 1954-83. His publications include *Cosmology* (1952); *The Universe at Large* (1961); *Relativity and Commonsense* (1964); *Assumption and Myth in Physical Theory* (1968); and (jointly), *Magic Squares of Order Form* (1982).

Joseph Mordaunt CROOK, F.B.A. Professor of Architectural History, Royal Holloway and Bedford New College since 1981, and previously Lecturer, then Reader in Architectural History, Bedford College. Public Orator, University of London since 1988. His publications include *The Greek Revival* (1968); *The British Museum* (1972); (jointly), *The History of the King's Works*, vol. VI, 1782-1851 (1973), *William Burges and the High Victorian Dream* (1981); and *The Dilemma of Style* (1987).

The late Very Revd. Sydney Hall EVANS. Dean of Salisbury, 1977-86. Dean of King's College, London, 1956-77, and previously curate, chaplain, and Warden of King's College postgraduate college at Warminster. Public Orator, University of London, 1972-74. d. January 1988.

Lord McGREGOR of Durris [Oliver Ross McGregor]. Chairman of the Advertising Standards Authority since 1980. Professor of Social Institutions, Bedford College, 1964-85, and previously Lecturer, then Reader, at Bedford College. Chairman, Royal Commission on the Press, 1975-77. His publications include *Divorce in England* (1957); (jointly) *Separated Spouses* (1970); and *Social History and Law Reform* (1981).

Leslie Philip Le QUESNE, C.B.E., F.R.C.S. Medical Administrator, Commonwealth Scholarship Commission since 1984. Professor of Surgery, Middlesex Hospital Medical School, 1963-84, and previously at the Middlesex Hospital from 1947. His publications include *Fluid Balance in Surgical Practice* (1957).

Gillian R. SUTHERLAND. Fellow of Newnham College, Cambridge, ince 1966. Her publications include *Elementary Education in the Nineteenth Century* (1971); (ed.) *Studies in the Growth of Nineteenth-Century Government* (1972), *Matthew Arnold on Education* (1973); *Policy Making in Elementary Education, 1870-95* (1973); and *Ability, Merit, and Measurement: Mental Testing and English Education, 1880-1940* (1984).

Sir William TAYLOR. Vice-Chancellor of the University of Hull since 1985, and previously Professor of Education, Bristol University, 1966-73, Director of the Institute of Education, University of London, 1973-83, and Principal of the University of London, 1983-5. His publications include *The Secondary Modern School* (1963); *Heading for Change* (1969); *Theory into Practice* (1972); *Research Perspectives in Education* (1973); *Research and Reform in Teacher Education* (1978); and *Universities under Scrutiny* (1987).

F.M.L. THOMPSON, F.B.A. Director of the Institute of Historical Research and Professor of History, University of London, since 1977, and previously Reader in Economic History, University College London, and Professor of Modern History, Bedford College. His publications include *English Landed Society in the Nineteenth Century* (1963); *Chartered Surveyors: The Growth of a Profession* (1968); *Hampstead: Building a Borough, 1650-1964* (1974); *The Rise of Respectable Society* (1988); and (ed.) *The Cambridge Social History of Britain, 1750-1950* (3 vols. 1990).

Brian L. TROWELL. Professor of Music, and Fellow of Wadham College Oxford, since 1988, and previously Lecturer in Music, University of Birmingham, Head of B.B.C. Radio Opera, and King Edward Professor of Music, King's College, London. His publications include *The Early Renaissance: Pelican History of Music*, II (1963); *Four Motets by John Plummer* (1968); and (ed.) *Invitation to Medieval Music*, III (1976), IV (1978).

William L. TWINING. Quain Professor of Jurisprudence, University College London, since 1983, and previously Lecturer in Private Law, Khartoum, Senior Lecturer in Law, Dar-es-Salaam, Professor of Jurisprudence, Queen's University, Belfast, and Professor of Law, Warwick University. His publications include *The Karl Llewellyn Papers* (1968); *Karl Llewellyn and the Realist Movement* (1973); (ed.), *Facts in Law* (1983); *Theories of Evidence* (1985); and (ed.) *Legal Theory and Common Law* (1986).

1

The Architectural Image

J. Mordaunt Crook

Architecture among many other things involves the formation of images: images of structure, images of status, images of power. The architectural image of London University – its visible presence, its corporate face – reflects only too well its episodic history and the daunting complexity of its organisation. Metropolitan and unitary from 1828; national and proto-federal from 1836; imperial from 1850; comprehensive from 1858; coeducationial from 1878; federal from 1900; increasingly confederal from 1929, 1978 and 1983 – London University is an educational giant which has often given the impression of living in furnished lodgings. Currently engrossing one-fifth of the United Kingdom's entire university sector – we have, incredibly, nearly 1,000 full Professors – the University of London boasts an architectural heritage which is, to say the least, mixed. Like the British Empire, our buildings seem at first glance to have materialised by accident; such is their diversity, the apparent chaos of the planning. In fact, planning there has been, in plenty: too many plans, and all of them unfinished.

A federal univeristy will have as many images as it has constituent elements. Plurality of status, plurality of place, plurality function: the result is a multiplicity of images. More than forty separate schools, colleges or institutes – many of them subdivided into a host of subsidiary

---

Footnotes: abbreviations

A.:	The Architect
A.A. Jnl.:	Architectural Association Journal
A.R.:	Architectural Review
B.:	The Builder
B.A.:	British Architect
B.N.:	Building News
C.E.A.S.:	Civil Engineer and Architect's Journal
C.L.:	Country Life
R.I.B.A.D.:	R.I.B.A. Drawings Collection
R.I.B.A. Jnl.:	R.I.B.A. Journal

units: from Kensington (Imperial College) to Stepney (Queen Mary College); from Cavendish Square (Heythrop College)[1] to Marylebone (Royal Academy of Music);[2] from Regent's Park (London Business School)[3] to Smithfield (Bart's Hospital);[4] from Camden Town (Royal Veterinary College)[5] to Campden Hill (Queen Elizabeth College; now King's College);[6] from Chelsea (Chelsea College, now also part of King's);[7] to Hampstead (Westfield College; now merged with Queen Mary College);[8] from New Cross (Goldsmiths' College)[9] to Bloomsbury (London School of Hygiene and Tropical Medicine);[10] from Bloomsbury

[1] Founded as a Jesuit college, Louvain, 1614; moved to England after the French Revolution; established at Heythrop, Oxon., 1926; transferred to Cavendish Square, as a school of London University, 1970.

[2] Designed by Sir Ernest George, 1910-11. See F. Corder, *A History of the Royal Academy of Music* (1922).

[3] Founded 1965; accommodated since 1970 in Sussex Terrace, designed by John Nash as part of his Regent's Park development, 1810-23.

[4] Sir N. Moore, *The History of St Bartholomew's Hospital*, 2 vols. (1910). V.C. Medvie and J.L. Thornton, eds., *The Royal Hospital of St Bartholomew, 1123-1973* (1974).

[5] Original 1792 building rebuilt 1936-7. Full status as a school of the university 1949, after which its Hertfordshire Field Station was developed according to plans by Devereux and Davis, *A.J.*, cxxvii (1958), 9. See *The Royal Veterinary College and Hospital* (1937).

[6] The 'Ladies Dept.' of K.C.L., 1885 onwards, began teaching in Observatory Avenue, Kensington and in Kensington Square; moved to Campden Hill 1915 (H. Percy Adams and C. Holden: *B.*, cx, 1916, 50 *et seq.*: ills. and plans), becoming King's College of Household and Social Service. Independent 1928; collegiate status as Queen Elizabeth College, 1953. After bombing (1944), it was rebuilt by Adams, Holden and Pearson (*B.*, clxxxvi, 1954, 119-24). Re-integrated with King's College, 1985. See N. Marsh, *The History of Queen Elizabeth College* (1986).

[7] Founded 1891 in Manresa Road, as South Western Polytechnic (J.M. Brydon, 1891-6; extended 1912 by F.G. Knight); from 1922 to 1956 Chelsea Polytechnic; from 1957 to 1963 Chelsea College of Advanced Technology; from 1960 Chelsea College, London; from 1966 a full college of London University; from 1985 part of King's College. See H. Silver and S.J. Teague, *Chelsea College: a History* (1977). In 1975 new halls of residence were begun in Wandsworth.

[8] Founded 1882 at 'Westfield' (2-3 Maresfield Terrace; now 4-6 Maresfield Gardens), the College purchased Kidderpore Hall (T. Howard, 1840-2) in 1890. Additional buildings: Maynard, Dining Hall and Skeel Library (R.F. Macdonald 1891; 1904-5); Chapman Wing and Orchard Building (Verner Rees, 1927; 1935); Chapel (P.R. Morley Horder, 1928); Refectory and Science Building (1961; 1962). See J. Sondheimer, *Castle Adamant in Hampstead* (1983). In 1989 Westfield College merged with Queen Mary College.

[9] Designed as the Royal Naval School by John Shaw, 1843-5; acquired by the Goldsmiths' Company in 1890 and presented to London University in 1905; extended by Sir Reginald Blomfield, 1907-8 (*B.*, xcv (ii), 1908, 188: ill.) and by Enthoven and Mock, 1965 (*B.*, ccx, 1966, 332-7). Partly destroyed 1940 and 1944. See D. Dymond, ed., *The Forge: the History of Goldsmith's College, 1905-55* (1955).

[10] Designed by Morley Horder and Verner Rees, 1926-9: 'One of the most successful designs in Portland Stone since [the days of] Vanbrugh and Hawksmoor', A.S. Gray, *Edwardian Architecture* (1985), 216. Funded by the Rockefeller Foundation, initially to the tune of £2,000,000. Previously the London School of Tropical Medicine, founded 1899 at Albert Dock Hospital.

again (University College Hospital)[11] to the City (Guy's Hospital);[12] and from Paris (British Institute)[13] to Egham (Royal Holloway College; now Royal Holloway and Bedford New College – Bedford having moved from Regent's Park). We even have outposts as far apart as Ashford in Kent (Wye College)[14] and Milport on the Clyde (Marine Biological Station, on the Isle of Cumbrae).[15]

The story of how this architectural kaleidoscope came into being is the story of the university itself. And that story, alas – as one of its historians has written – is 'a tangled skein of domination, ambition, intrigue, and disloyalty intermingled with some silver and gold threads'.[16] The story even has its own prehistory.

As early as the reign of Henry VIII, Sir Nicholas Bacon planned a university in London, funded out of the proceeds of the Dissolution of the Monasteries.[17] During the Comonwealth, 'A True Lover of London' suggested turning St Paul's Cathedral into a metropolitan university.[18] Lawyers have trained in the capital since the Middle Ages. And some form of medical education existed in London – as we all know – 'when Oxford was an obscure Saxon village and Cambridge [was] noted only for eels'.[19] Gresham College – the spiritual ancestor of London University, founded by Sir Thomas Gresham – survived from 1596 to 1768.[20] But the university as we know it only assumed architectural form with the building of University College.

In his famous letter to Lord Brougham of 1825, Thomas Campbell had called for the foundation of 'a great London University', placed 'centrically' in the metropolis. As to the buildings, 'all that would be necessary', he explained, 'would be to have some porticoes, and large halls independent of the lecture-rooms, to which [the students] might resort for relaxation.'[21] In other words the image of this, England's first modern university, was to be Greek, or at least Graeco-Roman: 'a palace for genius', as one of the founders put it, 'where future Ciceros should record the influence of that excitement which Tully declares he felt at Athens, when he contemplated the porticoes where Socrates sat, and the laurel-

---

[11] Designed by Alfred Waterhouse, 1898-1906, *B.N.*, lxx (1896), 671: ill. The Baroque Medical School on the corner of Gower Street and Huntly Street dates from 1907. See W.R. Merrington, *U.C. Hospital and its Medical School* (1976).

[12] H.C. Cameron, *Mr Guy's Hospital, 1726-1948* (1954).

[13] *L'Institut Britannique de l'Université de Paris* (1952).

[14] J.D. Sykes, *A Short Historical Guide to Wye College* (1984).

[15] Established 1970, in association with the University of Glasgow.

[16] T.L. Humberstone, *University Reform in London* (1926), 166.

[17] Campbell, *Lives of the Lord Chancellors*, ii (1845), 89.

[18] Sir E. Deller, 'London University Centenary', *The Listener* (1 July 1936).

[19] S. Gordon Wilson, *The University of London and its Colleges* (1923), 108.

[20] *Quarterly Rev.*, clxiv (1887), 34.

[21] *The Times* (9 Feb. 1825).

groves where Plato disputed.'[22] Appropriately, at the foundation-stone ceremony in 1827, a Latin oration was delivered by the architect himself: William Wilkins.[23]

Wilkins was an archaeologist turned architect, a scholar with a theatrical background, a Cambridge don with good connections and a weakness for polemic. During the 1820s, on a wave of enthusiasm for all things Greek, he became one of the best-known architects in England, Professor at the Royal Academy and a leading light in the Society of Dilettanti. But when his brand of archaeology was eclipsed by the Renaissance Revival of the 1840s – when Regency gave way to Victorian – his reputation collapsed.

Still, with a Corinthian portico no less than ten columns wide, one major and two minor domes, two sepulchral pylons, porticoed wings and a Doric entrance screen, Wilkins's scheme[24] – and his sequence of modifications after the initial competition of 1826[25] – was indeed a testimony to the cultural hegemony of the ancient world, Greek and Roman.[26] It was also an indication of the new university's rejection of Gothic as a symbol of all that was medieval, ecclesiastical, obscurantist and restrictive.[27] Cockerell's defeated design might have been more original,[28] but Wilkins's scheme struck the right archaeological note. Greek and Roman: the prototype for the columns of the central portico

[22] R.W. Liscombe, *William Wilkins, 1778-1839* (1980), 157.

[23] James Elmes called him 'perhaps the best educated classic that has honoured the profession . . . since Sir Christopher Wren', *C.E.A.J.*, i (1838), 248.

[24] Wilkins's original scheme: ill. Liscombe, *op. cit.*, pl. 84, exhib. R.A. 1827 (nos. 969-70) and 1828 (no. 1016). See also *The Age of Neo-Classicism* (1972), no. 1387; Britton and Pugin, *Public Buildings of London*, ed. Leeds (1838), 78-88. Wilkins later produced a *modified* design, ill. Leeds. opp. p. 77 and J. Summerson, *Architecture in Britain*, pl. 410. See also [Sir G. Gregory and A. Stratton], 'U.C.L.', *C.L.*, lxi (1927), 973: ills.

[25] Wilkins defeated Gandy, Atkinson, Davies, Wyatville and Cockerell – all of whom submitted classical schemes.

[26] Charles Kelsall's *Phantasm of a University* (1814) had suggested just such a combination of Greek and Roman elements: 'the artist who takes the spirit of the Grecian taste as his groundwork, at the same time engrafting with judgement the best parts of the Italian style on his designs will bid fair to attain to perfection in his art'. Others were less eclectic. One anonymous writer addressed the College Council as follows: 'Pray consider whether your University may not doff its three odious bonnetts for the sake of beauty as well as economy. Unless you build a pantheon in the air, a dome or cupola is horrible' [quoted, *C.L.*, lxi (1927), 974].

[27] Very few London University buildings were to be Gothic: exceptions being T.L. Donaldson's University Hall, Gordon Square (1849; now Dr Williams's Library); J.T. Emmett's New College, Finchley Road (1850, dem.; see J. Summerson, in *A. and B.N.* [20 Sept. 1935], 338-9); and Raphael Brandon's University Church of Christ the King, Gordon Square (built 1853 onwards, for the Catholic Apostolic Church; see [J. Betjeman], *The University Church of Christ the King*, 1965).

[28] D. Watkin, *C.R. Cockerell* (1974). Ill., N. Harte and J. North, *The World of University College London, 1828-1978* (1978), 26-7.

1. William Wilkins, The London University: unfinished scheme (1827).
(*Print: Sanders of Oxford*)

2. T. Roger Smith, University College: design for the completion of the Gower Street entrance (1895).
(*Building News,* lxviii, 1895, 48-49)

3. (*Above*) Sir William Chambers and Sir Robert Smirke, King's College, Somerset House river frontage (1829-35). (*Photo: National Monuments Record*)

5. (*Right*) Charles Holden, The Senate House (1933-38). (*Photo: National Monuments Record*)

4. Sir James Penethorne, University Offices, Great Burlington Street (1867-70). Now the Museum of Mankind. Headquarters of London University, 1870-1900. (*Photo: National Monuments Record*)

6. (*Top*) C.C.T. Doll (?), design for a University of London on the present Senate House site (1912). (*Estates Gazette,* 9 November 1912)

7. (*Above*) Sir Albert Richardson, scheme for extending Somerset House as a new University of London (1914). (*The Builder,* cvi, 1914, 13)

8. (*Top right*) Sir Albert Richardson, projected scheme for University of London, Bloomsbury (1926). (*Vincula,* ii, 1926, 12)

9. (*Bottom right*) Sir Edwin Lutyens, project for a University of London, Bloomsbury (1914). (*R.I.B.A. Drawings Collection*)

Ruffell Square

10. T.E. Colcutt, The Imperial Institute, South Kensington (1887-93; demolished, except for the tower). Headquarters of London University, 1900-36. (*Photo: National Monuments Record*)

11. W.H. Crossland, The Royal Holloway College, Egham, Surrey (1879-87). Now Royal Holloway and Bedford New College. (*Photo: Moreton Moore*)

12. Capt. G.S.C. Swinton (1859-1937). Lyon King of Arms: Chairman of the L.C.C. (*Photo: Scottish National Portrait Gallery*)

13. Charles Holden (1875-1960), Architect of the Senate House. (*Photo: National Portrait Gallery*)

14. Sir Ernest Graham-Little (1868-1950). M.P. for London University, 1924-50. (*Photo: National Portrait Gallery*)

15. Sir William Beveridge, later Lord Beveridge (1879-1963). Vice-Chancellor, 1926-28. (*Photo: National Portrait Gallery*)

was the Temple of Jupiter Olympius at Athens; for the lateral porticoes the Monument of Thrasyllus. And in one later scheme the architect added to the wings semi-circular Corinthian porticoes based on the Temple of Vesta at Tivoli.

Several of these features remained pipe-dreams. Indeed the early history of U.C.L. is an essay in architectural hypotheses: Wilkins's quadrangle remained unfinished for one and a half centuries. A whole string of architects – a veritable school of Gower Street Neo-Classicists – contributed to the College's later architectural history, built and unbuilt. First Professor T.L. Donaldson (interior staircase, Flaxman Gallery and Library, 1849-51);[29] then Professor T. Hayter Lewis [and J. Tavernor-Parry] (North wing 1870-1, 1878-81; South wing 1866-9, 1873, 1876);[30] then Professor T. Roger Smith (Gower Street front, 1893-5);[31] then Professor F.M. Simpson (Gower Street; Gower Place, 1912-15, 1923);[32] and finally Sir Hugh Casson (entrance, 1981-6).[33] What better way to celebrate the University's sesquicentenary than to complete the great portal of its first constituent college?

University College had been a Whig attempt to break the stranglehold of Anglicanism on higher education. King's College represented a Tory counter-attack: a reassertion of the educational values of the Establishment. But where? Hints were thrown out that a government site, even a royal property, might be suitable. The South Bank? St James's Park? Buckingham Palace? One scheme survives suggesting that the College might have found a home in Regent's Park. That was ruled out by local hostility: residents protested in *The Times* that one zoo was enough. 'Perfectly right', noted the Editor, 'a College in the park would be much worse than [a] menagerie of wild beasts.'[34] Instead the Government supplied an empty site on the edge of Somerset House, plus an architect to fill it: Sir Robert Smirke. At that stage Sir William Chambers's Somerset House (1776 onwards) was still unfinished, and Smirke had been toying with designs for its completion for some years. Like Wilkins, Smirke was a Greek Revivalist. Unlike Wilkins, he was a Government architect, and a protégé of many Tory patrons, including Sir Robert Peel.

The site of King's College – a strip of land between the Strand and the

[29] *Survey of London* xxi (1949), pls. 35, 37.

[30] *B.*, xl (1881), 81; Earl of Kimberley, *The New North Wing, U.C.L.* (1881), ill. Executive architects: Messrs Perry and Reade.

[31] *B.N.*, lxviii (1895), 48-9: ill.; exhib. R.A. 1894, no. 1705. Ill., Harte and North, *op. cit.*, 128.

[32] *B.N.*, cv (1913), 796-7: ill. and plan; B. cvi (1914), 49-52: ills. and plans; *A.* xciii (1915) 48, ill. and plan; *Architects and Builders Jnl.* 1.7 (1914); ill. and plan. See also J. Elliot Smith, *University of London, University College: new buildings for . . . Anatomy and . . . Physiology (1923)*.

[33] *Landscape Design* (May 1981), 22-3.

[34] *The Times* (24 Dec. 1828); drawings: R.I.B.A.D.

Thames, running parallel to Somerset House – was provided by the
Treasury at a peppercorn rent, in perpetuity, on one condition: the new
building had to be finished inside ten years. In particular the river front –
continuing Somerset House eastwards – had to be completed, according
to Sir William Chambers's late eighteenth-century designs, within five
years.[35] In other words, the Government struck a bargain: in return for a
central site, the infant college was to devote much of its private capital to
the completion of a public monument.

Such enforced expenditure left its mark. The river front was grand; but
the College building itself suffered from grinding economy.[36] It was not
until the 1870s that the chapel received its Byzantine decorations at the
hands of Sir Gilbert Scott[37] – an exotic interior, though perhaps less
enticing than the unexecuted Gothic design of 1859 by William Burges.[38]
The remainder of the building took aesthetic abstinence to extremes.
Pugin found an easy target in the entrance gateway to the Strand,
comparing it ignominiously with Tom Tower at Oxford.[39] 'This homely
gateway', snorted another critic 'might have been mistaken for one
leading to some mews, or to a porter-brewery'.[40] Within a decade of its
completion Smirke's Neo-Classicism had come to seem not only meagre
but hopelessly old-fashioned. It is 'such an arrant architectural nullity',
sneered W.H. Leeds in 1841, 'that its insignificance . . . shields it from
criticism, no-one [considers] it worth while . . . even to mention so
miserable a piece of design.'[41] By that date the Greek Revival had been
quite eclipsed by the new enthusiasm for revived Renaissance – a style

---

[35] Wearing his Office of Works hat, Smirke had in fact begun plans for completing
Chambers's design as early as 1825 (P.R.O. works 1/13, 383: 21 June 1825). For demands
to eliminate the eyesore of this incomplete façade, see *Gent's Mag* (1823), ii, 194 and J.W.
Croker, *Letter to the Earl of Liverpool proposing to finish the East Wing of Somerset House for National
Galleries* (1825). See also J.W. Hales, *The Site of King's College from 1552* (1881). Smirke's
estimate in May 1829 was £140,000, plus £10,000 for furniture. The College had only
£126,000 in hand. By the formal opening in 1831, £85,889 had been spent; but the river
front had not yet been begun, much internal work remained unfinished and College assets
totalled only £113,598. To complete the river front and Principal's house in accordance
with Treasury demand by June 1834, the College possessed only £6,000 of the £16,500
originally earmarked by Smirke for that portion of the work. On 26 April 1833 operations
were suspended after £6,339 had been spent on finishing only half the Thames frontage.
Frenzied efforts were made to obtain funds; work was restarted in June, and finished – only
a few months behind schedule – in April 1835, at the low cost of only £7,100 (*Gent's Mag.*
1829, i, 451; 1833, i, 450; 1835, ii, 644; F.J.C. Hearnshaw, *Centenary History of K.C.L.* (1929)
62, 78, 118).

[36] For plans and details, see R. Needham and A. Webster, *Somerset House* (1905), 271-2.

[37] Hearnshaw, *History of K.C.L.*, 159, 226-8.

[38] J. Mordaunt Crook, *William Burges and the High Victorian Dream* (1981), 40; G. Huielin,
King's College, London, The Chapel (1979).

[39] A.W. Pugin, *Contrasts* (1836), ill.

[40] *Library of the Fine Arts* (1831), ii, 276; *Athenaeum* (1831) 649: ill.

[41] *C.E.A.J.*, vi (1843) 193.

known, in diluted version, as Italianate. So when, a quarter of a century later, London University strove to express its expanding corporate role in architectural form, the image chosen was neither Greek, nor Roman, nor even Neo-Classic. It was to be unmistakably Renaissance.

The University of London had been set up in 1836 as an examining and degree-giving body: an umbrella organisation designed to disguise the rivalry between U.C.L. and K.C.L. It had no premises of its own. Indeed until 1901 it retained the status of what today would be called a quango. As regards acccommodation, it remained a government lodger until 1936. Its first headquarters was a set of rooms in Somerset House previously occupied by the Royal Academy.[42] Driven out by the Registrar General in 1853, it asked the Treasury for a home of its own. There was talk of a site in South Kensington: a choice that might have changed the whole focus of the University's architectural history.[43] But in the end the Government offered a base in Bloomsbury: a house in Byng Place – next to the present University Church – built by Cubitt as a theological college in 1832. This the University turned down flat: the situation was 'so inconvenient and remote'.[44] Instead it moved into a 'miserable garret' in Marlborough House, there to remain for three years, 1853-6, before transferring to the east wing in the forecourt of old Burlington House. Here extra rooms had regularly to be borrowed for examinations. Between 1867 and 1870 the University was even reduced to operating from an address more suitable to a gentleman's tailor: 17, Savile Row.[45]

Such frequent changes of address, complained the Senate in 1859, gave the University 'a temporary and provisional character', and lowered it 'in the Estimation of the Candidates, the Graduates and the Public'. To many people, Grote explained, the 'very existence' of the University 'is unknown'.[46] From 1867 the University of London had its own Member of Parliament, just like Oxford and Cambridge. But it did not have its own headquarters until 1870 – and even then it was leasehold, not freehold.

The architect chosen – by Government – for London University's first central focus was the future Sir James Pennethorne, heir to the practice of John Nash, and architect to the Office of Works.[47] At that date he was best known for his Palladian extension to Somerset House (1856). His first

---

[42] Part of the North range of Chambers's building, vacated when the R.A. moved to Trafalgar Square in 1837.

[43] The University demanded 'an appropriate Building in the metropolis, specially, exclusively, and permanently appropriated to its own use', Sir Douglas Logan, *London University: an Introduction* (1972), 54. Sir Henry Cole and Redgrave suggested South Kensington, V. and A. Guard Book 2510 (20 Feb. 1854). *Ex inf.* Dr G. Tyacke.

[44] See N. Harte, *University of London, 1836-1936* (1986), 102-3.

[45] *Ibid.*, 118.

[46] *Ibid.*, 116.

[47] For what follows, see *Survey of London* xxxii (1963), 435 *et seq.*; G. Tyacke, 'Sir James Pennethorne' (D.Phil., Oxon., 1987).

design for University Offices – approved in 1866 by W.F. Cowper, Russell's Liberal First Commissioner of Works – is now lost. It seems to have been Neo-Classical.[48] But within a few months Russell and Cowper were replaced by Disraeli and Lord John Manners – and their preferences were decidely Gothic. Pennethorne tactfully submitted a second design (which survives only in a faded photograph) in eclectic, Franco-Italian Gothic.[49] 'These days', noted the *Builder*, 'style is made to depend on political ascendancy'.[50] The University Registrar, Dr W.B. Carpenter, seems to have been willing to toe the line. But the Senate refused to be intimidated. Ornament in architecture, it protested, 'should be subservient to structural expression'.[51] And again, 'The Modern style of architecture [by which they meant Renaissance] would be preferable either to the Medieval or to the Italian Gothic'.[52] Such hostility to Gothic was hardly unexpected on the Buildings sub-committee: both Professors of Architecture at U.C.L. and K.C.L. were dyed-in-the-wool classicists. And neither had been invited to act as university architect. Pennethorne was instructed to scrap Ruskin and go back to Palladio.[53] 'Taking the front of Burlington House as a foundation',[54] as stipulated by the Senate, he produced a third design. This time – apart from a few suggestions by the only architect-M.P., Sir William Tite[55] – there was general acceptance, after an initial squabble about the sculpture.

England's first modern university had four faculties: Arts, Law, Science and Medicine. As figurative symbols the Senate chose Milton, Bentham, Newton and Harvey. No objection could be made to Harvey and Newton. But what about Bentham and Milton? Surely, suggested Lord John Manners, Justinian was wiser than Bentham? 'No man can be selected', replied the Senate, 'so suitable as . . . Bentham to represent the Faculty of Law in the University of London'. Well, might not Milton give way to Shakespeare? The Senate remained obdurate: the bard, though immortal, was insufficiently academic; he was relegated to a place inside, on the staircase. And controversy did not end there. High up on the central parapet appear representatives of 'ancient culture': Galen, Cicero, Aristotle, Plato, Archimedes and Justinian – Justinian replacing the Senate's rather obscure first choice of Tribonian. The East side is adorned with 'savants' or 'illustrious foreigners': Galileo, Goethe, Laplace,

[48] 'Plain classic', with a central Corinthian portico P.R.O. Works 33/1745; U.L. Archives, *Senate Minutes* (20 July 1870), 91. *Ex. inf.* Dr G. Tyacke.

[49] Drawings: R.I.B.A.D.'Unsatisfactory, weak in some parts, heavy in others, elegant in none', *B.N.* (7 June 1867), 397.

[50] *B.*, xxiv (1866), 664.

[51] Quoted by A.H. Layard, *Hansard*, clxxxvi (1867), 1234-5.

[52] *University of London Minutes of Committees* (1867-80), 225: U.L. Archives, Box 29, 'Accommodation, New Buildings, Burlington Gardens'.

[53] U.L. Archives, *Senate Minutes*, 27 March 1867, 27.

[54] *Ibid.*, 20 July 1870, 93.

[55] *Hansard*, clxxxviii (1867), 1263-4.

Leibnitz, Cuvier and Linaeus; the West side with 'English worthies': Hunter, Hume, Adam Smith, Locke, Bacon and Davy (Davy replacing Dalton).[56]

Boldly modulated in composition – designed to take full advantage of oblique viewing in a narrow street; polychrome in materials: grey, white and pink; logically and lucidly planned; richly decorated inside and out – Pennethorne's 'Senate House' (now the Museum of Mankind) was a triumph of eclectic classicism. Its language is Renaissance, but these are the forms of the Italian cinquecento seen through the eyes of late eighteenth-century France and early nineteenth-century Germany. The details may be Baroque, but the composition is Neo-Classical. By 1870, of course – the date of its completion – this sort of thing was out of date by a generation or more. Even so, it was well received.[57] Its opening, as Queen Victoria put it, marked 'a new era in the history of the University'.[58] *The Times* agreed that London University had at last arrived.[59] Alas, the domicile of a board of examiners – however august – hardly seemed quite the right headquarters for the University in its next metamorphosis as a mighty teaching conglomerate.

By the 1880s it was clear that the University of London did not belong specifically to London, nor was it really a university. It was no longer metropolitan. It was imperial. Bombay (founded 1857) and Sydney (founded 1850) were as much its responsibility as U.C.L. and K.C.L. 'The colleges teach, the University examines – examines . . . everybody in everything, without regard to age, sex, religion, colour, nationality.' In fact, noted the *Edinburgh Review* in 1886, 'the sun never sets over the British Empire or the papers of London University'.[60] Alas, it examined but it did

---

[56] Joseph Durham carved the Faculties; the sculptors of 'ancient culture' were J.S. Westmacott and W.F. Woodington; the 'savants' were by Patrick McDowell and E.W. Wyon; the 'English worthies' by William Theed, Jnr. and Matthew Noble. See *British Almanac and Companion* (1870), 132: ill. See also E. Walford, *Old and New London* iv (1890), 304-5; *B.*, xxv (1867), 854-5: ill. and plan.

[57] 'The details are severely classical, and the form sufficiently monumental for the institution [and] purposes . . . [Moreover] there is nothing about the building which can be called a sham . . . The two great halls in the wings [for lectures and examinations] which are appropriately lighted from the upper storeys, enabled [the architect] to get repose and dignity from an unpierced basement, and the requisite support to the centre containing the council room and other state apartments . . . All this is expressed in the exterior as truthfully as in any medieval building, and with an elegance that satisfies the most refined taste. The portico is perhaps the least successful part of the design, but its use is obvious, and there is nothing about it which seriously detracts from the beauty of the design.' J. Fergusson, *History of the Modern Styles of Architecture*, 2nd ed. (1873), 347.

[58] *I.L.N.*, lvi (1870), 533-4: ill.

[59] *The Times* (2 April p. 12; 9 May p. 6; 10 May p. 12; 12 May p. 9).

[60] *Edin. Rev.*, clxiv (1886), 245-6. It 'cries *urbi et orbi*, "come and be tested" . . . its crest should be a measuring rod and a mark of interrogation'. Prof. Hales, quoted in *P.P.* (1887), xxxix, 393. Hence the establishment in 1884 of an Association for Promoting a Teaching University for London.

not teach – or rather the teaching was beyond its control. Alone among the capital cities of Europe – except, that is, for Constantinople – London had no proper university of its own. 'The University of London', Matthew Arnold concluded, 'should be recast . . . the strangely devised and anomalous organisations of King's College and University College should be . . . *co-ordered* as the French say, with the University of London.'[61] Easier said than done.[62] By the 1880s U.C.L. and K.C.L. could only agree on one thing: they disapproved of the University of London. So they decided to declare U.D.I. – with or without the medical schools – by drawing an effective line between internal and external students, thus escaping the mob of seventy or so affiliated centres of teaching scattered all over the world. To do this they proposed to set up a new university altogether. This institution was to be known first as Albert Univeristy,[63] then as Gresham University,[64] then as Westminster University.[65] All three, as Lord Playfair put it, were to leave 'the London University out in the cold'.[66]

Now neither Albert University, nor Gresham University, nor Westminster University ever existed in even hypothetical architectural form. 'Colleges', it was solemnly observed, 'need not necessarily imply *buildings*'.[67] These were the hypotheses of administrators. And the complexities of Schleswig-Holstein were as nothing to the complexity of the 'London University Question'. The tensions between U.C.L. and K.C.L., between Internal and External systems, between Senate and Convocation, between central colleges and peripheral institutions, between metropolitan and cosmopolitan functions, between the coordinating power of the University and the disintegrative impulses of its constituent parts – all these resisted resolution throughout the 1880s and 1890s, and impeded interminably the emergence of a university with any physical focus, any collective architectural image.

Two Royal Commissions – the Selborne Commission (1888-9)[68] and

[61]　M. Arnold, *Higher Schools and Universities in Germany* (1882).

[62]　'University College . . . has no school of theology? – *That is so, it is founded on a strictly undenominational principle.* King's College has a school of theology, has it not? – *That is so; King's College is a Church of England institution.* It would therefore be quite impossible that those two institutions could be fused into one college? – *Quite impossible*'. (Minutes of Evidence, 'Royal Commission on a University for London', *P.P.* 1889, xxxix, 371).

[63]　Draft Charter, *P.P.* 1889, xxxix, 579-82.

[64]　Proposed by G.C. Warr, 1888: *P.P.* 1889, xxxix, 626; Draft Charter Considered: *P.P.*, 1894, xxxiv.

[65]　*The Times* (23 Nov. 1897) p. 6; (25 Nov. 1897) p. 14.

[66]　Playfair, in *Nineteenth Century*, xxxviii (1895), 700.

[67]　*Ibid.*, xxxi (1892), 251n.

[68]　'Royal Commission on a University of London', *P.P.* 1889, xxxix. Summarised in W.H. Allchin, *An Account of the Reconstruction of the University of London*, ii (1911). 'Quite the worst – the feeblest, least lucid, most self-contradictory – of all [commissions] it has been my lot to examine.' Hearnshaw, *King's College, London* (1929), 345, 347. See *Qtly. Rev.*, clxxiv (1842), 225-6.

the Cowper Commission (1892-4)[69] – and one committee of the Privy Council – the Cranbrook Committee (1891)[70] – were set up to find a way out of the 'horrible chaos' of this debate.[71] Unfortunately, they compounded that chaos by their own disagreements. Each recommended, sometimes by the narrowest of majorities, one university in London, not two.[72] But none of them supplied the magic formula which would guarantee agreement within the University itself.[73] The subject was debated at stupendous length in the columns of *The Times*.[74] Three successive Bills were introduced in Parliament, in 1895, 1896 and 1897. All failed. Not until 1898 was the London University Bill passed.[75] And that compromise Bill – creating a metropolitan university *with* an imperial dimension; teaching *and* examining – would never have succeeded without the joint efforts of two very determined men: Sidney Webb and R.B. Haldane.

Webb and Haldane: the Socialist and the Socialite; the Fabian and the Hegelian – they were the personification of the Lib.-Lab. pact. It was the foundation of the L.S.E. in 1895 which first drew Sidney Webb into the university orbit. Thereafter he was never far from the focus of academic power. Webb's dream of London University was distinctly inegalitarian: a two-decker structure owing more to Germany and America than to Oxford or Cambridge, staffed by low-paid lecturers and high-paid professors. At undergraduate level, what he called the 'internecine jealousy' and 'instinctive megalomania' of the colleges would be counterbalanced by intercollegiate Faculties and Boards of Studies.[76] At postgraduate level, research would be controlled by the professoriat and

[69] *P.P.* 1894, xxxi, xxxiv.

[70] Summarised in *The Spectator*, lxviii (1892), 262.

[71] *The Spectator*, lxi (1888), 164-5.

[72] See Playfair, *On Teaching Universities and Examining Boards* (1873) and 'A Great University for London', *Nineteenth Century* (1895), 699-705. See also the Royal Commission on Technical Education, 1882-4, *P.P.* 1882, xxvii; 1884, xxix-xxxi. Sir Philip Magnus spoke for many who feared the multiplication of degree-awarding bodies: 'the American system of graduation', *The Times* (24 April 1891) p. 14. No doubt he was thinking of the 370 degree-giving institutions in the U.S., thirty-five in Ohio alone, *P.P.* 1889, xxxix, 448.

[73] e.g. *The Times* (19 Oct. 1889), p. 7; (17 Feb. 1891) p. 13; (11 May 1891) p. 10; (18 May 1891) p. 8.

[74] e.g. *The Times* (5 April 1894), p. 8; (7 May 1895), p. 4; (26 July 1894), p. 10; (2 Aug. 1894), p. 11; (10 Aug. 1894), p. 11; (13 Dec. 1895), p. 8; (16 Dec. 1895), p. 14; (17 Dec. 1895), p. 8; (24 Dec. 1895), p. 15; (25 Dec. 1895), p. 5; (2 Jan. 1896), p. 9; (14 Jan. 1896), p. 10; (16 Jan. 1896), p. 14; (17 Jan. 1896), p. 7; (20 Jan. 1896), p. 10; (21 Jan. 1896), p. 6; (28 Jan. 1896), p. 3.

[75] See Hearnshaw, *King's College*, 406. 'I spoke for once', Haldane recalled, 'like one inspired.' Haldane, *An Autobiography* (1929), 126-8; Maurice, *Haldane* i (1937), 80-84. His speech persuaded Joseph Chamberlain. Asquith called it 'the best thing of its kind I have ever heard in the House of Commons.'

[76] Evidence to Haldane Commission, Report i, Minutes of Evidence para. 61, *P.P.* 1910, xxiii, 677.

concentrated on a university basis in 'the one or two highest colleges' –
making London 'the foremost postgraduate centre of the intellectual
world'. 'After a whole generation of conflict and controversy', Webb
complained in 1902, 'London has at last got its teaching university . . . Yet
the plain man remains unaware that the teaching university exists.' His
diagnosis was sound enough, but his remedy was mistaken. Instead of
building a university which would act as a visible focus of loyalty – and
thus as a magnet for donations and bequests[77] – he pinned his faith in the
publicity value of endowed research. 'What is needed', he concluded
firmly, 'is not more buildings but more professorships.'[78]

Lord Haldane made no such error. For thirty years or more he battled
obsessively for a unitary university, conspicuously set in its own
University Precinct. H.G. Wells once remarked that Haldane was rather
like a political butler: he 'carried his words on a plate'. 'Haldane doesn't
bark', noted one civil servant. 'He purrs'.[79] He certainly had a way with
committees. 'No one', it was said, 'can invest a subject in a more lucid fog.'
His vision of London University was indeed intoxicating: 'the chief centre
of learning in the entire Empire . . . the chief centre of learning for the
entire world':[80] an institution which balanced the centrifugal forces of
central administration with the centripetal thrust of collegiate autonomy.
Not for nothing was he the translator of Schopenhauer's *World as Will and
Idea*, 3 vols. (1883). He was Secretary of State for War; he was twice Lord
High Chancellor of England, Liberal and Labour. But universities were
his speciality: Scottish, German, American, English. 'I have lived for
universities', he wrote in old age, 'they have been more to me than
anything else'.[81] Beatrice Webb was not entirely taken in. For years she
saw Haldane at work – with Sidney Webb supplying the memos –
moulding the future of London University. And she saw it was all
vicarious power-play: a political world in miniature. 'He has always

[77] For this argument, see Sir H. Roscoe, *Life and Experiences* (1906), 351.

[78] S. Webb, 'London University: a policy and a forecast', *Nineteenth Century* li (1902),
916, 922, 929. 'We must abandon the simple ideal of equality, identity or uniformity
among professors, whether of tenure or salary, attainments or duties, time-table or
holidays. The principal professors, on whom mainly we must depend for research, should,
of course, have life tenure, high salaries and abundant leisure, whilst the bulk of the
university teachers required by so extensive an undergraduate population as that of
London will necessarily be engaged for short terms, earn only modest salaries, and work at
times and seasons convenient to those whom they serve'. *Ibid.*, 923.

[79] E. Ashby and M. Anderson *Portrait of Haldane at Work in Education* (1974), 102.

[80] R.B. Haldane, *The Nationalisation of Universities* (1920); Sir F. Maurice, *Haldane*, ii
(1939), 90-2.

[81] Ashby and Anderson, *op. cit.*, xiii, 1, 4. See also J.E. Lockwood, 'Haldane and
Education', *Public Administration*, xxxv (1957), 237-44; H.F. Heath, 'Lord Haldane: his
Influence on Higher Education and Administration', *Public Administration*, vi (1928), 350-
60.

delighted in power', she wrote, 'and the appearance of power . . . He . . . delights in the glamour of the great ones of the world . . . the City . . . Grand Society . . . aristocrats, plutocrats and social charmers . . . he loves to be 'in the know' . . . He is, in short, a *power* worshipper.' He was, she admitted, a remarkable administrator: he had just the right combination of energy, benevolence and cynicism. But he was a manipulator, not a communicator – a 'restless, lonely' bachelor; a *faux bon viveur* – it was the 'inner circles who loved him . . . towards the multitude and the press he was tactless'.[82] That tactlessness twice reduced Haldane's vision of a University Precinct to ruins. It had to be rescued by a man who understood public relations rather better: Sir William Beveridge.

It was Haldane, as much as anybody, who engineered the removal of the University's headquarters in 1900 from an annexe of Burlington House to a section of the Imperial Institute.[83] A new site for a new university; an imperial setting for a world-wide organisation. He persuaded Edward VII; he persuaded Lord Herschell – who happened to be both Chancellor of the University and Chairman of the Imperial Institute. The Institute itself, designed by T.E. Colcutt, was supposed in 1887 to embody the *idea* of Empire. Its style, remarked one critic in 1893 – without any sense of irony – is 'indescribable . . . [This] . . . is a building which is essentially Victorian . . . and . . . truly modern.'[84] Its eclecticism was indeed Victorian. But by the turn of the century it had become – in Edward VII's phrase – rather 'a useless white elephant'.[85] In 1899 the university had received – in return for surrendering its own central offices – a Government promise of accommodation commensurate with its new status.[86] 'Thirty years from hence', prophesied *The Spectator*, 'if civilisation is not pauperised by a general war to secure monopolies and seize swamps, the money required [for a totally new campus] will seem a trifle'.[87] Sadly, the chance was missed, and the palmy Edwardian years were frittered away in imperial lodgings in Exhibition Road, preparing evidence for yet another Royal Commission, this time under the chairmanship of Haldane himself. C.R. Ashby's design for a Fraternity House off Cheyne Row was not the least of the missed opportunities of this

[82] Beatrice Webb, *Our Partnership*, ed. Barbara Drake and Margaret Cole (1948), 95-8; Beatrice Webb, *Diaries, 1924-32*, ed. Margaret Cole (1956), 87-8, 171-2.

[83] The Eastern half, plus a temporary timber structure known as the Great Hall, built for the Institute's official opening by Queen Victoria. Details: *The Times* (29 July 1899), p. 15. For these negotiations, see R.B. Haldane, *An Autobiography* (1929), 142 *et seq.*

[84] R. Langton Cole, *British Almanac and Companion* (1893), 290; (1894), 289.

[85] U.L. MSS., 'Coordination and Developments Committee', Deputation to Treasury, 17 June 1926.

[86] Treasury Minutes, 16 Feb. and 13 July 1899. See *The Times* (26 May 1920), p. 7; (9 Oct. 1920), p. 6.

[87] *The Spectator*, lxxx (1898), 230-1, 851-2.

pre-First World War period.[88] In 1910 there was even a chance that London's memorial to Edward VII might actually take the form of a new London University campus.[89]

The University had been 'beguiled down to the wilds of South Kensington'[90] by the prospect first of inheriting the whole of the Imperial Institute Building,[91] and then by the dream of expanding all over Albertopolis – spearheaded by London's new *Technische Hochschule*, Imperial College. Now Imperial College was a project dear to both Haldane and Edward VII. It was born in 1907 as a result of Haldane's manoeuvres as Chairman of the Departmental Committee of the Board of Education in 1904-6. From the start it was a federation within a federation, and a federation with aspirations to autonomy.[92] Initially it took the form of a merger between two technical institutions: the City and Guilds College[93] on one side of Exhibition Road, housed in Waterhouse's mixed-classic building of 1881-94; and the Royal College of Science – itself a fusion of the Royal College of Chemistry[94] and the Royal School of Mines[95] – successively housed on both sides of the same road, in Fowke's *rundbogenstil* Huxley Building of 1872[96] and in Aston Webb's Baroque extensions of 1900-6[97] and 1901-13.[98] The absorption of so much

[88] From 1896 onwards, and especially in 1907-12, Ashby, Geddes and Lethaby were all involved in plans for a University Quarter centred on Crosby Hall. See A. Crawford, *C.R. Ashbee* (1986), 161; P. Kitchen, *A Most Unsettling Person . . . Patrick Geddes* (1975), 224; C.R. Ashbee, *Where the Great City Stands* (1917), 84-5, pl. 76; *University Halls of Residence, Chelsea and the Re-Erection of Crosby Hall* (1908), plans and ills.; *A.R.*, xxviii (1910), 14-19; R.I.B.A. Drawings Collection, *Catalogue*, i (1967), 34-5, pl. 26. In the event, the University Hall of Residence, Chelsea, incorporating Crosby Hall, opened in 1908, with plans for further extensions by Wratten and Godfrey. The Hall was extended in 1926 by the British Federation of University Women.

[89] A. Taylor Milne, 'Notes on the History of the University' 3, *Bulletin* (London University), 1972-3.

[90] Dr T.L. Mears, to the Haldane Commission, *P.P.* 1911, xx, 634.

[91] The Senate cited 'the size and dignity of the Institute building and its capacity for adaptation and expansion' U.L. MSS., 'Coordination and Developments Committee', [tipped in] Deputation to Treasury 17 June 1926.

[92] E.g. Lord Crewe's speech, 12 March 1914, opposing the unitary recommendation of the Haldane Commission, *Morning Post* (13 April 1914).

[93] Founded 1878 as the City and Guilds of London Institute for the Advancement of Technical Education; previously the Central Institute, and before that the Finsbury Technical College.

[94] Founded 1845, its original premises in Oxford Street were designed by James Lockyer.

[95] Founded 1851 as the Government School of Mines; 'Royal' from 1863, its first premises were in Pennethorne's Museum of Practical Geology, Jermyn Street.

[96] From 1881 the Normal School of Science and Royal School of Mines; from 1890 the Royal College of Science. Now the Cole Wing of the Victoria and Albert Museum.

[97] *B.*, lxxxvi (1904), 26; ill.; *A.R.*, xvii (1905), 256: ill.

[98] Wernher, Beit, Rhodes, Rothschild and Cassel were all involved in its funding. See also M. Argles, *South Kensington to Robbins: an Account of English Technical and Scientific*

technology into the structure of a reformed university was a complicated business, complicated enough to justify the setting up of the Haldane Commission in 1909. Once that Commission had been set up, however, Haldane made sure that its terms of reference extended to the restructuring and integration of the entire University.[99] When it reported, in 1913, its administrative recommendations were shelved, but its argument for geographical concentration had a permanent impact.[100] The solution to all problems, Haldane decided, depended on the acquisition of a new central site, and the erection of a permanent, symbolic building.[101] But where?

Education since 1851 (1964); [H.J.T. Ellingham], *Centenary of the Imperial College of Science and Technology . . . 1845-1945* (1945); A.R. Hall, *Science for Industry: . . . Imperial College . . . and its Antecedents* (1982).

[99] In 1907, the year of the foundation of Imperial College, the University had already asked the Government for a new site, *The Times* (20 Oct. 1920), quoting Site Committee report to Senate, 17 June 1914. That was soon after a scheme to extend the accommodation in the Imperial Institute by building a new Great Hall had been abandoned, *The Times* (30 June 1933).

[100] Much to the displeasure of K.C.L., 'the Haldane Commission was dominated and controlled by a small group of able and resolute men who were filled with that admiration and envy of Germany (mingled with fear of her) which prevailed in high places before the war. They believed in bureaucracy; they worshipped organisation; they loved system and consistency; they longed for centralisation and coordination; they loathed overlapping reduplication, and all the defects displayed by products of nature as distinct from products of logic; they were inspired by the confidence that comes from philosophical doubtlessness, and they were prepared for the ruthlessness which the enforcement of rigid principle requires. They had little respect for history or tradition; they tended to despise the antecedents and associations of the various colleges of the heterogeneous university; they envisaged everything from the central and official point of view; they dreamed of a 'university quarter' wherein, regardless of convenience or accessibility, offices, colleges, institutes and laboratories would be concentrated. In particular they lacked sympathy with King's, and were ready to sacrifice her on the altar of organisation.' Hearnshaw, *King's College*, p. 453-4.

[101] 'The University should have for its headquarters permanent buildings appropriate in design to its dignity and importance, adequate in extent and specially constructed for its purpose, situated conveniently for the work it has to do, bearing its name and under its own control' ('Royal Commission on University Education in London', *P.P.* 1911, xxii, 584. 'The site of the Imperial Institute is not sufficiently central for the University . . . its remoteness has occasioned much inconvenience and loss of time to those who are concerned with the working of the University and has exercised a harmful effect on its development. The buildings are shared with the Imperial Institute and are known by that name, and they have never become associated with the University in the minds of the public. The core of the fabric is in the hands of Your Majesty's Office of Works so that the University is not master in its own house . . . London, as a whole, cannot be made a university town like Oxford or Cambridge . . . But we think it is quite possible to create a university quarter in London, in which University life and interests would grow and develop, and students and teachers alike would find themselves in the atmosphere of a great seat of learning.' *Ibid.*, *P.P.* 1913, xl, 368. A true 'university quarter . . . would perhaps do more than anything else to impress the imagination of the great London public and to convince them that the University was a reality.' *Ibid.*, *P.P.* 1913, xl, 491.

Haldane had no doubt at all. He wanted Bloomsbury; in particular he wanted that part of the Bedford Estate which lay directly behind the British Museum.[102] And in 1912 he very nearly got it, even before his Commission had published its final report. Assuming the University was about to be reorganised – and that King's College would be forced by the Board of Education to move to Bloomsbury[103] – he felt free to set up a private group of Trustees to purchase the land from the Duke of Bedford.[104] £355,000 was raised in a fortnight.[105] A scheme was drawn up, just possibly by C.C.T. Doll, son of the architect to the Bedford Estate.[106] It showed how British Museum Avenue might become the approach to a great university quadrangle, thus – in effect – incorporating the façade of Burnett's Edward VII Galleries into a grand classical complex in Parisian, Beaux Arts fashion.[107] But Haldane was moving too fast. He had squared the Chancellor, Lord Rosebery; but he neglected even to consult the Vice-Chancellor, or the Senate, or Convocation – still less the L.C.C. The scheme collapsed, and the money was ignominiously returned.[108] Haldane had jumped the gun – 'in the manner', noted *The Times*, 'of clever, masterful people who wish to do business promptly'.[109]

That left the field clear for a whole gamut of schemes: Somerset House;[110] the Foundling Hospital;[111] the garden of Gray's Inn;[112]

---

[102] *The Times* (19 Feb. 1912), p. 4: plan showing four plots of land devoted to Great Hall; Senate House; Convocation, U.L.U., O.T.C., etc.; lecture rooms and library.

[103] In 1912 the Board of Education condemned the Strand site as inadequate and threatened fiscal sanctions unless another site was found: 'a thunderbolt out of the bluebook', Hearnshaw, *King's College*, p. 444. In 1913 the Haldane Commission peremptorily advised removal to 'the neighbourhood of U.C.', Huelin, *King's College*, p. 45-6.

[104] The Trustees were: Haldane, Milner, Rosebery and the financier Sir Francis Trippel, *The Times* (19 Feb. 1912), p. 4; (22 March 1912), p. 8.

[105] *The Times* (15 March 1912), p. 6; (21 March 1912), p. 4; (22 March 1912), p. 8; (25 March 1912), p. 8; (28 March 1912), p. 6.

[106] *B.* cv (1913), 264 (editorial hint regarding involvement of The Bedford Estate Office).

[107] *Estates Gazette* (9 Nov. 1912): ills. and plan.

[108] *The Times* (6 May 1912), p. 14; (9 May 1912), p. 6; (11 May 1912), p. 4; (14 May 1912), p. 7; (20 May 1912), p. 12. The L.C.C. claimed that the Duke of Bedford was asking three times the market price and – anyway – the Government had already promised to supply the University with suitable accommodation, *ibid.*, (3 April 1912), p. 4.

[109] *The Times* (14 May 1912), p. 9.

[110] *Pall Mall Gazette* (13 Nov. 1912). Though H. Heathcote Statham warned against its alteration, *The Times* (16 Dec. 1913), p. 6.

[111] *The Times* (5 April 1912), p. 2; (16 May 1912), p. 6 (plan); (13 Aug. 1912), p. 8. See also *The Graphic* (3 June 1912) (plan). The Senate Site Committee favoured this at one point, *The Times* (17 July 1912), p. 11; *Daily Telegraph* (16 July 1912). But the L.C.C. doubted the wisdom of destroying the old hospital buildings, *The Times* (28 July 1912), p. 12. Its use for the London Museum was also suggested, *The Times* (2 Aug. 1912), p. 7. This site was again considered in 1920 and 1927, *The Times* (1 Oct. 1920), p. 5; (7 Oct. 1920), p.

Pentonville Hill;[113] the Crystal Palace;[114] the Botanic Gardens in Regent's Park;[115] a South Bank site to the east of County Hall,[116] and another – now occupied by the National Theatre – next to Waterloo Bridge.[117] All these sites were rather more spacious than that offered by the Duke of Bedford. And in Albert Richardson's scheme of 1914 for a grandiose expansion of Somerset House this phase of university politicking produced at least one architectural vision of tantalising grandeur.[118] But all these ideas lacked Bloomsbury's trump-card, the proximity of the British Museum: 'the British Museum [Library] should be to the University of London what the Bodleian is to Oxford'.[119] That was the authentic voice of U.C.L. There were even two schemes to annexe the area *in front* of the B.M. as well, from Great Russell Street to beyond New Oxford Street.[120] King's might opt for the Strand; L.S.E. for the Aldwych; Imperial College and the external lobby for South Kensington; the L.C.C. for the South Bank. But Bloomsbury had a special magnetism, and on the very eve of the First World War it was the subject of one visionary scheme which might have given it for all time the status of an academic symbol: a scheme by no less an architect than Edwin Lutyens.

Surviving sketches by Lutyens, watermarked 1914, suggest that here was a scheme which might have married the Greek Revival of William

---

12; (6 Jan. 1927), p. 6; (2 March 1927), p. 18. In 1920 the price was estimated at £1,000,000, *Observer* (3 Oct. 1920); *The Times* (27 May 1922), p. 8; in 1927 at £1,250,000, *The Times* (2 March 1927), p. 13.

[112] *The Times* (4 April 1912), p. 11.

[113] *Islington Gazette* (12 Aug. 1913).

[114] *Daily Telegraph* (11 April 1912).

[115] Suggested as one of several urban improvements by William Woodward, *The Times* (10 April 1912), p. 4. The residents of Marylebone took fright at the idea, *ibid.* (15 May 1912), p. 10.

[116] 'The most splendid site in London' *The Times* (9 Aug. 1912), p. 8; 'room for half a dozen universities', *Birmingham Post* (9 Oct. 1913). For descriptions and views see *Daily Telegraph* (6 April 1912) and (28 June 1912); *Daily Graphic* (29 June 1912) and (20 July 1912); *The Times* (18 July 1912), p. 7; (19 July 1912), p. 4; (20 July 1912), p. 8.

[117] *The Graphic* (24 Jan. 1914) (plan); *The Times* (3 Aug. 1922), p. 4.

[118] *B.*, cvi (1914), 13 *et seq.* (plans and elevations by Richardson and Gill).

[119] *Westminster Gazette* (6 Aug. 1913). 'The intellectual heart of London', *The Times* (8 Nov. 1922), p. 7. 'Bloomsbury is inherently and fundamentally the intellectual pivot, not only of London, but of the Empire, and any attempt to shift it will be as futile as an attempt to shift the financial centre of London from the City to Kensington, or the theatrical centre from Piccadilly to the City', S.D. Adshead, Professor of Town Planning, U.C., in *Vincula* (*New Troy*), ii (1926), 174. For Bloomsbury and anti-Bloomsbury arguments, see *B.A.* (6 Sept. 1913) and (26 Sept. 1913) [E. Graham-Little]; *Westminster Gazette* (6 Aug. 1913) and (7 Aug. 1913) [Holford Knight]; *The Times* (9 May 1922), p. 8 and (10 July 1922), p. 8 [Sir G. Foster].

[120] By D.B. Niven, *B.A.* (29 March 1912): plan, and by H.J. Leaning *B.*, cxiii (1917), 163, 168: plan – designed to create 'collegiate repose' in 'one of the finest architectural courts in Europe', it was supported by the Duke of Bedford and by John Burns, M.P.

Wilkins with the Greek Re-Revival of J.J. Burnett.[121] Lutyens'
grandiloquent arrangement of porticoes, pylons, plinths and colonnades –
an elemental version of what he called the Classical High Game – conjures
up, even now, images of New Delhi in Bloomsbury.[122] The outbreak of the
First World War put an end to such dreaming. It did not, however, put an
end to the great debate. Indeed it magnified it out of all proportion. A
mighty new University of London was to be England's monument to
Imperial Triumph. At least, that was the idea of Major C.J.C. Pawley.
Backed by the Empire War Memorial League, Pawley dreamed of a
London which outshone Napoleonic Paris.[123] Lambeth Bridge as Empire
Bridge; Empire Avenue all the way from Millbank to Victoria; and
London University – King's College too – a Baroque extravaganza on a
riverfront site between the Tate Gallery and Westminster.[124] Some
people, remarked Lord Leverhulme, might think it 'mad' – but what were
a few more 'trifling millions' after a war costing £7 billion? Meetings were
held in Caxton Hall. The Duke of Westminster was willing to outbid the
Duke of Bedford. Canon Rawnsley of the National Trust rallied support to
the cause: he called it 'a monumental scheme of a gigantic type'.[125] But
such architectural histrionics were not to be taken seriously. The
predominant emotion in 1918 was not triumph but grief. Instead of a City
Triumphant, England settled for the Cenotaph and the Tomb of the
Unknown Soldier.

The situation at the end of 1918 was in reality rather desperate. The
Rector of Imperial College, Sir Alfred Keogh, had recently announced
that London University was 'the biggest thing in education on the face of
the earth'.[126] But where exactly was it? The debate on the site had reached
deadlock. King's College had rejected Bloomsbury.[127] University College

---

[121] The aged Beresford Pite had consistently argued for a Classical scheme to match the
British Museum – 'classical, academical, monumental and beautiful', *Daily Chronicle* (23
March 1912).

[122] R.I.B.A. Drawings Catalogue, *Lutyens* (1973), 37-8; *Lutyens*, Arts Council Exhibition
(1981) 186, no. 477: ill. This scheme is not mentioned in C. Hussey, *The Life of Sir Edwin
Lutyens* (1950), nor in A.S.G. Butler, *The Architecture of Sir Edwin Lutyens*, 3 vols. (1950).
Lutyens lived nearby, at 29 Bloomsbury Square, until the Summer of 1914.

[123] For further comparisons with Paris, see *The Times* (2 Mary 1922), p. 17.

[124] U.L. MSS., 27/4, drawing by Harold Oakley; *B.*, cxv (1918), 278 *et seq.*: ills. and
plan; *B.N.*, cxv (1918), 286 *et seq.*

[125] *B.*, cxv (1918), 255, 296, 298, 316, 331, 450. The scheme still had its supporters in
1922-4, e.g. Major Richard Rigg at the Royal United Services Institution, *The Times* (18
April 1923), p. 9; Captain G.S.C. Swinton of the L.C.C. Swinton, *London: her Traffic, her
Improvement and Charing Cross Bridge*, (1924); and Lutyens himself, *The Times* (29 July 1923),
p. 13; (31 July 1922), p. 6.

[126] *Daily Telegraph* (31 Jan. 1914).

[127] Where would K.C.L. go? 'Were they to go over the river?', the Principal asked his
students . . .' (Cries of 'NO!' and the singing of . . . 'One more river to cross'). Were they to
go to Bloomsbury? (Loud dissent). Were they to go to the Foundling Hospital? ('No, no',
and uproar). Wherever they went, they would require a great deal of money. (A voice, 'Go

had rejected South Kensington.[128] The Treasury had vetoed Somerset House.[129] Public opinion had dismissed the North Bank. And all parties, except the L.C.C., had rejected the South Bank. Already the British Museum and the National Shakespeare Theatre were jostling for position in Bloomsbury.[130] The Senate could not agree with Convocation, and neither could agree with the Board of Education, still less with the Treasury. 'There are so many conflicting interests', noted one observer, 'financial, educational, geographical, architectural, sentimental – that it is almost impossible to reconcile them, and the governing bodies of the various institutions which have a voice in the decision are so hopelessly divided that no agreement seems within sight. Who, then, will solve the riddle?'[131]

In 1919-20, H.A.L. Fisher, President of the Board of Education, set out to do so. Government offered to buy the Bloomsbury site from the Duke of Bedford for £425,000 and give it to the University. In return – and this was the snag – the University, and King's College, would have to raise money to erect new premises, and Government would take back the buildings of King's and the Imperial Institute. The University had five years to make up its mind, starting from April 1921.[132] It was, as A.C. Headlam observed, 'a strange sort of liberality'.[133] For the second time in a generation the University had 'the Governmental pistol' at its head.[134] Still, Fisher could count on the support of U.C.L., led by Sir Gregory Foster. He might even have persuaded King's, had he increased the paltry compensation of £370,000 which he offered to that beleaguered college.[135] But he reckoned without the L.C.C.; most of all, he reckoned without the L.C.C.'s Tory leader Captain G.S.C. Swinton (1859-1937) – soldier, artist, herald, town-planner, traffic engineer and polemicist

to Lloyd George'). Throughout the proceedings the students were very demonstrative with mouth organs, motor horns, bugles and other noisy instruments', *Commemoration Day*, *The Times* (4 July 1912), p. 6. Dr Burrows, however, seems to have been less opposed to Bloomsbury than his successor, Ernest Barker, *The Times* (13 May 1927), p. 17.

[128] E.g. *Westminster Gazette* (6-7 Aug. 1913); *The Times* (2 Feb. 1921), p. 11.

[129] *Westminster Gazette* (19 June 1914); *B.N.*, cvi (1914), 877. In 1913 the Government valued it at £3m, Hearnshaw, *King's College*, 455.

[130] Sir Hercules Read suggested the land to the North of the B.M. as the most suitable site for a National Library, cited by Swinton in *Nineteenth Century* cx (1921), 692.

[131] Philip Gibbs, 'Where Shall We Build the New University of London?', *The Graphic* (24 Jan. 1914): plan. 'Resistance to the settlement of the University of London site [question was] protean in its versatility', A.F. Pollard, *The Times* (4 Oct. 1920), p. 14.

[132] *The Times* (20 May 1920), pp. 15, 18; (2 Oct. 1920), p. 6; (10 Oct. 1920), p. 10; (10 Feb. 1921), p. 10; (28 Feb. 1921), p. 6; (17 March 1921), p. 12.

[133] *The Times* (9 Oct. 1920), p. 6. See also *The Times* (20 Oct. 1920), p. 18; (21 Oct. 1920), p. 11.

[134] *The Times* (27 Sept. 1920), p. 11: 'autocratic bludgeoning'.

[135] G. Huelin, *King's College*, 53. New buildings would cost three times as much, Sir E. Barker, *Age and Youth: Memories of Three Universities* (1953), 112-7, 128-30.

extraordinary.[136] The L.C.C. wanted Bloomsbury for housing. Swinton wanted a riverside site for the University,[137] or – failing that – Holland Park.[138] First he backed the North Bank; then he backed the South Bank; then he backed West Kensington – close to Albertopolis. He wanted something conspicuous on an expandable site, something monumental – after all he had been Chairman of the New Delhi Planning Committee.[139]

---

[136] Swinton's writings include: 'A Garden Road', *Fortnightly Rev.*, xci (1909), 514-25; *London: her Traffic, her Improvement and Charing Cross Bridge* (1924); 'The Troubles of London Traffic', *Qtly. Rev.*, ccxxiv (1925), 360-75; 'The Chaos of London Traffic', *Nineteenth Century*, lxiv (1908), 622-33; 'London Congestion and Cross-Traffic', *Nineteenth Century*, liii (1903), 821-33; 'The Traffic of London', *Nineteenth Century*, lviii (1905), 389-402; 'New Delhi', *Empire Rev.* (May 1931). Lutyens credited him with the invention of the green belt and the by-pass, *The Times* (18 Jan. 1937), p. 14; (23 Jan. 1937), p. 17; (2 Feb. 1937, p. 14. His later years were marred by illness, and he eventually committed suicide, *The Times* (20 Jan. 1937), p. 4; (21 Jan. 1937), p. 15. Swinton was a notable herald, and traced back his family – Swinton of that ilk – nearly 1,000 years to Aldred Edulfing, Lord of Bamburgh. He is said to have refused a mere knighthood.

[137] Swinton envisaged the university as part of a mighty redevelopment of the metropolis, centred on the Thames. 'Compared to the Thames the Seine and the Tiber are ditches. In its passage through Petrograd the Neva spreads out wide, and between Buda and Pest the great Danube pours a volume of water which no English river can equal. But the sweep of the Thames from Blackfriars to Westminster has possibilities greater than any of these. Imagine Charing Cross Station transferred to the other bank and finely rebuilt! ... [with] carriages ... from Paris, or Brussels, from Gibraltar or Rome ... from Jerusalem, Delhi, Peking or Vladivostock discharging on to it passengers ... of every race ... Alongside ... would be Waterloo Station, the landing-place of half the English-speaking peoples.' They would cross the Thames by a new Charing Cross Bridge, Swinton, 'An Empire War Memorial', *C.L.*, xlvii (1920), 41.

[138] 'The largest unbuilt-on-block of land in private hands ... Here [the University] could settle down permanently, grouping round the great historic house fine buildings widely spaced out amid trees and lawns, with power to expand all their activities as they choose. Here they could found a real university, comparable to Oxford or Cambridge', Swinton, *Saturday Rev.* (13 May 1921), p. 199. Lady Ilchester was eager to sell. And nearby were the Albert Hall, the Royal College of Music, the Imperial Institute, the Imperial College of Science and Technology, the Natural History Museum, the Victoria and Albert Museum, the Royal College of Art, *The Times* (15 Feb. 1921), p. 6; (7 Jan. 1921), p. 6. No wonder Holland Park seemed more suitable than Bloomsbury, *The Times* (4 Jan. 1921), p. 6. See also a letter by Sir Philip Magnus, *The Times* (19 Oct. 1920), p. 8. The case for Holland Park is made out in *Saturday Rev.* (Aug. 1921), editorial; *The Times* (22 Dec. 1920); (5 Jan. 1921), p. 6; (8 Feb. 1921), p. 6; (12 Feb. 1921), pp. 6, 10; (15 Feb. 1921), pp. 7, 11; (16 Feb. 1921), p. 7; (23 June 1921), p. 7; (11 July 1921), p. 6; (12 Oct. 1921), p. 7; (24 May 1922), p. 8; (10 June 1922), p. 6; (4 July 1922), p. 6; and in Swinton, 'The Site of London University', *Nineteenth Century*, xc (1921), 683-93; xci (1922), 890-901. The case for Bloomsbury is set out by Sir G. Foster in *The University of London: History, Present Resources and Future Possibilities* (1922), 24 *et seq.*

[139] 'Surely it is madness for a college or a university to bury itself away. Advertisement may be vulgar, but self-effacement is bad business. As a church is a challenge to unbelief, so is a University a challenge to ignorance. You must not hide the brightest light of education under a bushel. Even if there be recluses within it, the building must be vaunted to the world. Men must not be compelled to go to look for it. They must see it, and ask what it is', *The Times* (9 Aug. 1912), p. 8.

Alas, he wrote, the professoriat of U.C.L. 'are anxious that the University Quarter should cluster round them. The locality is unsuitable and the proposal contradicts all the recognised theories of zoning ... [a University] zone should be an example to all zones ... So far as the interests of town-planning are concerned these men [the professors of U.C.L.] are sinning against the light.'[140] By coordinating teaching and research – to say nothing of residence – on a strategically expandable site like Holland Park or the South Bank, the University might indeed have avoided the diseconomies of fragmentation and duplication which have bedevilled it ever since. Land in Bloomsbury was not even cheaper.[141] Nevertheless, Bloomsbury it was to be.

That decision (provisionally taken in 1920;[142] narrowly confirmed in 1927[143]) was a personal triumph for Sir William Beveridge,[144] Director of L.S.E. and Vice-Chancellor, and a personal defeat for Sir Ernest Graham-Little, M.P. for London University, champion of the Imperial External system, and lifelong supporter of King's and South Kensington against the omnipresent influence of U.C.L.[145] The anti-Bloomsbury faction very nearly won. King's College refused to move without adequate compensation.[146] Time ran out on the deal with the Duke of Bedford right in the middle of the General Strike.[147] With students demonstrating in the street, the Government returned the site, re-pocketed its £425,000, shrugged its shoulders while the Institute of Historical Research was

[140] Swinton, *London, her Traffic, etc.*, 38. 'The constituent college', warned Lord Dawson of Penn, 'will in effect absorb the university ... It will be [not the rape of Bloomsbury; merely] a case of peaceable penetration', *The Times* (10 April 1923), p. 8; (13 April 1923), p. 10.

[141] It was estimated that Bloomsbury would cost £36,636 per acre; Westminster £71,428; Holland Park £5,000, *The Times* (13 Jan. 1921), p. 6; (15 Jan. 1921), p. 10; (31 July 1922), p. 5. Another suggestion was Lord Mansfield's estate at Kenwood, Hampstead, *The Times* (16 July 1920), p. 9; (20 July 1920), p. 9.

[142] October 1920.

[143] By 21 votes to 18, Bellot, *V.C.H. Middlesex*, i (1959), 336.

[144] For Beveridge's career, see *The Times* (18 March 1963) and J. Harris, *Beveridge* (Oxford, 1977).

[145] E.g. *The Times* (18 Oct. 1920), p. 8; (2 June 1922), p. 6. For Graham-Little's career, see *D.N.B.*.

[146] 'Why should [K.C.L.] abandon the "air and waters" of the river bank with all its converging tide of humanity, for the frigid calm ... of ... Bloomsbury?' Sir E. Barker, *Age and Youth* (1953), 129-30. Barker likened Fisher's proposals to a game of musical chairs, in which K.C.L. was left standing, U.L. MSS. 'Coordination and Developments Committee', memo of 5 Nov. 1923, prepared late 1922. See also *The Times* (12 April 1923), p. 8; (26 March 1926), p. 15. The university was, in any case, inclined to take up a similar position *vis à vis* South Kensington, *The Times* (20 Oct. 1921), p. 7.

[147] *The Times* (18 May 1926), p. 8.

given notice to quit its temporary premises,[148] and berated the University for failing to make up its collective mind. 'Is it not an extraordinary situation', thundered Mr Winston Churchill, 'a great university . . . broken and paralysed by hostile action on the part of one of its colleges? . . . It is . . . lamentable . . . incomprehensible . . . madness.' 'The Council of King's College', replied Beveridge coolly, 'are as independent of [the University] as Russia is of [England]'.[149] In the end, in May 1927 – after the Duke of Bedford had raised his price by another £100,000 – 'a fairy godmother', as *The Times* put it, 'armed with uncounted gold', stepped in like 'a bolt from the blue': Beveridge returned from New York with a cheque for £400,000. The Bloomsbury site was in the bag at last, courtesy of the Rockefeller Foundation.[150]

Churchill himself well knew the imagistic power of architecture, and so did Sir William Beveridge. 'We make our buildings', Churchill once remarked, 'and afterwards they make us.'[151] Administratively speaking, the decks had been cleared at last. In 1924 Haldane – back in Government for the first time since 1915 – engineered the setting up of the Hilton-Young Committee (1924-6).[152] No longer was the Senate, in H.A.L.

---

[148] Professor Pollard's temporary I.H.R. buildings – appropriately Tudor in style – were adapted from existing wartime huts in the Summer of 1921, *The Times* (6 July 1921), p.9; (5 May 1922), p. 8; (10 May 1922), p. 8; (2 June 1922), p. 6. The University Union followed soon afterwards. Pollard encouraged staff and students to demonstrate, *The Times* (4 March 1926), p. 9; (12 March 1926), p. 13; (20 March 1926), p. 15; (22 May 1926), p. 8; (1 June 1926), p. 10; (18 June 1926), p. 10.

[149] U.L. MSS., 'Coordination and Developments Committee' [tipped in] 'Deputation to the Treasury, 17 June 1926'. At the time of the incorporation of King's College in 1908, Headlam hit upon a device which preserved its Anglican status in a secular university: a diarchy was established, enabling the College Council to remain autonomous. Barker wanted to 'scrap the whole of the Haldane Report', *ibid.*, Deputation of 14 March 1924. Philip Snowden simply wanted action: 'It is a perfect disgrace for the biggest city in the world not to have more imposing University accommodation and buildings than it has . . . This matter has been scandalously delayed now for years, and . . . it is high time it was settled', *ibid.*

[150] *The Times* (12 May 1927), p. 15. The Government made up the difference, and belatedly contributed additional sums in consideration of its long-standing promise to supply the University with accommodation. In 1926 Churchill had already offered half the purchase price of the Bloomsbury site for enlarging the University's unsatisfactory premises in Kensington, *The Times* (1 March 1926), p. 11; (9 March 1926), p. 10. Schemes were actually drawn up by William J. Walford, U.L. MSS., 'Coordination and Developments Committee', 17 Feb. 1926. Churchill disliked the idea of 'coaxing and weedling cash from the United States', 'Coordination and Developments', *op. cit.*, Deputation to Treasury 29 June 1926. In 1920 the Rockefeller Foundation had already given £1,000,000 to U.C.H. For negotiations with the Duke of Bedford, see *The Times* (20 Oct. 1926), p. 18; (23 Oct. 1926), p. 18; (13 Jan. 1927), p. 8.

[151] *A.A.Jnl.*, xl (1924), 44: in a lecture at the Architectural Association.

[152] 'Report of the Departmental Committee on the University of London', *P.P.* (1926), x. For the resulting University statutes, see P. Dunsheath and M. Miller, *Convocation of the University of London* (1958), 121-31.

Fisher's phrase, to be as anarchical as a Polish Diet.[153] After three Royal Commissions – Selborne, Cowper and Haldane; two governmental committees – Cranbrook and Hilton-Young; two Acts of Parliament – 1898 and 1926; and a whole battery of new statutes, the University of London was at last on the brink of visible autonomy. No university in the world had been so carefully investigated and so casually housed. Could the architectural profession rise to the challenge? The University Architect at this point was William J. Walford, a shadowy figure chosen inexplicably in preference to Sir Aston Webb.[154] But two other architects with U.C.L. connections had schemes in hand: A.E. Richardson and H.V. Lanchester. Lanchester's was Vanbrughian Baroque;[155] Richardson's was Parisian Beaux-Arts.[156] Symbolism, Lanchester explained – with a flourish of mixed metaphors – is one of the 'pillars of architecture', and this new university should be as 'a symbol or oriflamme striking the note of the place of architecture in the development of the age'.[157]

Beveridge was looking for something rather different. We need 'some inspired artist', he announced in 1927, 'who can embody [the very idea of a university, imperial and modern] in stone and steel and marble – not too much marble.'[158] In 1931 he set out to find him. With the Principal of the University, Edwin Deller, he examined more than a score of public buildings by upwards of a dozen architects. 'We went up and down the length and breadth of England and Wales', he recalled, 'seeing town halls and academic buildings, schools, hospitals and cathedrals. We enjoyed ourselves hugely.'[159] A short-list of four architects was drawn up. Four separate dinner parties were arranged at the Athenaeum.[160] At least one of the short-listed names was an architect of genius, Giles Gilbert Scott.

[153] E. Ashby and M. Anderson, *Portrait of Haldane at Work in Education* (1974), 158.

[154] In 1921 Walford was chosen 'to advise on . . . general layout . . . site and . . . style', U.L. MSS. 'Coordination and Developments Committee', 12 Oct. 1921. In 1927 he was appointed Surveyor and Manager of the Bloomsbury Estates, ibid., 'Minutes of the Site and Buildings Committee', 26 Oct. 1927.

[155] *Vincula* [*New Troy*] ii (1926), 158-9: ill.

[156] *Ibid.*, 172-3: ill.

[157] *Ibid.*, 158-9.

[158] *The Times* (12 May 1927), p. 19; (13 May 1927), p. 11; Beveridge, *Power and Influence* (1953), 185 *et seq.* 'Nothing shall be built on the Bloomsbury site that is not beautiful. Nothing shall be built that is not characteristic of London and of this age', *The Times* (17 Nov. 1928), p. 8: R.I.B.A. He dreamed of embodying in architectural form 'the clear-cut relevance of science, the lightheartedness and the solemnity of youth, the enchanted garden of the arts', Beveridge, *The Physical Relation of a University to a City* (1928), 15. It must not be 'mean or cramped or ugly. It must, like the Cathedrals of the Middle Ages, be the visible symbol of a faith . . . an enclosure of quiet courts and green spaces and great libraries and halls of learning . . . a visible sign to all men of the academic faith', *The Times* (10 May 1928), p. 18: graduation dinner.

[159] Beveridge, *Power and Influence, op. cit.*, 206.

But another had the backing of one of the Governors of L.S.E., Frank Pick.[161] Pick was overlord of London Transport, and his protégé was Charles Holden – architect of London's underground. Holden was a Romantic Modern: he called himself an 'anarchist Communist'.[162] Professionally speaking, he was a product of Arts and Crafts morality who progressed via eclectic mannerism to abstract modernity.[163] As a young rebel from Lancashire, suffocated by the pomp and circumstance of Edwardian classicism, he longed for a new architecture of function and pure form. Epstein and Walt Whitman became his idols. 'Come, you Modern Buildings, come!', he wrote in 1905. 'Throw off your mantle of deceits . . . we must put aboriginal constructive force into our work, and leave it to speak for itself: no mere ingenuity will suffice; tricky combinations of style and smart inventions are fool's play . . . The grave yawns for Architect's Architecture'.[164]

Holden's masterplan for London University (1932) envisaged a series of giant pylons, all the way from the B.M. to U.C.L.; a Temple of Learning a quarter of a mile long, axially arranged along a central spinal core and topped by gigantic terminal towers.[165] The advantage of a spinal plan – as opposed to the open courtyards which he first envisaged – lay in the fact that further units, or ribs, could be added to the 'backbone of knowledge' as need arose.[166] Holden was thinking not in terms of decades but in terms of centuries: a building programme of fifty years; a life-expectancy of five hundred; and an expenditure of £2-3,000,000.[167] To this new mega-campus would come Birkbeck College from Fetter Lane;[168] the Courtauld Institute from Portman Square;[169] the Institute of Archaeology from

[160] On the advice of Lord Crawford, Chairman of the R.F.A.C., Beveridge had plumped for a limited competition, U.L. MSS. 'Minutes of the Site and Buildings Committee, 18 Nov. 1927. Others called for an open competition, *A. and B.N.*, xxxv (1931), 231, 233.

[161] For Pick's concept of art, see Pick, 'Art in Modern Life', *Nineteenth Century* xci (1922), 256-64.

[162] He refused a knighthood and died in the small, semi-detached house which he designed for himself and lived in for fifty years, *A. and B.N.*, ccxvii (1960), 592: obit.

[163] See C.H. Reilly, *Building* (Sept. 1931) 396-401; B. Hanson, *A.R.*, clviii (1975), 348-56.

[164] [Holden], *A.R.*, xvii (1905), 258; xviii (1905), 27.

[165] *R.I.B.A. Jnl.*, 3rd ser. xliii (1936), 621-2: perspective by C. Hutton.

[166] *Ibid.*, xlv (1938), 634 *et seq.*: ills.

[167] *I.L.N.* (21 Jan. 1938), p. 86-7: ill.; *The Listener* (1 July 1936), p. 26. Holden prepared a view of 'The University from Russell Square in AD. 2014', when neighbouring leases had fallen in and the long-term plan had been completed, *R.I.B.A. Jnl.*, 3rd ser., xlv (1938), 640: ill. The Great Hall, *B.*, clviii (1940), 554: ill. was never built; the site remained empty until the 1980s.

[168] Bream's Building, 1883, C. Delisle Burns, *A Short History of Birkbeck College* (1924), 93: ill.

[169] Home House, designed by Robert Adam, 1775-7, *C.L.*, lxxii (1932), 428-33, 462-8.

Regent's Park,[170] and the Institute of Education from Southampton Row.[171] S.S.E.E.S. would come from King's;[172] S.O.A.S. would come from Finsbury Circus;[173] and the University Library, Senate House and Ceremonial Hall would come from South Kensington. Alas, there was no provision for centralised laboratories: these were to remain collegiate.[174] *Hinc illae lacrimae.* But Rockefeller had supplied the site; the Goldsmiths' Company were to provide the Library; the City of London the Great Hall; Samuel Courtauld the new Institute of Fine Art. The L.C.C. would help with Birkbeck College and the Institute of Education. 'London', announced *The Times* in 1932, 'reaches today a historic milestone . . . [it is to be] the home of an Imperial University.'[175] The Archbishop of Canterbury compared Holden's vision to Wren's St Paul's: twin witnesses to the glory of God.[176] The new shrine even had its martyr: Sir Edwin Deller, Principal of the University, went on an inspection of the site in November 1936 and was killed by a falling skip.[177]

'Timeless' was the quality aimed at. Abstract geometry outside; 'chaste dignity' within.[178] Far from being 'modern', the constructional techniques were quite traditional: no structural steel or concrete; all brick and marble, timber and masonry, even those skyscraping buttresses. A dauntingly permanent exterior, and an interior with an infinite capacity for rearrangement: the tower's steel bookstack, for example, is structurally autonomous and thus easily removable. Even the plumbing apparently aimed at eternity: these are 'the kind of soil pipes', wrote one critic, 'that one expects to see in the courts of heaven'.[179] Well, maybe. But 'timeless' the Senate House is not. In every line and every shape it bespeaks the eye of the 1930s. Its design was a compromise between

---

[170] St John's Lodge, Regent's Park, later part of Bedford College, J. Mordaunt Crook, 'The Villas in Regent's Park', *C.L.*, cxliv (1968), 22-5, 84-7.

[171] Opened 1907; formerly the London Day Training College.

[172] Founded 1915; Institute Status, 1932.

[173] The former London Institution, designed by William Brooks, 1815-19, A. Oswald, *C.L.*, lxxxix, 378-81. S.O.S. became S.O.A.S. in 1938.

[174] See *Nature* (9 July 1952). Twelve years previously, Oliver Lodge had floated a drastic solution: put the 'academic factories' on the periphery, but keep 'the humanising elements of education' at the centre, *The Times* (6 Oct. 1920), p. 6.

[175] *The Times* (27 July 1932), p. 13. 'The focus of [the University's] manifold activities . . . the visible sign and symbol of the pursuit of learning . . . in a vast city', *The Times* (12 May 1932), p. 10; (27 July 1932), p. 9.

[176] At a centenary service in St Paul's, *The Times* (1 July 1936), p. 11. There was also a luncheon at Guildhall and a reception at Lancaster House, *The Times* (1 July 1936), p. 17; (17 July 1936), p. 17.

[177] *The Times* (28 Nov. 1936), p. 9; (3 Dec. 1936), p. 7; (19 Feb. 1937), p. 16.

[178] *A. and B.N.*, cxlviii (1936), 306. Holden loved Portland Stone for its marmoreal qualities; the *Manchester Guardian* ran an article by James Bone on Holden and Deller's visit to the quarries of the Isle of Portland.

[179] H.M. Fletcher, *R.I.B.A. Jnl.*, 3rd ser. xlv (1938), 647.

classicism and modernity, and perhaps because of that, it was predictably popular with the professionals.[180] In the University's centenary year, 1936, Holden received the R.I.B.A.'s Royal Gold Medal. In 1938, when he unveiled Myerscough Walker's floodlit perspective, the R.I.B.A. audience broke into spontaneous applause.

Holden was an instinctive minimalist. His view of ornament was not negative but reductive. 'When in doubt', he used to say, 'leave it out.' He tried to do for architecture what Eric Gill did for typography.[181] 'It was not so much a matter of creating a new style', he explained, 'as of discarding those incrustations which counted for style'; all that 'surface embroidery empty of structural significance'. Freed of the mumbo-jumbo of traditional form, he felt able to concentrate on 'those more permanent basic factors of architecture, the plan, and the planes and masses arising out of the plan'.[182] True to his generation of 'early modernists', he tried hard to see architectural form as a product of necessity.[183] It was exciting, he tells us, to see the Senate House rising inevitably from its plan: the building, he claimed, 'almost designed itself'.[184] That was wishful thinking, and Holden surely knew it: he was too much of an artist to be a dogmatic functionalist.[185] Architectural design is always a matter of choice: choice from a number of equally valid solutions. The basis of that choice – in effect, the aesthetic impulse – is infinitely mysterious. But whatever its source, choice ultimately dictates the shape of a building. And as Holden's acoustic engineer, Hope Bagenal, remarked, every age 'will die for its shapes'.[186] The shapes of the 1930s are not our shapes, and even at the time Holden's shapes were not the shapes of A.E. Richardson,

[180] 'The design is mainly of our time, arising out of the natural expression of the plan. The very orderly disposition of the parts and the strong horizontal character of the whole [scheme gives] to the mass a classical basis, which together with the rhythmical disposition of the window openings and other essential features ... present[s] a neighbourly front to the British Museum and ... surrounding [buildings], without the necessity of columnar treatment', quoted in Humberstone, *New Buildings for the University of London*, 1933. 'Nobody better than [Holden] could strip a classical design to its essentials without leaving it looking naked', *The Times* (2 May 1960), p. 21: obit.

[181] *B.*, cxcviii (1960), 875: obit.

[182] *R.I.B.A. Jnl.*, 3rd ser., xliii (1936), 623: Gold Medal Presentation.

[183] 'Fitness for purpose', he believed, 'is more than a slogan, it is a creed; and, though it may not be the *last* word [in design] it is most certainly the first', *A.R.* clviii (1975), 348-56. Living in non-functional buildings is like 'asking for bread and being offered a dress-shirt' *R.I.B.A. Jnl.* xlix (1941-2), 130.

[184] *R.I.B.A. Jnl.*, 3rd ser., xlv (1938), 642. Even the drain-pipes were 'given a place of honour', *The Listener* (1 July 1936), p. 25.

[185] 'Style', he believed, 'should arise out of the solution of a particular problem, and the capacity of the architect to give visual aesethtic quality to that solution', *R.I.B.A. Jnl.* xlix (1941-2), 130. But our appreciation of architecture, he admitted, is ultimately a matter of aesthetics, *R.I.B.A. Jnl.*, 3rd ser., xlv (1938), 634.

[186] *A.A. Jnl.*, liii (1937), 294.

Max Beerbohm or Evelyn Waugh. Holden hoped to exemplify in his work 'the beauty in the soul of man in the industrial age'.[187] Richardson and his classical friends disagreed: they called it an academic 'ant-heap'; a 'Germanic' nightmare based on the 'molecular' or 'cellular formation of Assyrian palaces . . . Socialism in its most insistent form'.[188] 'Bleak, bland [and] hideous', Beerbohm exploded, a 'vast whited sepulchre.'[189] 'That gross mass of masonry', wrote Evelyn Waugh, 'its shadow and . . . vast bulk . . . insulting the autumnal sky.'[190] The Senate House was supposed to be England's answer to the American skyscraper.[191] Perhaps, they order things better in Chicago. Holden's interiors are grandly conceived and superbly finished, but – at least as regards exterior composition – his vision of embodied function outran his grasp of presentational design. He could handle an underground station brilliantly. But in Bloomsbury – at any distance less than half a mile – truly monumental form seems to have eluded him. Today – incomplete, marooned, melancholy as a beached whale – the Senate House seems timeless for all the wrong reasons.

Holden's master-plan collapsed with the onset of the Slump and the Second World War. Neither S.O.A.S. nor Birkbeck could raise the necessary funds. After 1935, and again after 1937, the original scheme was altered and replaced by a truncated version; the so-called 'balanced plan'. This in turn gave way to a piecemeal programme of separate buildings, cheaply built in steel and brick and loosely following the configuration of a Georgian street pattern originally designed for a totally different purpose. Bloomsbury descended to Subtopia.[192] S.O.A.S. (1938-46) was followed by Birkbeck (1939-51; 1964); Birkbeck by U.L.U. (1949-55; 1957)[193] and U.L.U. by the Warburg Institute (1957-8). S.O.A.S. still has one or two touches of vintage Holden.[194] Birkbeck was awarded a medal by the Worshipful Company of Tylers and Bricklayers.[195] And the Nuffield Swimming Bath at U.L.U. is not without antiseptic drama.[196]

[187] *R.I.B.A. Jnl.*, lxvii (1960), 383-4. Its design embodied 'a faith, a philosophy and an aesthetic principle', *ibid.*, xlv (1938), 634.

[188] T.L. Humberstone, ed., S.D. Adshead [A.E. Richardson], A.B. Knapp-Fisher, C. Doll, *New Buildings for the University of London* (1933). Humberstone called the design 'fantastically silly and megalomaniacal', Humberstone, *Torrington Square Saved!* (1938), 16.

[189] M. Beerbohm, *Mainly on the Air* (1946), 80.

[190] E. Waugh, *Put Out More Flags* (1942). During the Second World War it became the Ministry of Information, and there John Betjeman first encountered Miss Joan Hunter Dunn.

[191] Dr Maxwell Garnett called for a giant skyscraper, on American lines, a Cathedral of Learning like that at Pittsburg – double the height of St Paul's – a memorial to the Rockefeller Foundation's 'miracle of generosity', *The Times* (14 May 1927), p. 8.

[192] *A.J.*, cxxvii (1958), 5.

[193] Drawings: R.I.B.A.D.

[194] *B.*, clxx (1946), 7-9.

[195] *B.*, clxxxiv (1953), 877.

[196] *B.*, cxciv (1958), 346-9.

But the Warburg marks the last gasp of Holden's post-Georgian abstraction.[197] A comparison between the Warburg Institute and the Institute of Classical Studies (by Booth, Ledeboer and Pinkheard) is instructive.[198] Both were built in the mid-1950s. Both compromise previous traditions: Georgian Domestic on one hand, Scandinavian Modern on the other. One looks back, the other forwards – but neither looks very far. 'Holden', noted Ian Nairn in 1966, 'deserved better of old age than this.' The later buildings from his office – 'designed from God knows what backwater of the intellect' – were widely criticised (notably by Pevsner) as a geriatric retreat into Neo-Georgian.[199] Holden, once the darling of the avant garde, had become the whipping boy of the New Brutalists.

Brutalism arrived in Bloomsbury with the advent of Sir Denys Lasdun. Appointed in 1960, Lasdun inherited Leslie Martin's proposals of 1959[200] for the University Precinct – just as Martin had inherited Holden's proposals of 1932 and 1935-7, Abercrombie and Forshaw's County of London Plan (1943), and the County of London Development Plan (1957).[201] Holden and Abercrombie had begun with the concept of *tabula rasa*, even if Holden's programme was eventually forced to compromise with its Georgian context. Martin – with his principles of 'enclosure, seclusion and informality' – at least intended to follow the broad outlines of existing Bloomsbury, even if he envisaged wholesale replacement of terrace housing by a network of podiums, walkways and tunnels.[202] But Lasdun – facing conservationist pressures which mounted as his scheme progressed from 1965 to 1980 – had to try to accommodate Georgian brick and Brutalist concrete in an overall layout dictated by traffic flows, split-level development and high-density usage. Turning its back on the public, Lasdun's precinct faces inwards onto landscaped gardens; peripheral

[197] Drawings: R.I.B.A.D. 'Commonplace and trivial', J.M. Richards, *A.J.*, cxxviii (1958), 15.
[198] Criticism of elevational compromise by J.M. Richards, *ibid.*; architects' reply, *ibid.* (10 July 1958), 58-9. Judith Ledeboer had been one of the most rebellious young moderns at the A.A. early in the 1930s.
[199] Pevsner, 'Backyard Mentality', *A.R.*, cxxviii (1960), 446-8; I. Nairn, *Nairn's London* (1966), 114.
[200] *B.*, cxcvi (1959), 442-3; *A.R.*, cxxv (1959), 302, 357-8, *Daily Telegraph*, 26 Feb. 1959. Martin was appointed in 1957.
[201] Meanwhile the site had expanded. In 1951 the University had purchased another 13½ acres from the Bedford Estate, making a total of 35 acres between Euston Road and the B.M. Thanks to Rockefeller, U.C.L. had already bought up land between its own site and Torrington Place, *The Times* (16 Feb. 1932), p. 9. In 1914 the University had also bought All Saints, Gordon Square, closed in 1909, *The Standard* (2 March 1914).
[202] M.G.[irouard], *C.L.*, cxxv (1959), 458: ill. Woburn Square and the area north of Gordon Square will be destroyed – 'but the Georgian character of the area has been vitiated beyond redemption already, and the loss of these now isolated terraces would be a great deal more than counterbalanced by the gains'.

structures are all concrete strata and blocky service towers, echoing Holden's pylons: dogmatic, programmatic, uncompromising. His is a stern, uncomfortable aesthetic. 'Architecture', he reminds us, 'has other things to do besides consoling'.[203] As with Holden's scheme, the architectural world was hugely enthusiastic. But Lasdun's 'strong utopian impulse' – architecture as service; architecture as a metaphor for landscape – proved too strong and too utopian for popular consumption.[204]

What we see now – S.O.A.S., the Institute of Education and the Institute of Avanced Legal Studies – is but a rump, a utopian rump. Woburn Square has become a monument to a defunct planning ideology. Ironically, the projected building in the front line of this conservationist battle was the one institution in the University dedicated to the study of Fine Art: the Courtauld. It remained unbuilt. The University was left with a precinct which was doubly truncated: the conservationists defeated Lasdun just as surely as the Slump and the Second World War had defeated Holden. But – as the Irish would say – neither should have started from there. Both were prisoners of a totally unsuitable site: they paid the penalty of Haldane and Beveridge's commitment to Bloomsbury. And even as Lasdun's programme was stumbling to a halt, the magnet which had drawn the University to Bloomsbury in the first place was removed: the British Museum library was to be transported to St Pancras.

While the University was locking itself into an architectural cul-de-sac, the colleges were growing fast: too fast for their own architectural good. Expansion and reorganisation; mergers and rumours of mergers – associated with the names of Robbins (1963), Todd (1968), Murray (1972), Flowers (1980), Swinnerton-Dyer (1981) and Quirk (1982) – have all had an impact on the changing physical structure of our university. Particularly on the architectural face of medical teaching and scientific research.[205] The quintuple division which has emerged since 1983, centred on Bloomsbury, South Kensington, Mile End Road, the Strand and Egham, has itself produced a new wave of building on top of two previous waves of expansion: post-1945 and post-1963.

First into post-war expansion was Imperial College. From 1953 onwards – separately funded by the U.G.C. – it became the spearhead of a government-fuelled initiative in science and technology. Despite

[203] *R.I.B.A. Jnl.*, (Sept. 1977), 179, 366-7.

[204] For detailed analysis, see *A.R.*, clxvii (1980), 144-54; *B.*, ccxii (1967), 91-3; *A.D.*, li (1985), 4-5; *Interbuild*, xiv (1967), 24-6.

[205] E.g. 1950s work: by Easton and Robertson at Bart's Hospital, fronting Clerkenwell Road, and by Basil Ward and Lyons, Israel and Ellis at Hammersmith Hospital. The new School of Pharmacy in Brunswick Square, although begun in 1938, was only completed in 1959. New buildings for St George's Hospital Medical School – at Hyde Park Corner until 1976 – were not completed until 1984.

vociferous protests,[206] all but the tower of Colcutt's Imperial Institute was demolished and replaced by a series of sub-Meisian teaching blocks designed by Norman and Dawbarn, and sub-Corbusian halls of residence designed by Richard Sheppard and Partners.[207] Their mechanical, 1950s style façades seem slightly less tame today than they did in the 1960s – even so one occasionally sighs for the exuberance of their predecessors: the Imperial College Union, for instance, formerly the Royal School of Needlework, by Fairfax B. Wade (1898-1903; dem. 1963).

What Imperial College is to West London, Queen Mary College is to the East. And what the Imperial Institute was to Imperial College the People's Palace was to Q.M.C. E.R. Robson, best known for his work as architect to the London School Board, had projected a number of eclectic schemes[208] – with echoes of both the Crystal Palace and the Beaux Arts – before securing agreement for his executed design.[209] The rib-vaulted library was a classical version of the fourteenth-century Prior's Kitchen at Durham. The Queen's Hall (burnt 1931) outdid even Robson's Prince's Hall in Piccadilly. Opened by Queen Victoria in 1887, this 'happy experiment in . . . practical Socialism', as *The Times* put it, set out – in darkest Mile End Road – 'to sow the seeds of a higher and more humane

---

[206] E.g. *The Times* (4 Feb. 1956), p. 7 [Casson], (7 Feb. 1956), p. 9 [Richardson] (13 Feb. 1956), p. 9 [Betjeman], (27 Feb. 1956), p. 9 [Pevsner]; *C.L.*, cxix (1956), 329-30 [Hussey]; *R.I.B.A. Jnl.*, (Jan. 1956) [Goodhart-Rendel]. *The Times* itself defended Colcutt [3 Feb. 1956] p. 9, as did the Royal Fine Art Commission. But the Tory Government – backed by hard-line modernists e.g. J. Murray Easton; *The Times* (21 Feb. 1956), p. 9 – proved adamant. The eventual compromise, retaining the great tower, was suggested by Julian Huxley, *The Times* (10 Feb. 1956), p. 7.

[207] For plans of these designs, modified to include Colcutt's tower, see *C.L.*, cxxiii (1958), 244 and *Contract Jnl.* (13 Feb. 1958); exhib. R.A. 1960; *B.*, cc (1961), 5-8. 'There are most interesting architectural possibilities', noted [J.M. Richards] in 1956, 'in the juxtaposition of this richly-modelled piece of Victorian eclecticism and the plain, rectilinear buildings that will provide it with a new asymmetrical setting', *The Times* (22 June 1956). Fifty years before that, late Victorian Picturesqueness seemed wholly deplorable. 'The group, if so it can be called, formed by the City and Guilds of London Insitute, the Royal School of Needlework and the Imperial Institute, could not be paralleled on the Continent of Europe; a result so entirely, even so violently, unacademic would be abhorrent to cultivated taste in any country less wedded to liberty than our own', A.E. Street, *A.R.*, xvii (1905), 255: ills.

[208] People's Palace (Beaumont Trust) Prospectus, 1885: ill; *B.*, 1 (1886), 772: [not quite] a people's palace; there is rather a taint of aristocracy about it'. For another (unrelated) 'People Palace' design, by E.W. Godwin and J.P. Seddon – designed for a site on the Victoria Embankment, to the west of Waterloo Bridge – see *B.*, lii (1887), 250: ill.

[209] Great Hall, concert rooms, art galleries, gymnasiums, lecture and music rooms, winter garden, library, swimming baths, play rooms; statues by Verheyden; decoration and painted glass by Collinson and Locke, *The Times* (14 May 1887), p. 17; *B.*, 1 (1886), 772, 915: ills. and plan – exhib. R.A. 1886 no. 1683; *B.*, lii (1887), 716: ill. (Queen's Hall); *B.*, lvii (1887), 174: ill. (Library).

civilisation among the dwellers and toilers in [that] unlovely district'.[210] Thence grew the East London Technical College, the East London College, and eventually in 1934 Queen Mary College. Around Robson's original building has grown a complex of post-war blocks devoted to science and technology, themselves incorporating advanced structural techniques.[211]

Faithful to Sidney Webb's scale of priories, L.S.E. for many years preferred professors to buildings. 'Lack of space and higgledy-piggledy development has not', it was observed in 1958, 'prevented the L.S.E. from becoming a world-famous school of unique attraction. It is a phenomenon typical of London that this intellectual hub, that draws students from the ends of the earth, has no architectural existence at all.'[212] That was not quite true: during the 1920s and 1930s Beveridge made sure that L.S.E. was indeed 'that part of the University . . . on which the concrete never sets'.[213] And successive adaptations of existing buildings were occasionally imaginative. But it was not until the 1960s that L.S.E. moved – architecturally speaking – into the top league with two purpose-built tower blocks: the St Clement's Building and the Clare Market Building.[214]

Over on the other side of the Strand, the 1960s were equally dramatic – some would say architecturally traumatic. Ever since its foundation, King's College had coveted Somerset House. In a memorable outburst to the Haldane Commission in 1911, Dr T.L. Mears had challenged the government to do the honourable thing: 'Somerset House [is] the ideal

[210] 'The People's Palace is not to be merely a place of recreation, though rational recreation is itself a great civilising agency; in course of time it will encompass within itself the whole scheme of industrial life, providing for its toil as well as for its leisure. In this respect it is an institution of national importance', *The Times* (14 May 1887), p. 13. It was Barber Beaumont who in 1841 first bequeathed money for the project; it was Walter Besant who set out its Utopian programme; and it was the 'timely munificence' of Sir Edmund Currie which brought the project to completion. See G. Godwin, *Queen Mary College: An Adventure in Education* (1939); G.P. Moss and M.V. Saville, *From Palace to College* (1985).

[211] E.g. Nuclear Engineering Laboratory by Playne and Lacey, 1953; 1961, using pre-stressed (as opposed to reinforced) concrete members for the first time in the London area *A.J.*, cxii (1950), 110; Engineering Faculty Building by the same firm, *c.* 1958, using a steel frame and concrete grid; School of Biological Sciences (1976), a 'cascade' of steel and glass by the Playne Vallence Partnership (Fielden and Mawson; P. Vallence and A.J.S. Brown).

[212] *A.J.*, cxxvii (1958), 8.

[213] W. Beveridge, *The L.S.E. and its Problems, 1919-37* (1960), 28. The 'Old Building' (1920-22) was added to in 1928 and 1931-2. For Passmore Edwards Hall (1902, by M.B. Adams, editor of the *Building News*; reconstructed 1934), see *The Sphere* (31 May 1902): ills; J. Beveridge, *An Epic of Clare Market* (1960), 51: ill.; Sir S. Caine, *The Foundation of the L.S.E.* (1963), 80.

[214] By Cusdin, Burden and Howitt, *B.*, ccxviii (1970), (9), 69-71; *A. and B.N.*, v (1970), (3), 63. Cost £1½m.

spot [for King's] . . . Turn out the [Inland] Revenue'.[215] That was the cry
in 1912, in 1914, in 1918, in 1926, in 1944 – but the tax-gatherers hung on
grimly to the finest riverfront in London and one of the finest quadrangles
in the world. King's had to export its schoolboys to Wimbledon,[216] its
medics to Camberwell,[217] its theologians to Vincent Square,[218] its ladies
to Campden Hill.[219] It dug basements and built annexes, and waited.[220]
Then in the autumn of 1963 the Robbins Report appeared. Within two
days of its publication, the Principal, Sir Peter Noble, wrote to the U.G.C.
suggesting that an ideal site for expansion was right there, on the
doorstep: Somerset House.[221] The Government had other ideas: millions
of pounds were spent in building new universities in open fields. Instead of
Somerset House, King's got a new building in the Strand.

Two and a quarter million pounds worth of concrete; erected 1966-72;
architects: Troup and Steele; consultants: J. Murray Easton and E.D.
Jeferiss Matthews. 'The scale . . . character [and] colour', it was claimed
at the time, 'assimilate those of Somerset House, and in particular
maintain and emphasise the major horizontal motive. The façades . . . are
in the form of boldly moulded pre-cast concrete exposed structural frames
. . . finished in a coarse textured granite and white spar aggregate. It is
hoped this will weather in the same black and white tones as . . . Somerset
House . . . The new building seems almost to merge into the existing
varied street patterns . . . [Indeed it] respects its neighbours in a way
unusual for most modern buildings.'[222] Well it did not , and it does not.
When Sir Peter Noble retired as Principal of King's in 1972 it was said of
him that at his death two words would be found engraved upon his heart:
'Somerset House'.[223]

It was the reaction against such things which produced the wave of
post-functional thinking which we call Post-Modernism. The distance
between the Chemistry Building at U.C.L. (1970) and the Queen
Mother's Building at Westfield (1984) is rather more than the distance

[215] *P.P.* 1911, xx, 634.

[216] In 1897-9 King's College School moved from its basement quarters to premises in
Wimbledon designed by Banister Fletcher.

[217] In 1904-10 King's College Hospital moved from Portugal Street to Denmark Hill,
Camberwell, to buildings designed by W.A. Pike.

[218] Hostel, begun 1913, designed by Arthur Martin.

[219] See note 6.

[220] 'King's College, faced with the necessity of expanding on a non-expanding site,
solved the problem by constructing extensive laboratories underground. In the light of the
plans for its further development . . . this is seen to have been fortunate', *A.J.*, cxxvii,
(1958), 8.

[221] Huelin, *King's College*, p. 136.

[222] *B.*, ccviii (1965), 495; *Concrete Quarterly* (April-June 1972), 37-40: 'Manners in the
Strand'. The adjacent Macadam Building, if anything, is more Brutalist still.

[223] Huelin, *King's College*, p. 147. A poem by Prof. Eric Mascall deserves to be better
known:

from Bloomsbury to Hampstead. For *tabula rasa* read contextual values; for function read style. When W.H. Crossland's Royal Holloway College was opened by Queen Victoria in 1886, it had been greeted as in some sense a solution to the Victorian dilemma of style. 'Mr Crossland', it was remarked, has 'gone forward a great stride on the road to the creation of a new style.'[224] That was certainly wishful thinking. Crossland's synthesis of half-a-dozen Loire chateaux remains firmly rooted in the past. But it is not too fanciful to see just a little of that mimetic spirit in Sir Philip Powell's latest addition to Mr Holloway's campus: twenty million pounds worth of new buildings designed to take at least one part of London University into the twenty-first century.[224] From Chambord in Surrey to suburban Post-Modern: the architecture of London University continues to develop, if not at the centre, then surely on the periphery.

As we have seen, the architecture of London University is a mixed inheritance. One might be tempted to conclude: 'Happy is the university which has no architectural history'. But all is not total gloom: the Courtauld has moved to Somerset House, at last. In recent years we have certainly faced difficulties. But as H.A.L. Fisher promised in 1922, at a similar crisis in the University's history: 'commercial depression and industrial depression will not be with us for ever. Some day the sky will be clearer, and some day the funds will be forthcoming.'[225] Let us hope that when that time comes we do not make the same mistakes as our predecessors.

> Standing in the Strand at sunset, while the clock announced the hour,
> I beheld a monstrous building, like a dreadful ogre's tower,
> Musing to the dulcet accents of the soft pneumatic drill,
> I discerned upon its peak the noble legend HIGGS and HILL.
> 'Higgs and Hill'! my heart vibrated, every fibre felt the thrill,
> While my awestruck lips repeated 'Hill and Higgs! O, Higgs and Hill'.
> Dons replete with gin and Jaguars, students in your humble digs,
> Burying your mutual hatchets, join in praise of Hill and Higgs.
> Lives of great men all remind us, we can all for good or ill,
> Leave behind us concrete footprints, like the works of Higgs and Hill'.

ibid., 199. 'I am sure', announced H.M. the Queen, at its opening in 1972, 'that [this building] will add to the reputation of King's College.' The K.C.L. Association Magazine proclaimed, 'it takes the College into the space age'. In the quadrangle, as a final touch, was placed a statue by Barbara Hepworth entitled 'Ultimate Form', *ibid.*, 201-2.

[224] In marked contrast to Egham's earlier Brutalism, conceived by Sir Leslie Martin and Colin St John Wilson, *A.R.* cxxxiv (1963), 279.

[225] Sir G. Foster and H.A.L. Fisher, *The University of London: History, Present Resources and Future Possibilities* (1922), 46.

2

The Plainest Principles of Justice: The University of London and the Higher Education of Women[1]

Gillian Sutherland

My title 'The Plainest Principles of Justice', is a quotation from a speech made by that distinguished radical, George Grote, pleading, as Vice-Chancellor in 1862, for the admission of women to the University of London.[2] On that occasion the proposal was lost in the Senate by the casting vote of the Chancellor.[3] Three times in the ensuing years Convocation carried resolutions in favour of degrees for women, but only in 1877 was the Senate prepared to promote a Supplemental Charter, which was granted in 1878. Our knowledge of the content of Grote's speech is unfortunately fragmentary, culled from correspondence long after the event. But I hope it is not wholly implausible to suggest that this argument followed lines similar to those pursued in the two classic texts of nineteenth-century English feminist thought: Mary Wollstonecraft's *Vindication of the Rights of Women*, first published in 1792 and John Stuart Mill's *The Subjection of Women*, written in 1861, the year before Grote's speech, although not published until 1869. The core of the argument in each case was: women are human beings and no more to be denied the

[1] A version of this essay was first delivered as a lecture at Royal Holloway and Bedford New College in November 1986. In preparing both lecture and essay it has been a particular pleasure to begin to explore the archive so admirably looked after by Elizabeth Bennett; and to learn of and draw on the work being done on the history of Royal Holloway College by Caroline Bingham and on the history of Bedford by Marigold Pakenham-Walsh. I have also gained greatly from discussions with the historian of the University of London, Negley Harte. Negley Harte, *The University of London 1836-1986: An Illustrated History* (1986); Caroline Bingham, *The History of the Royal Holloway College* (1987).

[2] Negley Harte, *The Admission of Women to University College, London. A Centenary Lecture* (1979), p. 16.

[3] Emily Davies, *Women in the Universities of England and Scotland* (Cambridge, 1896), Appendix A.

benefits of education than any other members of the human race.[4]

Put like that it sounds simple, straightforward and blindingly, almost boringly, obvious. But if we embark on a further, more detailed examination of many people's notions of human nature, we find them to be profoundly influenced, although not always explicitly, by gender. Thus an examination of the debates about the higher education of women within the University of London, of the provision made, offers ways of examining some deep-rooted assumptions about both gender and higher education and the interaction of the two in nineteenth- and twentieth-century England. Such an examination offers, in particular, ways of exploring the perennial debate among feminists: is there such a condition as 'equal but different'; and ways of identifying more clearly some of the cultural encrustations which surround our notions of higher education. It can help us look at the hidden as well as the overtly prescribed curriculum, the associations, patterns of behaviour, whole life-style expected to go with the subjects formally studied and examined. It is with this cultural matrix that I want to begin.

The great, the revolutionary feature about the University of London was that it did not require residence of its students. It began in 1836 purely as an examining body. Even when, at the end of the nineteenth century, it acquired a teaching function, it still retained its external work and examining role.[5] This great fact allowed the separation of the questions of *how* and *in what context* you learnt, from the question of *what* you learnt.

The appropriateness of such a separation was hotly debated in nineteenth-century England. The pattern offered by Oxford and Cambridge – for some the model – was a residential, full-time one; and this was a very potent influence on one of the most celebrated contributors to the debate, J.H. Newman. In *Discourse VI* of his *The Idea of a University*, first published in 1852, he argued as follows:

> if I had to choose between a so-called University, which dispensed with residence and tutorial superintendence, and gave its degrees to any person who passed an examination in a wide range of subjects, and a University which had no professors or examinations at all, but merely brought a number of young men together for three or four years, and then sent them away . . . If I were asked which of these two methods was the better discipline of the intellect, . . . if I must determine which of the two courses was the more

---

[4] In her dedication of the *Vindication* to Talleyrand, Mary Wollstonecraft 'loudly demands *Justice* for one half the human race'. Mill wrote, 'The disabilities, therefore, to which women are subject from the mere fact of their birth, are the solitary examples of the kind in modern legislation. In no instance except this, which comprehends half the human race, are the higher social functions closed against any one by a fatality of birth which no exertions, and no change of circumstances can overcome.' (World Classics Edn., 1912, p. 449)

[5] Harte, *University of London*, pp. 68-76.

successful in training, moulding, enlarging the mind, which sent out men the more fitted for their secular duties, which produced better public men, men of the world, men whose names would descend to posterity, I have no hesitation in giving the preference to that University which did nothing, over that which exacted of its members an acquaintance with every science under the sun . . .

How is this to be explained? I suppose as follows: when a multitude of young men, keen, open-hearted, sympathetic and observant, as young men are, come together and freely mix with each other, they are sure to learn one from another, even if there is no-one to teach them; the conversation of all is a series of lectures to each, and they gain for themselves new ideas and views, fresh matter of thought, and distinct principles for judging and acting, day by day.

It is seeing the world on a small field with little trouble; for the . . . students come from very different places, and with widely different notions, and there is much to generalize, much to adjust, much to eliminate, there are inter-relations to be defined, and conventional rules to be established in the process, by which the whole assemblage is moulded together and gains one tone and one character.[6]

This is the most emphatic statement possible of the importance of a hidden curriculum; of the priorty to be attached to the socialising function of higher education. Here he is asserting that the process matters at least as much as the content. Indeed, he goes further, in claiming that sharing social life is even more important than sharing teaching.

What is the special relevance of this to the higher education of women? Why could we not re-state the core of Newman's argument like this:

when a multitude of young *men and women*, keen, open-hearted, sympathetic and observant, as young *people are*, come together and freely mix with each other, they are sure to learn one from another.

But free exchanges between the sexes had no place in Victorian notions of the behaviour appropriate to young ladies and young gentlemen together. Discussions between them were expected to be very carefully circumscribed indeed: a whole range of topics was taboo and chaperones were invariably expected to be present.

Let me try to illustrate the pervasiveness of such attitudes. The need to find chaperones was a feature of life at Bedford, at Royal Holloway College and at the Oxford women's colleges until the end of the First World War. At Cambridge it appears to have lasted even into the 1920s.[7] A.J. Munby, that extraordinary mid-Victorian barrister, fascinated – obsessed – by the detail of working women's lives, maintained that friendship between a man and a woman was only possible *across* class boundaries: that is to say, when the difference in social status between

[6] J.H. Newman, *The Idea of a University* (first published London 1852), Discourse VI, 'Knowledge Viewed in Relation to Learning', s. 9.

them was such that there could be no prospect of marriage. Having spent an evening alone in her room with a milliner called Louisa Baker, cosily drinking tea, discussing her employment prospects and the question of emigration to Australia, he reflected: 'With the men of her own class it would be indelicate to associate as friends; for modesty is an affair of *class* as well as sex, and with them such intercourse would certainly be misconstrued.'[8]

Nor were such scruples confined to the middle and upper classes. They exerted a powerful force on those aspiring to join the middle classes. In 1889 the newly appointed Principal of Homerton, the Congregational Training College for Teachers, found himself to be head of a dual institution, one for men and one for women. Since the elementary schools in which his students were destined to teach were mixed, he set out to try to integrate their training. He mixed classes, formed a Literary Society and held social evenings. Both the Literary Society and the social evenings had to be discontinued: the Literary Society because the girls objected – 'they could not speak freely before the men and therefore did not enjoy the meetings'; the social evenings because the men behaved badly. He concluded mournfully:

> The real objection to full freedom is that our men as a class are low in tone and few of the girls also and living in the same building we must regulate for the worst not for the best. It is a case of preserving the unfit from themselves.[9]

For poor Mr Horobin the shared social life presented more problems than the shared classes. Yet in the Newman – the Oxbridge – model of higher education it was a crucial part of the whole, in many ways the most crucial part. The colleges of Oxford and Cambridge were quintessentially male enclaves.[10] It was thus no straightforward matter to assimilate higher education for women to a model of higher education derived from Oxbridge. The University of Oxford admitted women to degrees only in

---

[7] Caroline Bingham, *Social Life in a Women's College: Royal Holloway College, the First Fifty Years 1887-1937*, Centenary Lecture 1986, pp. 23-4; Elizabeth Bennett, *Women's College Education – the Bedford Experience*, Centenary Lecture 1986, p. 19; I am indebted to Mrs Bingham and to Mrs Bennett for allowing me to see the texts of their lectures and to cite them. Vera Brittain, *The Women at Oxford* (1960), pp. 154-5. Ann Phillips, ed., *A Newnham Anthology* (Cambridge, 1979), p. 135.

[8] Derek Hudson, *Munby, Man of Two Worlds* (1972), p. 20 (1 February 1859).

[9] Homerton College, Cambridge, Archives, 'The Relationship of the Sexes at Homerton College', Mr Horobin's Memorandum on Dual Organisation, 1894. I am indebted to Homerton College for permission to quote from this.

[10] For various manifestations and the general importance of these, see Brian Harrison, *Separate Spheres: The Opposition to Women's Suffrage in Britain* (1978) esp. ch. 5, 'Clubland' and 'Women in a Men's House: the Women M.P.s, 1919-1945' *Historical Journal*, xxix (1986) pp. 623-54, esp. pp. 629-30.

1920; and the University of Cambridge did not do so until 1948.

But the Oxbridge model was not the only one available to nineteenth-century England. The Scottish universities had been doing things differently – and most successfully – for some considerable time. There teaching was shared but not necessarily social life.[11] In drawing clear distinctions first between residence and teaching and then between teaching and presentation for examinations, the new University of London brought even greater flexibility. This was a situation in which it was very much easier to argue for the admission of women to degrees.

To say this, however, is not to suggest that the University of London was untouched by, or in some special way insulated from, the social conventions of the day. Part of the campaign to admit women to degrees consisted of showing both that there was demand for higher education from women and that this could be expressed in an orderly and disciplined way. In 1868 a committee was set up, based on University College, to provide classes for 'ladies', analogous to those already provided for the men students of the College. This Committee spent a considerable amount of time on devices to keep male and female students separate, not only in the lecture rooms but in their comings and goings. Eventually it was agreed that lectures for men should begin and end on the hour, while those for women should begin and end on the half-hour. Practical considerations, such as the use of equipment, gradually brought a handful of shared classes. But there had to be separate entrances to these; and in the autumn of 1870 a whole new door was knocked into the Chemistry Laboratory, the Ladies' Association having given a guarantee to cover the cost of blocking it up again, if the female demand for chemistry were to fall off.[12] Propriety weighed even more heavily with the Council of King's College, who would have no ladies in the Strand, even coming and going on the half-hour. They responded to the Supplemental Charter of 1877 by opening their College for Ladies in Kensington in 1878.[13]

But perhaps the most interesting and telling manifestation of continuing male unease in the face of the idea of co-education – and one which affected Oxford, Cambridge and London alike – was the continuing pressure for the foundation of a 'Women's University', that is to say, not a women's college, which might be part of a larger, heterosexual whole, but a self-contained, degree-giving institution for women alone, situated well away from any male enclave. We may call this the *'Princess* phenomenon', or even the *'Princess Ida* phenomenon', depending on whether we prefer the images of Tennyson's poem, first published in 1847, or of the Gilbert and Sullivan operetta, first produced in 1884 and styled by composer and

[11] R.D. Anderson, *Education and Opportunity in Victorian Scotland: Schools and Universities* (Oxford, 1983), ch. 2 esp. pp. 29-30 and 35.

[12] Harte, *Women at U.C.L.*, pp. 12-13.

[13] Neville Marsh, *The History of Queen Elizabeth College* (1986), ch. 1 esp. pp. 7-8.

author, 'a respectful operatic *per*-version of the poem'.[14] I have wondered whether the notion exerted a fleeting influence on Emily Davies, the foundress of Girton, who sited her first establishment at Hitchin, equidistant from Oxford and Cambridge. Certainly we may speculate about the attractions of the idea for Thomas Holloway, in choosing his site at Egham and in framing Clause 2 of his Deed of Foundation:

> It is the Founder's desire that power by Act of Parliament, Royal Charter, or otherwise should ultimately be sought, enabling the College to confer degrees upon its students after proper examination in the various subjects of instruction.[15]

At first some of the Royal Holloway College students took London examinations as external students and others took Oxford examinations.[16]

National developments in the 1890s prompted a full-scale review of this. The schemes to make the University of London a teaching university, thereby establishing a framework within which Royal Holloway College might find an appropriate place, seemed to be gathering momentum at last. At the same time, both Oxford and Cambridge debated – and rejected – granting degrees to women.[17] In December 1897, therefore, the Governors of Royal Holloway College held a great public conference in London, at the Society of Arts. There were three questions on the agenda:

> 1. Is it desirable to apply for a separate Charter to enable Holloway College to confer degrees on its students?
>
> 2. Is it desirable to initiate a scheme for a Women's University of which Holloway College should form a part?
>
> 3. Is it desirable that Holloway College should be included in the proposed teaching University for London?

Over a hundred people attended; contributions were read from various distinguished absentees; and debate was animated.[18]

Nobody really argued for 1. – the separate charter. The case for 2. – the

---

[14] Quoted by Janet Soundheimer, *Castle Adamant in Hampstead: A History of Westfield College, 1882-1982* (1983) p. 7. For Tennyson's poem and its context, see John Killham, *Tennyson and 'The Princess': Reflections of an Age* (1958).

[15] Quoted on p. 3 of *University Degrees for Women: Report of a Conference convened by the Governors of Royal Holloway College and held at the House of the Society of Arts on Saturday, 4 December 1897* (1898) (henceforward *1897 Conference Proceedings*).

[16] Bingham, *Social Life*, p. 15.

[17] Harte, *University of London*, pp. 142-60; Brittain, *Women at Oxford*, pp. 106-8; Rita McWilliams-Tullberg, *Women at Cambridge: A Men's University – Though of a Mixed Type* (1975) ch. 8.

[18] *1897 Conference Proceedings*.

Women's University – was put in the main by men from Oxford and Cambridge who wished to extrude the women from those universities. The lead in arguing the case for 3. – involvement with a teaching University of London – was taken by Sophie Bryant, a distinguished member of Bedford College, the first woman D.Sc. of the University of London and, at that point, headmistress of the North London Collegiate School. 'There is', she declared:

> no demand in the schools for a separate University for women. The letter which has been circulated from the 150 members of the Head-Mistresses' Association stands in evidence. Indeed, I have never met with a woman who for herself wanted a Women's University. I have never even met with a woman who knew any other woman who desired to make use of such a University. Oxford, Cambridge, London (and the Northern Universities) fill the vision of aspiring students. The reason for this persistent preference is not, even in the abstract, hard to find. Most persons' ideal of learning is largely made up of a desire to be one of the learned, and to fulfil the accepted definition of learning, whatever that may be. The definition of learning must always be, in the main, what men make it, and there is therefore a strong permanent motive for taking that definition as we find it already established to begin with, though not to the exclusion of such share as our future success may give us in its development. Moreover on reflection it appears that, after all, the great variety of the work which men have to do in the world requires so much opportunity for specialization, side by side with general culture, in a man's University, that any qualitative peculiarity which later wisdom might discover as appropriate to a woman's course of study, would be a very small matter in comparison.[19]

There were many more contributions in similar vein. The Rev T.H. Grose, the Registrar of the University of Oxford, summed up: 'The scheme for the establishment of a separate University for women is dead. (Loud applause)'.[20] Alas, he was a little premature: the scheme surfaced quite seriously again in Cambridge in 1920.[21] But for Royal Holloway College, this discussion was decisive. Under the generalship of Emily Penrose, whose translation from the Principalship of Bedford to the Principalship of Royal Holloway College had been agreed just before the conference and was announced five days after it,[22] Royal Holloway College made successful application to become a school of the new teaching University of London. This course of action was followed also by Westfield College, which had been founded in 1882.[23]

In her powerful speech, Sophie Bryant had contended, 'we want what

[19] *Ibid.*, pp. 18-19.
[20] *Ibid.*, p. 41.
[21] McWilliams-Tullberg, *Women at Cambridge*, p. 157.
[22] I am indebted to Mrs Bingham for this information.
[23] Bingham, *Social Life*, p. 15; Sondheimer, *Castle Adamant*, pp. 57-9.

other people understand by higher education'. The point was under-scored by Arthur Sidgwick, who asked,

> How is the present education unsuited to women, I should like to know? Our experience at Oxford is rather curious in this respect: we ourselves began with the notion (being inexperienced and not having worked it out) of 'education adapted to women'; and the whole progress of our work has been towards realizing that the one thing wanted was systematic study and systematic study as it had been laid down by long experience for men. (Hear, hear.)[24]

There was, amongst the protagonists for women's higher education, a grave scepticism as to whether there could be such a thing as a higher education equal to but different from that provided for men. They could not be sure of parity of esteem until their opportunities were identical to those offered men. We can construe the debate about a 'Women's University' not only as a debate about higher education as a male enclave but also about the nature of equality. And if we pursue this further, we begin to see that there are two battle grounds. The first is the obvious one, the curriculum, both formal and informal. The second is participation in university government.

Argument about the formal curriculum centred on the question of whether there should be special 'women's subjects'. In the main, the supporters of women's higher education in the late nineteenth and early twentieth centuries set their faces against this. It was a position they had considerable difficulty in establishing in the early years, because of the absence of any systematic secondary education for girls. Thus at the beginning, Bedford, and, to a lesser extent Royal Holloway College and Westfield, had to do some very basic work with their students.[25] The need for systematic secondary education for girls was as pressing as that for higher education; and this helps to explain why the school section of the early Bedford College became so successful as to threaten the rest of the enterprise. But the objective remained the full curriculum and degree-level studies for the majority; and Emily Davies of Girton spoke warmly of Bedford's achievement in this respect at the great conference in 1897.[26] Arthur Acland, chairman of the Bedford College Council 1903-13 proudly told the Royal Commission on the University of London, sitting under the chairmanship of Haldane, in 1910, that Bedford aimed to be an institution

[24] *1897 Conference Proceedings*, p. 47.
[25] Gillian Sutherland, 'The Movement for the Higher Education of Women: its Social and Intellectual Context in England *c*. 1849-1880' in P.J. Waller, ed., *Political and Social Change in Modern Britain: Essays Presented to A.F. Thompson* (Hassocks, 1987) pp. 91-116; p. 107; Sondheimer, *Castle Adamant*, esp. p. 31; Margaret J. Tuke, *A History of Bedford College for Women, 1849-1937 (1939)* esp. *pp. 61-2, 115*.
[26] *1897 Conference Proceedings*, pp. 33-4.

strictly comparable to University College and King's.[27]

King's College for Women was the exception in this company. They had been slower than the other women's colleges to move towards full-scale degree-level work. They had also taken the lead in the development of an entirely distinctive women's course. 'Home Science'. The Management Committee for this course outlined their objective in 1910:

> We wish to attract the girl of the leisured class who, having left school, has both the time and the desire to follow some course of study which may be of practical use to her, either in home life or in social or philanthropic work.[28]

The representatives of King's College for Women also expounded their position to the Haldane Commission – and received a very tart response:

> We are doubtful whether the University should continue to bear the burden of supplying lectures in literary and scientific subjects, or instruction in music and the fine arts for the ladies of Kensington who can devote only their spare time to them, or as finishing courses of study for girls after leaving school.[29]

This condemnation, coupled with the success of Dr John Atkins in raising funds for Home Science, led to the transmogrification of King's College for Women into King's College of Household and Social Science, eventually to become Queen Elizabeth College.[30]

The other issue which raised questions of the most fundamental kind about the nature of equality was that of participation in university government. Many women hoped – and many men feared – that as women students took a full part in the life and work of a university, so their teachers, female as well as male, would take a full share in the government of the university. The sensitivity of the question was pinpointed very clearly once again at the conference of 1897. Mrs A.H. Johnson, of the Oxford Society of Home Students, was the only woman speaker to entertain the idea of a separate Women's University, and one of her grounds was the following:

> University men are not willing that women should share fully in the life of the universities. I don't mean to say they are not willing that women should go in for their examinations or have the advantage of the same education, because we know that they are, and since we began our work in Oxford we have all

---

[27] *Reports and Minutes of Evidence of the Royal Commission on University Education in London,* P.P. 1910, XXIII, P.P. 1911 XX, P.P. 1912-13 XXII and P.P. 1913 XI (henceforward *Haldane Commission*): P.P. 1911 XX qq. 7196-8.

[28] Quoted Marsh, *Queen Elizabeth College,* p. 38.

[29] *Haldane Commission,* P.P. 1911 XX f. 665 between qq. 9077 and 9078, Note by Sir Arthur Rucker and qq. 3924-7 (evidence of Miss Oakley); P.P. 1913 XI, para. 177.

[30] Marsh, *Queen Elizabeth College,* chs. 3, 4 and 5.

along been met with the greatest possible sympathy. But they are not willing that women shall share in the life of the University, or form part of its governing body, or be associated with men in all the higher work of the University. Therefore women will never be, so far as we can see, in the same position as the men who are managing the colleges for men. It may be right or it may be wrong, but the fact remains that we are no more liked now than when we began.[31]

Mrs Johnson's remarks certainly fitted the Oxford and Cambridge situations. And the London women found that the inclusion of the women's colleges as schools of the new University of London after 1900 did not rapidly bring a commensurate involvement in its government. The Haldane Commission was confronted with a petition from sixty-one of the sixty-eight women who by 1910 were recognised teaching officers of the University. They pointed out that there was only a single woman member of the Senate and complained bitterly that the present structure allowed 'no adequate expression by women of their views on University matters'. But on the remedy they were sadly divided. Twenty-nine were so opposed to the notion of positive discrimination that they had no proposal to offer. But a further thirty were prepared to contemplate some positive discrimination, at least in the short term, and argued for some Senate seats to be reserved for women.[32]

The outbreak of the First World War pre-empted any action on the Haldane Commission's Report; and the government only addressed itself again to the reconstruction of the central government of the University of London in the second half of the 1920s, following the report of the Hilton Young Committee. The revised constitution side-stepped the issue of the representation of women *per se*. But increased representation of institutions in the Senate gave the heads of the women's schools seats *ex officio*.[33]

The women's appetites had been whetted, of course, by the hard-won experience gained in the management of their own institutions. Long gone were the days when Erasmus Darwin could complain of the time taken in meetings at Bedford because ladies had no idea of committee work.[34] But this does raise questions about the ways in which colleges for women students only, staffed increasingly by women, related to the fierce preoccupation with equality. Just as twenty-nine of those recognised women teachers in 1910 could not bring themselves to contemplate any form of positive discrimination, colleges for women only could be seen as at odds with the determination to secure identity of treatment with men.

[31] *1897 Conference Proceedings*, pp. 52-3.
[32] *Haldane Commission*, P.P. 1911 XX qq. 3640-6.
[33] Tuke, *Bedford College*, pp. 194-5.
[34] *Ibid.* p. 89.

Why did they not concentrate all their energies on existing institutions, like University College?

While the ultimate objective might be complete equality, few, from the redoubtable Emily Davies onwards, denied that the real world was currently exceedingly *un*-equal in its treatment of men and women. Nor was transformation of this going to come overnight. In the meantime – in effect, in the forseeable future – women's colleges represented practical mechanisms for moving forward, for demonstrating the case for change. Since the existing institutions offered women little or no scope to show what they could do, they must create their own opportunities. Colleges for women might be described as crucial transitional devices.

This case was at its starkest and strongest when Bedford began in 1849. But the emergence of what might be called the 'U.C.L. option' after 1878 did not wholly undermine it. For a start, while the enthusiasts for women's education might see complete equality as an ultimate goal, not all their charges – or their charges' parents – were prepared to folilow all the way. As Margaret Tuke, the Principal of Bedford, pointed out to the Haldane Commission, many parents preferred a single sex college. She also went on to argue that such a college provided valuable opportunities for corporate life, more so than a mixed college.[35] This was a view shared by Emily Penrose, by Thomas Holloway, to judge from the terms of his Trust Deed, and by the Council of Westfield, where corporate life was given a distinctively Evangelical flavour.[36]

In this collective stand there are several strands which are worth unravelling. In the first place there was recognition – whatever the ultimate objectives – of the inhibitions engendered by the prevailing social conventions. Remember the problems Mr Horobin had with the Literary Society at Homerton. In the second place, there was acceptance of some part of Newman's argument about the contribution of shared debate and shared experience to the educative process. This was a view they held in common with many of those men who argued for London to become a teaching university.[37] But there was also here a strand of argument which related specifically to women. It was the claim that collegiate life was even more important for them than for men, given the pervasiveness of the nineteenth-century assumption that women's paramount duty was to their families. They were daughters, sisters, wives, mothers, before they were people. They had space and time for themselves and their own

[35] *Haldane Commission*, P.P. 1911 XX qq. 7212, 7215-6.

[36] *Bedford College Magazine*, 29 March 1896, p. 9 (Penrose); *Haldane Commission*, P.P. 1911 XX ff. 635-6 between qq. 8489 and 8490, Statement on behalf of Westfield College by Lord Alverstone and Miss Constance Maynard.

[37] See e.g. Acland's evidence to the Haldane Commission on the organisation of the University of London in general, P.P. 1911 XX qq. 7341-70. The Commission actually recommended the phasing-out of external degrees – Harte, *University of London*, p. 193.

concerns only when all other claims had been met. It took nine bitter years of conflict with her parents and sister before Florence Nightingale was able to begin to train to nurse.[38] In 1894 a letter to the *Bedford College Magazine* which began firmly, 'No girl can be happy whose sole object of existence is fancy work and novels', continued,

> Home duties must take precedence of all others, whatever our inclinations may be. An only daughter should be a companion to her mother, instead of shutting herself up to study languages, mathematics or any subject, however improving . . . Of course I am not speaking of those who have to earn their own living, when undivided attention to a profession renders severance from home unavoidable, but of girls who are not compelled by circumstances to leave home and make their own way in the world.[39]

Even in families which accepted the idea of education for women, notions of duty continued to press most powerfully.[40] It is worth remembering that Virginia Woolf's essay, *A Room of One's Own*, that incomparable evocation of the web of constraints surrounding women and inhibiting creativity, is a product of the 1920s, based on talks given at Newnham and Girton in 1928 and published in 1929.

Virginia Woolf recognised the attempt women's colleges made to give precious time and space to their students. She also recognised that they did so as perennially the poor relations. It is a cry still to be heard in Cambridge; other financial problems apart, Newnham has never quite lived down her description of its food! The cry of poverty also has peculiar resonance for London. From the creation of the teaching university in 1900 onwards, London has worried about the position of what it has come to call the 'small multi-faculty schools' – which in the main have consisted of the women's colleges. Bedford secured its place as a school of the reconstructed university in 1900 on the first round of negotiation. But Royal Holloway College and Westfield had to fight several rounds for their inclusion. And then they had to do it all over again in the second half of the 1920s, following the Report of the Hilton Young Committee.[41] There is a strong sense of *déja vu* in finding Bedford, Royal Holloway College, Westfield College and Queen Elizabeth College singled out for discussion in the Murray Report in 1972 and again by the Swinnerton-

[38] Cecil Woodham-Smith, *Florence Nightingale, 1820-1910* (1950) chs. III, IV and V.
[39] March 1894, pp. 10-11.
[40] Dame Margaret Tuke had had her own experience of this – see Victoria Glendinning, *A Suppressed Cry: Life and Death of a Quaker Daughter* (1969) esp. pp. 47-53.
[41] Sondheimer, *Castle Adamant*, pp. 57-8, 99-100; note the omission of all mention of Westfield and Royal Holloway College in the relevant section of the *Report of the Departmental Committee on the University of London, 1924-26 (Hilton Young Committee)* P.P. 1926 X, para. 57. Cf. also Gregory Foster's remarks to Margaret Tuke in 1907, quoted Tuke, *Bedford College*, p. 195.

Dyer Committee a decade later. The worries expressed by Murray about '"viability", both in terms of administration and more especially, of academic effectiveness' have an all-too-familiar ring.[42]

Gregory Foster, the Provost of University College, argued to the Haldane Commission in 1910 that the difficulties of the women's colleges were difficulties of size, not of gender.[43] But the former is a consequence of the latter. The 'smallness' of small, multi-faculty schools has its roots in their origins as women's colleges; and in this sense, if no other, gender continues to play a part in the patterning of higher education in the 1970s and 1980s, even if not exactly the part it played in the 1870s and 1880s.

Let me try to make the connections clearer. Historically, women's colleges have been small and for the most part, poor. They were small because the demand from women for higher education, though vital and consistent, was small both in absolute terms and as a proportion of the whole. As late as 1938-9 women represented just 23 per cent of the total university population of Great Britain. By 1962 the proportion had crept up to 25 per cent.[44]

Smallness of size contributed to poverty in that it limited income from fees. But in addition, with the single magnificent exception of Thomas Holloway, the women's colleges attracted no big benefactors.[45] Indeed, the veteran campaigner for women's education, Maria Grey, had written from her sick-bed to the great conference of 1897 that the scheme for a Women's University must be opposed if only because: 'This proposal will divert the funds, always so hard to get for educational purposes, especially women's'. And at that same conference, Emily Davies had pointed to what she hoped was the way ahead – state funding: Bedford being the first women's college to attract a grant from the University Grants Committee.[46]

This background and history constituted a relatively low base from which to expand. The women's colleges set themselves to respond to the call for expansion associated with the Robbins Report of 1963 as strongly as they could. The student populations of Royal Holloway College and Westfield College trebled in size between 1962 and 1973. And Bedford,

[42] *Final Report of the Committee of Enquiry into the Governance of the University of London* (*Murray Report*) (1972) paras 131 and 146 – from which the direct quotation comes. *University of London Committee on Academic Organisation* (*Swinnerton-Dyer Committee*) Second Discussion Document CAO/510, 28.5.1981, paras 45, 56-66.

[43] P.P. 1911 XX qq. 9571-4.

[44] *Report of the Committee on Higher Education, 1961-3* (*Robbins Committee*) *Appendix Two (A): Students and their Education* 1963 Cmnd. 2154-II, para. 13, Table 9.

[45] Sutherland, 'Higher Education of Women', p. 96; Janet Howarth and Mark Curthoys, 'The Political Economy of Women's Higher Education in late Nineteenth- and early Twentieth-Century Britain' in *Historical Research* LX (1987). See also Harte, *University of London*, p. 256, Table 6.4.

[46] *1897 Conference Proceedings*, pp. 30 and 34.

Westfield and Royal Holloway College followed Queen Elizabeth College in deciding to admit men as undergraduates.[47] But even trebling in size in a decade, with all the strains that that imposes, was not enough to turn a small school into a large school.

There was also an aspect of the expansion proposed by Robbins which presented peculiar problems for institutions with sizeable populations of women students. The Robbins Committee proposed a massive expansion in higher education as a whole, envisaging a student population in 1980 two and a half times the size of that in 1962. They did not specifically apportion the increases between men and women but in practice appear to have envisaged a more or less equal ultimate distribution between the sexes of the extra places. At the same time they proposed that the lion's share of the extra places should be provided in science and technology. These two sets of proposals pulled one against the other. As John Carswell has pointed out, in order to divide these 'extra places' in science and technology equally between men and women, 'the number of women studying that group of subjects at universities would almost have to treble in five years . . . and increase more than eightfold in less than twenty years.'[48] The Robbins Committee themselves had noted that the proportion of science students who were women was lower in 1962 than it had been just before World War II;[49] and with our time-scale of one hundred and fifty years we can see that social revolutions on the scale they apparently took for granted, take a little longer than two decades.

The colleges which began as women's colleges have a heroic record in the struggle to transform the trickle of women students in these fields into a stream.[50] But a stream cannot be transformed into a river overnight. Even a decision to fill every possible place with a male science student would not have solved all the problems and enabled even faster growth. In the first place, the Robbins Committee were over-optimistic about the speed with which the flow of male students reading scientific and technological subjects could be increased.[51] In the second place, such a decision would have raised very serious issues of principle. It could have entailed admitting some very marginal candidates while turning away others admirably well qualified in the arts and social sciences, wanting to study in fields in which the institutions concerned had most distinguished

[47] Marsh, *Queen Elizabeth College*, pp. 201-4; *Royal Holloway College Letter* 1974, Report from Council; Sondheimer, *Castle Adamant*, pp. 142-5; *Bedford College Old Students' Association Newsletter* no. 46, March 1964, 'College Notes'.

[48] John Carswell, *Government and the Universities in Britain. Programme and Performance, 1960-1980* (Cambridge, 1985), pp. 43-4.

[49] *Robbins Committee, Appendix Two (A)*, para. 15.

[50] Cf. the Principal's remarks in her Vice-Presidential Letter, *Bedford College Old Students' Association Newsletter*, nos. 51 and 52, 1969-70.

[51] Carswell, *Government and the Universities*, p. 45.

records of teaching and research. It would have been difficult to defend such a decision as equitable or conducive to equality. It would have marked a very clear departure from the notion of the varied and balanced intellectual community which the 'small' multi-faculty schools have defended so doughtily to inquiries from Haldane onwards.

Nationally, the response to the initiative of the 1960s has been impressive, despite the collapse of quinquennial planning in the early 1970s. The number of women taking scientific and technological courses in all forms of higher education more than doubled in absolute terms between 1962 and 1980; and as a proportion of the whole crept up from 14 per cent to 16 per cent.[52] The University of London has been bold in its efforts to achieve the economies associated with size, while not sacrificing the benefits, far more difficult to quantify, of study and research in a multi-disciplinary environment. To this outside observer at least, the line of descent from the the Bedford of 1910, described so proudly to the Haldane Commission by Acland and Margaret Tuke as exhibiting a range and variety of work appropriate to a modern university, to the Royal Holloway and Bedford New College of 1986, remains mercifully unbroken.

There remains the question of whether, in expounding the peculiar difficulty in responding to the thrust of government policy since the 1960s experienced by colleges which began as women's colleges, one is simply conceding at last the proposition that there are 'women's subjects'. I think not. Leaving aside all the questions about what *ought* to be the balance and range of disciplines appropriate in the higher education system of a developed country, it is surely right to register the practical problems entailed in any major change of direction. And if we do not reject our history and continue to concern ourselves with equality of opportunity for women, we need to ask ourselves why it is, when formal equality of access has been established so long, they 'cluster' markedly in certain academic disciplines.

After the surge of the last twenty years, women now make up almost 40 per cent of the university student population. But they are by no means evenly distributed. They are the dominant group in education-based studies, in language, literature and area studies, and in other arts subjects. They are a significant presence in medicine and dentistry, rather less so in biology and physics, and have only a toe-hold (9 per cent) in engineering. By and large, Royal Holloway and Bedford New College replicates the national pattern.[53]

Surely expectations differentiated by gender are still at work here, although in a much more subtle and less overt way than in the nineteenth century. In an important paper published in 1987, on the political

[52] *Ibid.* Appendix I, Tables 3 and 4.
[53] See Appendix, Tables 1 and 2.

economy of higher education for women in the late nineteenth and early twentieth centuries, Janet Howarth and Mark Curthoys explored the ambivalences of the late Victorian and Edwardian middle classes towards higher education for their daughters. For some families it represented an insurance policy against the failure of the girl to make a successful, that is, financially secure, marriage. Others feared higher education might actually reduce their daughters' chances of such a marriage.[54] The late nineteenth century thus saw the choice for women as lying between marriage and a career. The late twentieth century tends to see the choice as lying between children and a career; or if not an outright choice, a need to determine which has the priority.

Sense of a need to determine a priority and the tensions entailed in doing so, seem to affect both the subjects of study chosen by women and their career trajectories. In her 1984 Fawcett Lecture at Bedford, Tessa Blackstone, Master of Birkbeck College, quoted from a study of parental attitudes towards children's occupational choices. Their expectations and hopes were clearly differentiated by gender. Stress was laid on good prospects and security for boys; on interesting and flexible work for girls. When specified, these turn out to be the sorts of occupations thought to combine well with mothering, either because they are 'caring', or because of the hours worked and the possibility of part-time work. In the 1980s, she commented, despite 'leaving school with formal qualifications as good as, if not better than boys, most girls are still entering a remarkably narrow range of occupations'.[55]

Baroness Blackstone was looking across the whole range of educational qualifications and occupations. But the point holds good if we simply look at girls going to university, the subjects they choose and the jobs they go on to. It was underscored, anecdotally but most effectively, in the mid-1960s by the journalist, Jean Rook, writing of the experience of speaking at the Bedford Old Students' dinner. 'Absolutely all the old students, apart from myself, were headmistresses or housewives providing the headmistresses with material. This made for very salty conversation.'[56] For me the point was dramatised in a slightly different way about ten years later, in an aside to a conversation about Cambridge's efforts to extrude women in the 1920s. I was talking about the period with a woman who had lived through it, one I greatly admired – one of the first twelve women to be appointed to university posts in Cambridge and one of the first married women Fellows of a Cambridge women's college. 'Ah, you

---

[54] For the full reference, see n. 45 above.

[55] Tessa Blackstone, *Mistresses, Masters, Professors and Vice-Chancellors: Prospects for Women in Education*, The Fawcett Lecture, delivered at Bedford College, January 1984. I am grateful to Baroness Blackstone for permission to quote from this.

[56] *Bedford College Old Students' Association Newsletter* no. 47, January 1965.

young things', she said, 'children as well. That's having your cake and eating it.'

Identifying, bringing out into the open such assumptions about women's need if not to choose, at least to determine priorities, may help us to make more sense not only of the 'clustering' of women in certain groups of disciplines but also of the distribution of women in academic posts. Women may form almost 40 per cent of the student body nationally; but only 15.6 per cent of the people who teach them are women. These women university teachers are clustered not only in certain subjects but also by status. They are overwhelmingly concentrated in the lower grades. Only 2.4 per cent of Professors are women, while 17.5 per cent of the Lecturer grade are women. Here Royal Holloway and Bedford New College runs slightly ahead of the national average: 19 per cent of its academic staff are women, including 8 per cent of the professoriate.[57]

We may have left behind the starkness of the nineteenth-century situation, the extreme versions of the notion that men and women have 'separate spheres'. But attitudes to higher education, its function and purpose in our society are still in important ways shaped by gender, often more so than we care to admit. Recognising these attitudes clearly is the essential first step. Only then can we decide whether we want to change them and if so, how. In the last one hundred and fifty years the University of London and Bedford and Royal Holloway have had a distinguished record in challenging many of the barriers preventing women from gaining access to higher education, guided by a strong sense of 'the plainest principles of justice'. Challenging inequalities resulting from the differences in expectation of men and women remain for the University to face in the future.

[57] See Appendix, Tables 3 and 4. See also the analysis, 'Co-Education 105 Years On', by the Provost, Sir James Lighthill, in the *University College London, Annual Report 1983-4*, pp. 23-9. I am grateful to Negley Harte for drawing my attention to this.

Appendix

Table 1: Subjects Studied 1984/5 in UK Universities, by Sex

SUBJECT GROUP	TOTAL NO STUDENTS, UK AND OVERSEAS, IN 000s	UK STUDENTS AS A PERCENTAGE OF THE TOTAL	
		MEN	WOMEN
Education	3.6	26	63
Medicine, dentistry & health	28.1	50	45
Engineering & technology	34.6	77	9
Agriculture, foresty & veterinary science	4.7	57	40
Biological, mathematical & physical sciences	58.1	64	31
Administrative, business & social studies	57.0	50	42
Architecture & planning	4.0	55	33
Language, literature & area studies	31.1	29	67
Other Arts	20.6	44	50
TOTAL	241.7	54	39

Source: *Universities' Statistical Record, University Statistics 1984-5*, published on behalf of the University Grants Committee (Cheltenham, 1986) vol 1, *Students and Staff*, p. 6, Table E.

*Table 2: Proportions of Women Students, by Subject Groups,
at Royal Holloway and Bedford New College 1985-6*

SUBJECT GROUP	WOMEN STUDENTS AS A PERCENTAGE OF FULL-TIME EQUIVALENT NUMBERS
Physical and Biological Sciences	
Physiology	64.0
Biochemistry	53.7
Mathematics	50.8
Biology (inc. Botany and Zoology)	41.8
Chemistry	30.4
Statistics/Computer Sciences	26.1
Geology	23.1
Physics	11.6
Social Studies	
Psychology	74.9
SPSS	53.8
Geography	45.2
Language-based Studies	
French	85.1
English	81.2
Italian	69.2
German	60.1
Classics	41.5
Other Arts	
Drama & Theatre Studies	64.6
Music	57.9
History	53.7

Source: Royal Holloway and Bedford New College Planning Office, by kind permission.

Table 3: Full-time Academic Staff, by Subject Group, Status and Sex, UK 1984-5

SUBJECT GROUP	TOTAL	WOMEN	WOMEN AS A PERCENT-AGE OF THE TOTAL
Education			
Total	1952	445	22.8
Professors	110	8	7.3
Readers & Snr Lecturers	380	34	8.9
Lecturers	1392	365	26.2
Others	70	38	54.3
Medicine, dentistry & health			
Total	8777	2142	24.4
Professors	953	25	2.6
Readers & SLs	2079	264	12.7
Lecturers	4570	1305	28.6
Others	1175	548	46.6
Engineering & technology			
Total	6256	273	4.7
Professors	459	2	0.44
Readers & SLs	1073	4	0.37
Lecturers	3673	163	4.4
Others	1051	104	9.9
Agriculture, forestry & veterinary science			
Total	1009	182	18.0
Professors	91	—	0
Readers & SLs	203	6	2.9
Lecturers	566	116	20.5
Others	149	60	40.3
Biological, mathematical and physical sciences			
Total	12017	1337	11.1
Professors	1039	10	0.96
Readers & SLs	2393	65	2.7
Lecturers	7328	861	11.7
Others	1257	401	31.9
Architecture & planning			
Total	443	29	6.5
Professors	42	—	0

SUBJECT GROUP	TOTAL	WOMEN	WOMEN AS A PERCENT-AGE OF THE TOTAL
Readers & SLs	91	4	4.4
Lecturers	297	21	7.1
Others	13	4	30.8
Administrative, business & social studies			
Total	7517	1248	16.6
Professors	760	23	3.0
Readers & SLs	1448	97	6.7
Lecturers	4871	926	19.0
Others	438	202	46.1
Language, literature & area studies			
Total	3383	836	24.7
Professors	351	16	4.6
Readers & SLs	620	94	15.2
Lecturers	2210	600	27.2
Others	202	126	62.4
Other arts			
Total	2801	392	14.0
Professors	344	17	4.9
Readers & SLs	625	16	2.6
Lecturers	1752	297	17.0
Others	80	32	40.0
Research workers in libraries & museums	37	9	24.3
ALL ACADEMIC STAFF			
Total	44192	6893[1]	15.6
Professors	4150	101	2.4
Readers & SLs	8914	614	6.9
Lecturers	26679	4657	17.5
Others	4449	1521	34.2

[1] Percentage of total women academic staff in the various grades

Professors	1.5
Readers & SLs	8.9
Lecturers	67.6
Others	22.1

Source: *University Statistics 1984-5*, vol. 1, p. 51, Table 25.

Table 4: Academic Staff at Royal Holloway and Bedford New College 1985-6,
by Status, Sex and Subject Group

(a) Status	TOTAL	WOMEN	WOMEN AS A PERCENT- AGE OF THE TOTAL
All grades	272	52	19.1
Professors	34	3	8.8
Readers & SLs	76	15	19.7
Lecturers	128	34	21.0

(b) Subject group	TOTAL	WOMEN	WOMEN AS A PERCENT- AGE OF THE TOTAL
Biological, mathematical and physical sciences	157	15	9.5
Arts	83	30	36.1
Administrative, business & social studies	31	7	22.6

Source: Royal Holloway and Bedford New College Planning Office, by kind permission.

3

The Humanities

F.M.L. Thompson

The Humanities, according to a leading article in *The Times Higher Education Supplement*, are under siege.[1] Beset by apparently formidable forces drawing their strength from utilitarianism, philistinism, and indifference, the humanities feel neglected, unappreciated, and extremely vulnerable. They eye the future apprehensively, invoking without much conviction outlandish symbols, hoping against hope that F.T.E.s, performance indicators, or citation indexes may be friendly enough talismen to protect them from mortal injury. There is no danger that they will disappear without trace. There will always be men and women sufficiently determined, sufficiently resourceful, sufficiently talented, and sufficiently crazy to see that Mycenaean studies are not forgotten, that historical research goes on, or that philosophical speculations take place. Individual, freelance, scholars and writers, however, are not quite the same thing as great university departments. They may have been practically all that existed before 1836 to create and sustain such subjects as literature, history, or geography, but the idea that they might be all that exists after 1990 is decidedly alarming. The notion sounds fanciful. But for many it is no longer unthinkable that some Arts subjects may vanish from some universities, may perhaps disappear altogether from universities and polytechnics, just as Natural Philosophy, once the handmaiden of Mathematics, and Mental and Moral Science, once the most modern and progressive subject in the London B.A. degree, have long since vanished, unlamented and unremembered. It becomes the more thinkable as more funds are handed out to subjects like information technology and communication skills, while the question of what information is to be processed and what for, and what thoughts are to be communicated, are ignored.

Some might feel that it is untoward that the celebration of the 150th anniversary of the Faculty of Arts in the University of London should fall

[1] *The Times Higher Education Supplement*, 'Humanities under Siege', 12 Sept. 1986.

at a time of such gloom and despondency, which are bound to blight the feast. On the contrary, no time could be more appropriate. It is a reminder not to be complacent, not to rest upon laurels, but also not to panic. The University, after all, or more particularly University College which of course was the University for the first eight years until 1836, caused considerable alarm and consternation in establishment circles when it was created, because of the threat which it posed to the moral and religious basis of learning. There followed more than half a century during which the University, the teaching colleges, and perhaps particularly the humanities, were rather a disappointment and source of worry, less because the moral foundations of education were not undermined than because unmistakeably high-level teaching and scholarship failed to emerge, except patchily. In the last hundred years there has scarcely been any period of more than ten consecutive years during which the University has not been in crisis and in process of being pulled up by its roots for inspection by some external or internal enquiry. Crisis, alarm, despair, and bewilderment are parts of the normal atmosphere in which the University and its academics have lived. Yet it is in the last hundred years, and especially within the last sixty or so, that the Humanities have flourished and grown in stature, putting in place the Arts hypotenuse, as it were, of the Oxford-Cambridge-London triangle, and raising London to that international class in the Arts to which it already belonged in, for example, Medicine, Science, or Engineering. This is not to say that the present crisis, with its ominous hints of intellectual discrimination and prejudice armed with financial muscle, is not grave and more serious than any that have gone before. It is to say that the Arts have a well-proven toughness and vitality, a record of resilience, and an unexpectedly youthful profile, all of which point to more practicality and rapport with contemporary trends than the reputation of humane studies for other-worldly detachment would suggest, and all of which imply capacity to ride out spells of rough weather.

The craft which rides the rough seas is in one sense vast, sprawling, gangling, ill-coordinated and barely seaworthy; in another sense it is so small and compact as to be puny, a dinghy among the great ships. The twenty Boards of Studies among which the academic oversight of subjects in the Humanities is currently distributed hint at the diversity and complexity of the Faculty of Arts. Several of the Boards, on the model of Classics or Romance Languages, have responsibilities for whole families of related but separate disciplines, while it is safe to assume that the Board of Studies for Oriental and African Languages and Literature shelters not one family but so many different and mutually incomprehensible tribes that it is inconceivable that they can communicate with one another, except in English. All in all, well over thirty distinct departments of learning shelter under the Arts umbrella; the total number of institutionally distinct departments, within the eight Schools of the federal University which operate in the Faculty, is of course much larger than that. Such multiplicity suggests intellectual richness. It also suggests that administrative confusion and chaos is never far below the surface. An extreme case is illustrated by architecture and geography, subjects which have always been in a state of fruitful identity crisis, driven forward by tensions between the aesthetic and the technical, the humane and the scientific, posing problems that university administrators find hard to handle. The result is that both architecture and geography appear to belong to the Faculties of Science and of Social Sciences (Economics) as well as to the Faculty of Arts; positions full of possibilities for advantageous manipulation, but carrying the risk of being nobody's pigeon. Of lesser importance is the utter failure of the attempt of the academic managers to marshal the straggling forces of the Arts into two compact groups, one under the banner of Languages and Literature, and the other under that of Historical and Philosophical Studies. This scheme of the early 1970s looked good on paper. But the individuality and independence of the diverse disciplines failed to generate any enthusiasm for an institutionalised expression of common interests and concerns on the lines of this bipartite division. I am myself, of course, a prime culprit in this abortive affair, having been chairman of one of the two Academic Advisory Boards for a dozen years without holding a meeting. Unfortunately it was an unpaid sinecure.

The Faculty of Arts, then, presents a picture of a large, individualistic, ill-disciplined army, marching towards a common objective of critical, humane, studies, but by so many different routes that it is beyond the capacity of one single person to trace them all, let alone understand them all. The paymasters, on the other hand, see no difficulty in reducing the horde to order. Viewed through accountants' spectacles the whole proud array and broad sweep of the Arts has been brusquely and efficiently compressed, in the ugly terminology of our times, into little more than a couple of Cost Centres, one labelled 'Language-based studies' and the second 'Other Humanities'.

It is true that some part of Cost Centre 36, 'Creative Arts', is within the Faculty, but the greater portion has a separate Faculty of its own, Music. And the two definitionally problematic subjects, architecture and geography, each have a separate Cost Centre of their own in the great scheme of things which is to take care of higher education into the 1990s, numbers 26 and 29, and some small fraction of these represents the humane elements in those two disciplines. In essence, however, the whole of the Faculty of Arts has been squeezed into Cost Centres 34 and 35, in terms which cannot fail to strike many people as dismissive and as appearing to treat most of the humanities as an insignificant residual category composed of the pursuits of cranky scholars who are not studying proper subjects worthy of individual recognition. To be sure, it is purely for financial purposes that authority finds it expedient to distinguish between pharmacology and pharmacy and to maintain separate records of the numbers of teachers and students in each subject, while content to remain statistically ignorant of and financially indifferent towards any distinction between philosophy and history, or classics and English. It is a chastening thought that these great areas of human knowledge, an inheritance of thousands of years of intellectual endeavour, can be summarily boxed into a mere couple of cost centres out of the 37 amongst which the academic activities of a university are now divided so that they can be kept under surveillance. It has to be admitted, however, that the Faculty of Arts seems much easier to handle if it is thought of as the contents of a couple of bureaucrats' boxes rather than the flowering of thirty or more separate disciplines, each with its own subject matter, its own techniques, its own traditions, its own achievements, and its own history.

The Faculty may have the stature of a dwarf, but it develops the strength of a giant. In a well-known recent exercise related to the selective funding of universities the U.G.C. awarded brownie points to departments which were thought to be outstanding in their research. The methods of assessment are unknown and the results have been widely questioned. Nevertheless, if it can be assumed that erratic and bizarre judgements were randomly distributed as between subjects, it is not without interest to observe that out of the forty-eight stars scattered around the University of London one half were contributed by the Humanities. Further, if those Institutes which were pronounced to be 'of national importance', in the same exercise, are counted as having been accorded super-stars – and as the Director of one of the Institutes I am not averse to such arithmetic – then more than half of London's tally of brownie points comes from the Faculty of Arts. Comparisons cannot be made with other universities in absolute numbers, for whereas London's federal structure meant that History, for example, had a chance of scoring seven times, once in each of the Schools with a History Department, in every other university it only had the chance of scoring once. Comparisons in relative terms, however, are no more unreliable than the underlying data, and they show that in Oxford and in Cambridge, and in all the other British universities taken together, Arts subjects contributed one-third or less of the stars. London is a very large university and it would be surprising, and disgraceful, if it did not have many excellences in many fields of knowledge; but the message that it is particularly strong in the Humanities is not often heard. When it is added that the Arts, in terms of student numbers, form less than a quarter of the University, and in terms of cost probably absorb little more than 10 per cent of the University's annual expenditure, a picture emerges of an extremely strong, productive, and cost-effective Faculty.[2]

[2] U.G.C. letter 4/86 of 27 May 1986, Appendices A and C. *Developmenmt of Higher Education into the 1990s* (1985) p. 51.

This message would not have surprised the founders of the University in the least, but would probably have astonished and dumbfounded any Victorian observer of the academic scene in London. The truth is that the original Faculty had the stature of a giant and the strength of an infant, and remained feeble for most of the rest of the nineteenth century. The University, which until 1900 was purely an examining and degree-giving body, started life in 1836 with no more than three Faculties, Medicine, Law, and Arts; this was also the structure in the two teaching colleges, King's and University College, and it simply mirrored the conventional organisation of the departments of knowledge at the time. Every university-level subject which was neither medical nor legal, therefore, came under the Arts umbrella. Thus, the ordinary or pass degree of Bachelor of Arts established in 1837 comprised examinations in Mathematics and Natural Philosophy – a portmanteau term for arithmetic, algebra, geometry, plane trigonometry, mechanics, hydrostatics, hydraulics, pneumatics, and astronomy, requiring among other matters a knowledge of permutations, annuities, the eleventh book of Euclid (but only so far as proposition 21), the motion of falling bodies in free space, the forcing-pump as well as the common pump, the apparent motion of the heavens round the earth, and proofs of the Copernican system – in Chemistry, Animal Physiology, Vegetable Physiology, and Structural Botany, with Classics, Greek and Roman History, the History of England to the end of the seventeenth century, and translation from and into either French or German thrown in for good measure. All these subjects were compulsory. Having surmounted that hurdle a candidate might elect to go on to an Honours degree, and could choose between four branches: Mathematics, Classics, Chemistry, or Animal and Vegetable Physiology.[3] In this manner Arts staked its claim to the entire span of knowledge, for medicine and law were in a different category as professional studies; and teaching had to struggle as best it might to cope with this vast syllabus. So matters continued until 1858 when parturition occurred and a separate Science Faculty with a separate B.Sc. degree was established.

The original London B.A., you might think, looked more like O Levels in ten or a dozen subjects than the crown of a university education, and the Honours degrees like pale anticipations of A Levels. You would be entirely right. To pass in English History it was necessary to say 'what three essential principles of our government were established by the Commons in the reign of Edward III?' and also to mention 'by what remarkable events the reign of Elizabeth was distinguished?'– itself, admittedly, a question which would much later occupy the entire career of a distinguished Astor Professor at University College – while if one could

---

[3] *Papers Relating to the University of London*, P.P. 1840, XL, Regulations for Degrees in Arts, pp. 215-51. *University of London Calendar*, 1844, pp. 24-36.

grapple with the problem 'If 144 excavators clear 18 yards of tunnel per week, in what time should we expect 120 yards to be cleared when the number of hands was trebled?' one was on the way to a B.A. Honours in Mathematics.[4] Teaching was geared to what was expected in examinations, and was naturally an exercise in imparting large volumes of facts and sticking closely to a handful of textbooks or the familiar round of set passages from Homer, Plato, Thucydides, Cicero, Tacitus, and Virgil. This was an activity calling for much memorising and mental agility from students, but little intellectual effort; and it was an operation in which competent pedagogues well versed in the arts of cramming could do well, but it neither required nor was likely to foster scholarly eminence.

Nevertheless, at its inception the degree scheme was an innovation of outstanding audacity, just as the distribution of professional posts in the teaching colleges was revolutionary in its coverage. The older universities may not have been sleeping quite so deeply in the early nineteenth century as is commonly supposed, but they were certainly dozing comfortably in their classical chairs, and the signs of life evidenced by the early eighteenth-century establishment of the Regius Chairs in History had long since ceased to disturb the tranquil routine. It was, therefore, a dramatic assertion of the independence and modernity of the new university when both King's and University College appointed professors of English, of French, and of German. This was the first time, in this country, that modern languages were recognised as worthy of a place in a university as subjects that could be studied seriously and not merely as social accomplishments that might come in handy in social converse or in the pursuit of other more elevated scholarly enquiries. The new university, of course, pioneered in other modern subjects, notably in the physical sciences, although these were not completely unknown in Oxford and Cambridge; but in the core area of the Humanities languages expressed the innovatory thrust, and marked out for London the leading position it has retained ever since both in developing the scope of the original language studies and in extending the range of languages which are treated as something more than a means of everyday communication with the peoples of the world.

The novelty of modern languages was surpassed by the originality of elevating English language and literature to the status of a degree, or at any rate a matriculation, subject. Something of the daring in this step can be gathered from the remarks of Dr Thomas Arnold, Headmaster of Rugby, who had been appointed a member of the first Senate in 1836. He thought that every candidate for the B.A. should 'bring up' for examination, among other offerings, 'some one treatise or work on moral philosophy, together with some one history or work of poetry, to be taken

---

[4] P.P. 1840, XL, B.A. Pass Examination, English History, 1840, pp. 306-7; B.A. Honours Examination in Mathematics and Natural Philosophy, 1839, pp. 242-3.

from a list drawn up by the University.' 'The poetry', he continued, 'must of course always be read in a foreign language; an examination in an English poet would be absurd and impracticable.'[5] He may well have been right. The University, at least, found it quite impossible to imagine what the contents, structure, or purpose of any organised study of English Literature might be, and the only safe place that it could find for English in the hierarchy of examinations was in the guise of a paper on 'the Grammatical Structure of the English Language' in the matriculation, which was the test for admission to the degree courses.[6] The subject rested in this lowly, but honourable, estate until 1859. Honourable, because it shared the position with English history which was likewise for schoolboys, not undergraduates, a not unworthy companion. Honourable also because the University's matriculation, given the long list of institutions at home and later overseas which became eligible to enter for its degrees, quickly became established as the country's first and premier school-leaving examination, used throughout the English-speaking world and forerunner of the School Certificate, Higher School Certificate, and G.C.E. O and A Levels.

In 1859, as a consequence of the separation of Science from the Arts and the reconstruction of the B.A. degree that became necessary, English found itself promoted to the high table, at first to a place in the 1st B.A. or Part I as senior partner in a single subject called 'English Language, Literature and History', and soon after to a place, under the same label, in the B.A. Finals. At the same time the academic ascent was completed with the emergence of the possibility of taking Honours in English, a process that involved taking further papers, one in Literature, and one in History, on subjects covering identical chronological periods whose limits were changed from year to year in a most disconcerting fashion.

Thus in 1884 candidates grappled with English History and English Literature between 1547 and 1579, while for 1885 the periods jumped to 1727-60, only to fall back for 1886 to 1642-60. Sometimes these special periods ran ahead to look at 1750 to the present '(excluding living writers)', and sometimes they dropped back to Chaucer's England, a splendidly random ringing of the changes which doubtless provided teachers and students alike with invigorating mental exercise.

The dignity of Honours degree status, however, should not be confused with the substance. The candidate who answered ten questions in three hours on English Literature, 1547-79, by for example tracing 'the origin of our early dramatic literature', giving 'instances from the literature of this period showing the strength of loyalty and personal attachment to the

[5] P.P. 1840, XL, letter from T. Arnold to the Chancellor [Lord Burlington], 31 May 1837, p. 192.

[6] P.P. 1840, XL, Examinations for Matriculation in 1839, p. 241. The paper in English History for the same examination is at p. 237.

Queen in the days of Elizabeth', and stating 'the chief modifications in the form of English prose', and in another three hours disposed of English history by describing the origins of the Court of High Commission, describing 'the means taken by the Crown . . . to secure Parliamentary support', and estimating 'the position of English commerce' and stating 'any measure taken for its advance', besides dealing with another seven similar historical questions, had undoubtedly amassed a great deal of knowledge. How much understanding he had acquired must be questionable.[7]

If the movement of English up the formal academic escalator appears slow, that of History was a tortoise to its hare. It was considered fair enough to expect some knowledge of the national history from seventeen- and eighteen-year-olds at matriculation, but after that history was simply an adjunct to the classics, or, as we have seen, a companion to English literature. When one subject addressed the question 'who wrote what, and when?' and the other 'who did what, and when?' these alliances were very sensible. The fragmentation of History was completed by the inclusion of constitutional history in the Law degree. This was in fact dispersal rather than fragmentation, since there was no pre-existing unitary subject called History, with generally accepted territorial limits, which could have been broken up; the dispersal merely recognised the generally subordinate and service functions which historical studies were fitted to perform. Only in 1896 were the several strands of historical study brought together to form a separate branch of knowledge, which London called Branch IV in its Pass degree and Branch VI in its Honours degree; History had been patched up into an entity, fittingly enough largely by scissors and paste methods, and brought to the starting gate for its mad rush to eminence in the twentieth century.[8]

These slow and stately gyrations and evolutions in the formal degree structure in part reflected the divorce between teaching and examining which was the essence of the University from 1836 to 1900, so that there was no necessary relation between what the University chose to examine and what the professors and others in the colleges were teaching. But in part they did genuinely reflect the teaching professors' own conceptions of the nature of their subjects. The very idea of the University had been revolutionary in the 1830s, but its implementation had from the first been restrained by giving power to a government-nominated Senate dominated by Cambridge men; the Senate continued throughout the nineteenth century to ensure that its panel of examiners was largely composed of Oxford and Cambridge divines, some of them College Fellows and many of them public school headmasters. It was not until the 1890s that a few of the university examiners began to be appointed from the ranks of the

[7] *University of London Calendar*, 1859, p. 46; 1868, p. 50; 1885, pp. 69, xlv-vi.
[8] *University of London Calendar*, 1896, pp. 50, 57.

London colleges' own professors. Although a few of the earlier examiners had been very eminent in their fields – the economist Nassau Senior examining in Political Economy, the apostate classicist F.A. Paley in Classics and Ancient History, and the constitutional lawyer and theorist A.V. Dicey in Constitutional History, for example – it would be possible to argue that the body of examiners, with its Oxbridge ties, had a vested interest in seeing that their examination questions sustained a conservative and unadventurous interpretation of their subjects, in order to keep the upstart University in its place and restrain unwelcome competition with their *almae maters*.[9] This certainly became a standing source of conflict between teachers at the two colleges and the University authorities from the 1870s onwards, a running sore which gave rise to acrimonious debate in the 1890s and which was only partially and temporarily lanced by the reforms of 1900 that converted London into a teaching university.

All the same, it was not simply institutional imperfection and friction which caused what looks like stunted or retarded development in the Arts subjects after the fine dawn of the 1830s. Quite simply, the seeds then scattered did not have the capacity to produce flowers. The people did not exist who were capable of turning ideas that were fine on paper into the realities of rigorous, organised, well-defined academic disciplines, and the potential students did not exist who wished to study such subjects. English was a mild case in point. The Reverend Thomas Dale, the first Professor of English at University College, took some interest in grammar and philology, but a strictly didactic attitude towards literature which he maintained should be studied solely for the moral lessons it imparted. He left Gower Street rather rapidly, and when he turned up a few years later as the first professor of English at King's College he brought his moral messages with him. With the appointment of the Reverend F.D. Maurice at King's in 1840 the outlook for literature brightened considerably. He taught the subject through the study of actual texts for the first time, agonising over the propriety of using unbowdlerised versions of Chaucer and Shakespeare's *King John*, and used literature and political history in tandem to present a coherent and uplifting story of the forging of English national identity through the labours of the rising middle classes.[10] This imparted some intellectual content to the subject and lifted it off the rote-learning floor; but Maurice single-handed could not get English fully airborne, and he was not the kind of systematic thinker who could even begin to visualise the task of mapping out the aims, the methods, and the contours of a subject, which has to be tackled in making a collection of intellectual interests into an academic discipline. University College had

---

[9] Examiners were listed in the *University of London Calendar*, starting in 1844.

[10] Alan Bacon, 'English Literature becomes a University subject: King's College, London as Pioneer' *Victorian Studies*, 29 (1986), 591-612.

to wait until 1865, when it returned the compliment by gaining Henry Morley from King's, to find its first successful professor of English, and Morley made a considerable mark not only by lecturing to women and pressing forward the cause of university education for women at a crucial point in the 1860s, but also in advancing his subject with his massive survey of English language and literature, *English Writers*, which helped in providing the discipline with foundation texts.[11] Thus London made distinct contributions to the development of English into a true university subject. But pulling off this trick required more scholarly weight than London could muster, and in fact it was to be the example of Oxford in the late 1880s which definitely propelled English studies into their modern orbit.

History in London was a much more sickly plant, largely left as a tiresome extra chore for whoever chanced to be teaching classics or English. It is true that King's obtained a distinguished historian, Samuel Rawson Gardiner, as professor in 1872. Gardiner published between 1863 and 1901 a great multi-volume history of the early Stuarts and Cromwell, based on careful use of primary sources; and after he had left King's for All Souls he produced in 1889 a volume of documents, *The Puritan Revolution*, which in association with Stubbs's earlier *Select Charters* and G.W. Prothero's slightly later *Select Documents of the Reigns of Elizabeth and James I*, were to provide the core for the study of constitutional history from original documents and hence formed a key element in the rise of History as a discipline. As a historian Gardiner regarded himself as primarily a gentleman-scholar of private means, which indeed he had been quite literally for twenty years before accepting his first academic post, at King's; and he then took his lecturing duties as lightly as possible, so that he could get on with his serious work at home. This, you may say, neatly anticipates the life-style of many modern professors and lecturers and is not at all remarkable. But Gardiner seems to have kept his lectures, which he gave to the girls of Bedford College as well as at King's, and his research in separate compartments, and he apparently had no interest in trying to lift the undergraduate study of History out of its conventional and boring rut. Other nineteenth-century History professors of note were notable, like E.S. Beesly who was at University College for over thirty years from 1860, for the rarity of their appearances in the lecture room. In his case this afforded ample time to become the first British academic to be in close touch with bricklayers and other trade unionists, to establish a reputation as the leading home-grown socialist intellectual, and to sustain the labour newspaper of the day, the *Beehive*, with a steady flow of leading articles.[12] Excellent activities, precedents which have had many

---

[11] Negley Harte and John North, *The World of University College London, 1828-1978* (1978), p. 77.

[12] S. Maccoby, *English Radicalism, 1853-1886* (1938), pp. 121, 122, 207-8. Harte and

twentieth-century followers; but their contribution to the development of the subject was not apparent to contemporary generations of students.

History in London was all but invisible when the thirty-four-year old A.F. Pollard made his entry in 1903, fresh from the highly efficient and disciplined collaborative scholarship of the *D.N.B.* which he had helped to edit and write in the 1890s, and determined to transform university study of the subject into something equally purposeful, rigorous, and indispensable for any educated person. His methods, and even his concepts, may be questioned; but it is impossible to quarrel with his view that History, at that time, was 'the Cinderella of the Arts', or indeed with Sidney Webb's more sweepingly dismissive reference to 'the dwindling Faculty of Arts' also made in 1903.[13] History was at least represented, however nominally, by three professors and six lecturers, and had expanded in staff numbers since the 1830s with the arrival of the new colleges of Bedford, Westfield, Royal Holloway, and East London. Dwindling here was an absence of intellectual growth. In some other subjects it was a case of the vanishing trick: the first Professor of Spanish at University College left in 1830 to take part in the July Revolution in Paris, and the subject was not to be taught again until 1964.[14] But above all what had dwindled was the prospect which Thomas Arnold had perceived in 1837, that the new University should provide a new, demanding, and enlightened 'general or liberal education' through a marriage of the modern subjects, history, languages, poetry, and philology, with the traditional mathematics, classics, and logic.[15]

Arnold had foreseen from the beginning a rift between examination syllabuses determined by the University and courses of study settled by the teachers, when he wrote: 'We must thus either shape our examinations according to the system of instruction actually pursued by other institutions, or we must risk the appearance of dictating to them their course of study.'[16] This correctly identified a problem which was to rumble on until the Saunders reforms of the late 1960s permitted the teachers of the separate colleges to devise their own 'School-based' degree syllabuses; whereupon a new problem arose, of the possible balkanisation and devaluation of the London B.A. degree. Meanwhile Victorian professors were sometimes irked by the failure of the degree examination syllabus to correspond with what they wished to teach, and especially at King's could become so considerably irked that they refused to teach to the syllabus or to enter their students for the London degree. Thus academic obstinacy and institutional oddity in part account for the fact

North, *World*, p. 104.

[13] A.F. Pollard, *The University of London and the Study of History*, his 1904 inaugural lecture, cited in his *Factors in Modern History* (1st edn. 1907, 3rd edn. 1932), pp. 231-5.

[14] Pollard, *Factors*, p. 254. Harte and North, *World*, p. 39.

[15] P.P. 1840, XL, T. Arnold to the Chancellor, 31 May 1837, pp. 191-2.

[16] *Loc. cit.*

that many nineteenth-century London students spent a year or two at King's or University College and then moved on to take their B.A.s at Oxford or Cambridge. This behaviour, reminiscent of the peripatetic habits of German students and therefore perhaps welcome to the spirits of some at least of the University's founders, was so general among the more able and ambitious students on the Arts side that a more deep-seated cause may be suspected. The majority of the distinguished students listed by the centenary historians of both colleges completed their undergraduate studies at Oxford or Cambridge; it was characteristic that the one London man to reach the top of the Civil Service before 1914, becoming Permanent Under-Secretary at the Home Office, had been at King's and then at Trinity, Oxford.[17]

Just as the University was a free-market institution whose degree examinations, on certain undemanding conditions, could be taken by anyone who paid the fees, and towards which the colleges in London were free to adopt a take-it-or-leave-it attitude, so also the colleges themselves were free-market institutions whose professors mainly collected only a fee income, per student and per course, and were naturally disinclined to regard their academic work as a full-time occupation if they had the slightest talent which could attract other income. Sauce for the goose was sauce for the gander, and students adapted to the free-market situation, paying only for those courses they wanted and staying at a college only for as long as it suited their interests. It rather looks as though the nineteenth-century market place directed a stream of able young men to the London colleges who required topping up before they were ready to go on to tackle Greats at Oxford or the moral science Tripos at Cambridge, and another stream of the less able or less wealthy who were content to stay the course and take a London B.A. The high ability stream, it may be surmised, were those who were excluded from the conventional public-school route to Oxbridge, for a variety of financial, social, and religious reasons; for them Victorian London served as a kind of superior sixth-form college, an Oxbridge feeder that broadened and deepened the narrow and socially exclusive intake of Isis and Cam.

Paradoxically, the brave new university experiment of the beginning of Victoria's reign, founded to break the monopoly of the older universities, to challenge alike their religious discrimination and their neglect of learning and of modern subjects, ended her reign as a virtual dependency of Oxbridge. Among the consumers of higher education, London's student body was continually creamed off by Oxbridge; and among the producers, the great majority of London's teachers were supplied by

[17] H. Hale Bellot, *University College London, 1826-1926* (1929), pp. 363-6; F.J.C. Hearnshaw, *The Centenary History of King's College London, 1828-1928* (1929), pp. 336-9, 396-7; Jill Pellew, *The Home Office, 1848-1914* (1982), App. B, p. 208 – he was Sir Dalzell MacKenzie Chalmers (1847-1927), a member, among many other things, of the Lord Chancellor's Sleeping Sickness Committee.

Oxbridge. In 1901 the University as such acquired for the first time a Faculty of Arts, composed of the newly-instituted category of 'recognised teachers', then seventy-five in number. About 70 per cent of this Faculty had first degrees from Oxford or Cambridge, and a mere dozen had London first degrees; a select band which included Gregory Foster, then lecturer in English at University College and at Bedford and later the first Provost of University College, and J.W. Adamson, lecturer in educational theory and practice at King's and author of a history of English education which was for long a standard work.[18] In outline what had happened was that Oxford and Cambridge had been roused from their intellectual torpor, in some measure spurred on by the threat of competition from London, and had been forced out of their institutional archaism, in the series of university reforms that began in the 1850s, and had recaptured the academic initiative. Scholarly distinction and intellectual life were thus added to a social reputation that had never been dimmed, and London missed its early Victorian opportunity. In late Victorian London the tables had been turned, and the stirrings towards the establishment of single-subject Honours degrees in the Humanities in the 1890s, which were to mark the path of twentieth-century advance, were largely responses to and imitations of the Honours Schools of Oxford and the Tripos schemes of Cambridge, in which the first decisive moves had been made. Unsurprisingly, the majority of London professors seem to have lived in Oxford or Cambridge as members of those cultural societies, paying fleeting visits to their lecture rooms to count their students and collect their fees.

The road from the dependent status of 1901 to the glittering prizes of the 1986 brownie points was, naturally, paved with good intentions: and with great visions, such as those of Pollard, who saw History as the queen of Sciences, the school of administrators and statesmen, and London as the place where its full development could be realised; of Sir Israel Gollancz, who abandoned a Cambridge fellowship to come to King's College in 1903, drawn to London by his wish to be close to the newly-founded British Academy that, as its first Secretary, he aspired to build into a national institution, and by his desire to try out his great talents as a populariser of English literature on a really wide audience; of T.W. Arnold, who had a mission to make London the great imperial centre for the study of oriental languages and Islamic culture; or of Margaret J. Tuke, who looked forward in 1911, when splendid new buildings were going ahead in the magnificent site which had just been acquired in Regent's Park, to turning Bedford College into 'a complete University College' for women, quite different, as she said, 'in our aims and work from, say, Newnham College at Cambridge or Somerville College at

---

[18] *University Calendar*, 1901, Vol. II, pp. 53-8. *A Short History of Education* (1919), and *English Education, 1789-1902* (Cambridge, 1930) were J.W. Adamson's most used books.

Oxford', more 'a kind of little University to ourselves,' equal to any in Arts and in Science.[19] There were many more. There were others who virtually invented new subjects from the vantage point of their London chairs. R.W. Seton-Watson, not content with inventing most of the new nation states of Central and Eastern Europe after the First World War, invented East European studies, first at King's and then at the newly-created S.S.E.E.S. J.G. Robertson, splitting a chair in German between Bedford and University College between 1903 and 1933, played the chief part in making London into the leading centre for German studies in Britain, feeling confident enough of London's future to turn down the offer of a chair at Cambridge in 1910. W.P. Ker, professor of English at University College form 1889 to 1922, had energy left over from shaping the English Honours degree in the early 1900s to invent Scandinavian Studies, and virtually expired uttering the words 'Do not forget the Danish tongue'. Sir Sidney Lee, who in 1913 became the first professor of English at the East London College, had of course already invented the *D.N.B.* and went on to invent the modern style of royal biography, documented and replete with oral evidence, in his lives of Victoria and Edward VII. While Sir Allen Mawer, the second Provost of University College, may be ranked as co-inventor of the study of English placenames. Cyril Burt, whose invention of the I.Q. turned out, alas, to have been a shade too inventive, can be safely left to the Faculty of Education; but I must regretfully accept, being an economic historian myself, that the invention of economic history, in which London had such a notable role in the interwar years with R.H. Tawney, Lilian Knowles, Eileen Power, and others, and a tradition stretching back to the appearance of historical elements in H.S. Foxwell's rendering of political economy, probably belongs in the Faculty of Economics.[20]

[19] Pollard, *Factors in Modern History*, p. 250, and Memoir by V.H. Galbraith, *Proceedings of the British Academy*, XXXV (1950), pp. 257-74. Sir Israel Gollancz, Memoir in *Proceedings of the British Academy*, XVI (1930), pp. 426-8. T.W. Arnold, Memoir in *Proceedings of the British Academy*, XVI (1930), pp. 452-7. Margaret J. Tuke, evidence to the *Royal Commission on University Education in London (the Haldane Commission)*, Evidence, P.P. 1911, XX, qq. 7195-6.

[20] R.W. Seton-Watson, Memoir, *Proceedings of the British Academy*, XXXVII (1951), pp. 350-3 – he was, of course, reliant on the work of the equally distinguished Sir Bernard Pares in the establishment of the School of Slavonic and East European Studies in 1932 as an independent Institute. J.G. Robertson, Memoir, *Proceedings of the British Academy*, XIX (1933), pp. 366-9; W.P. Ker, Memoir, *Proceedings of the British Academy* XI (1924-5), pp. 416-17; Sir Sidney Lee, Memoir, *Proceedings of the British Academy* XV (1929, pp. 458-9; Sir Allen Mawer, Memoir, *Proceedings of the British Academy* XXIX (1943), pp. 438-9. Economic history questions appeared in the examination papers on Political Economy set by Foxwell, e.g. in 1896, *University Calendar*, 1896, p. ci, while they had not appeared in the days when Nassau Senior or his successor, Jacob Waley, were the Political Economy examiners, e.g. *University Calendar*, 1858, p. cli, *University Calendar*, 1868, p. cxiii-iv. Economic History, of course, sits on the frontier between the Humanities and Social Sciences and tends to be disputed territory.

In addition, no university could aspire to memorability without accumulating a gallery of eccentrics and a store of legends. The more erudite examples ranged from Sir Ernest Barker, who during his time as a classics lecturer at King's recorded the distressing effects produced by the short skirts of the young ladies in his class – sadly he did not live to see the mini-skirt – to C.E.M. Joad, the Birkbeck philosopher who so impressed the B.B.C. that they promoted him to be a professor, and whose mental agility and air of profundity delighted millions of wartime listeners to the Brains Trust, while his lapse in travelling by train without a ticket convinced them that academics were human as well as useful. Dame Lillian Penson, that formidable scholar and academic politician who put Bedford firmly on the map and dotted those parts of the map of Africa which were coloured red with offshoots of London University, was in a class of her own as the first woman Vice-Chancellor in Britain and the only known Head of Department to insist that all her academic staff wear gloves while lecturing.[21]

Strong personalities, large women and big men, were an important ingredient in the forging of London's reputation; but by no means the sole factor. The twentieth-century flowering of excellence, no less than the twentieth-century expansion in size, have been part of the national history of university education, alternatively encouraged and admired, and distrusted and starved, by governments and public opinion, in an academic variation on the stop-go theme which has served Britain for so long as a substitute for policy – a story which it would be out of place to attempt to describe, let alone explain, here. Certain of the features in the changing national environment, however, were of particular importance to London: women, salaries, and professionalisation may be singled out.

By the end of the nineteenth century women formed more than a third of the student body of University College. Although King's kept them at arm's length physically and institutionally in their Ladies' Department in Kensington, women were similarly important there. Bedford, started in 1849 as a kind of sixth-form college for girls, began teaching for London degrees as soon as they were opened to women in 1878. Westfield (1882) and Royal Holloway (1887) were also making their presence felt, contributing to London's outstanding role in pioneering university education for women. It is notable, however, that the Haldane Commission thought, in 1911, that only Bedford among the women's colleges was capable of becoming strong enough to take a place alongside King's and University College as a fully-fledged 'constituent college' of

---

[21] Sir Ernest Barker, Memoir, *Proceedings of the British Academy* XLVI (1960), pp. 344-5. C.E.M. Joad (1891-1953, *Who Was Who, 1951-60*; he was Reader in Philosophy at Birkbeck College, 1930-46. Dame Lillian Penson (1896-1963), *Who Was Who, 1961-70*. London also provided the first woman professor in the country when Caroline Spurgeon became Professor of English at Bedford College in 1913.

the University, remarking of Westfield and Royal Holloway that, while admirable, 'they are both residential colleges organised more upon the lines of the colleges of Oxford and Cambridge than on those of the Scotch or German universities which the University of London reconstituted [on Haldane lines] would resemble.' The 1911 Report continued, harshly revealing the durability of administrative views of geography, by asserting that: 'The Royal Holloway College, moreover, is so far distant from London that it cannot hope effectively to give or gain strength either through its students or its teachers by a more intimate connexion with the University than it now possesses.'[22] The colleges survived Germanic logic rather better than they have weathered monetarist economics.

Medical education and qualifications had been among the chief goals in the women's fight to get into the universities; and in King's Ladies' Department domestic science figured prominently as eminently suitable for females, although Bedford did not think of it as a proper university subject.[23] But while women did study these subjects, and some of the natural sciences, their strong preference for the Arts, for English, languages, history, or the classics, had rapidly become apparent. The great potential power of women as a motive force for growth in the Arts in London was that, unlike the men, they had nowhere else to move on to. As long as able men students migrated to Oxford and Cambridge to complete their degrees, the London colleges had little incentive to raise the standards of their courses and no market for more specialised or higher-level degrees. Women students, by contrast, once they were inside the London colleges, could not realistically plan their education with the expectation of escaping to Oxbridge, for the number of places at the new women's colleges there was minute. The general effect was that London was in a better position to attract and retain able women than able men; that it had a more stable body of students likely to stay for a full three years and for whom it was therefore worth providing different and better courses; and that the pressures of student demand became more focused on the nature and quality of complete degree packages, rather than on the utility and attractiveness of individual lecture courses. There was, to be sure, some risk that some girls would treat London as an inexpensive finishing school, just as some boys treated it as a sixth form on the cheap. It was voiced by A.J. Butler when he was considering the offer of the chair of Italian at University College in 1898. 'No students, no pay; no pay, no lectures; no lectures, no students!' he wrote. 'Still, if I could come in my own time (which would probably be about 5 p.m.) and were not expected to hold forth more than twenty-four or so times in the year, nor to give assistance to young ladies about to spend a winter at Rome in acquiring a

[22] *Haldane Commission*, Report, P.P. 1913, XL, p. 67.
[23] *Haldane Commission*, Evidence, P.P. 1911, XX, q. 7206.

colloquial knowledge of the language, I think I could be of some use.'[24]

All the same, the women were in general serious students intent on getting B.A.s, for personal satisfaction or to go into teaching, and their presence helped push the colleges and the University into the teaching and degree reforms that gathered momentum from the 1880s and led to the specialised Honours degrees that ruled unchallenged as the essence of the B.A. from the early 1900s until the 1970s. The more frivolous and wealthy girls on the whole did not fancy London, as the professor of Mathematics at Royal Holloway explained in accounting for the absence of non-resident students at the college: 'Englefield Green', he said, 'is a place which has in the past been inhabited by rich people, and I do not think, as a rule, as far as my experience goes, that very rich people's girls are very anxious to attend a University College.' An opinion echoed by his Principal's view that 'I do not think that the people who would naturally attend a University College exist very largely in the neighbourhood of . . . Egham.'[25] At the same time women, dedicated rather than wealthy, moved into university teaching, by no means exclusively in the women's colleges. One-fifth of the first Faculty of Arts, in 1901, were women; and one-third of this admittedly small group had London degrees, compared with less than one-sixth of the male lecturers, so that in this sphere one may depict women as spearheading the University's recognition of its own products. By 1921, in the aftermath of war, a quarter of the teachers in the Faculty were women, and by 1939, on the eve of war, the proportion had grown to 30 per cent; since then, in the aftermath of decades of feminism, it has fallen back to about its 1921 level.[26]

The influence of women, as teachers and as students, has been very considerable. It would be wrong to claim, however, that it was decisive in propelling the Arts onwards and upwards, for women did not begin to move into positions of power and authority in the academic structure until the 1930s. Butler's 1898 letter pointed to the two matters which were to be decisive: salaries and full-time work. Unsalaried professors tended to work part-time, and if they did devote their lives to scholarship their devotions did not take place in college. A stroke of good luck might break the pattern. Richard Quain, the surgeon, left University College a small fortune in 1887, and because of his conviction that medical men ought to have a liberal education a large part of the bequest was earmarked for the endowment of a chair of English, to the great and enduring benefit of the subject and perhaps in less visible ways to the benefit of medical practice.[27] Quain had links with University College from his early career;

---

[24] Quoted in Harte and North, *World*, p. 106.

[25] *Haldane Commission*, Evidence, P.P. 1911, q. 8626.

[26] *University Calendar*, 1901, Vol II, pp. 53-8; 1921, pp. 118-21; 1939, pp. 202-12; 1986, entries for Classics, English, Germanic Languages, History, and Romance Languages.

[27] *D.N.B.* Richard Quain (1800-87).

more unpredictable was Amelia Edwards's action in 1892 in endowing a chair of Egyptology expressly for occupation by Flinders Petrie, the virtually unschooled son of a roaming railway surveyor, who had started digging about in the pyramids in 1883 and had developed, single-handed, techniques of scientific excavation and methods of dating. Thus, almost by chance, Egyptology received its first academic recognition in Britain, and University College in due time acquired Petrie's great teaching collection for housing in the converted stable in which it still rests.[28] These developments were exceptional, and in any case Egyptian archaeology when stretched as far as the god Min was not a fit subject for undergraduate study. More typically the scholarly life of Victorian London as a city, which was extremely vigorous and innovative, went on in voluntary and specialist learned societies, and in the chambers of gentlemen scholars; some of the circle might dash off a lecture now and then if they happened to have a connexion with the university, but that was not the centre of their loyalties.[29]

The new teaching University of London in 1900 made the crucial move that was to lead to the transformation of this situation, when it ruled that anyone called a professor must have a guaranteed annual salary of at least £600 before being eligible for acceptance as an 'appointed teacher' and professor of the University. This was less than one-third of the salary of the first Principal of the University, under the new dispensation – a differential which has become somewhat eroded over time – but was still sufficient for jogging along.[30] It was not riches, but it was on a par with the incomes of keepers of collections in the British Museum and the Victoria and Albert, and with first-class clerks in the Treasury, who were superior beings. Above all, it set a modestly attractive goal for an academic career, and in return demanded full-time work within the slightly elastic definition of 'full-time' to which academics have subsequently become adjusted.[31] From this everything else followed: university teaching

[28] Sir Flinders Petrie, Memoir, *Proceedings of the British Academy* XXVIII (1942), pp. 315-7.

[29] A case in point was the Philological Society, a centre of activity for generations of English scholars. W.P. Ker (University College), R.C. Latham (University College), J.W. Hales (King's College), R.C. Trench (King's College) – later Archbishop of Dublin – were active members, but the main impetus came from F.S. Furnivall. Furnivall was a typical University College student in that he completed his degree at Trinity Hall, Cambridge. Called to the Bar in 1849, he spent most of his life as a freelance scholar, secretary of the Philological Society and founder of the Early English Text Society. He was chiefly responsible for conceiving the project of a New English Dictionary and for the work on it from 1857 to 1879, when it was taken over by Sir James Murray with the support of the O.U.P. What became the *O.E.D.* might, therefore, through the Furnivall-Philological Society-University College links have been the London English Dictionary: R.W. Chambers, *Philologists at University College*, pp. 22-5, in R.W. Chambers, ed., *University of London, University College, Centenary Addresses* (n.d. *c.* 1928).

[30] Negley Harte, *The University of London, 1836-1986* (1986), p. 177.

[31] *Whitaker's Almanack for 1910*, pp. 179-200.

became a career, just as college tutoring had become a career in Oxford and Cambridge after the marriage bar for fellows was lifted in 1877. In Oxbridge career dons turned to devising honours degrees that would provide job satisfaction and professional justification for their work, and produced character-building recipes well adapted to teaching from authorities and curbing the influence of research professors, and ideal for turning out men to run the country and the empire. In London career professors, backed at first sketchily and by the 1930s more adequately by lecturers grouped in departments and enlisted in a profession with promotion prospects, turned also to professionalising their work and to producing the honours degrees which full-time occupations made possible. Being mainly Oxbridge people in exile, and hence naturally dissatisfied with the way things were done in their old universities, their concept of honours degrees was slightly different and placed more stress on keeping up with the latest research, to which they expected to contribute themselves, and on putting young minds through their critical paces.

Devotees of Parkinson's Law will glimpse here an excellent example of work being created to fill the staff time available.[32] It would be nearer the mark to say that the intellectual case for organising knowledge in distinct disciplines, each with its own honours degree as the vehicle for conveying its fundamental message, had existed for some little while; and that the opportunity for translating this into academic practice was created by the funding of a body of professionals dedicated to the task. A.F. Pollard was among the most dedicated, and the History degree which he did so much to shape may be offered as an exemplar of the process, without implying that it was or is exemplary. The story is peculiarly apt, since Pollard was not funded when he arrived at University College in 1903 as Professor of Constitutional History without stipend, but became funded with a regular salary from 1907 while in the middle of organising the new system of intercollegiate teaching and lecturing to deploy the combined resources of all the colleges to lift the refurbished History degree out of limbo and into the limelight.[33] The degree, with its 'seamless web' approach leading to

[32] C. Northcote Parkinson spent the most productive parts of his career at Liverpool and as Raffles Professor of History in Singapore, but perhaps his most formative years were as a postgraduate at King's College.

[33] Intercollegiate lecturing in English seems to have preceded that in History. It was referred to enthusiastically by Gregory Foster in 1911 (*Haldane Commission*), *Evidence*, P.P. 1911, XX, qq. 9580, 9673, though he may have had in mind no more than co-operation between University College and Bedford College; oddly, since Pollard was sitting beside him at the time also giving evidence, Gregory Foster does not seem to have heard of the elaborate system of intercollegiate teaching in History, drawing in teachers from King's College, the London School of Economics, Royal Holloway College, Westfield College, and King's College Women's Department, as well as University College and Bedford College, which was in operation from 1904 (*University Calendar*, 1904, Vol. II, pp. 266-9).

the culminating point of studying a limited topic in depth from original documents, was recognisably similar to the present syllabus, which differs more in the range of choice than in underlying structure: the contents of the bottles have altered more than the labels on them. In explaining the purpose of the study of History Pollard returned to Thomas Arnold and the origins of London University, and spoke out for the provision of a 'liberal education' as the essence of a university, in contrast to the then current fashion of emphasising the need for more technical education to counter economic competition from Germany.[34]

Plus ça change. In 1837 a 'liberal education' meant a basic grounding in all the arts and science subjects, ancient and modern. In the 1900s it meant, at university level, coming to grips with the variety of subject matter and method encompassed by one single Arts discipline. In either case it was seen as offering education for intelligent living and working, not as a form of vocational or professional training. This was not idle or pious talk: it represented what students wanted. Pollard himself recognised that it was necessary to look to the quality of teaching in schools in order to ensure the flow of students into the subject, and with that end in view he was instrumental in founding the Historical Association in 1906; it is something to which university teachers are turning with renewed concentration in the 1980s. In the event student numbers increased from general causes rather than as a response to individual efforts. All the same, the Arts subjects more than held their share of the total. The number of London's internal students increased sixfold between 1902 and 1939, roughly from 2,000 to 12,000; in the same period the number reading History, for example, grew from a handful (in 1905 there were five finals candidates; in 1906, nine) to nearly 300. In the great post-1945 surge, with its Robbins accelerator, in which London's student numbers peaked in 1981 at just over 55,000, the Arts subjects held a fairly steady 25 to 30 per cent in the multi-faculty colleges.[35]

This was the hard evidence of strong student demand for what the Arts had to offer; a demand that was admittedly largely determined by specialisation at school, and was influenced by almost everything except precise knowledge of what particular Departments or Colleges had on offer, but nevertheless a demand for something other than a crude meal ticket or passport to a specific career. It was a demand for specialised, single-subject, honours degrees, which became firmly established as the core of all the Arts subjects by the 1930s. In providing these degrees the teachers became more specialised, more professional, more involved in research. This was the context in which the great personalities flourished. It was also a context in which individuals came to identify more with their discipline and their profession in its national network of learned journals

[34] Pollard, *The University of London and the Study of History*, pp. 240-1.
[35] Pollard, *Factors*, pp. 235, 254; Harte, *University of London*, pp. 26, 34.

and conferences, and less with a particular college or university of which they might be only transient members. Byzantine London was a peculiarly difficult university to identify with. The countervailing force came from the Senate Institutes, grown from the single seed planted in 1921 in the Tudor Huts of Malet Street to the eleven which still survive today, and all of them save for our ally in Advanced Legal Studies within the Arts orbit. These Institutes have gone with the grain of the tendency of research-based professional academics to think and live in terms of communities of scholars that transcend university boundaries, by becoming not just London University centres but national and international centres in their fields. The community of scholars does not simply exist in the abstract, in journal articles and book reviews, or assemble once a year in a *Small World* conference: it may be viewed every day in the I.H.R. common room, the Classical Studies seminar room, or the Warburg library. By the 1960s it had become quite usual to refer to the Institutes in words first used by Sir Douglas Logan as 'the jewels in the crown of London University', a possibly unguarded phrase when jewels are a security risk.

The years from 1900 to the early 1950s have sometimes been referred to as the period of the great revival of the Arts in London.[36] Since there was so little there to revive, it is better to think of this as the first rise of Arts, the period of take-off. The drive to maturity from the 1950s entered the 'age of mass consummation', to employ the happy words of an exam script of 1966, at about that time. Maturity has its perils. In the 1970s fears were expressed that Arts subjects might, or perhaps already had ossified, there was much talk of relevance, not yet *passé* as a buzz-word, and there were worries about the marketability of students with Arts degrees. Some even pretended not to know what they were for. Retracing steps to the 1870s and 1880s, two-subject degrees were laboriously re-invented, meeting with no more than moderate success. More helpfully and constructively, honours degrees were scrutinised, overhauled, and given a new look, some of them going college-based. The worries, though not unfounded, were largely misplaced. Arts degrees are, and will remain, relevant not in any vocational sense, and not through going into contortions to make their subject matter highly contemporary or otherwise trendy. They are relevant because they provide a training in learning how to find things out, how to select and marshal evidence and distinguish probabilities from mere opinions, how to conduct reasoned argument and test hypotheses, and how to express conclusions. To be sure, these are skills which may be acquired in other ways also, through other disciplines, although clarity of expression is not a readily identifiable product of information technology, as anyone who has wrestled with a computer

---

[36] For example by V.H. Galbrdaith in his Memoir of A.F. Pollard, *Proceedings of the British Academy*, XXXV (1950), p. 260.

manual can testify. In any case, while you can lead a horse to the water . . .
In the Arts these qualities can be acquired through the study of subjects
which students in large numbers happen to find interesting and attractive.
They are scarce and valuable skills, and they sell well in the job market. It
is very easy to consider the Civil Service stupid, in its continued preference
for recruiting Arts graduates and its persistent Oxbridge bias.[37] But it
would be difficult at the same time to condemn Marks & Spencer or Shell,
John Lewis or Ford Motors, Natwest or Sainsbury, as they scramble in the
annual milk-round to collar the most promising Arts graduates.

More worrying, maybe, is the tendency of academics to become so
professionalised that they talk only to each other and make their subjects
so abstruse that they are unintelligible except to a handful of fellow
specialists. This has been a general tendency in the world of learning, in
no way peculiar to the Arts or to London, and is a necessary consequence
of the cumulative effects of increasing specialisation and refinement of
methodologies. Some subjects, indeed, deliberately set out to drive
unqualified practitioners and amateurs out of their field, and to annex
fields of knowledge in the best-approved manner of closed-shop
professions like medicine, the law, or architecture.

'Everyone thinks that he or she can write history and biography
without any preliminary training or any specific research,' Pollard had
remarked in 1904, 'and the public will buy any book if the author
possesses a handle to his or her name'.[38] One aim of the London History
School was to put an end to this lamentable state of affairs, and some, who
apparently have not noticed the Pakenham family, think that in the 1980s
this has been achieved with the extinction of amateurism and the total
annexation of the production of history by academic historians.[39] That is
an erroneous view. Besides, not all history produced in the universities is
monographic or unreadable, and London has its share of those who reach
a public with an unsatiable appetite for the subject: Neale's *Queen Elizabeth*
was a best-seller in the 1930s, and it is not without its successors (as well as
its detractors).

The Arts, indeed, need to communicate with the public and not keep
their intellectual riches to themselves. London has never been backward
in doing this. Classics, cruelly characterised as having become 'self-
absorbed and self-enclosed, and thus doomed to self-destruction' in this

[37] *Whitaker's Almanack for 1986* records that out of 22 Permanent Secretaries or
equivalent heads of the main Whitehall departments, one had a London degree, a B.A. in
English, while twelve had Oxford and seven had Cambridge degrees. In the larger
population of what Whitaker defines as 'Public Offices' there are 62 Chairmen, Directors,
or the equivalent of the various authorities, of whom 14 have London degrees, six of which
are in the Arts: the holders are chiefly to be found in the museums and gallery world.

[38] Pollard, *Factors*, p. 251.

[39] David Cannadine, 'The State of British History', *Times Literary Supplement*, 10 Oct.
1986, pp. 1139-40.

century, after losing its Victorian function of equipping future statesmen with a fund of Latin tags, in fact flourishes on a strong, if minority, interest in the ancient world. And as almost incidental by-products it has contributed A.E. Housman, who wrote *A Shropshire Lad* while Professor of Latin at University College, and Louis Macniece, who was a lecturer in Classics at Bedford College in the 1930s, to the store of poetry which Thomas Arnold had said could never be examined. Sir Mortimer Wheeler, whose contributions to archaeology need no rehearsal, was one of the earliest telly dons as well as the founder of London's Institute; the one did as much to make archaeology one of the public's, and the fund-givers', darlings, as the other did to advance its techniques and achievements. Anthony Blunt, Director of the Courtauld from 1947 to 1974, was already widely known for his work in making the history of art generally accessible, long before he became notorious. Sir Nikolaus Pevsner, Professor of the History of Art at Birkbeck until 1969, created the incomparable guides which every discerning traveller has in hand when looking at *The Buildings of England*. Huw Wheldon, an L.S.E. graduate, brought art history, architectural history, and much else besides, to millions of viewers.[40] While inside the Slade art is created, and the incomparable, since the days when Augustus John was a student, easily outshines the indigestible. And so one could go on.

There is a record here of successful communication with the world outside the university. It is one which is being well maintained. Not only is there no shortage of telly dons, but of much greater importance there is no shortage of the development of fresh approaches in the Arts, sometimes within old subjects like classics, sometimes in new subjects that emerge from older ones, like linguistics, which are exciting for the public as well as the academics. Self-congratulation or self-absorption are not part of the tradition of the Faculty of Arts in London. Those brownie points, transitory as they may seem, are firmly grounded. The Faculty may seem to exist only on ceremonial occasions, when its Dean takes the stage to present honorary graduands. But it has great strengths, great achievements, and a great future.

---

[40] R.P. Graves, *A.E. Housman: The Scholar Poet* (Oxford, 1979), esp. chaps. 5 and 6. Sir R.E. Mortimer Wheeler, Memoir, *Proceedings of the British Academy*, LXIII (1977), pp. 486-97. Sir Nikolaus Pevsner (1902-83), (Sir) Anthony Blunt (1907-84), Sir Huw Wheldon (1916-86), *Who's Who* (v.d.).

4

Laws

W.L. Twining

A comprehensive history of legal education in England has yet to be written.[1] The story is complex and could be constructed in a number of ways. On almost any interpretation it would make depressing reading. One outstanding feature, which Max Weber and others have emphasised, is the very minor role played by the universities both in the formation of the legal profession and in the development of the common law. Weber treated this as the distinguishing characteristic between the modes of

This is a revised version of a lecture delivered at Queen Mary College on 28 October 1986 as part of the sesquicentennial celebrations of the University of London. In the course of preparing the lecture I have benefited from help and advice of numerous individuals and institutions. Professor Michael Thompson, Negley Harte and Andrew Lewis provided invaluable advice and material. David Sugarman joined me in interviewing Professors Albert Kiralfy, L.C.B. Gower, Sir Jack Jacob, George Keeton and Lord Wedderburn, all of whom provided invaluable information insights and correctives. Professors Antony Allott, Francis Jacobs, Jeffrey Jowell, Michael Zander and Graham Zellick supplied me with a mass of information about the five London law schools. Members of the External Division and Judith Maynard, Secretary of the Board of Studies in Law provided invaluable assistance. Among others to whom I am indebted are Dr John Baker, Professor F.R. Crane, Jacky Gorringe and Professor Robert Stevens. This lecture is a celebration, interpretation and commentary, rather than a descriptive history. However, in the course of its preparation, I acquired sufficient material to form a small archive. This will in due course be deposited in the Institute of Advanced Legal Studies in the hope that it will be of help to real historians.

[1] Standard accounts include: L.C.B. Gower 'English Legal Training', *Modern Law Review*, 13 (1950), 137, B. Abel-Smith and R. Stevens *Lawyers and the Courts*, (London, 1967); *Report of the Committee on Legal Education* (1971), Cmnd. 4595 (Ormrod Report). The modern history of legal education in England, 1800-1980 is currently being re-interpreted by David Sugarman, see especially 'The Legal Boundaries of Liberty: Dicey, Liberalism and Legal Science', *Modern Law Review*, 46 (1983), 102 and 'Legal Theory and the Common Law Mind: The Making of the Textbook Tradition' in *Legal Theory and the Common Law*, ed. W.L. Twining, (Oxford, 1986). There are, of course, many particular studies, too numerous to mention here.

thought of civil law and common law systems.[2]

The standard overview – as presented by Gower, irreverently glossed by Abel-Smith and Stevens, and given respectability by the Ormrod Report of 1971[3] – can be briefly restated as follows: civil law was studied at Oxford and Cambridge from an early date, but the study of English Law did not become firmly established in the universities until the late nineteenth century. Systematic study of law was never accepted by those in power as a necessary preparation for practice; indeed its desirability was often questioned. Today a law degree is the normal first stage for qualification as a barrister or solicitor, but we remain one of the few countries in the world in which a law degree is not a necessary qualification for practice. We are not here concerned with the history of entry to the legal profession; however, in assessing the contributions of the University of London in the field of law, it is worth remembering the limited and ambiguous role that university law faculties play in preparation for practice and in professional life. They have never had a monopoly, or anything approaching one, over legal education. Law schools run by the professions, private crammers and, more recently, polytechnic law schools (some of which, unlike the universities, are directly involved in professional training) all play a significant part. Similarly, unlike the continent of Europe, legal scholars have made an extremely modest impact on legal development.[4]

In this standard account, the foreshortened history of the discipline of law in the universities emerges as a series of false starts and disappointed expectations. From the Middle Ages until the late sixteenth century the Inns of Court were the only centres for the study of English law. In their heyday they were vigorous intellectual communities, which served to provide a general education as well as professional training. But the educational functions of the Inns atrophied, especially after the Civil War, and for a long time such legal education as there was rested on apprenticeship and self-education.

Blackstone's lectures, and the creation of the Vinerian Chair, in the period 1753-65 failed to institutionalise the teaching of English law at Oxford. So did the establishment of the Downing Chair at Cambridge in 1800. The Faculty of Arts and Laws at University College, founded in

---

[2] Max Weber *Law in Economy and Society*, ed. M. Rheinstein (Cambridge, Mass., 1954), ch. VII.

[3] Above n. 1.

[4] Their influence has increased in recent years but, as Brian Simpson remarked: 'Any attempt by the academics to displace the higher judiciary from their central place as expounders and modifiers of the law seems to me to have always been foredoomed to failure. In the absence of some quite radical scheme of modification the judges, and in particular the members of the Court of Appeal and the House of Lords, are hardly likely to abdicate their status in favour of the professors. Why should they?' A.W.B. Simpson 'The Survival of the Common Law System' in *Then and Now, 1799-1974*, 63-4, (1974).

1826, is sometimes said to be England's first modern law school. But, as we shall see, the story of Law in London in the nineteenth century is a rather sad tale of missed opportunities and promise unfulfilled.

1846 rather than 1836 is often treated as the start of modern legal education in England.[5] In that year a Select Committee on Legal Education was set up by the House of Commons and produced a remarkable report in three months.[6] What it found amounted to an almost total vacuum:

> It revealed that there was virtually no institutional law teaching of any kind in England, with the exception of Professor Amos's teaching at University College, London [which had stopped in 1834]. At Oxford, Dr Phillimore, the Professor of Civil Law, had ceased to lecture because there were 'few or no attendants'. The Vinerian professor had at most thirty-eight students because there were no degrees in Common Law. The Downing Professor of Law at Cambridge informed the Committee that 'there are at present no lectures given, and no attendance whatever.'[7] The Regius Professor of Civil Law at Cambridge continued to lecture because attendance at his lectures was a necessary requirement for a degree in Civil Law, but there were no examinations. Apart from attendance at these lectures, the only qualification for a degree was lapse of time, 7 years for a Bachelor and 12½ years for a Doctor's degree. At the Inns of Court, there was no formal instruction, and no test of proficiency of any kind before Call to the Bar.[8]

The examination which intending solicitors were required to pass under the 1843 Act served 'merely as a guarantee against absolute incompetency',[9] and the Committee had almost nothing good to say about the operation of articles.

In the Committee's view, the consequences of this situation were serious: there was no guarantee of minimum competence in either branch of the profession; there was 'a hypercritical attention to the technicalities'[10] and a lack of concern for general principle; there was no class of jurists of eminence concerned with the systematic exposition and reform of the law;[11] and there was inadequate provision for the study of law for 'the unprofessional student.'[12]

[5] E.g. Ormrod, 5.
[6] *Report from the Select Committee on Legal Education*, 25 August 1846, B.P.P. Vol X, p. 1.
[7] iv.
[8] Ormrod, 5. This contains a useful, and generally accurate, summary of the *Report*.
[9] 1846 Report, xvi.
[10] Id. xxxix (quoting R. Bethell Q.C.).
[11] lvii.
[12] lviii. The Committee concluded: 'That the present state of Legal Education in England and Ireland, in reference to the classes professional and unprofessional concerned, to the extent and nature of the studies pursued, the time employed, and the facility with which instruction may be obtained, is extremely unsatisfactory and incomplete, and exhibits a striking contrast and inferiority to such education, provided as

The Committee saw the solution in the institutionalisation of legal education. They put forward three main proposals:

1. A great expansion of university legal education in England and Ireland through the creation of new chairs and a proper system of examination for law degrees; systematic law teaching should be revived in Oxford and Cambridge and extended in London.[13]

2. The Inns of Court should combine to form 'a special institution', a College or 'Law University' analogous to the College of Surgeons or Physicians. There should be an examination on entry to the Inns, a formal system of lectures and a public qualifying examination for call to the Bar.[14]

3. Intending solicitors should be stringently examined both prior to admission to Apprenticeship and by a final examination that should be 'conducted more in reference to general principles than technicalities'.[15] There should be separate provision for classes suited to the needs and situations of articled clerks, to supplement articles, but with some provision for attendance at certain classes in the Inns of Court and for exemption on the basis of attendance at University lectures.

In 1971 the Ormrod Committee commented: 'The history of legal education in England over the past 120 years is largely an account of the struggle to implement the recommendations of the 1846 Committee and the effects of that struggle.'[16] This oversimplifies the story and, read out of context, exaggerates the significance of the 1846 Report in respect of both originality and influence.[17] Nevertheless, the Report was prophetic in a number of ways, including anticipating exemptions, stringent Law Society Finals, and some common training for barristers and solicitors. Its more immediate significance was two-fold: first it made a sharp distinction between 'the practical and mechanical side' of legal study and 'the higher and doctrinal' side and argued strongly that the role of university law faculties was to concentrate on the latter.[18]

Secondly, it accepted that some aspects of the practical side could be the subject of formal instruction and examination, but recommended that these should be the responsibility of separate institutions. As the Ormrod Committee observed, the most striking difference between our system of education and training and that of most other countries (and, one might

it is with ample means and a judicious system for their application, at present in operation in all the more civilised States of Europe and America' (lvi).

[13] lvii-lix.

[14] lix-lx.

[15] lxi.

[16] Ormrod, 8.

[17] For details see Abel-Smith and Stevens, Gower, and A.H. Manchester *Modern Legal History* (1980), 54-66.

[18] The contrast between 'higher' and 'technical' studies pervades the report; see e.g. xlvii-xlviii.

add, other professions) is 'the existence of independent law schools run by the profession itself' which play a part in the education of future professional lawyers (particularly of solicitors).[19]

Such thinking had three interrelated consequences: first, it institutionalised some extremely dubious distinctions between theory and practice; education and training; and knowledge, understanding and skill. Secondly it further marginalised the contribution of the universities not only to professional formation, but also to legal practice and the operation of the legal system. We now have a four-stage structure of legal education and training: the academic stage, the vocational stage, apprenticeship (articles and pupillage) and continuing legal education.[20] The universities produce a significant, but not overwhelming, majority of those who satisfy the requirements of the academic stage;[21] unlike the polytechnics they play almost no part in conversion courses for non-law graduates and in the vocational stage; their contribution to the rapidly developing field of continuing legal education is growing, but uneven.

Thirdly, questions about the educational objectives of law degrees, the role of law schools and the identity of academic lawyers are endemic matters of controversy in most countries. The structure of our system has excluded a number of options: it rules out the possibility that university law faculties can emulate English medical schools, German law faculties or the Harvard Law School – all of which have been put forward as models in the past 150 years. On the other hand, legal education is largely demand-led and a significant percentage of students sees the law degree as a passport to a professional qualification, though not necessarily to practice. Thus the influence of the legal profession is mediated through students' expectations, some of which are unrealistic or unsuited to a university environment. Accordingly, despite the yearnings of some law teachers, it is virtually impossible for a law faculty to seek to be an institution which is single-mindedly devoted to pure science or liberal education or systematic law reform or to serve as a guerrilla base. The market pressures against this are too strong. Yet, at least since the rise of full-time teaching, academic lawyers have consistently rejected 'the trade school model'. They have also regularly insisted that a law degree can

[19]   Ormrod, 3.
[20]   See further W. Twining 'The Benson Report and Legal Education: A Personal View' in *Law in the Balance*, ed. P.A. Thomas (Oxford, 1982), ch. 8.
[21]   The most comprehensive figures are to be found in J.F. Wilson and S.B. Marsh, *A Second Survey of Legal Education in the United Kingdom* (1981). On the basis of projected intake quotas for 1983-4 Wilson and Marsh predicted that the output of law graduates in England and Wales would be universities 2455 (66 per cent), polytechnics 1238 (34 per cent) (Table 43 at p. 45). These figures did not take account of the revival of the External LL.B., the Licence of the University of Buckingham, graduates with mixed degrees who proceed to a professional qualification and non-law graduates who take the Common Professional Examination.

serve equally well as a general education and as a foundation for law practice. University law schools, especially since the Second World War, have been hybrid institutions serving a variety of constituencies and uneasily juggling with competing purposes. Similarly the individual law teacher has to struggle with often irreconcilable demands to be an Expositor, Craftsman, Liberal Intellectual, Scientist or Censor. Pessimists call this falling between stools;[22] optimists call it creative tension. This is the situation of the London law faculties.

The Benthamite Vision and the Austinian Gloss

Once upon a time there was a man named Henry Tonks, who was Slade Professor of Fine Art at University College from 1917 to 1930. In 1922 he painted an enormous canvas depicting Jeremy Bentham in the foreground, considering the architect's plans for University College, watched by Henry Brougham, Thomas Campbell and Crabb Robinson who are very much in the background.[23] An irreverent wag once said of the picture that its 'lack of artistic distinction is overshadowed by historical inaccuracy.' For Bentham is about twice the size of the others; yet he is not officially recognised as a founder of the college and played a minor and rather obscure role in its establishment. He took, as it were, a back seat. For many years the painting hung at ground level in the North Cloister. Unfortunately in 1985 it was vandalised – whether by a historian, an aesthete or a common or cloistered vandal is likely to remain a mystery.

I confess that I was that irreverent commentator;[24] but not, I hasten to add, the vandal. I hereby retract my judgement. For in preparing this essay I have learned that the curious perspective of the painting was due, not to incompetence, but because it was intended to hang under the dome of the Flaxman Gallery and to be viewed from below.[25] In short, for years we have been looking at it from the wrong angle. There may be a moral there. Furthermore, like this essay, the picture is a celebration, which should not be judged by conventional standards of either History or Art. Indeed, only in a naively literal sense is it true that Bentham was not among the founders of University College. In spirit the institution was, and in important respects still is, Bentham's College.[26] He departed in

[22] L.C.B. Gower 'The Future of the Legal Profession', *Modern Law Review*, 9 (1946) 211, at 218.

[23] N. Harte and J. North *The World of University College, 1828-1978*, 8-9, 108-12.

[24] W. Twining 'Why Bentham?', *The Bentham Newsletter*, no. 8 (1984), at 36.

[25] Harte and North, 67. The picture has recently been returned to its intended place in the Flaxman Gallery.

[26] Professor J.L. Montrose, one of the most imaginative pioneers of modern attempts to broaden the study of law, entitled his Presidential Address to the Bentham Club in 1950, 'Return to Austin's College'. No irony seems to have been intended.

1832, but he has never left us. Much the same is true of John Austin. Seen from a narrow institutional angle, his tenure of the Chair of Jurisprudence was a disaster. But in the perspective of intellectual history, Austin's ideas, even more than Bentham's, were the single most important force in academic law for nearly 150 years – not only in the University of London, but also in England and much of the common law world.

The story is a sad one: Austin narrowed down Bentham; the followers of Austin narrowed down Austin and the opportunity was lost to create a genuinely systematic, interdisciplinary, critical intellectual tradition in academic law. It is only recently that Bentham, rather than Austin, has belatedly been recognised as the true 'Father of English Jurisprudence' and that what passed as the Austinian Expository approach to the study of law is acknowledged to be a sadly impoverished interpretation of the vision of that tragic figure.[27]

In assessing the contribution of a great university one must, of course, take account of the achievements of successful individuals – teachers, scholars, alumni and even administrators and entrepreneurs. One must also try to make some assessment of its contributions to national life – a much more elusive form of enquiry. I shall touch on these. But a university is above all a house of intellect; its currency is ideas. So I make no apology in placing the ideas of our two leading thinkers in the foreground and in inviting you to consider Bentham's and Austin's visions of law and of its study, as it were, from below. Then continuing the allegory, let us consider an alternative model – that of Austin's brilliant and engaging colleague, Andrew Amos, our first Professor of English Law. I shall present these as symbolising three different visions of what might have been.

First, then Jeremy Bentham. Whether one loves or hates him, accepts or rejects his ideas – or like most Bentham scholars one is caught in a posture of deep ambivalence – one cannot ignore him.[28] He is there, larger than life and more persistent. He presented a vision of a science of law and of its potential that is clear, comprehensive, coherent and intellectually ambitious. The composition is classical and its outline can be sketched quite simply. The foundation is a theory of value – utility – by which all human institutions, practices, designs and actions are to be judged. It is opposed not only to deontological moral theories (especially all versions of natural law and natural rights), but also to intuitionist, irrationalist and sceptical theories of value. It underpins and suffuses all of Bentham's work.

The second element is an epistemology and a theory of language, embodied in his theory of fictions. This was the basis of Bentham's method of classification and precise conceptual analysis characterised by

---

[27] W. Twining 'Academic Law and Legal Philosophy: The Significance of Herbert Hart', *Law Quarterly Review*, 95 (1979), pp. 557-60.

[28] Twining (1984), 44-7.

John Stuart Mill as 'the method of detail'.[29] The theory of fictions had its roots in English empiricism, but has subsequently been recognised as anticipating, to a remarkable degree, developments in analytical philosophy associated with, for example, Russell, Wittgenstein and J.L. Austin.[30] It is no coincidence and highly significant that Bentham's approach to conceptual analysis was explicitly the starting-point of the work of our greatest contemporary legal philosopher, Herbert Hart.[31]

Thirdly, Bentham had a somewhat mechanistic view of the nature of man and of man in society. In the eyes of many, the Achilles heel of his general approach lies in his psychology and social theory.[32] This may indeed make him vulnerable to criticism from the perspective of the sociology of law; yet psychology and social theory are widely acknowledged to be among the least developed aspects of the discipline of law today.

Fourthly, in politics Bentham was – especially in later life – a genuine radical, who tried to steer a clear path between reaction and piecemeal reform on the one hand and violent revolution and anarchy on the other.[33] It is a curious feature of secondary juristic discourse that legal positivism, of which he is one of the leading exponents, is still often treated as inherently amoral and conservative. Yet, if the term 'critical' is to be given other than a narrow and contingent meaning, Bentham must surely count as a critical theorist.

All of these ingredients underpin Bentham's theory of law and legislation. This was positivist, instrumentalist and normative.[34] It was positivist in two important senses: first, he insisted that laws are human artefacts, created by the will of men with the power to impose that will (the sovereign). Laws are posited by man (*nomos*) rather than immanent in nature (*physis*). Secondly, he insisted on a sharp distinction between law as it is and law as it ought to be – a distinction he considered to be essential for clarity of thought in the service of utility. His main concern was normative: one needs to have a language for accurately expounding, describing and analysing actual laws (and their context and their consequences) in order to criticise, evaluate and improve them. The science of legislation is a technology concerned with the design, creation,

---

[29] J.S. Mill 'Bentham', in J.M. Robson, ed., *Collected Works of John Stuart Mill*, 10 (Toronto, 1969), 75.

[30] E.g. H.L.A. Hart *Essays on Bentham* (Oxford, 1982), 11, 128; Ross Harrison *Bentham* (1983), ch. 3.

[31] See especially Hart's inaugural lecture H.L.A. Hart 'Definition and Theory in Jurisprudence', *Law Quarterly Review*, 70 (1954), 37, reprinted in H.L.A. Hart *Essays in Jurisprudence and Philosophy* (Oxford, 1983).

[32] For a more sympathetic view of Bentham's psychology see Mary Mack *Jeremy Bentham: An Odyssey of Ideas, 1748-1832* (1962).

[33] *Op. cit.*, n. 24.

[34] See generally H.L.A. Hart *Essays on Bentham* (Oxford, 1982).

and evaluation of institutions and laws as instruments of utility.[35]

The story of poor John Austin, the first Professor of Jurisprudence in London, has recently been retold in no less than three books.[36] There are several interpretations. In nutshell form, the one that I favour can be restated as follows. Austin was a committed utilitarian, but his followers played down or overlooked this aspect of his thought. He shared Bentham's concern for conceptual analysis, but his epistemology and his conception of language were both closer to common sense and cruder than those of his master. Politically he was a strange mixture of reformist and reactionary; but, more important, his primary concern in jurisprudence was scientific rather than critical. Austin's command theory of law was in general outline and structure very similar to Bentham's; but it was also much simpler and more vulnerable to criticism. For over a hundred years it was the chief target of critics both within and outside the positivist tradition. It was Austin's simple command theory, rather than Bentham's, that was the target of Hart's *Concept of Law* that in 1961 launched the most important modern version of English legal positivism.[37]

In this view, Austin was a poor man's Bentham and, if the commentators are to be believed, the first Professor of Law at King's, the ill-fated J.J. Park, was an inferior version of Austin (Park is said to have been appointed *because* he was an opponent of Bentham).[38] Yet it was Austin rather than Bentham who came to be called 'Father of English 'Jurisprudence' and whose received ideas not only dominated the teaching of jurisprudence, but provided the theoretical justification – such as it was – for our dominant tradition of academic law.[39]

There are two crucial distinctions that are relevant to interpreting this aspect of our intellectual tradition. The first is the distinction between Expository and Censorial Jurisprudence.[40] In *A Fragment on Government* Bentham wrote: 'To the province of the *Expositor* it belongs to explain to us what, as he supposes the Law *is*; to that of the *Censor* to observe to us what he thinks it *ought to be*'.[41] Bentham gave a central place in his science to exposition; but he made it clear that he cast himself in the role of censor: 'The business of simple *exposition* is a harvest in which there seemed no likelihood of there being any want of labourers; and into which, therefore, I had little

---

[35] *Ibid.*

[36] W. Morison, *John Austin* (1982). W.E. Rumble, *The Thought of John Austin: Jurisprudence, Colonial Reform and the British Constitution* (1985). L. and J. Hamburger, *Troubled Lives; John and Sarah Austin* (Toronto, 1985).

[37] H.L.A. Hart *The Concept of Law* (Oxford, 1961).

[38] R. Cocks *Foundations of the Modern Bar* (1983), 42-3, 50.

[39] E.g. Sugarman (1986) at 37-44.

[40] The *locus classicus* is J. Bentham, *A Fragment on Government*, ed. J.H. Burns and H.L.A. Hart, *Collected Works* (1977), preface.

[41] *Fragment*, 397.

ambition to thrust my sickle.'[42] Furthermore, unlike Austin and many later law teachers, Bentham did not insist that systematic exposition of the 'is' must always *precede* criticism.[43]

Strikingly absent from this dichotomy is a third character, the ordinary legal practitioner – let us call him the craftsman – concerned to advise on, apply, manipulate, and argue about and within the law as it is. As we shall see, the biggest deviation from the Benthamic model is that academic law in London – and indeed in England – has concentrated almost entirely on exposition and craft; academics have sporadically been involved in criticism and reform, but *systematic* intellectual criticism and design, along the lines of Bentham's Science of Legislation, or some functional equivalent, have been neglected, sometimes explicitly rejected.

A second important distinction, to be found in Bentham but more fully articulated by Austin, is between General and Particular Jurisprudence.[44] Particular jurisprudence is concerned with a single system or body of law. General jusrisprudence is, according to Austin, 'the science concerned with the exposition of the principles, notions, and distinctions which are common to (maturer) systems of law' – including notions and distinctions and principles which are necessary to any system.[45] For Bentham, 'the *Expositor* is always the citizen of this or that particular country: the *Censor* is, or ought to be, the citizen of the world.'[46] Both Bentham and Austin, therefore, in different ways, saw the scientific study of law as transcending the study of particular systems. Bentham chose the role of Censor, Austin that of Expositor. Both were mainly concerned with general jurisprudence.

In this regard, the cosmopolitan spirit of Bentham and Austin has always been part of the London tradition. So far as I can tell, at every point in our history there has been firm resistance to pressures to confine legal studies to a parochial concern with English law.[47] The particulars have changed, but at different times London has emphasised, and has

[42] *Id.*, 404.

[43] Below n. 61.

[44] J. Austin *The Province of Jurisprudence Determined*, ed. H.L.A. Hart, (1954); J. Bentham *Introduction to Principles of Morals and Legislation*, ed. J.H. Burns and H.L.A. Hart, CW. (1970), 294-5 (*Jurisprudence Local-Universal*). These recent reappraisals bring out the fact that Austin was more concerned than Bentham to develop an empirical science that was close to the facts of legal practice and based on political economy. His successors both obscured this distinctive emphasis and, more strikingly, down-played or ignored Austin's broader political and moral concerns. Rumble and others have also shown how Austin's enterprise departed much further from Blackstone's than did Bentham's (e.g. Rumble, 227 n. 101). I am grateful to David Sugarman for this point.

[45] Austin, 367.

[46] *Fragment*, 398.

[47] E.g. G.W. Keeton 'University College, London, and the Law', *Juridical Review*, 51 (1939), 118; A.N. Allott, 'A Short History of the Teaching and Investigation of Law at the School of Oriental and African Studies'. (Unpublished Ms., May 1986.)

been in the forefront of, general analytical jurisprudence, international law, Roman law, modern civilian systems, socialist legal systems, oriental and African laws, laws of the European Community, and international trade. Intellectually as well as institutionally ours has been a cosmopolitan tradition. Yet I think that it is fair to say that often in the treatment of those subjects, the significance of the distinction between general and particular expository jurisprudence has been obscured. For Austin, the foundation of all study of law and its claim to be a science lie in general jurisprudence. Bentham proposed a School of Legislation; Austin argued for a School of Law; what we have are Faculties of Laws.

Bentham's views on legal education were never published and need not concern us.[48] Austin's were set out in his well-known prefatory lecture on 'The Uses and Study of Jurisprudence'.[49] Using the Prussian system as a model, he suggested that the preparation of a 'theoretico-practical' lawyer should be divided into two stages – what we would now call the academic and the vocational. The first stage should take place in a Law Faculty, the second in lawyers' offices. The Law Faculty would provide a systematic grounding both for intending practitioners and for those destined for public life in legislation or administration. London would be a particularly suitable place for this, because teaching would either be carried out by practitioners or under their supervision. 'In England, theory would be moulded to practice'.[50]

The emphasis would be on general expository jurisprudence – with logic as a necessary foundation and a strong emphasis on Roman law. Austin was prepared to concede some place to the study of English law, but it occupied a restricted and subordinate place in his curriculum. This would include logic, the general principles of jurisprudence and of legislation (the two involving ethics generally), international law and the history of English law. Significantly, he pointed out that: 'In the Prussian Universities, little or no attention is given by the Law Faculty to the actual law of the country.'[51]

Austin narrowed down Bentham by giving a subordinate place to the normative, critical science of legislation; by down-playing the idea that understanding law is essentially an inter-disciplinary endeavour; and above all by putting exposition of the law as it is at the core of the academic enterprise. Austin's followers and successors diluted and narrowed his vision in some crucial respects: they substituted the detailed study of English law (Particular Jurisprudence) for Austin's more rigorous and scientific General Jurisprudence.[52] The study of logic dropped out of the

[48] The most important source for Bentham's views is 'Proposal for a School of Legislation' Bentham Mss, U.C. CVII, (*c.* 1794).
[49] Above n. 44.
[50] Austin, 390.
[51] Austin, 381.
[52] See generally, Morison ch. 5.

curriculum and, insofar as Austinian analytical jurisprudence survived, it was banished to separate courses labelled 'Jurisprudence', which became increasingly seen as a subject apart, rather than being the necessary foundation and starting point of all particular study, providing both a map of the discipline of law and a methodology for systematic exposition of principles.

Andrew Amos: An Alternative Model?[53]

The first Professor of English Law, and Austin's only colleague was Andrew Amos, a successful barrister with a rising reputation. He was by all accounts a brilliant and engaging figure. Shelley's friend at Eton, a wrangler at Cambridge, a keen classical scholar, a lively and conscientious teacher, he could not be accused either of anti-intellectualism or of indifference to education. Yet he can usefully be made to symbolise a significantly different approach to the study of law. John Baker has vividly evoked the image:

> He loved the fire and thunder of actual litigation, and felt the intellect most usefully engaged when exploring problems casually thrown up in the course of forensic warfare. Order and analysis and deep reflection were necessary for writers of books; but there was no more place for them in the classroom than in the courtroom. The very first lecture (1828) gave a sufficient foretaste: opening with the law of maritime accretion – by any reckoning an odd way to begin a general survey of English Law – he proceeded to tenures, followed by a discussion of contingent remainders and executory devises and conveyancing problems associated therewith; then finally, presumably somewhat late at night, he outlined the history of the forms of action, illustrated (doubtless to gasps of amazement) by the writs *de ventre inspiciendo* and *de pipa vini carianda*.[54]

What is significant here is not the contrasts in personality and teaching styles of Amos and Austin, but rather the differences and the similarities in their conceptions of legal education: Austin was concerned with the patient, systematic search for general principles and universal truths. The approach was abstract, dry and analytical. Amos's objective was 'emphatically practical';[55] his presentation was anecdotal, unsystematic, even disorderly and his subject-matter was largely based on first-hand

[53] This section draws heavily on John Baker's admirable lecture 'University College and Legal Education, 1826-1976' (1977) *Current Legal Problems*, 1-13 and Hale Bellot *University College London, 1826-1926* (1926). A collection of Andrew Amos's papers survives: U.C.L. Ms Add. 90 (seven boxes). A clear summary of Amos's approach, based on his evidence to them, is given by the 1846 Select Committee of Legal Education, op. cit. at p. viii.

[54] Baker, 2-4, citing Amos's 'Introductory Lecture'.

[55] A. Amos, *An Introductory Lecture upon the Study of Law*, delivered in the University of London, 2 Nov. 1829.

experience, 'such as no person is competent to teach but a barrister familiar with the practice of the Courts'.[56] In his lack of concern for systematic theory and for general principle, Amos may have mirrored the prevailing attitude of barristers of his day. Yet his enterprise was an exercise in intellect. He invited students to argue with him about difficult points of law. It has been suggested that his approach was a forerunner of the American case method. It would be more accurate to say that it anticipated the problem method – for the focus was on problems rather than on the texts of reported cases. And the problems were derived from, and presented in the context of, actual practice. Austin's central focus was general jurisprudence, his model product was the scientifically educated lawyer; Amos was particularistic, his model the courtroom advocate.

It is tempting to set up Austin and Amos as symbols of the difference between 'theoretical' and 'practical' approaches. But here they merely illustrate the inadequacy of such distinctions. For the similarities between them are as important as the differences. The Utilitarians and University College were concerned with 'useful knowledge' and Austin, no less than Amos, saw his enterprise as a preparation for practice. They also shared the same arena, the classroom; both saw their enterprise as laying a foundation rather than providing a substitute for apprenticeship. Furthermore, Amos may have taught a few tricks of the trade *en passant*, but his aim was to stretch the minds of his students intellectually. His problems were exercises in argument and analysis based on logic. Both were concerned to develop *skills* of analysis rather to purvey *information*. This is particularly significant in the light of subsequent developments, especially since Amos, the practitioner, was even less concerned than his colleague with 'coverage' – the unfortunate obsession, which through the medium of the professional examinations was to blight both academic and practical legal education.[57]

Thus we have four possible models or ideal types for the role of the law teacher: Bentham's Censor, whose subject is the Science of Legislation; Austin's Scientific Expositor, whose subject is general analytical jurisprudence; the more modest Particular Expositor, concerned to describe accurately (with or without systematic search for underlying principle) the law as it is in a given legal system; and the Craftsman, symbolised perhaps imperfectly by Amos, whose aim is to develop even within the University the intellectual and other skills of the practitioner. A fifth, largely more recent role, is the External Observer whose concern is to understand law in society from an external point of view, which may involve the perspective of sociology or political economy or some kind of history.

[56]Cited Baker, 3.

[57] There is, admittedly, a marked contrast between Amos's accounts of his intentions and practice and the markedly pedestrian factual questions that he set in examinations. Examples of the latter were appended to his Introductory Lecture.

It is, of course, artificial to suggest that these perspectives are mutually exclusive or necessarily in competition with each other. Are they not complementary and should not a balanced system include all of them? Should not one Faculty contain latterday Benthams, Austins and Amoses – and others besides? But these are useful concepts for analysing many of the tensions and conflicts over priorities within academic law. They are certainly more illuminating than the crude distinction between 'academic' and 'practical'.

In the University of London, three of these five perspectives have been generally excluded completely or at best treated as marginal. Thus at no time has Bentham's Censorial (Jurisprudence or) Science of Legislation nor some non-utilitarian counterpart provided the basis for systematic instruction on a significant scale. Much of what passes for criticism or policy analysis would have been rejected by Bentham as caprice.[58] The formal teaching of practical skills has been almost entirely confined to the professional law schools and then only recently and in a rudimentary form. The marginality of historical jurisprudence and sociology of law throughout the history of English legal education gives the lie to the claim that the primary objective of some degree programmes is the understanding of law in society.[59] All of these have from time to time had a place in our academic culture, and L.S.E. in particular has consistently emphasised the links between law and the social sciences.[60] But by and large the discipline of law has been concerned with two types of exposition: at the lowest end, has been the acquisition of particular detailed information of the kind that has been traditionally tested in professional examinations; at the higher end, the central concern has been with digging out, analysis and application of the more abstract concepts and the general principles that are thought to provide coherence and system in legal doctrine – what might be called applied particular jurisprudence. Even at L.S.E., leading proponents of broader, critical approaches, scholars such as Kahn-Freund and Wedderburn, have insisted – unlike Bentham – that exposition and analysis of the law as it is must *precede* criticism or sociological study.[61]

[58] J. Bentham *Introduction to the Principles of Morals and Legislation* ed. Hart and Burns, *CW* (1970), 21-22n.
[59] It is beyond the scope of this lecture to explore controversial questions about the extent and the nature of the relative marginalisation of broader approaches to legal education in our intellectual tradition. Suffice to say that the story is a complex one and at no stage did more extreme versions of the Expository Orthodoxy go unchallenged.
[60] John Griffith, 'Law at L.S.E.', *L.S.E.* (June, 1979); Cyril Grunfeld, 'Reflections of a Convenor' (1978).
[61] E.g. O. Kahn-Freund, 'Reflections on Legal Education', *Modern Law Review*, 29 (1966), 121 at 129; confirmed by Professor Lord Wedderburn (interview, October, 1986). Compare the more cautious statement by Kahn-Freund and Wedderburn in the Editorial Foreword to the first book in the 'Law in Society Series', D.W. Elliott and H. Street, *Road Accidents*, 1968. For a different view, see W. Twining and D. Miers *How To Do Things With*

Laws in London, 1836-1908

1836 is not a very auspicious moment at which to begin our story.[62] By then, the two stars of University College, Amos and Austin, had both resigned; in 1833 Professor Park of King's had died at a young age. They had been replaced by competent, but uninspiring part-timers.[63] More important, law teaching was revived at the Inns of Court in 1833 and it soon became apparent that neither University College nor King's was able to compete with them in attracting students. The first degree in English law in the country was instituted on the foundation of the University, but the first graduating class with LL.B. in 1839 totalled only three.[64] All were from University College and none from King's. Brave efforts were made to keep the enterprise going with very few students, but the 1846 Committee on Legal Education was rather generous in suggesting that University College was the only institution in the country to provide 'any considerable facilities for legal education'.[65] At that time there were only two part-timers and a handful of students.

Throughout the second half of the nineteenth-century Law in London languished for lack of students. Reforms in the 1860s and 1870s and beyond enabled University College to attract some men of distinction, such as Sheldon Amos, Bund, Bolland, Hunter, Murison, Scrutton, Pollock, and Taswell-Langmead and later Holdsworth – but they failed to attract students and few lasted long. For example, at U.C.L. in 1867-9 the largest class in any subject (Roman law) had eight students;[66] in 1890-1 there were only thirteen students attending classes. Baker reports that in the fourteen years prior to 1909 the College had produced a total of only nine graduates in law.[67] For most of this period the situation at King's was no better and was often worse. Hearnshaw, the often acerbic author of King's centenary history, paints a depressing picture of repeated failures to form viable courses; and for long periods the Chair of Law was perceived as a sinecure. Law was not the only subject in difficulties in this period. For example, Hearnshaw reports: 'In February 1854 the Reverend Richard Jones, who had slept in the Chair of Political Economy

Rules, 2nd ed. (1982), ch. 2 (attacking the fallacy of The Way of the Baffled Medic – prescription before diagnosis).

   [62] The main sources for this section are for U.C.L.: Baker (1977), Bellot (1926), Keeton (1939); for King's: F.J.C. Hearnshaw *The Centenary History of King's College, London, 1828-1928* (1928), 91; Gordon Huelin *King's College London, 1828-1978* (1978); Cocks (1983). It is fair to say that the history of laws at King's is less well-documented than that of U.C.L.

   [63] For details, see Bellot Ch. 4 (and Charts) Hearnshaw at 98 ff.

   [64] For details see Harte (1986) 106; Baker 5-6.

   [65] At vii.

   [66] Bellot, 327.

   [67] Baker, 8. Figures for the period 1838-1900 are set out in Harte (1986) at 106 and 139. The bulk of LL.B. graduates before the inter-collegiate system was established seem to have been external students.

since 1833, woke up and announced his wish to retire. The Council placed no obstacle in his path and expressed no thanks for his inactivities.'[68]

Hale Bellot attributes this unhappy situation to the lack of full-time teachers: 'In law, as in history and economics, in fact, the professors were little more than visiting lecturers whose emoluments were not sufficient to procure a greater share of their services, and whose activities were inadequate to the creation of a flourishing school of studies in any of their several departments.'[69] Others emphasise the competition from the professional schools, despite or because of their poor quality: for, says Baker, in the days before local authority grants, they offered a quicker and cheaper crash course than a law degree.[70] Perhaps more fundamental than those inter-related factors was the point that academic law had failed to find any recognisable role: academic legal education was not seen as a serious form of general education nor as a valuable preparation for practice nor, as Austin envisaged, as a preparation for public life.

Thus we must be careful to set some claims in perspective. London rightly boasts the first degree in English Law, but University College produced only 135 LL.B.s in the nineteenth century; the numbers for King's are substantially less.[71] A majority of those who earned LL.B.s studied privately. Again one of the proudest claims of the University is that it provided opportunities for many classes of students who had previously been denied access to University education, especially Jews, Catholics, Protestant Dissenters and women. Women were first allowed to study Jurisprudence at University College in 1873, but the first woman law graduate took her degree in 1917.[72] It is advisable not to make both boasts in the same sentence.

The Inter-Collegiate Heyday, 1908-1965

The situation was transformed after the Haldane reforms of 1898;[73] these launched the University of London Mark III.[74] The turning-point in law came in 1906-08 when, under the aegis of the University of London,

[68] Hearnshaw, 243.

[69] Bellot, 331.

[70] Baker, 7.

[71] Personal details of the Law Graduates of U.C.L. are collected in a valuable unpublished document by J.H. Baker: *University College London: Faculty of Laws, List of Graduates, 1839-1930* (1969-70) (Copy on file at I.A.L.S.).

[72] Baker, 7. Women were first admitted to the legal profession in 1922, Abel-Smith and Stevens, 192-4.

[73] The main published sources for this section are Keeton (1939), Gower (1950), Edward Jenks 'English Legal Education, 1885-1935'; *Law Quarterly Review*, 51 (1935), 162. In addition I am greatly indebted to Professor George Keeton for permission to draw on a personal memoir (September, 1985) and an extended interview in August, 1986.

[74] Harte, 158.

King's, University College, and the recently formed London School of Economics agreed to pool their resources in a tripartite scheme of lectures leading to an LL.B. degree of the University of London. This inter-collegiate system of teaching lasted until the 1960s and survives today at postgraduate level in the Master of Laws.

Numbers picked up after the introduction of the tripartite system, very rapidly at King's – mainly among evening students; more gradually at U.C.L., who attracted mainly day students. During this period, L.S.E. law students began to be treated as internal students and L.S.E. academics began to make their distinctive contribution to law teaching. To start with nearly all of the teaching was done by part-timers. Only at L.S.E. were there any full-time posts at all. After the First World War student demand for law increased significantly and between 1919 and 1931 a great advance was made by the establishment of five new full-time chairs and three full-time readerships, mainly financed through the U.G.C.[75] They were filled by some notable scholars.[76] Part of the stimulus for this 'revolutionary change',[77] as Keeton called it, appears to have come from Sir William Beveridge, who in the late 'twenties proposed that all law teaching should be transferred to L.S.E.[78] The case was a strong one: L.S.E. had by far the best law library and almost the only full-time teachers; the tripartite system of lectures made life difficult for students who had to move continuously between the three centres. It also upset college time-tables. However, not surprisingly, King's and U.C.L. resisted – after all, each had been teaching law for almost exactly a hundred years (whenever they had students to teach), and U.C.L., in particular, could point to an extremely distinguished list of names, even if the incumbents had been paid almost nothing and most had not stayed for very long. The outcome was that the need for full-time teachers was accepted at King's and U.C.L. as well as at L.S.E.

Professor George Keeton remembers the period 1930-9 as the happiest years of the Inter-Collegiate system.[79] For the first time there was a body of full-time scholar-teachers of law who were dedicated to the enterprise. They were young, keen, proud of what they were doing and determined to work within the Inter-Collegiate system. Until the late thirties the

---

[75] Jenks, 171-2.

[76] The incumbents of the Chairs were: 1919 Commercial and Industrial Law – H. Gutteridge; 1924 English Law – E. Jenks; 1920 International Law – E.P. Higgins; 1930 Legal History – T.F.T. Plucknett; 1931 Roman Law – H.F. Jolowicz. In addition, three Readerships in English Law were established in this period: U.C.L. – G.W. Keeton; K.C.L. – H. Potter; L.S.E. – W.I. Jennings. Other notable pre-1939 appointments included: R.S.T. (later Lord) Chorley; H. (later Sir Hirsch) Lauterphacht; A.T. (later Lord) McNair; D. (later Sir David) Hughes Parry; and W.A. Robson.

[77] Keeton (1939) at 133.

[78] G.W. Keeton (interview); Professor A. Kiralfy (interview).

[79] G.W. Keeton, letter to author (17.9.85). Interview.

enterprise was quite small (averaging about fifty students a year for the full-time degree), but in respect of both teaching and scholarship the quality was outstandingly high. There were inevitably conflicts, but the three Heads of Department – of whom Hughes Parry was the acknowledged leader – worked as a team and managed to resolve them amicably. By modern standards teaching loads were heavy, especially in respect of spread of subjects.[80] In 1931 Keeton recalls being asked by Jolowicz to teach equity and trusts, and both the newly introduced course on English legal system and evidence, which he had never studied, to the evening students. He was also asked to 'look after' U.C.L. students in English law – a further six subjects. In 1938 Gower resigned his position at University College, partly because he was expected to cover six or seven subjects.[81]

Others who were students and teachers during this era confirm Keeton's picture of harmonious co-operation, of a generally high level of teaching and some remarkable achievements in scholarship, exemplified by the establishment of the *Modern Law Review* and by the publications of individuals such as Jennings, Jolowicz, Keeton, Lauterpacht, Plucknett, Potter and Robson.[82] No doubt a great deal of this story of unpretentious institutional development and individual excellence is attributable to the work of some outstanding long-serving Heads of Department: Sir David Hughes Parry was Head of Department at L.S.E. for nearly thirty years; George Keeton was Dean at U.C.L. from 1939-54; and Harold Potter who was Head of Department at King's from 1930 until his untimely death in 1950, in the words of the college history, 'worked to build up the Faculty virtually from nothing into one which by the time of his death was more than pulling its weight in the life of the College.'[83]

In retrospect four features of this period stand out. First, the genuinely inter-collegiate nature of the enterprise. Secondly, given its modest scale it was remarkable what was achieved in both scholarship, teaching and public influence. Thirdly, by 1939 most of the work had been taken over by full-time teachers. Yet the number of full-time teachers responsible for teaching day and evening classes in the internal LL.B., for the LL.M., (as well as evening external students) never exceeded fifteen before 1939.[84] Fourthly, throughout this period the LL.B. degree catered uniformly for several very different constituencies: full-time day students who usually came straight from school; and internal evening students, (including

---

[80] *Id.*

[81] Professor L.C.B. Gower (interview).

[82] E.g. Professor A. Kiralfy (interview), Professor F.R. Crane ('A Note on the London Law Faculty, 1930-85', communication to author); Professor Sir Jack Jacob Q.C. (interview).

[83] Huelin (1978) at 112.

[84] These figures are approximate, partly because the distinction between 'part-time' and 'full-time' teachers was not always a sharp one.

articled clerks, a few admitted solicitors, and members of the legal staffs of government departments and private sector enterprises). There were also three classes of external students: students in university colleges in the U.K.; students in law schools overseas that were in a special relationship with the University of London; and independent external students.[85] I shall return to deal in more detail with the story of the External LL.B. and special relationships – for it is in this area perhaps more than any other that the University of London made a distinctive contribution to legal education.

During the Second World War the London law schools were dispersed: initially L.S.E. went to Peterhouse, Cambridge; U.C.L. to Aberystwyth and K.C.L. to Bristol. Harold Potter nobly kept his evening class for students from the Estate Duty Office going in London.[86] After a year U.C.L. moved to Cambridge and King's followed in 1941. Technically speaking the inter-collegiate system did not operate during the war; naturally resources were pooled, and some lectures were shared with the diminished Cambridge Law Faculty, but this was an emergency arrangement rather than a continuation of the system.[87] During this period servicemen, prisoners-of-war and others were able to read for the external LL.B. and a significant number succeeded.[88]

After the war, the three heads of department Parry, Keeton and Potter were keen to revive and develop the inter-collegiate system. But, largely because of an increase in numbers of students and staff and the need to give younger teachers opportunities to teach their own courses, the system came increasingly under strain.[89] More and more parallel lecture courses developed. At the same time, the common undergraduate syllabus and examinations required approval of all three departments in regard to any change in curriculum and methods of assessment. This provided a rigidity that was increasingly resented. Eventually, following the reforms in the University, associated with the Saunders Committee of 1965-6, the present system of special regulations was introduced in the mid sixties. This allows each College Law Faculty to have its own curriculum and methods of assessment in the LL.B., although they are all under the aegis of the University of London. This granting of 'dominion status'[90] to the colleges allowed much greater flexibility in a time of rapid expansion, and facilitated the establishment of a new Faculty of Laws at Q.M.C. in 1965

[85] G.W. Keeton 'The Revision of Courses for the LL.B. in London', *Jo. Soc. Pub. Teachers of Law* (NS.) 1 (1948), 189.

[86] G.W. Keeton (interview).

[87] Keeton (interview).

[88] Harte, 238-41.

[89] Keeton (letter to author, *op. cit.* n. 79), Kiralfy (interview).

[90] Harte, 264-65. One of the most significant results of the introduction of Special Regulations was that internal and external candidates no longer took examinations that were common to all students.

and the introduction of a distinctive undergraduate course in law at S.O.A.S. (B.A. 1975, LL.B. 1976) in 1975.

1965-86

The last twenty-one years have seen an enormous expansion and diversification of laws in London. Many flowers have bloomed and each school has developed its own distinctive programme and strengths. In 1983 a committee of the Heads of University Law Schools listed fourteen important changes and trends in the discipline of law in the previous fifteen years.[91] The University of London, mainly through its five law schools, has both participated in and contributed to nearly all of these changes.[92] For example:

a.   The *scale* of the enterprise increased at both undergraduate and post-graduate levels;(i)[93]

b.   There was a trend towards *diversification* within and between under-graduate law degrees;[94]

---

[91]   Heads of University Law Schools, *Law as an Academic Discipline*: A response to the Leverhulme Report and the U.G.C. Letter on a Strategy for Higher Education into the 1990s (March, 1984). An abbreviated version was published in The Society of Public Teachers of Law *Newsletter*, Summer, 1984.

[92]   Material on the history of the five London Law Schools is collected in the 'archive' mentioned in n*.

[93]   Some indication of the changes can be obtained from the following figures for the University of London:

    (a)   *LL.B.* (internal):
        Intake: 1965/6   309; total undergraduate law students: 755
                  1983/4   441; total undergraduate law students: 1186
              (Source: *Law as an Academic Discipline*, Appendix)

    (b)   *LL.M.* (internal)   *Candidates*   *Passes*
        1974   237   171
        1985   419   289

    (c)   *Institute of Advanced Legal Studies*
        Students registered for postgraduate work in the University of London.
        1965/66   337
        1984/85   573
                  (I.A.L.S. *Annual Reports*)

[94]   Some examples of diversification are as follows:
    (a)   Each of the five schools has its own curriculum for the three year LL.B. (London) (internal) (for details, see the prospectus of each law school). These have diverged both from each other and, even more strikingly, from the curriculum as it stood at the end of the inter-collegiate period.
    (b)   In addition to the three year LL.B., there are several distinctive undergraduate degree programmes offered by individual schools. For example:
        (i)   *King's*: joint four year programme in English and French Law leading to both the LL.B. (London) and the Maitrise en Droit of the University of Paris I.

The POLITICAL.TOY-MAN.

16. Brougham hawking shares in projected University of London, July 1825. Cartoon by Robert Cruikshank. (*British Library*)

17. T.H. Huxley, F.R.S. (1825-95), lecturer at the Royal School of Mines, creator of the first science degrees. (*Imperial College*)

18. Duel between the Duke of Wellington and the Earl of Winchilsea, Battersea Fields, March 1829. (*King's College*)

19. Sidney Webb, Lord Passfield (1859-1947), co-founder of the London School of Economics. (*Photo: National Portrait Gallery*)

20. H.A.L. Fisher (1865-1940), President of the Board of Education, 1918-22. (*Photo: National Portrait Gallery*)

21. R.B. Haldane, Viscount Haldane (1856-1928), Secretary for War, 1905-12, Lord Chancellor, 1912-15 and 1924, chief author of 1898 Act and chairman of 1909-13 Royal Commission on the University. (*Photo: National Portrait Gallery*)

22. Dame Lillian Penson (1896-1963), Professor of Modern History, Bedford College, 1939-63, Vice-Chancellor, 1948-51.

(*Photo: University of London*)

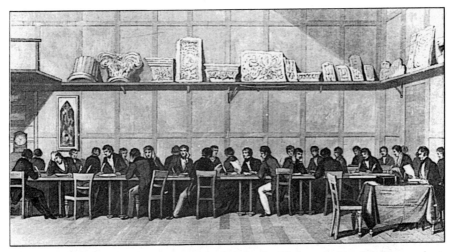

23. Matriculation examination, July 1842, in the University's original premises in Somerset House. V.A. Huber, *The English Universities*, ed. F.W. Newman, III (1843)

24. Women graduates receiving their degrees from the Vice-Chancellor, Sir James Paget, in Burlington Gardens, 1891. (*The Graphic*, 23 May 1891)

25. Westfield College students, July 1885, outside the original premises in Maresfield Gardens, Constance Maynard (Principal, 1882-1913) seated centre. (*Photo: Westfield College*)

26. Bedford College in Baker Street, students in the Art Studio, 1890s. (*Photo: R.H.B.N.C.*)

27. Bedford College in Regent's Park, students in the new Chemistry Laboratory, 1913. (*Photo: R.H.B.N.C.*)

28. Cartoon, *c*. 1860, showing the University of London on the side of Scientific progress in the battle with religious reaction. (*Huxley Papers, Imperial College*)

29. Sir James Paget, F.R.S. (1814-99), lecturing on anatomy at St. Bartholomew's Hospital Medical College, 1874.

(*Pictorial World*, 25 July 1874)

30. The Institute of Historical Research in the 'Tudor Cottage', Malet Street, 1920s. (*Photo: Institute of Historical Research*)

31. Sir Mortimer Wheeler, F.B.A., F.R.S. (1890-1976), Director of the Institute of Archaeology, at the excavation of Maiden Castle, mid 1930s. (*Photo: Institute of Archaeology*)

32. The Auto-Icon of Jeremy Bentham (1748-1832), displayed in University College London with Bentham's actual mummified head at its feet, *c.* 1948. (*Photo: University College London*)

c. There has been increased emphasis on *European Law*;(iii)[95]

d. The range of *standard* subjects has greatly expanded (for example Administrative Law, Family Law, Labour Law, Revenue Law and Planning Law are found in nearly all London degrees).(iv)[96]

e. There has been an increased involvement in *continuing legal education*, especially in the last three years;(v)

f. The *computer* has begun to make an impact;(vi)

g. Some *four year* degrees have been introduced;(ix)[97]

h. There have been several new institutes and research centres.[98]

The same committee projected a series of likely developments in the next ten to fifteen years.[99] It is difficult to believe that all or most of the London law schools will not be involved in all of them. The H.U.L.S.C. Report painted a picture of a discipline in the process of rapid expansion and change that started in the mid 1960s and continues today. Change has

(ii) *L.S.E.*: Degree of Bachelor of Laws with French Law (for which candidates are eligible to enter for a Diplome d'études juridiques of the University of Strasbourg) and Degree of Bachelor of Laws with German Law (which includes a certifying Examination of the University of Hamburg)

(iii) *Queen Mary College* has a joint B.A. in Law and Politics and particular strengths in Commercial Law and Intellectual Property.

(iv) *U.C.L.* has recently introduced a provision enabling undergraduates to opt for a four year programme leading to the LL.B.

(v) *S.O.A.S.* has a number of distinctive undergraduate degrees with a unique emphasis on oriental, African and Comparative laws and connections with other disciplines, including anthropology, languages, religious studies and economics.

(c) Perhaps the most significant diversification has taken place in the LL.M. (internal). In 1965 thirty options were listed in the Regulations; in 1986 eighty-two options were listed, of which seventy-one were examined (source, Senate House).

[95] All five programmes leading to the LL.B. (internal) include at least one course relating to the E.E.C. The majority also contain at least one course on foreign or comparative law related to Europe. In 1986-7 there were courses in the internal LL.M. relating to E.E.C. and laws of particular European countries.

[96] The main exceptions in 1985-6 were (a) the S.O.A.S., LL.B., which has more emphasis on oriental and African laws and less on specialised English law subjects and (b) Planning law, which received more emphasis at L.S.E. (a full option on Land Development and Planning Law) than in the other LL.B. curricula.

[97] See above n. 94.

[98] See below, text at 00.

[99] The H.U.L.S.C. Report stated: 'Significant developments in legal education in the next ten-fifteen years are likely to include:

(i) continuing pressure to expand the range of subjects and to adopt broader approaches within the LL.B.

(ii) similar pressure at postgraduate level, especially in respect of inter-disciplinary work, research training and expanding fields such as foreign law in relation to commerce, trade and economic development

been uneven and not as radical nor as systematic as some of us would wish. The economic climate has slowed and frustrated, but not entirely halted, expansion. For law is currently one of the most buoyant of disciplines. Considerable damage has recently been done to libraries and to the age-structure of the law-teaching profession, yet it is probably true to say that at no stage in its history has the overall picture of legal education and training in the United Kingdom presented such a vibrant diversity of activities or such a range of opportunities. Within London many of these activities are taking place in the five constituent law schools, but three distinctive features of the federal University should be singled out: the External System; the LL.M.; and the Institute of Advanced Legal Studies.

The External System

From its inception until 1900 the University was only an examining and degree-conferring body.[100] The sharp separation of teaching and examining functions paved the way for what is arguably London's most important contribution to higher education: the external system. In 1985-6 there were 24,500 students registered for external degrees in six main subject areas. It is estimated that about 75 per cent of these were actively studying. Law is by far the biggest subject, with about 75 per cent of all

   (iii) possibly, an expansion of mixed two-subject honours degrees
   (iv) possibly, a more substantial legal input into other general, non-vocational degree courses
   (v) a continuing increase in the demand from other disciplines for legal inputs into vocationally oriented courses
   (vi) more emphasis on computer applications to legal education and research, not solely in respect of information retrieval, but also, for example, in the development of 'expert systems'
   (vii) a rapid expansion of continuing legal education and of part-time studies, for the legal profession and for a great variety of other groups; it is particularly significant that from 1985 continuing legal education for solicitors in England and Wales will be compulsory for the first three years of practice
   (viii) developments in teaching of practical skills, simulation exercises and clinical legal education
   (ix) changes in the nature and environment of legal practice including increasing complexity, shifts in markets for legal services and the varying impacts of information technology will continue to exert pressure on the legal education system to anticipate and adapt to changing conditions.
           Law as an Academic Discipline (1984), para. 6.

[100] I am grateful to members of the External Division of the University of London, especially Andrea Kelly, Sam Crooks and Jenny Shelburne for help with this section. Other sources relied on include: Bruce Pattison *Special Relations: The University of London and New Universities Overseas* (1984); The University of London: *The University's Policy for the External System* (Policy Statement, July 1983); The University of London: *The External System: A Background Paper* (unpublished policy statement, 1986). A.M. Carr-Saunders *New Universities Overseas* (1961); Eric Ashby *Universities: British, Indian, African* (1966); I.C.M. Maxwell *Universities in Partnership* (Edinburgh, 1980).

enrolments. In 1985, 358 LL.B.s were awarded to internal students; in the same year 298 graduated with External LL.B.s.[101] Given a high wastage rate, there are overall many more candidates (at undergraduate level) in the external programme than in the five London Law Schools.[102]

The scale of the enterprise is not, of course, the main reason for the significance of the external system. At different stages in history, it has served a variety of functions, both for individuals and for other educational institutions. For example, for long periods it met needs that today are largely catered for by such admirable institutions as the C.N.A.A., the Open University and the Common Professional Examination. During the Second World War hundreds of servicemen and prisoners of war were able to continue their studies by reading for external degrees.[103] Today, at least three very different categories of students avail themselves of the opportunities offered by the external LL.B.:

a. Well-qualified people, often graduates, seeking to advance already established careers or to change career or more generally to pursue an academic interest in law;

b. Educationally disadvantaged people, often with minimum qualifications, who see the degree (based, as it is, on the principles of open entry and freedom in respect of methods of study) as providing opportunities denied by conventional insitutions;

c. School leavers, in several countries in the Far East and Africa who have been unable to obtain a university place in their own country.[104] The

[101] Figures supplied by Senate House.

[102] In June, 1985 the figures for *candidates* for the LL.B. were as follows:
Intermediate: Internal: 415 (including 8 absent); External: (a) Home: 894 (168 absent); (b) Overseas 1292 (399 absent).
Part I: Internal: 374 (8 absent); External: Home: 472 (90 absent); Overseas: 291 (78 absent).
Part II: Internal: 331 (2 absent); External: Home: 288 (28 absent); Overseas 105 (13 absent).
These figures exclude mixed degrees. (Figures supplied by Senate House.)

[103] A note supplied by Senate House reads:
EXAMINATIONS IN PRISONER OF WAR CAMPS, 1942-5
'The University of London provided 1,305 different examination papers to prisoner of war camps – over a fifth of the total. Only eleven other Examination Boards exceeded 100 papers, the next largest being the Royal Society of Arts with 324 papers.
Examination papers were sent by air mail via Lisbon from May 1942 to March 1944, when the arrangements had to be suspended owing to the plans for D-Day. The Lisbon air-route was resumed in July 1944 but did not prove satisfactory under the different conditions and a new quicker air-route via Sweden was begun on 9 September 1944 and continued until the last despatch on 7 April 1945 when the scheme came to its anticipated end with the victorious advance of the Allied Armies and the over-running of the prisoner-of-war camps in Germany.' See further, Harte (1986) at 238-41.

[104] Andrea Kelly (letter to author 17.10.86, cited with permission).

LL.B. is not only by far the most popular external degree, but 'laws has been the pioneer for the rest of the external programme' – especially in the last few years.[105]

Perhaps even more significant than provision for individual students has been the contribution of the external system to institution-building. Between 1849 and 1949 'all university colleges created in England and Wales . . . automatically spent their apprentice years under the aegis of the London External Degree System'.[106] From 1850 students of institutions in the British Empire were eligible to register for London degrees and from 1858 this facility was extended to students anywhere in the world. After the Report of the Asquith Committee in 1945, London created a scheme of special relationships with eight colleges in Africa and the West Indies, which proved to be one of the great success stories of the late colonial period. So far as law is concerned the actual numbers of students who graduated with the External LL.B. under this scheme were quite modest, but law faculties in four countries spent their formative years in special relationships and several others, formally outside the scheme, were heavily influenced by the London model.[107]

During the period of decolonisation the scheme of special relationships gradually ran down as university colleges became fully independent universities. The external degree system, however, continued to flourish, with registrations reaching a peak of 34,198 in 1970.[108]

This rise in numbers led to the conclusion that the University was overreaching itself. During the early seventies it was decided to wind down and severely to limit the system. First, it was decided to cease to register home students enrolled in full-time courses in public educational institutions and to abdicate this role to the C.N.A.A. and the Open University. Private External students were still enrolled in the U.K., but

---

[105] *Ibid.*

[106] 'The External System: A Background Paper', *op. cit.* n. 100.

[107] The law schools directly affected were: Gordon College, Khartoum (later University of Khartoum); University College, Gold Coast/Ghana (later University of Ghana, Legon); University College, Dar-es-Salaam (via Makerere College, Uganda; subsequently Dar-es-Salaam became a constituent college of the University of East Africa and then the independent University of Dar-es-Salaam). Law Faculties developed after the attainment of university status in the University of the West Indies, and in a more complicated way, at the institutions that became Makerere University, Kampala and the University of Nairobi. The Law Faculties of Hong Kong, Singapore, Malaya (Kuala Lumpur), Malawi and the first generation of Nigerian Law Faculties could be said to have belonged to the same family of law schools, without having been part of the special relationship system. for details, see Pattison (1984) 133-6; L.C.B. Gower *Independent Africa: the Challenge to the Legal Profession*, Cambridge, Mass. (1966); J. Bainbridge *The Study and Teaching of Law in Africa* (South Hackensack, New Jersey 1972).

[108] 'The External System: A Background Paper', *op. cit.*

the degree was no longer actively promoted. Later it was announced that, starting in 1977, the University would cease to register overseas students.

It is hardly surprising, given the continuing demand, that these decisions caused consternation in a number of quarters, especially overseas. Subsequently it was acknowledged that while necessary at the time, the decision to cease overseas registration seemed ungenerous retrospectively in the light of the University's long history of work in the Commonwealth and of the [Government's] decision in 1980 to raise overseas student fees for those studying in Britain.[109] Accordingly in 1982-3 the process of winding-down was reversed and a brand new policy was formulated. This period of retrenchment provided an opportunity for a fundamental rethinking of the system. The new scheme differs from the old one in several key respects. For example, the new External System is entirely self-financing; London University teachers are involved in providing instruction for external students; revision of syllabuses has been institutionalised; the academic support provided by the university is being significantly enhanced in a number of ways; there is to be a greater emphasis on continuing education and distance learning; and the way has been opened for a measure of exchange between school-sponsored degrees on the one hand, and External syllabuses and modes of study on the other.[110]

Clearly all of these new developments have particular significance for law which has by far the largest, indeed a disproportionate, share of enrolments for external degrees. It is impossible to do justice to this large and immensely important subject here. But it is far too important to say nothing about it.

Special Relations

My very first examiners' meeting was a direct experience of a special relationship. It was 1959 and I was a Lecturer at the University of Khartoum, which two years previously had become an independent university. This was to be one of the first occasions on which our students would be given a Khartoum degree.

The Sudanese were ambivalent: they were proud to be independent of London, but they were fearful for the prestige of their own degree – at home as well as abroad. A few facts stick out in my memory about the occasion. The examiners' meeting was held in London, at K.C.L. Nearly all of the External Examiners were well-known London law teachers: Coulson, Crane, De Smith, Gower, Graveson, Grunfeld, Keeton, Lloyd,

---

[109] S.B. Crooks paper on 'External Fund-Raising' for the Working-Party on the Development of the External System (1986), (quoted with permission).

[110] See references in notes 1, 9 and 10 above.

Nokes, Schwarzenberger.[111] I had not met most of them before. Nearly all had taken the trouble to turn up and were very gracious. I was dazzled. The meeting lasted less than an hour, largely because the internal examiners' marks and judgements were accepted almost without question. Then we recessed to drink champagne at the retirement party for a thirty-year-old lecturer who had inherited an estate in Scotland. I decided on the spot to emulate him – and I left Africa and duly retired to the U.K. shortly after my thirtieth birthday. Like me, he is still teaching.

Later, in 1961, I was involved in negotiations with the University of London over the syllabus for the London LL.B. in the new Law Faculty in Dar-es-Salaam – which in October 1986 celebrated its twenty-fifth anniversary. We were more concerned in Dar to innovate and to localise and we tended to grumble about the constraints of the special relationship. But, in looking through my old papers I find that nearly everything we proposed was accepted – including a course on the constitutions and legal systems of East Africa and a general mandate to study local law where this was feasible.

Sir Eric (later Lord) Ashby has said that 'the link with the University of London was one of partnership, not merely of patronage.'[112] Under the special relationship, a fair degree of leeway was given in adapting course content to local conditions, but London 'was uncompromising in resisting any departure from the pattern of the degree'.[113] The foundation of this attitude was a concern to maintain 'standards'; but, as Ashby points out, there was a tendency to lump together under the idea of 'standards' three quite separate ideas': academic excellence or quality; the particular methods and criteria by which such quality was assessed; and curriculum (the structure and pattern of degrees – notably with emphasis on single subject honours).[114] The outcome was that concern for quality – largely supported by nationalist leaders and public opinion – at times resulted in a somewhat rigid 'consolidation of orthodoxy'.[115] Nevertheless, Ashby concludes, the system of special relationship avoided what were seen to be historic mistakes in the development of Indian universities, and the 'supreme merit' of enabling the Asquith colleges to be accepted as full members of 'the international family of universities.'[116]

Generally speaking, my experience in Africa – especially in Khartoum

---

[111] The names of the External Examiners for 1958 are listed in the University of Khartoum *Calendar* (1959).

[112] Ashby (1966) at 235.

[113] *Id.* 238.

[114] *Id.* 259-60.

[115] *Id.* 258.

[116] *Id.* 259.

and Dar-es-Salaam – confirms Ashby's analysis.[117] We chafed at some of
the constraints that we felt were imposed by London, but the students in
particular were concerned with the international and local recognition of
their degrees. Moreover, it is striking that when the university colleges
became independent universities relatively few changes in structure,
methods of assessment and, to a lesser extent, course content were
introduced. Even Dar-es-Salaam, by far the most radical of the new
African law faculties, did not deviate far from the London model in respect
of course structure, quality and methods of assessment; insofar as it did, it
pioneered adjustments that became quite commonplace in English law
faculties after 1968 – such as half-courses and continuous assessment.[118]
No doubt in the early stages there were some inhibitions about making too
radical a break for fear of jeopardising the reputation of the degree; but I
suspect that a far greater constraint was the limits of the imagination and
expertise of the innovators. Writing of the early days of Ibadan in Nigeria,
its first Principal, Dr Kenneth Mellanby, summed up why relatively few
modifications were ever requested of London:

> First we had to use existing textbooks. Secondly, many courses (e.g.
> mathematics, chemistry) are of universal applications and there is no specific
> 'African' version. Thirdly, most of our staff, both African and European, had
> insufficient experience of Africa to be competent at the outset to modify their
> courses.[119]

In the case of law, the special relationship system did not so much serve
to put a brake on localisation – inevitably a slow process – as to limit
American influence, which was much more pronounced in countries
outside the special relationship system, such as Ethiopia and Liberia.

The institutional history of the system of special relations has been
relatively well-researched and proclaimed.[120] The more complex human
story of individual candidates for external degrees – both the successes
and the failures – remains largely unexplored; it deserves more attention
from social historians and students of education.

There can be no doubt at all of the historical and contemporary
importance of the external system in providing educational opportunity,
in institution building, and in meeting a variety of specific needs and

[117] For details, see William Twining 'Legal Education within East Africa' in *East
African Law Today*, 115 (1966). British Institute of Int. and Comp. Law, London; and 'The
Camel in the Zoo' in Issa Shivji (ed.) *The Limits of Legal Radicalism* (Dar-es-Salaam, 1986).
[118] For details, see Twining (1966).
[119] *Minerva*, I (1963), 153 cited Pattison (1984) at 162. Professor Gower suggest that
'increasingly in the post-war period the failure of Commonwealth universities to adapt to
local conditions was due to their reluctance to put forward proposals rather than London's
reluctance to accept suggestions' (letter to author, 6 January 1987).
[120] Especially Ashby, Carr-Saunders, Maxwell and Pattison, *op. cit.* n. 100.

demands. From a purely intellectual and educational point of view the merits of the system have not been so clear-cut. Consistent attempts have been made to maintain standards in all three senses distinguished by Ashby. The external LL.B. has gained widespread international recognition, but there have been costs: for example, a certain rigidity and conservatism; painfully high failure and wastage rates; few Upper Seconds and almost no Firsts – though I am pleased to say that one First was awarded in 1986, the first for many years.

The revival and reform of the external system provides a great opportunity to make external degrees more interesting, flexible and up to date. For its potential to be realised it must be adequately funded, so that its operation can be properly monitored, new forms of distance learning and educational technology can be fully used and, above all, that it should be adapted to the human and educational needs of students of different kinds. As an outside observer, I see two dangers which, are both associated with the 'London disease' of spreading academic resources too thinly and making a virtue of parsimony. The External System is too important to be left entirely to a handful of dedicated administrators and the voluntary efforts of academics who contribute over and above their ordinary duties as full-time scholar-teachers in the various Law Schools.[121] The new external system also needs active support, financial as well as professional, not only from law teachers, but also from any body concerned with improving access to legal education and the legal profession, both in this country and elsewhere.[122]

A Prose Poem in Praise of the LL.M.

Once upon a time, long, long ago the LL.M. was a quiet gentlemanly affair: a handful of academically promising students working largely on their own and meeting occasionally with their tutors. Over the years it growed and growed and became internationalised. Student numbers increased, new courses developed – often as an outlet for individual teachers seeking a less constricting forum than the three year LL.B. for the development of their interests and ideas. Despite this expansion, for many years it was seen as a sideshow, a hangover from the days of the inter-collegiate system – at best a pleasing avocation, at worst a diversion from

[121] Professor F.R. Crane points out that the involvement of senior London law teachers declined significantly after the introduction of Special Regulations (letter to author, December 1986). Individuals who teach or examine for external degrees are paid *pro rata*, but participation is not part of their contractual duties and normally no allowance is made in respect of their duties in their respective shcools. What is surely needed is a small group of full-time academic staff (perhaps on temporary secondment) who can devote themselves single-mindedly to this important enterprise.

[122] The Commonwealth Legal Education Association is currently engaged in a study of Access to Legal Education and the Legal Profession in the Commonwealth.

the serious enterprise of teaching undergraduates.

Then the LL.M. was privatised. From a marginal sideshow it has developed into a juristic bazaar with nearly 500 students from over fifty countries; there are at present over eighty courses on the books ranging from child law and juvenile justice to Chinese, Islamic and African law – and, indeed, space law. It has been said that according to present projections, the rate of growth of numbers of lawyers in the United States relative to population is such that by about A.D. 2050 there will be more lawyers than people in that country. Some fear that, according to present trends, there will be more courses than students in the LL.M. by the year 2000. Others see this as evidence of the vitality of Laws in London.

The main impetus for reform has come from the imposition by Government of a requirement to charge differential fees for overseas (non-EEC) students. Within a relatively short time those who had opposed differential fees on principle found themselves, largely by economic necessity, acting as sales persons and recruiters for their own institutions. As one who has consistently opposed this provision, I have to admit that one good result of the policy – perhaps the only one – is that it has led to an enormous improvement in the LL.M. Decaying courses that had sat untouched on stalls for twenty years were revised or dropped; brand new glossy products – some produced not far from here – come off the presses almost weekly. Finance officers tremble when students, quite rightly, demand value for money. Tutors prepare proper reading-lists and course materials; teaching in the LL.M. counts as part of one's teaching load; the Institute of Advanced Legal Studies buys books. British Council representatives complain that their time is taken up by over-eager sales persons claiming to represent well over 100 British institutions of higher education. It is rumoured that in one of the fringe subjects students are wooed with beer in the 'Jeremy Bentham'; yet down the road, the story goes, a lecturer stands on the table in front of a packed room and tries to deter people by saying: 'Go away – if all you want is to get rich quick' . . . to which the students reply: 'So we do and so do you.' For it is widely, though erroneously, believed that the LL.M. is a profit-making enterprise.

It would not be appropriate on a celebratory occasion to pursue some of the more controversial aspects of this matter here. For whatever reason, it is clear that in recent years the LL.M. has been enriched and tightened up into one of the largest, most varied and most genuinely cosmopolitan postgraduate programmes in the world. For better or worse, it *is* a bazaar – an extraordinarily diverse group of clients in search of a variety of wares and services from a pretty diverse group of stall-holders. In the first few weeks of term, new postgraduates are advised to shop around and sample what is on offer, before committing themselves. The record is said to be held by one keen student, who starting at 10 a.m. on Monday managed to attend forty-five lectures and tutorials by Friday evening, including three different courses on intellectual property, a private tutorial on Mongolian law and a small seminar discussing the meaning of the auto-icon.

Like all bazaars, the fascination lies in the diversity of the customers and of the wares on offer. In time, one hopes that most people find something to suit their needs. There are, of course, some carpers who would homogenise the enterprise by creating a monopolistic superstore along the lines of Sainsbury or Marks and Spencer. To my mind this is a mistake. Rather we should celebrate the LL.M. for what it is: five law schools, over a hundred academics and practitioners, and students from all over the world jostling together – often in friendly competition – in a great big, booming, buzzing marketplace of ideas and information, lightly regulated in an incomprehensible way by the invisible hand of that great poker player of academia, Senate House.

The Institute of Advanced Legal Studies[123]

In 1986 the University of London has eight Institutes and Centres devoted wholly or partly to the advancement of our discipline. These are:

The Institute of Advanced Legal Studies
Centre of European Law (K.C.L.)
Centre of Law, Medicine and Ethics (K.C.L.)
Institute for Economics and Related Disciplines (L.S.E.)
Centre for Labour Economics (L.S.E.)
Centre for African Studies (S.O.A.S.)
Centre for Commercial Law Studies (Q.M.C.)
Centre for the Study of Socialist Legal Systems (U.C.L.)

Few will contest the proposition that the most important of these is the Institute of Advanced Legal Studies, which celebrated its fortieth birthday in 1986 with a visit from the Chancellor. In 1934 one of the two conclusions of the very disappointing Atkin Committee on Legal Education was that there was a need for an institution which would be a national headquarters for academic research and would promote the advancement of knowledge of the law in the most general terms. 'The natural organ for this purpose will be found in the establishment of an

---

[123] The main sources for this section are Institute of Advanced Legal Studies, *Annual Reports*; I.A.L.S., *Report of the Policy Review Sub-Committee* (Chairman, Sir Robert Megarry) (May, 1986); Sir David Hughes-Parry 'The Institute of Advanced Legal Studies' *J.S.P.T.L.* (N.S.) (1949) I, 183; Lord MacMillan *A Man of Law's Tale* (1952) at 217-18; Aubrey Diamond 'Willi Steiner and the Institute of Advanced Legal Studies', *The Law Librarian*, 15 (1984), 46-7; *Report of the Legal Education Committee* (Atkin Report) 1934, (Cmd 4663); Gower 'English Legal Training' (1950) *op. cit.*, n., above. I am grateful to Professor Aubrey Diamond, Professor Sir Jack Jacob Q.C., Muriel Anderson and Barbara Tearle for information used in this section; the opinions expressed are my own.

Institute of Advanced Legal Studies.'[124] This proposal was all that remained of the more ambitious plans for a Legal University of London, which had been revived by Harold Laski who was a member of the Atkin Committee. The Government took no action on the recommendation, but after the War Professor David Hughes Parry persuaded the University of London to set up such an Institute. This was in 1946.[125]

Forty years on the institute is well-established as an important centre both nationally and internationally. Within the University of London it plays an absolutely pivotal role, both symbolically and practically, in sustaining inter-collegiate co-operation in our discipline. It houses the best law library in the university and one of the three best in the country. It is the headquarters for many visiting scholars from all over the world, for approximately 700 graduate students, for the Board of Studies, and for all law teachers in the university.[126]

Without the Institute laws in London would be fragmented and drastically impoverished. It is also fair to say that the significance of the Institute lies as much in its future potential as in its past achievements. For, it is a widely held view, which I share, that it has a long way to go before it fulfils its promise. For much of its history, the Institute has not had funds to match its aspirations.[127] Only in respect of its building – which was given to the University by Sir Charles Clore – can it be said that it has ever been adequately provided for. Its greatest achievement is the library; yet, in 1983-4 approximately sixty law schools in the United States (and several in Canada) were reported to have more books than are at present in the Institute Library. Harvard has nearly 1,500,000 volumes; the Bodleian Law Library about 290,000; I.A.L.S. has 174,000, slighly fewer than Emory University Law School, and slightly more than Hofstra.[128] Allowance must be made for the crudity of such statistics; also for 'rationalisation', which is Newspeak for cutting costs. This prevents

[124] Atkin Report, *op. cit.* n. at 13.

[125] The Institute celebrated its fortieth birthday in October, 1988. Some historians give its date of birth as 1947 (e.g. Harte (1986), 247) or 1948 (Abel-Smith and Stevens (1967), at 185). The University of London formally decided to establish it in 1946; it began work in 1947 and was formally opened by the Lord Chancellor on June 11, 1948. The phenomenon of a person celebrating their thirty-ninth birthday in several successive years is quite familiar; on a generous interpretation of history the Institute has a unique opportunity to celebrate its fortieth birthday for three years in succession.

[126] Other achievements of the Institute include *The Index of Foreign Legal Periodicals* (1960-83); *List of Current Legal Research Topics*; the annual W.G. Hart Workshop; the *University of London Legal Series* and miscellaneous bibliographical and special publications (for details, see *Annual Reports*).

[127] Many of the constraints were foreseen by Sir David Hughes-Parry in 1947 (*op. cit.* n. 123.

[128] The main sources for these figures are David A. Thomas, '1983-84 Statistical Survey of Law School Libraries and Libraries', *Law Library Journal* (1984-5), 77, 575; I.A.L.S. *Report of the Policy Review Sub-Committee* (1986).

wasteful, necessary and useful duplication. It also creates or obscures vacuums of responsibility, especially in interdisciplinary areas such as law and psychology, law and social history, American legal history, legal education and training, forensic science, access to justice, and many other areas where legal practice intersects with broader worlds of practical affairs. This is just not good enough for what aspires to be the second best academic law library in the country.[129] There is no point in allocating blame – indeed there are many individual heroes and heroines in the Institute's history: but this clearly represents a collective failure of imagination and of will on the part of both the academic and the legal communities over a period of forty years.

The Institute organises or hosts many valuable academic activities, but it has never quite achieved the aim of becoming the national headquarters for academic law.[130] In this respect we could still learn a lot from our neighbours in the Institute of Historical Research. The I.A.L.S. is both inter-collegiate and international; it has some way to go before it is a centre for sustained interdisciplinary research. Again, it has long been recognised that the Institute has great potential for strengthening the ties between the academic and practising branches of the legal profession. This is reflected in the composition of the Committee of Management and in some valuable occasional seminars; but what has been achieved to date falls far short of what could be.

This is not captious carping by a disgruntled academic. For much the same assessment was made in a report of a Policy Review Sub-committee chaired by Sir Robert Megarry in 1986. This concluded that the Institute 'has yet to develop into what it should be and was originally intended to be, the national centre for research with a wide spectrum of scholarly activities'.[131] This remarkable document, which represented an unexpected *volte face* from an essentially pessimistic and defensive approach, was unanimously and enthusiastically endorsed by the Committee of Management and the Board of Studies and, despite the chill economic and political climate, steps are currently being taken to implement its recommendations.

One of the most important recommendations of the Ormrod Committee that has yet to be implemented, is that there should be an Institute of Professional Legal Studies, which would be a means by which universities and other institutions could be involved in professional

[129] The modesty of our national aspirations can be gauged by comparing the latest S.P.T.L. 'Statement of Minimum Holdings for Law Libraries in England and Wales' (revised 1986), *Legal Studies* (1986), 6, 195-215 with equivalent documents in other common law countries.

[130] On 'rationalisation' within London, see Megarry Report, *op. cit.*, Appendix A.

[131] *Id.* 5. Unlike some London Institutes, the I.A.L.S. does not register research students; it provides services to postgraduates registered in the various schools, but does not itself earn any income from fees.

education and training in a co-ordinated way.[132] It is a constant source of amazement to visitors from abroad that in England the university law schools are almost totally uninvolved in professional training after the academic stage. As I have argued elsewhere, there is also an unmet need for research in, and systematic development of, the direct teaching of professional skills.[133] The Institute of Advanced Legal Studies, in addition to aspiring to be an excellent library and centre of research, can perform a vital role in strengthening links with the practising profession. Twelve years after the Atkin Report the University of London implemented a recommendation that had been ignored by government. Fifteen years after Ormrod seems a good time to revive another idea that has not yet found official favour.

Conclusion

When full histories of legal education in England and in this University come to be written, three themes ought to be treated as central.

The first is economic: during the past 150 years academic law has been perceived and treated as a low-cost enterprise. For the first hundred years in London nearly all teaching was left to parsimoniously remunerated part-time teachers. A major change came with the shift to full-time teachers. But staff-student ratios have always been among the worst, research funding has been almost non-existent, and professional training today is Ormrod-on-the-cheap. Some heroic feats have been achieved with minimal resources; but the potential of our discipline is far from being realised. Recently the climate of opinion has begun to change. In 1983 the Heads of University Law Schools argued that while law remains one of the most cost-effective subjects, nearly all recent developments in our rapidly changing discipline involve at least some increases in unit costs. This message has been reiterated in 1986 by a forceful report of Australian Law School Deans, by the Policy Review Committee of the I.A.L.S. and, in more muted terms, even by the U.G.C.

The second theme is political. The often dismal history of legal education and training in England has been in part a story of failures of co-operation. At crucial points – for example, in 1846; in 1900; in the series of abortive attempts to establish a great Legal University in London and, more recently, in the Ormrod and Benson exercises, the main interest groups – the Inns of Court, the Solicitors and the academic community – refused to co-operate. One result was that Government was freed from sustained pressure to provide public funding on the same scale as for other professional subjects, such as medicine or engineering.

[132] Ormrod Report, *op. cit.*, n. at pp. 88, 98, discussed in Twining (1982) *op. cit.*, n. at 209-13.
[133] 'Taking Skills Seriously' *Commonwealth Legal Education Newsletter*, 44 (1986), appendix.

The uneven history of laws in the University of London illustrates a converse pattern. For some of the main success stories – the inter-collegiate system, especially in the inter-war years; the External system; the Institute of Advanced Legal Studies; and the recent strengthening of the LL.M. – are all instances where the constituent colleges, while maintaining their distinct identities, have been able to sink their differences and engage in joint enterprises of the University of London. The twin factors of our geographical location and the opportunity to pool the resources of five law schools remain our greatest source of potential strength.

Perhaps the most important lesson of history is that legal education, in this country and in most parts of the world, has tended to be demand-led. The scale and nature of the enterprise of academic law are largely determined by the popularity of the subject, rather than by the ideas of planners or academics or governments. Legal education in London in the nineteenth century languished for lack of students. Today the high demand for legal education is a remarkable international phenomenon. In this country law is better protected than most disciplines by the buoyancy of demand, both at home and overseas. There is, of course, a constant tension between what students want, or think they want, and what their teachers think they ought to want or want to offer them. But an institution such as ours is well-placed to resolve many of these tensions if we stand firm on a single principle. Over time law teachers can exert proper control over their situation only if they have imagination, the will and the persistence to reiterate an uncompromising message to colleagues and administrators, to the legal profession, to providers of funds – both public and private – and, above all, to our students: 'We demand excellence.'

Today this may sound like crying in the wilderness. We are living in a period of cuts, and of official incomprehension, hostility and ineptitude. Morale is low. The legal profession is experiencing what may prove to be an historic series of traumas. We have been damaged, but largely because of buoyant demand we have not been maimed. Indeed never in our history have laws in London been stronger. Nevertheless, the last fifteen years have been very painful, for all of us. Students, younger teachers and libraries have been among the main victims. There are two main responses to this kind of adversity: one can stonewall: or one can counter-attack. The revival of the External System and the recent report on the Institute of Advanced Legal Studies represent the latter approach. They deserve our full support. In this regard I am reminded of two precepts of Lord Butterworth, one of the most successful Vice-Chancellors in recent years. In the seventies, he used to say to me: 'My boy, in a period of stop-go, stop-go, always be ready to go.' Later, when the cuts came, he said to us: 'When everyone else has their heads beneath the parapet, that is the time to CHARGE!'[134]

[134] Reconstructed and cited with permission.

5

The Sciences

Sir Hermann Bondi

There was plenty of outstanding research and scholarship, and some university-level teaching, in London for hundreds of years before the city acquired a university. Indeed, many notable scientists were associated with the new University from the start in 1836, and much innovatory teaching and examination of the sciences went on for more than twenty years before a separate Faculty of Science and a first degree in Science were established. Initially the University, if not wholly committed to the idea of the unity of all knowledge, since its arrangements acknowledged the independence of the disciplines of Law and Medicine, held to the view that all knowledge which was not strictly vocational or practical belonged to a single family. Thus in the University's early years mathematics, chemistry, and physics were subjects within the Bachelor of Arts degree, and in institutional terms the Faculty of Arts embraced all those sciences which were not para-medical. To us this may look like a confusion of obviously separate branches of knowledge and enquiry, but it is no more confusing or inconsistent than the contemporary, twentieth-century, continental European usage of the terms 'science' and 'scientific' to include what we think of as 'humanities' or 'arts', a usage very reasonably justified on the grounds that 'science' refers to all branches of learning involving systematic thought and disciplined research.

During the time that the boot was on the other foot, and 'arts' was understood to include 'science', several individual scientists in a number of institutions associated with the University – the Royal College of Chemistry, the Royal Institution, the Department of Science and Art, and the Government School of Mines, as well as in King's and University Colleges – were making notable contributions to advancing the frontiers and methods of experimental science, and to the creation of completely new areas of scientific enquiry, which were to lead to the declaration of scientific independence in 1858. The nature and subject matter of mathematics, chemistry, physics, or botany have long pedigrees and have long been well understood in the world of learning and by the educated public. Their contents, methodology, and theoretical structure were becoming more sophisticated and complex, and at the same time new subjects were being invented or defined as a result of pioneering research in, for example, electricity, heat, magnetism, organic chemistry, or geology. This expansion of knowledge lay behind the coming of age of science. It was the work of many people in many countries, an international community of scientists, among whom the London scientists were outstanding. The critical part played by London can be seen from the careers of some of the key people. Sir Charles Lyell, a geologist, was one such person. He had only a brief period at the University, at King's College in the 1830s, but it was a very influential and productive period of his life. I am often struck by the difficulty of the subject of history. Before you can appreciate the contribution that somebody made, you have to put yourself into the frame of mind of those who preceded him and his contribution. The greater that contribution, the more it has changed our mode of thought, the less we can imagine that one could have thought as people did, as the most intelligent and imaginative did, before the contribution of the particular person in mind. In this case, what was so outstanding about Charles Lyell was that he first saw the challenge to explain and interpret geology in the light of the present. His slogan was: 'The present is the key to the past'. Indeed this was diametrically opposed to the widely current opinion at the time, that the shape of the Earth's surface and its rocks had been formed by a series of unimaginable catastrophes going on in quite a different way from the way that the Earth's surface is changing now. The moment you talk about an unimaginable past, you rob yourself of the real ability to interpret, to understand and to fathom what has been going on. It is only when you have totally exhausted the possibility of accounting for what you observe, through the action over long periods of the forces we see at work today, that you might conceivably be driven to a catastrophic theory. But in geology, as you know, Lyell is essentially the one we support, the one who turned geology, in a certain sense, into a science. He was never more effective in his propaganda activities than during his period at King's when he lectured in a most active manner and gave popular lectures to many. University College and King's College were founded under very different auspices; one without any religious affiliation, the other as Anglican, yet their subsequent work and their subsequent development was remarkably similar. It is interesting that Charles Lyell, who was born in 1797 and lived to 1875, gave his most effective lectures at King's and that the content of them was thought questionable from the point of view of faith, but that he was nonetheless a member of the staff. Much later in life, be became one of the early supporters of Darwin, and is said to have arranged for the publication of the work of Wallace and of Darwin. He came to King's when he was not much over thirty.

My second giant of the past was born in 1825: Thomas Henry Huxley. He was a long-term member of this University and held the Chair of

Natural History at the School of Mines for thirty-one years, having before that already been a lecturer there. There is no doubt that the bulk of his work was done in this University. He was the leading figure in securing the establishment of the separate Faculty of Science in 1858 and the introduction of the new degree of Bachelor of Science, steps of central significance in the nineteenth-century reordering and systematising of the structure of knowledge. The recognition of Science as a separate and distinct branch of knowledge was undoubtedly a practical as well as an intellectual necessity, although some might say that the institutional separation of Arts and Sciences, which Huxley helped to ensure, was not an unmixed blessing. Huxley's astounding amount of research in biology, particularly perhaps in the comparative anatomy of different animals, was his chief claim to personal distinction. He was of course one of Darwin's greatest supporters and probably the most outstanding publicist of Darwin's views. He was also a great writer, not just of technical work, but of work of wide public interest. He became a Fellow of the Royal Society when he was only twenty-six. The titles of some of his books sound modern: *The Course of Phenomena of Organic Nature*; *Zoological Evidence as to Man's Place in Nature*; *Science and Culture*; *Evolution and Ethics*; one could very well publish under such titles today. He had a great interest in elementary education and worked hard to improve it.

My third giant, James Clark Maxwell, was born in 1831 and died in 1879. He became a Fellow of the Royal Society at the age of thirty and spent five years at King's College from 1860 to 1865. Those were the most fruitful years of his life as far as scientific research was concerned. It was while at King's that he perfected his theory on gases. It was while at King's that he published the equations of electro-magnetism that bear his name. To non-physicists it may be necessary for me to stress what a tremendous figure he was in physics, in theoretical physics certainly the greatest figure of the nineteenth century. His equations are as important, as relevant, as much trusted as they ever were. And in such a rapidly advancing subject as physics, to say that about any work a century and a quarter later is quite astounding. He resigned from King's College to devote himself to the care of his family's estates in Scotland and then was recalled from this exile albeit in his own country. I cannot really call it retirement because he was only in his late thirties at the time. He was recalled from there as the first Cavendish Professor in Cambridge to create and build up the Cavendish Laboratory, a tremendous task. He spent the last eight years of his life in Cambridge. He also was a great writer: *Theory of Heat*, written in 1871, evidently while he was on his Scottish estate; and the *Treatise on Electricity and Magnetism* which came out in 1873 not long after he went to Cambridge, and is still to my mind the best text book on the subject. Both describe work that he did while he was at King's.

My fourth figure stretches into this century, Sir William Ramsey (1852-

1916). He held the Chair of Chemistry at University College from 1887 to 1913. He was a towering figure in chemistry. He made many contributions to organic, inorganic and physical chemistry but is perhaps best known for his discovery of and work on the inert gases. Some of the discoveries were in collaboration, but I do not think there is any other figure in chemistry to whom one can give the honour of having added a complete column to the periodic table of elements: helium and neon, argon and crypton, zenon, and even radon. He also wrote a great book: *The Gases of the Atmosphere: the History of their Discovery*, which was written in a popular style in 1896. He was one of the earliest Nobel Laureates (1904) and became a Fellow of the Royal Society when he was in his mid-thirties.

There seems to me a link between these four giants, a link it is well for us to ponder. They were each researchers of the highest calibre. If they had done nothing but write their research communications, we would hold them in great honour. But every one of them also regarded it as his duty and as something that had a justified call on his time to write books that any educated person could understand. This is not an easy task. This is not a task that one can carry out at speed. It needs deep thought and it is highly integrative. It brings knowledge together. Again it reminds me of the subject of history. In history more honour is given to a great integrative work of scholarship that brings much knowledge together than to the discovery of this or that fragment of a letter or correspondence, however illuminating, which one could call research. Today in science we are so wedded to research and the results of it, however few might understand it, however highly specialised it is, that we give no honour and therefore no incentive to devote time to integrative work. I think modern science is the poorer for this attitude. The separation of science and the educated general public is often noted, and deplored. I do not think it is the fault of the public, it is that we do not follow the example of the people I have spoken about and give enough time and encourage young people to give enough time, effort and mental work to what is needed to make our subject intelligible to others.

It is remarkable that at least some of the four scientists I have discussed and several of the other figures who follow later were appointed to their positions very young in life. They were outstanding people – no doubt they showed at least some of their brilliance relatively early, but do please reserve some of your admiration for the appointing committees. Remember that in those days there was no retiring age. If you appointed somebody at the age of thirty, he might be with you for half a century. Even if your choice was good, this might not be ideal. True the expectation of life was less than it is now, true there were some tragic cases of early death (Maxwell was one of them); true that a number of people left London for elsewhere, be it Scottish estates, or whatever; yet such events could not be foreseen by the bodies that appointed them. In appointing people of that capacity, of that brilliance, and may I say of that character, so early in life the University of London has something in its history of which it can justly be proud.

One of the difficlties in this country has been, and again it sounds a very modern remark, to give enough value to the experimental part of science which effectively is an application of engineering. The necessity of treating the practical and experimental part of science as an integral part of the education of a scientist is not something that has always been understood. Thomas Graham, a Professor who was first at Andersons University in Glasgow and then came to London as the second Professor of Chemistry at University College in 1837 when only thirty-one years old but already an F.R.S., introduced the first practical teaching in chemistry anywhere in the world, and he really revolutionised the teaching of the subject. Physics, I regret to say, had to wait rather longer. Again it was at University College that practical classes in physics were first introduced, by George Casey Foster, Professor there for nearly forty years; he established them immediately on his arrival in 1865, at the age of thirty. These were real revolutions.

I wish to draw attention to some of the statistics on the University of London and the Royal Society – statistics drawn from the data for which I am most grateful to Dr Berridge. It is pleasant to know that in 1837 there were, outside the medical field for which I have no figures, four Fellows of the Royal Society active in the University of London. One was Professor of Chemistry at King's College, another Professor of Chemistry at University College, a third Professor of Physics at University College and a fourth Professor of Physics at King's College. This is very nice symmetry and it shows how eminent this University had become when it was still only a year old.

One of the great figures at King's College was Sir Charles Wheatstone who straddled the divide, if there is one, between science and engineering. He was Professor of Experimental Philosophy from 1834, again in his very early thirties. He was very active in establishing telegraphy, but as a pure scientist he was also the first to study how rapidly impulses travel along wires and he worked on many such topics. Similarly Professor Williamson at University College, who was Professor of Chemistry there for thirty-eight years from 1849 to 1887, first in practical chemistry and then in general chemistry, came to University College when he was only twenty-five and had to wait several years before he became an F.R.S.

I am not sure whether there was a practical chemist at the same time but chemistry was then supposed to include both. Professor Williamson worked very successfully on molecular structure and did a great deal to introduce the science degree as we have it today.

At King's there had been a rather older man, Daniell, best known to the public as the inventor of the Daniell Cell, the first practicable source of electricity and therefore essential to the beginning of electrical engineering. He was born in 1790 and was Professor at King's College from 1831 to 1845. He became an F.R.S. when he was only twenty-three. He did a great deal of work on the atmosphere and he may well have been the first person to state that all the extremely complicated behaviour of the atmosphere must be explicable in terms of physics and chemistry. When you take a subject that had looked totally mysterious and set it within what boundaries of knowledge it must become explicable, a major contribution has been made.

A different school, a school of thought, a school of work that started with somebody whose association with this University was more geographical than anything else, is exemplified by Sir Francis Galton (1822-1911) who did an enormous amount in founding the whole subject of human inheritance, and studied various human characteristics. He introduced finger-printing, for he discovered that this was a characteristic of each of us. He was the one who first started mental testing. He was the first one to point out what a tremendous amount of knowledge could be received from the study of identical twins. He was a great believer in eugenics, which is now viewed as rather more doubtful. He started the whole statistical school of genetics which is still so important, but he was also very active in meteorology. He was the first person to draw weather maps and introduce the term anticyclone. In addition to founding his first laboratory close to University College, he was a student at King's College. One who was very much influenced by him was Karl Pearson (1857-1936), a Professor at University College from 1884 to 1933. He is well-known to anybody in the subject as, in a sense, the father of modern statistics and as the person who introduced statistical experiments in biology. He introduced that enormously misused and misunderstood chi squared test. But it is perhaps not right to blame somebody for having produced something the mechanics of which can be taught but the inherent meaning of which we seem to find much more difficult to get across, even if today we have many mindless applications of his important invention. He too was a great author: *The Ethics of Free Thought*, was one of his books. He worked together with Wheldon, the Profesor of Zoology, and it was a very fruitful co-operation. He also got going the subject of experimental psychology. In our own time, G.B.S. Haldane was Professor at University College from 1933 to 1957, a good span of time. He was born in 1892 and lived until 1964. His contribution to genetics, to evolution, his introduction of the whole idea of gene linkage, were formative influences in science.

Peter Medawar spent a sizeable period at University College. He is best known for his work on the subject of immunology but also contributed greatly to the philosophy of science. I am an admirer both of the content and the title of his book where he described science as 'the art of the soluble'. I think this is one of the happiest expressions I have heard and I have greatly admired what he has done in this field, a field that so many successful practising scientists ignore but a man of his stature, a Nobel Laureate, pursued with great vigour. University College had the great school of Physiology with A.V. Hill and Andrew Huxley.

Let me now move from the life sciences themselves to the subject of crystallography, where J.D. Bernal was such a formative influence. For much of his life, over thirty years, he was Professor at Birkbeck College with numerous students who became eminent, and exerted great influence, through using crystallography as a method to study the structure of substances and the nature of liquids, and as an instrument for advancing the understanding of life and its origin. In the same field we had Kathleen Lonsdale, who was on the staff of University College for many years. She came from Bedford College and was one of the earliest women Fellows of the Royal Society. It is strange to think that that happened only as relatively recently as 1945. She was rightly honoured at a very early stage for her outstanding work in this field.

At King's, in the first half of the century, there are two names I particularly want to mention, both Nobel Laureates: Charles Barkla and Edward Appleton. Both had a fruitful part of their career at King's; Barkla a relatively short period from 1909 to 1913 and Appleton twelve of the most fruitful years of his life. Barkla worked on x-rays and established many of their properties, notably features characteristic of individual elements, thereby creating an enormously useful tool for research. Edward Appleton is the man to whom we owe most of our early knowledge of the upper atmosphere and especially of its electrical properties, establishing the notion of the ionosphere as we call it. In the same field there was Sydney Chapman, Professor at Imperial College from 1924 to 1946, and V.C.A. Ferraro who was Professor at Queen Mary College from 1952 to 1974 where he went after he had been a Reader at King's College.

In my own work I have been a tremendous admirer of Sir Henry Massey who, for nearly four decades, was Professor at University College. His work on atomic collisions alone would have secured his fame and honour in physics, but he then went on, initially on his own, to create the British scientific space effort. This was a great feat of innovative thinking, of creating something new by a man, who when the space age dawned, was no longer that young – having been born in 1908.

There were many more in the band of innovative and remarkable people: Ambrose Fleming of University College whose thermionic valves ruled electronics for the first half of this century and O.W. Richardson who did much to explain what went on in them. Richardson was at King's College from 1924 to 1944 and received the Nobel Prize while there in 1928. In London we also had one of the great mathematical thinkers of our time, Alfred North Whitehead, who was at Imperial College for ten years. He had worked with Bertrand Russell on *Principia Mathematica*. Afterwards he did a tremendous amount on his own on the foundations of mathematics and on the nature of thinking. *Modes of Thought* is one of his most famous books. It is perhaps not so well-known that Lord Penny, who became a force in the land, was a Reader at Imperial College from 1936 to 1945. I suspect that for the last four of these years Imperial College did not see such a lot of him, but it was his base, the place where he had also been a student. Lord Blackett (Patrick Blackett) must of course be mentioned. He was the man chosen to lead the Physics Department at Imperial College when the enlargement and growth of this was decided upon in 1953. He was there for twelve years. He had already been famous for his outstanding work on cosmic rays for which he received the Nobel Prize. He was not young when he came to Imperial College being in his mid-fifties. Since he had been for many years a professional naval officer his physics career was perhaps not quite as long as one might have thought. After he arrived at Imperial College, and while engaged on the enormous administrative task of helping the growth of the institution, he began to found a completely new school of investigation in geophysics. He achieved this not in his early days, but when he was at Imperial College.

A great school of this University is the School of Biophysics which was founded by J.T. Randall at King's College. He arrived in 1946 as Wheatstone Professor of Physics and in 1961 became Professor of Biophysics, a department that was very much his creation. I must also mention Maurice Wilkins, who received the Nobel Prize for the work he did in that Department, which also had Rosalind Franklin who died so tragically young. Some people started whole schools: Sir Ian Heilbron in chemistry at Imperial College; Ernest Chain, biochemistry at Imperial College; Donald Hey, organic chemistry at King's College. A great chemist, Sir Harry Melville, was Principal of Queen Mary College from 1967 to 1976. Queen Mary College, incidentally, has another very interesting characteristic as being the place where aeronautical engineering, at the join between science and engineering, made a fine beginning. H.H. Read did fundamental work on the origin of granite and of other materials, metamorphic rocks and the like, and was Professor at Imperial College for sixteen years. David Brunt created meteorology as an academic subject at Imperial College and had an outstanding school. Nearer our time, Professor Wibberley of Wye College did much to make land use and agricultural economics, and now planning, academic subjects.

At Royal Holloway and Bedford New College the activities in science are closely connected with Sir William McCrea, who was born in 1904 and is still a very creative scientist. He was at Royal Holloway for twenty-two very active years where he had as his colleague Professor S. Tolansky, F.R.S. Coming back to Imperial College, in the whole movement of turning optics, from what many considered to be a dead subject, into a modern, highly active one, Dennis Gabor had a very major part for which he received the Nobel Prize. But McCrea, who had earlier been a Reader and Assistant Professor at Imperial College, was an oustanding man in stimulating whole lines of research in theoretical astronomy and has made the most remarkable contributions.

The relation of the University to the Royal Society can be depicted in figures. In 1837 there were four Fellows in the University. By 1861 an interesting situation had arisen because by that time there were a large number of Fellows of the Royal Society in the medical institutions and hospitals. In that year, according to my count, there were twenty-three Fellows attached or linked in some way to the great hospitals of the City, while there were nineteen outside the medical field at teaching colleges. Forty years later the number of medical ones had diminished slightly to twenty-one, but those who were in ordinary teaching positions numbered thirty-two, plus five more who had retired: the retiring ages and the greatly increased expectation of life had begun to have an influence.

Let me finish by paying tribute to one particular person, at a particular school of this University not yet mentioned in my talk – the London School of Economics where that outstanding person and great hero of mine, Karl Popper, became Professor of Logic and Scientific Method in 1946 and held the Chair until his retirement twenty-three years later. It is remarkable that this philosopher of science (who also made great contributions to the philosophy of politics and of history) was brought to this country by the London School of Economics. No scientist should think that that great institution has no connection with science. Popper's philosophy has been inspiring and fruitful, and has taught us all a great deal about the nature of science and what we should honour scientists for: not for being right because in the end we are all wrong, it is not the business of a scientist to be right, but for being stimulating, for being creative, for being ready to be tested and disproved by experiment, for influencing others, for being innovative. The achievement of this University in being innovative, in contributing to the shaping of modern science, and in keeping the ways open for future as yet unknown developments, has been by no means inconsiderable. In many areas it has been decisive.

6

Medicine

L.P. Le Quesne

The 150 years since the foundation of the university have seen profound, accelerating change and development in all the sciences, none more so than in those related to medicine.* But the story of medicine in the university comprises more than its contribution and response to these developments, for, with its inescapable involvement in the day-to-day treatment of the sick, it also reflects the great changes that have taken place over this period in society and in the provision of health care. And there is a further strand in the story, for the history of medical education in London long pre-dates the foundation of the university, as at the time of this event there were in existence a number of medical schools which looked askance at the formation and claims of this new institution.[1]

From the time of their foundation, in some instances dating back to the twelfth century, the great London hospitals had been centres of medical education, based on the apprenticeship system. Throughout the eighteenth century this practice had increased and developed, with students being attached to individual teachers, to whom they paid fees. In due course this led, through the pooling of fees, to the formation of medical schools, each of these being essentially an off-shoot of its parent hospital,

*For their help and advice in the preparation of this lecture I am deeply grateful to Mr Negley Harte; Dr Malcolm Godfrey; Sir John Ellis; Mrs Gillian Roberts, the Academic Registrar, and the staff of the Academic Department in the Senate House; to the staff of the University Library; and to many other friends and colleagues too numerous to mention.

[1] For detailed accounts of the history of medicine within the University see: (a) H.H. Bellot, 'The University of London', *The Victoria History of the County of Middlesex*, vol. I (Oxford, 1969), 315-44; (b) Todd Report, Appendix 14, F.G. Young, 'The Origin and Development of the University of London with Particular Reference to Medical Education'.

For a more general review of the development of medical education in the 19th century see: (a) C. Newman, *The Evolution of Medical Education in the Nineteenth Century*. (Oxford, 1957.); (b) C. Singer and S.W.F. Holloway, 'Early Medical Education in England in Relation to the Pre-History of London University', *Med. Hist.* (1960), iv. 1-17. G. Rivett, 'The Development of the London Hospital System, 1823-1982' (1986) contains much background information relating to the medical schools.

which owned and controlled it.

In the early years of the nineteenth century, none of the existing schools provided an organised, comprehensive course, the students frequently enrolling at different schools for various courses. The teaching which they received at these schools was largely confined to the clinical aspects of medicine. For the study of anatomy, which, because of inability to preserve the cadaver, in those days took place only during the winter months, the students attended private schools, the most famous of which was the Great Windmill Street School,[2] run by John and William Hunter. Influenced no doubt by the circumstances in which they worked and reflecting the altogether coarser nature of life in the metropolis in those days, the majority of students were, by our standards, uncouth and boisterous. As readers of the novels of Dickens will know, this aspect of medical student behaviour continued well on into the nineteenth century.

At that time there was no single examination giving entry into the profession of medicine, which was based on an hierarchical structure, though this was rapidly breaking down. At the top were the physicians, licensed by the Royal College of Physicians,[3] 'eminent, distinguished and proud' men, who 'advised rather than did'.[4] Below them were the surgeons, whose origin was in the manual crafts rather than learning, their status being guarded by the Royal College of Surgeons.[5] Finally,

During the period covered by this lecture there were five important, relevant government enquiries, three concerned with the University and two with Medical Education in general, as detailed below. Throughout the text they are referred to by the name in brackets, thus (Todd Rep.): (a) Rep. Roy. Comm. Advancement of Higher Ed. in London. (The Selborne Rep.) 1889. [C5709], xxix. 323; (b) Rep. Roy. Comm. for proposed Gresham Univ. in London (The Gresham Rep.) 1893-4 [C7259] xxxi. 807; (c) Rep. Roy. Comm. Univ. Educ. London (The Haldane Rep.) (i) 1910 [Cd. 5165], xxiii. 639. (ii) 1911 [Cd. 5527], xx. 1. (iii) 1911 [Cd. 5910], xx. 453. (iv) 1912-3 [Cd. 6015], xxii. 581. (v) 1913 [Cd. 6717], xl. 297; (d) Rep. Inter-Departmental Committt. on Med. Schs. H.M. Stationery Office. 1944. (The Goodenough Rep.); (e) Rep. Roy. Comm. Med. Ed. (The Todd Rep.) 1967-8. [Cmnd. 3569], xxv, 569.

[2] For an account of this school see: G. Gordon-Taylor and E.W. Walls, *Sir Charles Bell, His Life and Times* (Edinburgh and London, 1958).

[3] The Royal College of Physicians of London was founded in 1518. The requirements for obtaining the Fellowship of the College were a classics degree from Oxford or Cambridge, followed by an examination, conducted in Latin until 1820.

[4] 'In the words of one of the Acts of Parliament they were "profound, sad, discreet, groundedly learned and deeply studied in Physic". They were eminent, distinguished and proud, they advised rather than did, and they were not paid – they were reimbursed for their expenses and accepted presents in gratitude for advice. Their left hand did not know what their right hand was doing when gold was quietly passed into it, even though that right hand might be very well able to look after its own interests.' Newman, p1.

[5] Originally united with the barbers in the Company of Barber Surgeons, founded in 1540, in 1745 the surgeons broke away to form the Company of Surgeons, becoming the Royal College of Surgeons of London in 1800, and changing its title to that of the Royal College of Surgeons of England in 1843. The customary qualification in the early years of the nineteenth century was M.R.C.S., requiring a course in anatomy, and attendance for

there were the apothecaries; originally retail druggists, over the years they had acquired the right to prescribe, in so doing becoming the forerunners of the modern general practitioner; their status was formalised by the Apothecaries Act of 1815.[6]

Despite the many disparities between these three branches of the medical profession, there was one striking similarity in that in no instance did the licensing bodies have any authority over the schools, nor did they have any responsibility for the selection of students and the nature and content of the teaching, so that there was no organic connection between the teaching and the examination. In the early years of the nineteenth century there was increasing dissatisfaction with this state of affairs, and it is a reflection of this dissatisfaction that medical men were closely involved with the movements that led to the foundation of University College,[7] originally called London University, in 1825, and also that of King's College in 1828.[8] It is of interest that a number of these men, like Charles Bell, had received their medical education in Edinburgh, where, since the middle of the eighteenth century, there had been a more coherent system of medical teaching, closely related to the University.

The foundation of these two colleges marks the beginning of the story of medicine in the University of London, for both colleges had a Faculty of Medicine, with professors in all the main subjects, both planned a coherent course of study in one school, both planned to acquire a new hospital, expressly organised for student teaching, and the medical members of each college were insistent that to achieve their aims the colleges must have university status, with the right to grant degrees.

It is altogether appropriate that this lecture should be delivered in this School, for not only did The Middlesex Hospital nearly become the teaching hospital for University College,[9] but in the early days students from both University and King's Colleges walked the wards of The Middlesex Hospital. Furthermore, not only was Sir Charles Bell,[10] a

one year at the surgical practice of an hospital; frequently these were preceded by up to five years apprenticeship, often with a general practitioner.

[6] The Society of Apothecaries was founded in 1617. The Apothecaries Act, 1815, conferred on the Society the right to give a qualification to practise medicine – the L.S.A. This was changed, in 1907, to the L.M.S.S.A. (Licentiate in Medicine and Surgery of the Society of Aopthecaries).

[7] For a full account of the early years of University College, see H.H. Bellot, *University College London, 1826-1926* (1929).

[8] For a full account of the early years of King's College, see F.J.C. Hearnshaw, *The Centenary History of King's College, London, 1828-1928* (1929).

[9] See Gordon-Taylor and Walls, pp. 141-3; also H. Campbell Thomson, *The Story of the Middlesex Hospital Medical School* (1935) 23-4.

[10] Charles Bell (1774-1842). After qualifying in Edinburgh, Bell moved to London, where he taught in the Great Windmill Street School. Surgeon to the Middlesex Hospital, 1814-36, during which period he was the first Professor of Surgery at University College, 1828-30. He was one of the founders of the Middlesex Hospital Medical School in 1835. In

surgeon on the staff of the Hospital, the first Professor of Surgery at University College, but the first Professor of Medicine was a Middlesex physician, Sir Thomas Watson, and in addition three of the inaugural professors in the Medical Faculty at King's were on the staff of The Middlesex Hospital.[11] A distinguished Middlesex student, Sir Anthony Home, incidentally the first Middlesex man to be awarded the Victoria Cross, in a memoir written many years later, wrote of one of these three men that he . . . 'was refined in appearance, belonging to a family of university distinction. He united this with the suggestion of a don, and of one translated to an uncongenial soil. Perhaps a life-long pasture on Greek roots might have been naturally to his taste. He did not invite questions at the bedside, nor do I think that I ever heard him make a clinical remark during his round'.[12]

Of the original intentions of the founders of these two new medical schools, only one, the construction of two new hospitals, was attained within a few years. In 1830, after previous unsuccessful attempts through Parliament, University College lodged an appeal to the Crown Council for incorporation as a university. The application was strongly opposed by the long-established but slumbering schools of medicine in Oxford and Cambridge and by the existing medical schools in London. This opposition was cogently expressed by the leader writer in the *Medical Gazette*, who wrote of the application: 'All of this is exceedingly contemptible: the Council of London University know – or ought to know – that, as a medical school, their institution was wholly uncalled for; that there were, and are connected with the great hospitals in London, schools at least as good as theirs'.[13] Four years later, ninety-nine physicians and surgeons from the London schools, including such illustrious names as

1836 he was invited to the Chair of Surgery in Edinburgh, a post he held until his death. A distinguished surgeon, he made important contributions to our understanding of the nervous system. A gifted artist, he produced a series of splendid anatomical drawings, and also of soldiers wounded at Waterloo. Gordon-Taylor and Walls's book is an attractive account of his life and times.

[11] Herbert Mayo, Surgeon to The Middlesex Hospital, Professor of Anatomy and Physiology; Francis Hawkins, Physician to The Middlesex Hospital, Professor of the Practice of Medicine; Sir Thomas Watson, Physician to the Middlesex Hospital, Professor of Forensic Medicine.

[12] Sir Anthony Home, 'Fifty Years Ago, a Retrospect', *Middlesex Hosp. J.*, 13 (1909), 6-22. The individual in question was Dr Francis Hawkins. Sir Anthony Home was awarded the V.C. in 1858, for gallantry in the Indian Mutiny.

[13] *Medical Gazette*, 6 (1830), 377-9. The article contains another oft-quoted passage 'As to the rest, if appending a few letters after their names be considered by young gentlemen as an advantage, we would advise the physicians and surgeons connected with the hospital schools forthwith to confer diplomas. We should thus have "Masters of Medicine and Surgery" in the University of St Bartholomew's – in the United Colleges of Guy's and St Thomas – or, what would come nearer the mark, in London University at Mile End Road.'

Astley Cooper[14] and Richard Bright,[15] petitioned the King not to grant the privileges of a university 'to the medical school in Gower Street', stating 'that the London University resembles in no respect the ancient universities of England; that it is a joint-stock association, founded and supported by money subscribed in shares, which may be bought and sold in the market, like those of canals, gas-works and other speculative undertakings . . .'[16]

As is well-known, this opposition was partially successful, and in 1836 the University of London was constituted solely as an examining body, with powers to give degrees to students from University and King's Colleges, and to any other colleges in the United Kingdom approved by the Privy Council. It is true that in the case of medical schools such an application required the approval of the Senate as well as that of the Privy Council, but the University had no power of inspection, nor of control of appointments to the staff, nor of teaching in the schools, which remained free to accept and teach students for whatever qualification they chose, a consequence which was to have a profound effect on the development of medicine within the University for over 100 years.

All the principal London schools were recognised by the Senate and Privy Council,[17] but this made little difference to them, the majority continuing as isolated teaching institutions, dominated by the clinical staff, the attitude of most of whom was essentially empirical not academic. Although in many respects similar, the medical schools of the University and King's Colleges nonetheless differed from the others in that they were integral parts of these multi-faculty colleges, and they continued to appoint professors in the main subjects, including medicine and surgery. These clinical appointments were modestly salaried, part-time posts, and the duties were solely teaching. The declared objects of these two colleges

[14] Astley Paston Cooper, (1768-1841), F.R.S. 1802; P.R.C.S. 1827 and 1836. Distinguished surgeon and anatomist. Lecturer in Anatomy, St Thomas Hosp. Med. Sch., 1789-1825. Surgeon to Guy's Hospital 1800 until his death.

[15] Richard Bright, (1789-1858), M.D. (Edinb.) 1812; F.R.S. 1821. Physician, later consultant physician to Guy's Hospital, 1824 until his death. Pioneer in correlating clinical findings with those at autopsy, notably in the case of Bright's Disease (nephritis).

[16] *Med. Gaz.*, 14 (1834), 147-151.

[17] In London the eleven schools founded by 1835 were recognised, together with six private schools; recognition was granted to thirty schools elsewhere in England, to sixteen in Ireland, and three in Scotland, where a number of individual teachers were also recognised (Univ. Calendar, 1844). In 1850 the Charter of the University was modified to enable it to grant degrees to students not only from Colleges in the United Kingdom, but also 'in any of Our Colonies or Possessions abroad or in Our Territories under the Government of the East India Company'. By 1898, 106 medical schools were recognised, twenty-two in London, forty elsewhere in England, twelve in Scotland, twenty-one in Ireland and eleven overseas. (Univ. Calendar, 1898-9.) The reorganisation of the university in 1900 restricted the schools geographically to, in broad terms, Greater London.

were confined to teaching and there was at that time no concept, at least in the field of medicine, that the professors should undertake research, it being considered apparently that this was an extra-mural, intellectual activity that they might indulge in if they so wished. This is well illustrated by Lord Lister,[18] who graduated from University College in 1852 with a Gold Medal in the M.B., and was later Professor of Surgery at King's: he carried out the researches which led to the introduction of antiseptic surgery in a room in his own house in Glasgow. Nonetheless, we should remember that it was Liston,[19] Charles Bell's successor as Professor of Surgery at University College, who carried out the first major operation under anaesthesia in this country, at University College Hospital, in 1846.[20]

One of the first acts of the Senate of the new University was to set up a committee to draw up regulations for degrees. Amongst the first of these were the M.B. and M.D., the latter, no doubt reflecting the origins of medicine in the humanities rather than the sciences, including, until 1885, a paper in logic and moral philosophy. The first examinations for the M.B. degree were held in 1839. Prior to starting studies for this degree students had to be eighteen years old, and to have passed either the University Matriculation Examination, or obtained an arts degree from a university recognised by the University of London. There were two examinations after two and four years study in recognised institutions. The emphasis in the first examination was on the basic subjects such as anatomy, botany, and materia medica, whereas in the second it was clinical subjects, but there was not the same clear-cut distinction between clinical and pre-clinical subjects as later became customary.

[18]Joseph Lister (1827-1912), M.B. (London), 1852; F.R.C.S., 1852; F.R.S., 1860; Professor of Surgery, Univ. of Glasgow, 1860-9; Univ. of Edinburgh, 1869-77; King's College, 1877-92. The founder of antiseptic surgery. He performed the first operation using this technique on August 12, 1865. Unsuccessful applicant for the Chair of Surgery in University College, 1866. His invitation to the Chair at King's in 1877 resulted from a memorial to the Council of the College signed 'by all the staff of the medical department with the exception of the surgeons, and one unimportant professor.' (Hearnshaw, p. 299.) President of the Royal Society, 1894-1900, the only other surgeon to have held this position being Benjamin Brodie (1858-61).
[19] Robert Liston (1794-1847). M.R.C.S., 1816; F.R.C.S. (Ed.), 1818; F.R.S., 1841. Surgeon to University College Hospital, and Professor of Surgery, University College, 1835 until his death. A brilliant, dexterous surgeon, renowned for the rapidity of his operating.
[20] The operation, a mid-thigh amputation, was performed on 21 December 1846. The anaesthetic, ether, was administered by a chemist, William Squire, who later qualified as a doctor. It was not strictly the first operation under ether in England, as two days previously James Robinson had extracted a molar tooth under ether anaesthesia, in a house in Gower Street, now marked with a plaque. For a full account of Liston's operation see F.W. Cock, 'The First Operation under Ether in Europe – the Story of Three Days', *Univ. Coll. Hosp. Mag.*, (1910) 1. 127-44.

Although the impact of this degree was less than hoped for, it is nonetheless a landmark in medical education in London, for it was the first comprehensive medical qualification available to students at the London schools, and it was the first to require a defined general educational standard prior to embarking on the course of study. Of great interest is the fact that whereas the papers contained case-commentaries there was no clinical examination as we know it today. This is undoubtedly a reflection of the fact that in those days the art of medicine was largely based on an analysis of the patient's symptoms, with little or no examination of the patient. But all of this was about to change, for the foundation of the University coincided with the great burgeoning of modern, scientific medicine. At that time the leading centre of medicine in Europe, indeed the world, was Paris, where one of the outstanding figures was Laennec, the inventor of the stethoscope.[21] This development led directly to the realisation of the importance of examination of the patient, to the correlation of physical signs with the changes found at autopsy, and hence a rational concept of disease. It was not long before this new learning was brought to London by physicians who had studied in Paris, and this is reflected by the introduction of clinical examinations into the M.B. in 1852.

Alongside this growth of clinical medicine was the development of the scientific basis of medicine, exemplified by the work of the great French scientists, such as Claude Bernard.[22] Later in the century leadership in the field of the medical sciences passed to Germany, where, in contrast to the scene in London, medicine was embedded in the universities, with strong academic departments, headed by great figures such as Virchow, the founder of the concept of cellular pathology.[23] These fundamental changes in our understanding not only of disease, but of the structure and functioning of the body, together with the increasing importance of the

[21] Théophile Réné Hyacynthe Laennec (1781-1826). M.D. (Paris), 1804. Appointed physician to the Hôpital Necker in 1816, and Professor at the College de France, 1822. In 1819 published his book, *De l'auscultation mediate*, describing the use of the stethoscope.

[22] Claude Bernard (1813-78). Originally a pharmacist's assistant, before qualifying as a doctor in Paris, 1839. M.D. (Collège de France), 1840; Professor of Physiology, Collège de France, 1852; Foundation Professor of Physiology at the Sorbonne, 1855; elected to the Academie Française, 1868. One of the greatest physiologists; discovered the hepatic synthesis of glucose, the digestive activity of the external pancreatic secretion and the presence of vasomotor nerves. Formulated the concept of the *milieu intérieur*. The first French scientist to be honoured with a public funeral.

[23] Rudolf Ludwig Karl Virchow (1821-1902). M.D. (Berlin), 1843; Professor of Pathology, Würzburg, 1849, moving to the chair in Berlin in 1856. In his famous book, *Die Cellularpathologie* (1858) he set out his doctrine of '*omnis cellula e cellula*'. An outstanding figure in nineteenth century medicine, he made contributions in several areas of pathology, describing leukaemia, the factors contributing to thrombosis etc. A man of strong views, he was politically active in the City Council and the Prussian Lower House, often opposing Bismark.

basic sciences in relation to the study of medicine, were reflected in the content and pattern of teaching in the London schools, and also in the form of the examinations. Thus, the 1850s saw the introduction of microscopy into various branches of medicine and medical teaching, and in 1860 the University introduced a Preliminary Science Examination, entitled an Examination in Mechanical and Natural Philosophy, but consisting essentially of physics, chemistry and biology. There was, however, no concomitant change in the structure of the schools to encompass these profound changes in the nature of the study of medicine. The middle decades of the century saw the gradual decline and disappearance of the private medical schools, with the concentration of teaching in the main medical schools, but in them the teaching of these new subjects, and of anatomy, physiology and pathology was carried out not by professionals in these areas of learning, but as the part-time occupation of junior members of the hospital staff, 'gentlemen who', as succinctly stated by Lord Justice Fry, 'take up their subject, not as their main work in life, but as a παρεργον; they deliver lectures for a short while, but look to practice as physicians as the ultimate object of their ambition'.[24]

In contrast to these small, poorly staffed departments of basic sciences in the traditional medical schools – departments which could in their teaching reflect the great changes in medicine, but were unable to make any significant contribution to them – in University and King's Colleges these departments were *ab initio* an integral part of multi-faculty colleges. The first proper physiology laboratory in the country was opened at University College in the 1870s and the same period saw the flowering of the great physiology school in this College, headed by Michael Foster,[25] who left to found the Department of Physiology at Cambridge. He was followed in the chair by a former pupil of Claude Bernard, J.S. Burdon-Sanderson,[26] who attracted a host of outstanding workers to the

[24] The Selborne Rep., para 1068. Lord Justice Fry was Vice-President of U.C.L. and a member of the Senate.

[25] Michael Foster (1836-1907). Qualified from U.C.L. 1858; M.D., 1859; F.R.S. 1872; Professor of Practical Physiology, University College, 1869; Praelector of Physiology, Trinity College, Cambridge, 1870; Professor of Physiology, University of Cambridge, from 1883. In collaboration with T.A. Huxley developed practical laboratory work in physiology, and introduced practical physiology classes to Cambridge.

[26] John Scott Burdon-Sanderson (1828-1905). Graduated from Edinburgh. M.D., 1851; F.R.S., 1867; Medical Officer of Health, Paddington, 1854-67; Physician to The Middlesex Hospital and Brompton Hospital, 1860-70; Professor of Practical Physiology, U.C.L., 1871; Jodrell Professor of Physiology, U.C.L., 1874; first Waynflete Professor of Physiology, Univ. of Oxford, 1882; Regius Professor of Medicine, Univ. of Oxford, 1895-1903.

Department, amongst them being Victor Horsley,[27] one of the founders of neurosurgery, before himself moving to Oxford to found the school of physiology in that university.

Alongside, and interwoven with this permeation of science into medicine, the nineteenth century saw profound demographic and social changes, which greatly influenced medicine and medical education. In the years 1811 to 1891 the population of the United Kingdom more than doubled, and these years saw the transformation of the country from an essentially rural, agricultural community to an essentially urban, industrialised society.[28] Associated with this change was the growth of a wealthy, educated middle class, whose background was in industry and the professions, not the land; a cadre of people who were aware of and interested in the development and benefits of the new sciences, amongst them medicine. One manifestation of this growing concern with medicine was the movement to protect the public from the activities of untrained practitioners, leading in 1858, to the foundation of the General Medical Council, with powers to define acceptable degrees and diplomas, and to publish a register of appropriately qualified doctors. Although not primarily directed to its improvement, the foundation of this Council had a profound influence on medical education, for within a few years the Council had developed the concept that a qualification leading to inclusion of the holder's name on the register should indicate a safe doctor who could, on the day he qualified 'practise any branch of his profession on a suspicious public without too much risk'.[29] This concept undoubtedly raised the standards of general medical practice, but at the same time it led to a confusion, still not completely resolved, between the requirements and purposes of an examination leading to a professional diploma, with legal implications, and those of a university degree, which must, or ought to be, related to academic attainments.

The development of the middle classes, the spread of education, and the realisation of the increasing potential of medicine – a potential which was certainly real in terms of diagnostic achievement, but, as yet sadly inadequate in terms of treatment – led to an increasing demand for doctors. From 1858 onwards the Medical Register shows a steady increase in their number, with over 35,000 doctors on the register by the end of the century. Given this increasing number of doctors, the prestige of the London schools, and the growing importance attached to a university degree in general, one might have expected that throughout the century

[27] Victor Alexander Hadden Horsley (1857-1916). Student at U.C.H.M.S., F.R.C.S, 1880; F.R.S., 1886; physiologist, Director of the Brown Institute, 1884-90; Surgeon to Univ. Coll. Hosp. and National Hosp. for Nervous Diseases. One of the founders of neurosurgery.

[28] D. Thomson, *Europe Since Napoleon*. (1985), Ch. 7.

[29] Newman, p. 200

the London M.B. would have come to play an increasingly important role in the London schools, but such was not the case. In the first forty years following its inception only 795 students obtained this degree, that is about twenty each year, and it was not until 1884 that over fifty obtained it, and 1894 before 100 did so.[30] To this total of graduates must, of course, be added the number of students, increasing towards the end of the century, who came to London from Oxford and Cambridge for their clinical training; nonetheless it remains the fact that throughout the century, and indeed long after, the majority of students at the London schools qualified by means of some diploma other than the London M.B. Following the introduction in 1866 of the Conjoint Diploma of the Royal College of Physicians and Surgeons, a diploma specifically devised for the rapidly growing cadre of general practitioners, the 'safe' doctors of the General Medical Council, London students increasingly qualified with this diploma, though it is true that a number of them subsequently obtained a university degree.[31]

There were a number of reasons for this failure of the M.B. to make a real impact on the schools. The level of secondary education of many of the students was so poor that many failed the essential preliminary hurdle of the Matriculation Examination. Similarly the failure rate in the Preliminary Sciences Examination in its first twenty-five years was nearly 50 per cent,[32] reflecting not only the poor standard of the secondary education but also the poor quality of the teaching of these sciences. The whole series of the M.B. examinations were considered to be both more difficult and more academic than the alternative roads to qualification, so that in effect the M.B. came to be considered as an honours course, reflected in the fact that in the latter years of the century the number of those obtaining the higher degrees of M.D. or M.S. amounted to approximately 50 per cent of those obtaining the M.B. each year.[33] A further factor was that the Conjoint Diploma and a number of other qualifications could be obtained by a shorter course, a factor of great importance in that, at least in those years, to achieve a medical qualification was for many a means to social and financial betterment; and parents were often unable or unwilling to invest in this process more than was necessary. Finally, the staff of the hospitals, who owned and

[30] Figs. from Univ. Calendars.

[31] As late as 1933-7 85% of London students obtained Registration on a Conjoint Diploma, and only 7% with a university degree. Many students subsequently went on to obtain a university degree, but over half the students qualifying from the London schools in this period never obtained a university degree (Goodenough Report, Appendix C, Tables A & B). It was only following the introduction of the new University regulations for the medical course, in 1973, that the great majority of London students obtained Registration on the basis of the M.B., B.S. degree.

[32] Selborne Rep. Append. 17.

[33] See Univ. Calendars.

controlled the schools, were intimately involved in the affairs and welfare of the Royal Colleges rather than those of the university; with the existence of the Conjoint Diploma they saw no reason why they should seek to shape the teaching at the schools to university reqirements, with the result that there was no coherent relationship between this teaching and the requirements of the M.B.[34]

This lack of an effective relationship between the schools and the university was not confined to medicine, and by the '70s there was widespread and increasing dissatisfaction with the purely examining role of the university. This led to a series of movements and events which in due course transformed the university, and eventually the medical schools. Before considering these changes there is one other topic to which I must refer. The university was founded to admit students 'of all classes and denominations without any distinction whatsoever'. Without specifically saying so this certainly did not include women. However, within a few years there was an increasing demand for the higher education of women, marked by the foundation of Bedford College in 1849; this demand included the opportunity for women to study medicine.[35] The first English woman to qualify in this country was Elizabeth Garrett, known after her marriage as Elizabeth Garrett Anderson.[36] In 1861 she persuaded Mr Hawes, a surgeon to The Middlesex Hospital, to arrange for her to study in the Medical School; she

[34] In 1885 the two Royal Colleges, of Physicians and Surgeons, petitioned to obtain incorporation as 'The Senate of Physicians and Surgeons', with power to grant medical degrees. In rejecting this proposal the Selborne Commission, para. 4, argued that it could not be accepted 'without either conferring the power of giving such degrees upon colleges which have no academical character, or creating a new examining and degree-giving university in a single faculty: neither of which innovations appears to us in itself desirable.'

This close association between the teaching hospitals and the Royal Colleges continued for many years. 'The old order did not change and give place to the new either quickly or gracefully. This was made clear to me when in 1944, shortly after the publication of the Goodenough Report, I was lunching at one of our medical schools. Next to me was a leading surgeon who pointed out that the London teaching hospitals had clinical facilities which were known all over the world and the two Royal Colleges conducted examinations which led to diplomas which were registrable qualifications. Where, I was asked very pointedly, did the University impinge on medical education at all?' (Sir Douglas Logan, University of London, Report by the Principal, 1946-5, p. 35) (see also note 30).

[35] The first English woman to qualify as a doctor was Elizabeth Blackwell (1821-1910). Born in Bristol. Emigrated to New York with her parents, 1832. Graduated M.D. in the Univ. of Geneva, New York State, 1849. Returned to U.K., and her name placed on Medical Register (1859) as she had obtained her degree prior to the passage of the Medical Act (1858). In 1875 became the first Professor of Obstetrics and Gynaelology in the London Medical School for Women.

[36] Elizabeth Garrett Anderson (1836-1917). Qualified L.S.A. in 1865, being admitted to the examination only because her father threatened legal action if her entry was refused. M.D. (Paris) 1870. Senior Physician (1866-92) to the Elizabeth Garrett Anderson Hospital, which she founded. Closely involved in the foundation of the London Medical School for Women, being on its staff 1875-1905. First woman member of the B.M.A.

gained honours in every subject for the first M.B. exam, whereupon her male colleagues manoeuvred her removal from the School. Undeterred, she continued her studies in a number of other institutions, and in 1865 obtained the Licentiate of the Worshipful Company of Apothecaries. Inspired by Elizabeth Garrett, Sophia Jex-Blake,[37] who had failed in her attempt to achieve admittance of women to the medical school in Edinburgh, founded the London Medical School for Women in 1874. Although initially no hospital or examining body would accept their students, in 1877 the Royal Free Hospital accepted their students for clinical work, and in the following year the university opened all its faculties to women, becoming the first university in Great Britain to grant medical degrees to women, though it was not until the late 1940s that all the medical schools in London opened their doors to women.[38]

Returning to the nineteenth century, it would be inappropriate to go in detail into the complex manoeuvres and discussions, including two Royal Commissions,[39] which surrounded – indeed often obscured – the movement to transform the examining into a teaching university, in which the staff of the schools had some real involvement in its activities. Medical men took a leading part in the proceedings of both Commissions, of interest being the discussions, still of relevance today, of the correct relationship between a university degree and a professional qualification. Of greater importance is the appearance, in the Gresham Report, the second of the Royal Commissions, of an overt discussion for the first time of the place of research in a university, particularly in the field of medicine. The Commission concluded surely to the great benefit of the university, that 'any . . . limitation of research to institutions specially set apart for that purpose would tend to lower the academic character of the schools of the university and the standard of teaching'.[40]

As a result of these prolonged negotiations, the university was reorganised in 1900 under new Statutes, all the medical schools being admitted as Recognised Schools. Although the university had the power to inspect them, in practice the schools remained essentially independent entities, with their own finances, and this change had only a limited impact on the schools, illustrated by the fact that the historian of the Middlesex Hospital Medical School gives it no more attention than an insert simply stating that: 'It should be noted that when the University of London was reconstituted in 1900 the Middlesex Hospital Medical

---

[37] Sophia Louisa Jex-Blake (1840-1912). In 1869 accepted as a medical student by Edinburgh University, but later Court of Appeal ruled they had acted *ultra vires* in so doing. Obtained M.D. (Berne) 1877, and right to practise medicine. Settled in Edinburgh, where she founded the Women's Hospital and School of Medicine, which closed in 1894 when the University admitted women.

[38] As a result of a recommendation of the Goodenough Rep.

[39] The Selborne Rep., the Gresham Rep.

[40] Gresham Rep., para 23.

School became a School of the University'.[41] An important feature of the reorganised university was the introduction of the Boards of Studies, in which the teachers in the various disciplines from the various schools could, for the first time, meet to define courses of study and the related exams. In the broad field of medicine and related sciences seven Boards were established, many more being added in later years.[42] The three main boards in medicine immediately set about a thorough revision of the regulations for the M.B., which, except for the introduction of the Preliminary Sciences Examination, had remained essentially unchanged since 1839, and this resulted, in 1904, in the introduction of the new M.B., B.S. course and examination, with its formal separation of pre-clinical from clinical studies, and with separate examinations in medicine, in surgery, and in obstetrics and gynaecology.

The early years of the twentieth century were in fact dark days for the London Medical Schools. The intake into the schools had fallen from about 650 per annum in the 1860s to some 250 in 1905-9. In part this was due to a general decline throughout the country of the number of students entering medicine, but there was a more serious reason. With the ever increasing importance and complexity of the sciences related to medicine, the schools, which were financially solely dependent on the fees of the students, were finding it increasingly difficult to meet the cost of the requisite laboratories, equipment and staff. Although, since the reorganisation in 1900, many of the staff of these departments were now appointed teachers of the university, they remained poorly paid servants of the school, and many left to work elsewhere, resulting, in most of the schools other than University and King's Colleges, in small poorly equipped, poorly staffed departments. The problems of such small departments had been recognised for some time, and as early as 1870 *The Lancet* had recommended the amalgamation of pre-clinical departments, stating bluntly, 'The amalgamation of the medical schools in London is, we think, one of the most important and pressing questions of the day. All scientific men are convinced of the absurdity and practical impossibility of carrying on scientific teaching in eleven separate institutions in

---

[41] Campbell Thompson, p. 91.

[42] The original boards related to medicine were those of Preliminary Medical Studies, of Intermediate Medical Studies, of Advanced Medical Studies, of Dentistry, of Pharmacy, of Hygiene and Public Health, of Physiology and Experimental Psychology (Univ. Calendar, 1900-1). In 1951-2 the Medical Boards were reduced to two, those of Preclinical Studies and Advanced Medical Studies. In 1968-9 the Board of Preclinical Studies was disbanded, and those of Medicine and Postgrad. Med. Studies (disbanded 1984-5) formed, preceded by those of Pathology (1947-8) and Microbiology (1966-7). The Boards of Studies in Surgery, and in Obstetrics and Gynaecology were founded in 1968-9, followed by that of Community Medicine in 1974-5. The dates indicate the first appearance of the Boards in the Univ. Calendar.

London.'[43] The Gresham Commission had indeed recommended amalgamation of the pre-clinical departments,[44] but because of the competition between schools for students, and the certainty that neither University or King's Colleges would join such a scheme, nothing was done.

Despite this, the first forty years of this century saw the full flowering of the traditional London schools, dominated by their prestigious, part-time clinical staff, essentially isolated from the university, with the teaching almost totally confined to the wards of the great London hospitals, which were still abundantly supplied with patients from the local population and by referral from their alumni. From our present standpoint it is easy to criticise these schools, but we should not overlook the exceedingly high clinical standards of their staffs, the many, distinguished contributions they made to clinical medicine, notably in the field of neurology in which they lead the world, and the fact that even if they failed in general to impart scientific curiosity in their students, they trained generations of doctors with high standards of clinical competence and professional conduct.

During these years of apparent stability and assurance we can discern the origins of the forces and concepts, both social and academic, which in the years since the last war have brought about such great changes. Heralding the birth of the concept that the health of the community should not be dependent upon charity and market forces but is a direct concern of the state, the passage of Lloyd George's National Insurance Bill in 1911 was a direct forerunner of the Beveridge Report (1942) and the foundation of the National Health Service (1948), a political transformation which has had, and continues to have, profound consequences for medical education.

Coincident with the controversy surrounding the passage of Lloyd George's Bill, the University was being examined by yet another Royal Commission, arising from the dissatisfaction with the 1900 reorganisation. The Chairman of this Commission was Lord Haldane, a distinguished Liberal politician, a man deeply concerned with university education, who in his youth had been greatly influenced by the German university system. Because of the outbreak of war in 1914 the recommendations of the massive report of his Commission were never adopted,[45] but in the field of medicine they had a seminal influence, and a direct line of thought can be traced from Haldane through the Goodenough Report (1944) on Medical Schools to the 1968 Royal Commission on Medical Education (the Todd Report). In the pre-clinical sphere Haldane was greatly influenced by the evidence of Ernest

[43] *Lancet*, ii (1870), 544.
[44] Gresham Rep. p. 848.
[45] Haldane Rep. The passages referring to medicine will be found in Cd. 6015 and Cd. 6717. See Note 1.

Starling,[46] the distinguished Professor of Physiology at University College, who, in his evidence, wrote:

> The medical schools, however efficient, are essentially of the nature of 'trade schools'. As the boy leaves a secondary school to enter a medical school the standard which is at once set before him is professional success. The teachers of sciences with whom he first comes in immediate contact, in many cases not of marked ability, are in all cases in a position of inferiority to the clinical staff, whose servants they are. The work which is expected of these scientific teachers is to get the students under them as quickly as possible through the various Preliminary and Intermediate examinations, so that they may be passed on to the clinical work of the wards. The whole idea of the first three years, the most impressionable time of the student's career, is not educational but professional.[47]

Given evidence of this nature and his own cast of mind, it is not surprising that Haldane recommended a strengthening of the traditional scientific departments. In this, of course, he was not breaking new ground, and it was in the clinical field that his report was of the greatest importance.

In this area Haldane was greatly influenced by Abraham Flexner,[48] who had just completed his well-known study of medical education in America and Europe, and by Sir William Osler,[49] Regius Professor of Medicine at Oxford, formerly Professor of Medicine at Johns Hopkins, and himself greatly influenced by German medicine. Both of these men, whilst admiring their clinical standards, deplored the lack of scientific content in the London Schools. As Flexner put it:

> There is no certain or direct interaction between the fundamental scientist and the clinicians; except in the region of morbid anatomy, some elementary bacteriology, and physical chemistry they barely touch. The clinician lacks the time, even if he has the training, which will enable him to bring to bear upon clinical problems the artillery which the chemist and the pharmacologist are forging.[50]

[46] Ernest Henry Starling (1866-1927). Qualified at Guy's where he became Demonstrator of Physiology; M.D. (Lond.), 1889; F.R.S., 1899; Jodrell Professor of Physiology, U.C.L. 1899-1923.

[47] Haldane, Final Rep. (1913) para 231.

[48] Abraham Flexner (1866-1959) American educationalist. In 1910, he published, for Carnegie Foundation, a critical report on American medical schools, followed in 1912 by a similar report on European medical schools. The substance of these two Reports was consolidated in his book, *Medical Education, a Comparative Study*, (New York, 1925).

[49] William Osler (1849-1919). Qualified M.D. (McGill), 1870; F.R.C.P., 1884; F.R.S., 1898; Professor of Medicine, McGill 1874; Univ. of Pennsylvania (Philadelphia) 1884; first Professor of Medicine, John Hopkins Med. Sch. 1889, where he organised the first modern, clinical academic unit, based on both clinical and laboratory work; Regius Professor of Medicine, Univ. of Oxford, 1904-19. A great teacher and bibliophile.

[50] Haldane, Final Rep., (1913) para. 248.

Both Flexner and Osler stressed the self-perpetuating effect of this situation, and the need to found clinical academic units with salaried staff. As Haldane put it in his report:

> The essence of (their) contention is that in a University Medical School the principal teachers of clinical medicine and surgery in all their branches ought to be university professors in the same sense as the principal teachers of chemistry or physiology . . . If this is once admitted the rest follows. It is simply in each case a question of appointing a university professor and arranging that his department shall be so organised that he will be able to do his work.[51]

Shortly after the First World War the first five clinical professors in this sense were appointed.[52] It was, however, to be sixty years before this recommendation was to be fully accepted, and sentences essentially identical to those of Haldane can be found in the Goodenough and Todd Reports, save for the implication that it was a simple matter. But in the inter-war years, nurtured in part by the University which, in 1929, was reorganised into its present structure, and in part by the University Grants Committee, there was a strengthening of the pre-clinical departments, which, though in most cases remaining small, increasingly became true university departments, making important research contributions, such as the synthesis of stilboestrol by Charles Dodds,[53] the discovery of penicillin by Alexander Fleming,[54] and the fundamental discoveries in the field of immunology by Peter Medawar.[55] Each of these represent a significant advance in their respectve fields, but they have a wider significance. Hitherto the applications of science to medicine had,

[51] Haldane, Final Rep., (1913) para. 253.

[52] Prof. Sir Francis Fraser, St Bartholomew's H.M.C., Medicine; Prof. H. Maclean, St Thomas's H.M.S., Medicine; Prof. Dame Louise McIlroy, Royal Free Hospital S.M., Obst. and Gynae; Prof. F.S. Langmead, St Mary's H.M.S., Medicine; Prof. C.A. Pannet, St Mary's H.M.S. Surgery; these five appointments were made 1920-2.

[53] Edward Charles Dodds (1899-1973). Ph.D. (Lond.) 1925; M.D. (Lond.), 1925; F.R.C.P., 1945; F.R.S., 1942); P.R.C.P., 1962-6; Courtauld Professor of Biochemistry, the Middlesex Hospital Medical School, 1925-64. His synthesis of stilboestrol in 1938, the first synthesis of a non-steroidal compound with biological activity of a steroid hormone, led to the therapeutic use of steroids.

[54] Alexander Fleming (1881-1955). M.B. (Lond.), 1908; F.R.C.S., 1909; F.R.C.P., 1944; F.R.S., 1943; Professor of Bacteriology, St Mary's H.M.S., 1928-48; Principal, Wright-Fleming Inst, of Microbiol., 1946-54. His isolation of penicillin in 1928 led to the development of the whole range of antibiotics. Received Nobel Prize in 1945 jointly with Howard Florey and Ernest Chain.

[55] Peter Medawar (1915-87). F.R.S., 1949; Professor of Zool., Univ. of Birmingham 1947; Jodrell Prof. of Zool. and Comparat. Anat., U.C.L. 1951; Director, Nat. Inst. for Med. Res., 1962-71; Nobel Prize for Medicine, 1960. His fundamental observations on the host versus graft reaction led to the development of tissue and organ grafting and the whole concept of cellular immunity.

except in the important fields of public health and surgery, been largely confined to the elucidation of disease processes and the functioning of the human body, with little direct application to therapy as opposed to diagnosis. But each of these discoveries had, within a comparatively short while, important therapeutic applications, and as such are heralds of the striking advances in treatment which are such an exciting component of modern medicine.

The growth of scientific activity in London Schools was also stimulated by the Medical Research Council, founded in 1913.[56] This is nowhere more dramatically illustrated than in the work of Sir Thomas Lewis who from 1916 to 1945, whilst on the full-time staff of the Research Council, was a member of the clinical staff of University College Hospital and the Medical School.[57] His scientific contributions still stand as landmarks in their field, but of greater significance was his bringing of scientific investigation to the bedside. He was the founder of modern clinical science, and it has been this application of the scientific method to the whole range of medical activity, including therapy, which has transformed medicine within the last fifty years.

Largely determined by the concepts originating in the second decade of this century, the past forty years have seen greater changes in the Faculty of Medicine than at any time in its history, but before turning to them I would like to mention an important extra-mural achievement of the Faculty. Arising from the recommendations of a Government Commission on University Education in the Colonies set up in 1943,[58] the Faculty, in the twenty years after the War, took on the responsiblity, through an extension of the system of external degrees, of nurturing through their formative years the new medical schools in Jamaica, in Ibadan and in Khartoum. The subsequent achievements of these schools is testimony to an enterprise in which the Faculty of Medicine can take great pride.[59]

The changes in the domestic scene are without doubt most strikingly

[56] The Medical Research Council was founded in 1913, as the Medical Research Committee. It was renamed the Medical Research Council in 1920. See: F. Dainton, *Reflections on the Universities and the National Health Services. Nuffield Provincial Hospitals Trust* (1983) ch. 3 for a full account of the formation of the M.R.C.

[57] Thomas Lewis (1881-1945). B.Sc. (Cardiff), 1902; M.B., B.S. (Lond.), 1905; M.D. (Lond.), 1907; F.R.C.P., 1918; following qualification, house-surgeon to Horsley (see note 27); Ass. Physn., Univ. Coll. Hosp., 1913; Physn., 1919; appointed to W/T staff of M.R.C. 1916, the first clinician to hold such an appointment; Head of the Dept. of Clin. Res. at U.C.H.M.S., 1919, the first 'unit' outside the main laboratories of the M.R.C. and the first clinical unit. Made outstanding contributions to knowledge of mechanism of heart, of its diseases and of pain. The father of modern clinical science. Founder of the Med. Res. Soc.

[58] Rep. on Univ. Ed. in Colonies (The Asquith Rep.) 1945 [Cmd. 6647], iv. 673.

[59] See: B. Pattison, *Special Relations: The University of London and New Universities Overseas, 1947-1970* (1984) for a full account of this enterprise.

shown by the great growth in the numbers and strength of the University, academic departments within the schools, especially in the clinical field. This is clearly illustrated by the increase in the number of Appointed Teachers, notably in the clinical field. Without question this growth of academic staff was largely stimulated by the Goodenough and Todd Reports, but at the same time it reflects a real change in the climate of thought, affecting not only the university but the N.H.S. staff, with the schools becoming increasingly permeated by scientific endeavour and achievement. Although no doubt the changes were not as fast and as great as some might have wished, the years 1950-75 were in many respects golden years, with a sense of ever-expanding horizons, both intellectual and financial. They were years in which many members of the staff of the Faculty were in the forefront of medical advances, as indeed they still are, leading the field not only in this country but throughout the world. To single out from such a broad spectrum of achievement any one individual is invidious, and such a choice must be largely personal, but it is doubtful if any one individual made a more pervasive contribution than Sir Austin Bradford Hill,[60] Professor of Medical Statistics at the London School of Hygiene, who was a leader in the application of statistical methods to the medical and biological sciences, and in the development of that very powerful research tool, the controlled trial, which has projected scientific accuracy into the field of therapy. His work was also of importance for another reason, in that it focuses attention on the growth and great achievements during this period of the distinguished postgraduate schools and institutions of the Faculty, a contribution which from the constraints of space alone are not described in more detail.[61]

A marked feature of this growth of scientfic activity has been a broadening of its scope. On the one hand this is shown by what may be called the increasing depth of medical research, so that Virchow's concept of cellular pathology has been extended not only into the chamber of the cell, but, with the growth of molecular biology, into the gene itself. On the other hand, there has been the outward extension of the medical sciences into the wider fields of the behavioural sciences, into all aspects of community medicine, and increasingly into the fields of preventive medicine. Whilst the former has seemed to rivet the attention of the

---

[60] Austin Bradford Hill (1897-   ). Ph.D. (Lond.), 1926; D.Sc. (Lond.), 1929; F.R.S., 1954; Reader in Epidemiology and Vital Statistics, Lond. Sch. Hyg. & Trop. Med., 1933; Prof. of Med. Statistics, 1945-62.

[61] (a) The London School of Hygiene and Tropical Medicine, founded 1924; originally the London School of Tropical Medicine, founded 1899. (b) The Royal Postgraduate Medical School, founded 1931. (c) The British Postgraduate Medical Federation, founded 1945. (i) Todd Rep. Appendix 14, para. 28-37. (ii) For a full account of the early years of the R.P.M.S., see: C.C. Booth, 'Medical Science and Technology at the Royal Postgraduate Medical School: the First 50 Years', *Brit. Med. J.*, 291 (1985), 1771-9.

student more firmly to the laboratory and the bedside, the latter has widened his horizons, and with that the horizons of the medical schools. The concerns and sphere of interest of a medical school now extend not only far beyond the walls of a single hospital, but into the community itself, a development facilitated by legal separation of the schools from their parent hospitals in 1948.[62] This widening in the scope of medicine has been reflected in the reconstruction of the medical curriculum in 1973, a consequence of which has been that for practical purposes all the students now qualify with a university degree, thus after 150 years achieving the aims of the original founders. Further, reflecting both the growing scientific content of medicine and the problems, already referred to, of combining a professional qualification with a university degree, a growing number of students have obtained in addition a second degree, a B.Sc., a valuable development sadly retarded by present financial constraints. As a yet further reflection of the widening perspectives of medicine, the University has instituted a degree in nursing studies, heralding the concepts of a school of medicine concerned not only with the education of doctors, but also with that of the many other professions involved in the provision of health care.[63]

Just as the nineteenth century medicine and medical education were influenced by changes in society, so it has been in recent years. In contrast to the great growth of the inner cities in the previous century, largely as a result of developments in transport the last ninety years have seen a steady decline in the population of Inner London, which is now over 50 per cent less than at the turn of the century.[64] Inevitably this has led to the increasing development of hospitals and medical services in the growing fringes of the city, a change which has been greatly accelerated in recent years by the policy of the N.H.S. to equalise the availability of health care throughout the community. As a consequence the medical schools have increasingly come to utilise more peripheral hospitals for the training of their students. Initially, influenced by their experience of dispersal of their clinical students during the years of the Second World War, the schools actively sought to place their students in such hospitals on educational grounds, but recently, and increasingly, they have been forced to do this as the result of the effect of the N.H.S. policy decisions on the clinical practice in the principal university hospitals. There is a limit to which

---

[62] Prior to 1948, except for St Bartholomew's H.M.C. and the London School of Medicine for Women, the London Medical Schools were effectively owned by their associated hospital. Partly as a result of a firm recommendation in the Goodenough Rep., and partly owing to the formation of the N.H.S., all of them became incorporated, and separately affiliated to the university in 1948.

[63] B.Sc. in Nursing Studies, introduced in 1977. In conformity with this concept, the university set up a Working Pary in Health Studies, under the chairmanship of Sir John Ellis, which produced its final report in 1987.

[64] O.P.C.S. Census Report, 1981. County Rep., Gt. London. Pt 1. H.M.S.O. 1982.

such dispersal of students is beneficial, and it is believed by most Deans that this limit has been reached, if not exceeded.

In contrast to these social influences, with their tendency to disperse the educational activities of the schools, the main thrust has been towards concentration in their growing scientific and research activities. One of the main themes of the Royal Commission on Medical Education (the Todd Report, 1968) was that, with the growing complexity of the medical sciences and with their ever-accelerating rate of advance, it was increasingly difficult for small academic departments to achieve their full role, whilst at the same time there was an increasing need for the medical sciences to be closely integrated with multi-faculty colleges with their strong departments of basic science. Restating the theme of the leader in *The Lancet*, 100 years previously, the report stressed the problems of small medical schools, and recommended that the twelve general medical schools and twenty-three postgraduate schools and institutes should be amalgamated into six large schools, each incorporated with a multifaculty college. Given the long history of many of the schools it is not surprising that these radical proposals were not welcomed with open arms, and in fact they led to little in the way of concrete change. But within a few years the economic problems facing the country introduced a new factor which sharpened the need for the University to concentrate its resources and for the N.H.S. to focus even more sharply on its policies of resource allocation. Faced with these twin problems the university set up, under the Chairmanship of Lord Flowers,[65] a further Working Party which, although adopting a different pattern from the Todd Report, again put forward a plan for the amalgamation of the schools into larger units. The resulting complex negotiations of the early years of this decade are so close to us that it is difficult to see them in perspective. For this reason I do not intend to consider them in any detail,[66] and will simply say that, faced with these challenges the nettle was grasped, and the schools of the

[65] *London Medical Education: a New Framework. Report of a Working Party on Medical and Dental Teaching Resources* (1980). Simultaneous with the study of this working party, the London Health Planning Consortium produced a report entitled *Towards a Balance: a Framework for Acute Hospital Services in London, Reconciling Services with Teaching Needs* (1980). There was some cross-membership between these two groups, 'to facilitate as far as possible a complementary approach by each body' (L.H.P.C.). It is of interest that the Todd Report (para. 488) recommended the setting up of a Joint Committee between the University and the N.H.S. to review essentially the same range of problems as that covered by these two working parties, but with powers of implementation. This proposal was rejected by the University on the grounds that it threatened the academic independence of the University. (Sen. Min. July 1969, para. 5899.) For response of the Univ. to Flowers Rep. see: Reps. of J.P.C. to Senate, *Sen. Min.*, (Oct. 1980) mins. 245-76; (March, 1981) min. 747-75; (Dec., 1981) min. 483.

[66] For a fuller account see: L.P. Le Quesne, '*Medical Education in London: the Last Forty Years*' *Proc. Roy. Soc. Med.* 80 606-14.

Faculty were reorganised in a new pattern involving the fusion with multifaculty colleges of some but not all of the schools.

This reorganisation is now nearly complete. It is too early as yet to assess its success, yet it is, perhaps, fair to say that it has provided the university, which educates one-third of the medical and dental students in the United Kingdom, with a variety of powerful schools with the potential to exploit and lead the exciting advances in medical science, though this potential is undoubtedly weakened by the increasing cuts in university finance, which we must hope are only temporary. However, if our schools are to fulfil their true role, there is a further requirement, for they require not only powerful scientific departments but also powerful university hospitals, with adequate resources both financial and clinical, a requirement which depends upon identity of purpose and close collaboration between the university and the Health Services. But to achieve this requires resolution of an antithesis. The mains pressures on the Health Service relate to the provision of health care for the here and now. Not only is an adequately conceived and supported university hospital an essential component in the provision of this care, but with its concern, in collaboration with the medical school, for research and teaching it has responsibilities not just for today but also, and just as importantly, for tomorrow.

7

Theology

Sydney Evans

If we accept the maxim that 'Nothing comes from nothing' we are likely to be led on to ask the question for which there is no scientific answer, 'Why is there something and not nothing?' The maxim and the question are relevant in matters of the microcosm as well as in the mysteries of the macrocosm. 'How comes it that there *is* a Faculty of Theology in the University of London?' To this question there *is* an answer: an answer which calls into use both the language of historical fact and the language of theological faith.

The historical fact is relatively straightforward. The fact is embedded in the University of London Act of 1898. That Act provided that 'there shall be eight Faculties in the University, i.e. Theology, Arts, Laws, Music, Medicine, Science, Engineering, Economics with Political Science.' The Act provided that the first Schools of the University 'shall be University College, London, and King's College, London'. Within the Faculty of Theology the following institutions were given recognition: Hackney College, Hampstead; New College, Hampstead; Regent's Park College; Cheshunt College; the Wesleyan College, Richmond; the London College of Divinity, commonly called St John's Hall, Highbury. By the same Act a Board of Studies in Theology was established as one of thirty-two Boards. The Degrees of Bachelor of Divinity and Doctor of Divinity were regulated.

But as we all know, what the University of London is celebrating is 150 years of academic activity, not just eighty-eight years since the passing of the University of London Act of 1898. The period of 150 years dates from the sealing of the Charter of 1836 – an event which itself was not so much a beginning as the culmination of a series of incipient beginnings. That story has been succinctly unravelled by a former senator, Professor H. Hale Bellot, and can be found in the first volume of the *Victoria County History for Middlesex*. He described the initiatives that led to the founding in 1825 in Gower Street of an institution called 'London University' – 'designed', he writes, 'to supply the shortcomings of Oxford and Cambridge and to effect a reform of medical education in England'. It offered 'higher education free of religious tests, a non-resident system that substantially reduced costs, with teaching organised upon professorial lines after the Scottish pattern'.

This now internationally famous institution (U.C.L.) brought into being by the efforts of Jeremy Bentham, Henry Brougham, James Mill and Joseph Hume with deliberate exclusion of theological studies or religious affiliation, inevitably in the climate of the early nineteenth century provoked counter-action. The *Evening Standard* of 19 June 1828 announced that a meeting would be held at Freemasons Hall in Great Queen Street on the following Saturday to establish on Christian and constitutional principles a great metropolitan school to be called 'King's College'. 'With such a seminary in a prosperous position', the writer declared, 'there will be neither motive nor excuse for any parent to inflict upon his offspring the disgrace of education in the infidel and godless college in Gower Street.'

In the chair at that meeting on 21 June was Arthur Wellesley, Duke of Wellington. Among the company on the platform were two archbishops, seven bishops and a number of prominent laymen. A letter from Sir Robert Peel was read expressing regret at his unavoidable absence. The full story has been told in detail by Professor Hearnshaw in his *Centenary History of King's College, London*, published in 1929, and briefly retold recently by Dr Gordon Huelin in his readable account of 150 years, published in 1978.

If the founding of University College provoked a powerful intervention into higher education in London from distinguished representatives of the Establishment in both Church and State, the protagonists of King's College were themselves not without opponents. Because a duel fought by a Prime Minister in Battersea Park is such an eccentric episode in the eventual emergence of a Faculty of Theology in the University of London, this bizarre encounter deserves to be remembered. To understand the provocation we need to remember that a Bill of Emancipation of Roman Catholics in this country, supported by the Duke of Wellington and Sir Robert Peel, had alienated some of the ultra-Protestants, especially the Earl of Winchilsea. Winchilsea, who hitherto had supported the idea of a new college based on the King's faith, suddenly became suspicious that the college was being promoted for the clandestine training of young Jesuits. A letter appeared in the *Standard* from Lord Winchilsea announcing that he had cancelled his subscription to the King's College Appeal because the Duke of Wellington was associated with its foundation. The Duke gave him two opportunities to retract and apologise, which being refused the Duke issued a formal challenge: 'I now call upon your Lordship to give me that satisfaction for your conduct which a gentleman has a right to require and which a gentleman never refuses to give.'

Elizabeth Longford tells the tale at some length in her life of

Wellington. I quote only the event itself. Lord Hardinge was the Duke's second; Lord Falmouth was second for the Earl of Winchilsea. John Hume was the Duke's doctor.

Before giving the Duke his pistol Hardinge unfolded a piece of paper and from it read Winchilsea and Falmouth a lecture which drew tears to Falmouth's eyes. The Duke stood with a good-natured expression during this performance. Finally the two pistols were in the principals' hands and cocked.

'Then gentlemen, I shall ask if you are ready', said Hardinge, 'and give the word fire, without any further signal or preparation.' There was an instant's pause. 'Gentlemen, are you ready? Fire!' Hume's eyes were fixed in agony on his friend, whose blood he might in another moment be staunching, and he did not notice that Winchilsea kept his right arm glued to his side. The Duke noticed, and instead of hitting Winchilsea's leg fired wide. With a seraphic smile Winchilsea then raised his pistol as if in blessing and fired it off into the air. (Before acting as his second Falmouth had made Winchilsea promise on his honour, if he survived the Duke's shot not to fire back. Falmouth had always considered Winchilsea to be 'completely in the wrong'.)

Having stood the Duke's fire, Winchilsea felt that honour permitted him to apologize for the *Standard* letter. Falmouth produced a draft apology which he read aloud to the Duke.

'This won't do,' said the Duke in a low voice to Hardinge 'it is no apology.' For though the word 'regret' appeared the word 'apology' did not. Hume promptly pencilled in the words 'in apology' and initialled them, 'J.R.H.'. This the Duke accepted. He bowed coldly to the two peers . . . and cantered off the field. It had been a good morning for a Prime Minister

But we must leave the 'field of Battersea'. What was in fact established by the University Charter of 1836 was an examining body appointed by the Crown with power to grant degrees. It had no teachers and was accommodated in offices in Somerset House. This stange compromise was the solution adopted to enable the granting of degrees by a procedure which would override the opposition of King's College to any union with University College and avoid the absurdity of creating two degree-conferring universities in the metropolis. All candidates for B.A., LL.B., B.Med. and M.D. in the first examinations in 1839 came either from University College or from King's College. There was no theological option in the Faculty of Arts and no degree of Bachelor of Divinity.

As a member of the Senate, Arnold of Rugby led a powerful group which wished to make a knowledge of the Greek Testament and Scripture history compulsory for an arts degree. The proposal was vehemently opposed by the Benthamites. The Home Secretary when appealed to declared himself in favour of an optional paper in Greek Testament but opposed to a compulsory paper. Forceful letters were exchanged. Arnold was defeated. Believing as strongly as John Henry Newman that religion is the only sound basis of national education, Arnold resigned from the Senate, and for some years King's College held aloof from the arts degrees of the new university. When eventually in the University of London Act, 1898, degrees in divinity were established, not in the Faculty of Arts but in a distinct Faculty of Theology, following the Scottish rather than the Oxford and Cambridge pattern, the reason for this decision was, I imagine, a recollection of those 'old unhappy far-off things, and battles long ago'.

But if King's College held aloof in the early years, the opportunity of affiliation to the new university was seized by a number of colleges and schools in the provinces, and notably by those seminaries in which Roman Catholic priests and dissenting ministers received their training. The House of Lords in 1834 had rejected a Universities Admission Bill which would have opened Oxford and Cambridge to dissenters. Within five years no fewer than sixteen educational establishments besides the two London Colleges received authority from the Crown to issue certification of attendance and good conduct, qualifying their holders to sit for degrees in arts and in law. Even more numerous were the recognised medical schools. Hearnshaw comments: 'the University of London became not a teaching institution for the metropolis but a board of examiners for the empire'. From these beginnings developed what was to become one of London's greatest services to the furtherance of opportunities for higher education – the nurturing of colleges in the provinces and overseas in a special relationship until they grew into fully-fledged autonomous universities.

For all its achievements, the compromise of 1836 understandably failed to satisfy the proper ambitions of would-be university promoters and teachers. Towards the end of the nineteenth century voices for change became more insistent. The need for an autonomous teaching university to replace an examining board appointed by the Home Secretary and answerable to him led to many more unhappy years of wrangling between conflicting interests. Eventually men of the calibre of R.B. Haldane and Sidney Webb pressed through the preparation of a 'London University Commission Bill'. From this came the all-important Act of 1898 which among much else established a Faculty of Theology; significantly for future development it provided no funds for the salaries of professors, readers or lecturers in this discipline.

The ancient universities of England and Scotland were founded by the authority of the medieval Latin Church of the West to guarantee teaching standards in the *studia generalia*. They were guilds of scholars open to all nationalities for the pursuit of the humanities and at least one of the higher studies of theology, law or medicine. The aim of such a system was to produce holy and well-learned men to serve both Church and State. Entrance to the advanced studies required successful negotiation of the *trivium* and *quadrivium* of the arts faculty. Following the Reformation in England the universities largely became 'finishing' schools for Anglican gentry: the emphasis changed from the scholarly to the social virtues, though sound learning was not wholy abandoned. However, for a long time Oxford and Cambridge colleges remained closed against all who were not prepared to claim to be Anglicans.

This vacuum of opportunity stimulated the founding of Dissenting Academies, studied by my friends Dr Geoffrey Nuttall and Dr Gordon Huelin. In his published lectures on *New College, London and its Library* Dr Nuttall names no fewer than thirty such institutions. The ejectment of the Nonconformists from the Church of England in the summer of 1662 was the signal for the setting up of Dissenting Academies, so called after the celebrated Academy in Geneva founded in 1559 by John Calvin. Originally set up to provide training for intending ministers of religion, many of these academies admitted sons of Nonconformists who were not intending to follow that precise vocation. It is claimed that some three hundred of their pupils became sufficiently distinguished to be included in the *Dictionary of National Biography*.

One such Academy came into being in London in Hoxton Square about the year 1700. The theological tutor, Dr Joshua Oldfield, in his *Essay towards the Improvement of Reason* affirmed Hebrew, New Testament Greek, and ethics to be necessary ingredients in the curriculum. An earlier Academy in Newington Green counted Daniel Defoe among its students. In 1730 a group of Congregationalists of strict Calvinist persuasion, meeting in a hostelry of this name, formed a *King's Head Society*. This group founded Homerton College. In 1850 Homerton College joined with Highbury College and the Coward College to lay foundations in the Finchley Road of a building known to many of us as New College – one of the Divinity Schools named in the Act of 1898. For more than a century New College flourished as a Christian community of theological learning and gave the Faculty of Theology in recent years such scholars and friends as Principal John Huxtable and Dr Geoffrey Nuttall. The unique New College collection of theological books gathered in from Dissenting Acadamies is now safely housed in Dr Williams's Library.

Other London-based enterprises in theological education must be mentioned. Sir Thomas Gresham, a City mercer, established what was probably the first major endeavour in the field of what is customarily called adult education. In his will dated 1575 he left money to the Mercer's Company for the setting up of seven lectureships: one of these was in divinity. His former house became Gresham College. The statutes prescribed that the Divinity Professor should deal with matters of theological controversy 'especially those wherein the Church of England differs from the common adversaries, the papists and other sectaries'. Divinity lectures on this foundation continue to be given in the Barbican Centre – but with a less restrictive prescription.

Controversy does, however, throw up new initiatives. The London College of Divinity was an Anglican evangelical reponse to the theological debate fired by the publication in 1859 of Charles Darwin's *Origin of the Species* and in 1860 of the volume of essays by seven churchmen entitled *Essays and Reviews*. To ensure that there would be clergy whose trainng would be based on the Bible and Thirty-nine Articles of Religion a wealthy evangelical, Alfred Peache, provided money for a college known originally as St John's Hall, Highbury. Wilson Carlisle, founder of the Church Army, was once a student there. During Hitler's war the Principal, Dr Donald Coggan (later to become Archbishop of Canterbury) had the task of evacuating the students from the bombed buildings to a temporary home at Ford Manor, later to new buildings at Northwood before the College's eventual move to become St John's College, Nottingham.

Of all the theological institutions in London which have contributed to the maintenance and development of the University Faculty of Theology, without doubt the most attractively housed was the Wesleyan College opened in 1843 on the top of Richmond Hill in an estate of ten acres. Richmond became a recognised School of the University in 1909. Among the treasures of its library was John Wesley's personal collection of books.

Many streams from the high country of theological exploration and education flowed into the river of the incipient and later developing Faculty of Theology, and many distinguished and devoted scholars gave their best to the cause of Theology in the University without any personal remuneration except examining fees when they were examiners. But something in the geology of circumstances deepened the channel and extended the banks of the tributary that sprang up in the Strand.

From the opening of the college on 8 October 1836 until the passing of the King's College London (Transfer) Act of 1908 the college had the characteristics of a liberal arts college with Christian and Anglican foundations and principles. In the sciences, arts and medicine the college was served by teachers of notable standing in their subjects in spite of the College's endemic shortage of money to pay the bills. Some study of divinity was from the start required as a basic element along with classics, mathematics and English. At the end of three years a College diploma known as Associateship of King's College (the A.K.C.) was awarded to those who had satisfied their examiners and had received testimonials from their teachers of satisfactory conduct and regular attendance at chapel. A distinct theological department for the training of ordinands was not introduced until 1846 with the appointment of three Professors of distinction and variety – one 'low' and one 'broad' and one 'high' – Alexander McCaul, Frederick Denison Maurice and Richard Chenevix Trench.

Throughout the nineteenth century the Principal of the College was an Anglican in Holy Orders. The Charter of 1829 provided that 'no person who is not a member of the United Church of England and Ireland as by law established shall be competent . . . to fill any office in the College except only the Professorships of Oriental literature and modern languages.' It does not require a deep knowledge of the currents of thought in the nineteenth century to perceive the limitations imposed by this religious requirement in an institution of higher education. One anecdote that makes the point tells of the appointment of a particular candidate for the Chair of Greek on the grounds that he was the only one applying who both knew the Greek alphabet and was prepared to subscribe to the Thirty-nine Articles!

The liberation of the College from these shackles was the achievement of the last two clerical Principals: Archibald Robertson, who conceived the solution, and Arthur Cayley Headlam who carried it through. They perceived that the College was becoming a 'poor relation' on the periphery of a developing metropolitan university.

The King's College (Transfer) Act, 1908, was a triumph of imaginative ingenuity that achieved continuity of tradition with creative change, placing the secular departments under a Delegacy appointed by the Senate of the University and so eligible to receive Treasury funding, and maintaining the original Council of the College, with its Charter which secured the College's right to the Strand site, and continuing to be responsible for the Theological Department and the training of ordinands. The last clerical Principal, Arthur Cayley Headlam, added to that responsbility the new office of Dean of King's College and Head of the Theological Department until he was translated from London to the Regius Chair at Oxford. From then on the Principal has been a layman appointed by the Crown, and the Dean a cleric appointed by the Council; and some reflecting on the College motto have found it matter for research whether the *Sancte* was always represented by the Dean or the *Sapienter* always represented by the Principal! It speaks well for the relationships between successive Principals and Deans that this condominium held the College community together as one body in spite of different sources of income and separate governing bodies. Students, I believe, were conscious only of belonging to one college. The worship in the College chapel, the optional but popular Monday morning divinity lectures available for students of all faculties, the lectures frequently given to theological students on Friday mornings by teachers from other faculties, the equal membership of the Students' Union and partnership on the river and at Mitcham secured that *Sancte et Sapienter* were never divorced but enriched by reciprocal proximity.

The University Faculty of Theology, therefore, was fed from these several tributaries of teachers and students as I have briefly indicated. Apart from these independent sources of supply there would have been no University Faculty. The story for the next half-century is the story of the search for solutions as one by one each of these seminaries was faced with the threat of closure by fluctuations in the number of fee-paying students, the retirements of stalwarts on the teaching staffs, the increase in the salaries of university teachers. The inability of these recognised Schools of Divinity to raise their own salaries to the minimum required by the university to secure the status of recognition carried with it the inevitable loss of the right to enter students as internal students for the university examinations.

It is interesting to read the minutes of the early meetings of the new University Faculty of Theology and Board of Studies. Recognised teachers from the various colleges (A.E. Garvie and Charles Gore among them) worked together to promulgate the syllabus to be negotiated by students for the first examination for the London B.D. The requirement was formidable: no easy option here! The syllabus was a kind of academic pentathlon, requiring of the candidate the ability to handle ancient languages, Hebrew and Greek; textual and literary criticism and exegesis of ancient texts; the history of doctrine and the history of Christian institutions (in particular the early Church and the Reformation); and philosophy of religion. By 1939 to the degrees of B.D. and D.D. had been added those of M.Th. and Ph.D.

Every few years academics feel the itch and the urge to revise the syllabus. Theologians were no exceptions. Methods of awarding honours in theology have varied from time to time, and syllabus structures have been altered. The original Intermediate Examination required by the university consisted of seven papers to be taken at the end of the first year: Elementary Hebrew; two papers on St Mark's Gospel – translation and grammar in one, subject matter and exegesis in the other: Plato's *Apology* and *Crito*, translation and subject matter: Cicero's *De natura deorum*, translation and subject matter in one paper, grammar and retranslation in the other; and finally elements of logic with the option of elements of psychology and ethics if logic had been taken in matriculation. Substantially (but without the Latin) that was the first-year syllabus into which I was plunged as a teacher when I was demobbed from the Royal Air Force in January 1946, and four days later found myself Chaplain of King's College. New Testament Greek alone was a demanding intellectual assault course for veterans returning from four or five years in uniform. After 1960 the University no longer required the passing of an Intermediate Examination as a visa for entering the last two years of study for the B.D.

But the periodical itch and urge to revise the theological syllabus is not just an academic pastime. Revision is demanded by the impact on theological thinking of the changing world of thought in the university at large. During this period of 150 years that we are celebrating, the 'acids of modernity' had been eating into the foundations of received tradition. New questions raised by a century and a half of scientific enquiry and critical method had challenged many assumptions on which theological teaching had previously been based. The title deeds of Christianity had been subjected to searching investigations into historical origins, historical relativity, historical truth. The structure of theological language, the nature of symbolic communication, the validity of God-talk in a culture increasingly one-dimensional in its assumption about what constitutes reality – all this became grist to the mill of a modern faculty of theology. What has changed in the task of theological teaching can be measured partly by syllabus content, but even more by teaching methods, essay subjects and examination questions. All this is tough going for a student who comes to feel that his or her teachers are cutting off the branch of the tree of knowledge against which the ladder of their faith has hitherto rested. In an ideal world theology should be a second degree for students who have learned to sharpen their critical faculties on less emotive material.

The most serious problem facing the Faculty of Theology as a result of its dependence on its affiliated schools was, as I have indicated, the increasing difficulty experienced by these independent schools, as their stalwarts reached the age of retirement, in finding the money for replacement of teachers competent to receive university recognition. The University authorities were aware of the long-term implications of this problem for the future of theology as university teachers' salaries continued to rise. Not only were they aware, they were greatly concerned, and not least for the future of the External B.D. But during the 1930s there seemed no way, without giving hostages to fortune, in which public money could be injected into independent schools, even to subsidise teaching given to their students specifically for university courses.

What is clear to me is that the changes that have in fact taken place since 1945 could not have happened had there not been a sufficient ground swell of desire to find a solution among members of the Academic Council, the Senate and the Court of the University. But the main thrust towards a solution came from Sir David Hughes Parry, a non-conformist who later became Moderator of the Presbyterian Church of Wales. Although he ceased to be Vice-Chancellor in July 1948 be remained a member of both Court and Senate, becoming chairman of the Finance and General Purposes Committee which controlled the Senate Vote. He was not a great admirer of the Established Church, but this did not prevent him from being a personal friend of Dean Walter Matthews, himself the most distinguished graduate from the Faculty of Theology, and also at that time a member of the Senate. I suggest that the continuing existence of the Faculty of Theology owes more to the mutual liking and trust of these two outstanding men than can ever be documented.

What started the ball rolling was a request from the Board of Studies in Theology in 1943 that the Senate should make the Samuel Davidson Chair of Old Testament Studies a full-time post. The Chair had been created as a result of a small benefaction to the University in 1925. The post was only part-time owing to the inadequate income of the Trust Fund. The Court in 1944 concurred with the Senate providing the additional money required to make the post full-time. The Chair had been located at King's from 1930 and held by an eminent scholar, Samuel Henry Hooke, until 1946, when he was succeeded briefly by Alfred Guillaume; in 1948 William Duff McHardy was appointed to the post. King's College accommodated him in the room that had been put at the disposal of his predecessors.

The next important push to keep that ball rolling came in a letter to the Senate in 1946 over the signatures of Sir William Halliday and Canon Eric Abbott – a joint request from the Delegacy and Council of King's College for financial help for theological teaching. What is important about this letter is evidence that it had been written only after consultation with the other theological schools. The Court consulted the University Grants Committee. Their response was negative, fearing a precedent that would open the door for applications from other schools if a grant was made to King's College Theological Department. Nevertheless action followed. The University chose to follow the Samuel Davidson precedent and to finance additional unattached chairs in theology from the Senate vote. In 1948 the Chair of Philosophy of Religion, held since 1945 by Edwin Oliver James, who had been appointed by the Council of King's, was made an unattached University Chair in the History and Philosophy of Religion: the holder continued to be housed in King's but both he and the Samuel Davidson professor gave lectures in the Senate House which were open to the students of all four theological schools.

This timely move on the part of the University to help the Faculty of Theology was not without its difficulties. Administratively, unattached or 'floating' professors, as they came to be called, did not comply with normal regulations: they were without departmental libraries and without academic control. Professor McHardy, I recall, was far from content with the arrangement and never really felt at home at King's in spite of the hospitality and facilities provided. But this discontent served a purpose. It focused attention on the need to find a more satisfying long-term solution to the underlying problem.

What went on behind the scenes I have been unable to discover: but the Senate and the Court returned to the charge, and ultimately in distributing the grant for the quinquennim 1957-62 the Court included in the Senate vote provision for additional theological posts at King's College. For this to have happened a continuing discussion must have taken place between interested parties over several years. I have no doubt that Hughes Parry was still active in promoting the cause, and so was my predecessor as Dean, Canon Eric Abbott. Evidence that a solution in principle had been arrived at as far as the University was concerned can be gleaned from his 1955-6 Report as Principal, in which Sir Douglas

Logan expressed himself as follows:

> After giving much thought to the problem I am convinced that, if we are to develop a Faculty of Theology worthy of the University, it cannot be done by adding still further to the number of professors who are not officially attached to any School. The only course is to build up a proper teaching and research cadre in a non-denominational, multi-faculty School which is in receipt of grant from the Court. I hope that development on these lines will be feasible in the coming quinquennium.

That Eric Abbott had been active in the matter became clear to me when it was made known that I was to succeed him as Dean in January 1956. Abbott had not only reconstructed the Theological Department at King's after the war years of dispersal at Bristol, but had made it a condition of accepting appointment as Dean that the Council would support him in developing a post-graduate fourth-year college away from London to provide a new and needed dimension in the preparation of students of King's College who were ordinands. His pastoral concern for the Department and the College was matched by his concern for the future of the University Faculty of Theology. The writing was on the financial wall for the Theological Department at King's as well as for the London College of Divinity, Richmond College and New College. But any proposal for a radical change in the Headlam Constitution of 1908 would need the active cooperation of both Council and Delegacy, of both Principal and Dean. Principal Noble had, it appears, at that time been unwilling to consider radical change such as would upset the equilibrium of the condominium of the College. That canny Scot seems to have taken the line: 'Better the anomaly you know than the alternative you don't know'.

When I was asked in 1956 to succeed Eric Abbot, that rare and agile spirit, on his departure to Oxford to become Warden of Keble College, I was blissfully unaware that I would be required to fulfil the triple roles of surgeon, executioner and midwife. But so it was. I could see no future for a University Faculty of Theology unless it was located in King's College: I could see no future unless the teachers were on the University pay-roll. This seemed to indicate the setting up of a non-denominational Faculty of Theology such as Sir Douglas Logan envisaged, under the Delegacy, in partnership for as long as may be with the Council and the staff of the Theological Department.

After a crucial conversation with Sir Douglas Logan to discover whether a solution along these lines would be acceptable to the University, and encouraged by him, I took to Principal Noble a proposal for new chairs in theological subjects, financed by the University, established within the Faculty of Arts in King's, the individual holders of the chairs forming a joint teaching Faculty of Theology with teachers in the Theological Department under the chairmanship of the Dean of

King's College, who was Dean of the whole college as well as Head of the Theological Department.

Would the Principal of King's College, not yet *Sir* Peter Noble but destined to become Vice-Chancellor, be willing to negotiate such an enterprise to save the University Faculty of Theology? He was willing! May full credit be given to him for choosing to embark on such a hazardous voyage in spite of his earlier misgivings and reluctance. I had explained that I saw this proposal as a temporary arrangement for a number of years to enable two teams of teachers to work together in common cause until such time as a new Charter for King's College should be required and with it the end of the Headlam solution of 1908 which had proved such a creative success. I knew myself in all this to be 'mine own executioner'. In future a Dean of King's College would be a different sort of animal!

The new pattern was put on the loom with remarkable speed. At both college and university level it was accepted as a promising programme. This could not have happened without Sir Peter Noble's active support or without the strong encouragement of Sir Douglas Logan, Sir David Hughes Parry and others who backed the proposal on the Academic Council and the Senate. In the College there were, of course, those who regretted the necessity for change, but the Delegacy, the Council and the Joint Professorial Board eased the passage of the scheme. Mr Peter Shaw, Secretary of the College, Mr David Hunter Johnson, Treasurer of the Council, and Mr Myles Tempany, Bursar of the College, were indispensible in working out details of organisation and finance.

Once the change had been made the professors petitioned for lecturers, and strange as it may now sound there was money made available for several new appointments. Professor S.R. Sutherland, who was to become Principal of the college in 1985, arrived at the same time, as did his successor in the Chair of History and Philosophy of Religion, J.S.K. Ward. When the number of Appointed and Recognised Teachers on what I will refer to as the Delegacy component of the Faculty became more numerous than the component from the Council side it was right for me to cease to be Dean of the combined Faculty and to allow the Faculty to choose its own Dean.

As I reflect on the years during which all this change and development took place, culminating in the consequential drafting of a new Charter for the College, I am amazed at what happened, the speed with which it happened and the absence of rancour. Meanwhile, during the whole period from 1955-75 the study of theology within the college was exciting: teachers and students were jointly engaged in what felt like exploration of truth rather than the mere accumulation of knowledge. The problems presented by the tradition were faced with critical openness within a community in search of the truth, however disconcerting for previously unexamined inherited ideas it might prove to be.

I would like to emphasise the importance of this sense of community between teachers and students, a sense strengthened here by the vocational commitment to the teaching profession or to ordination of the majority of the students, strengthened also by the accessibility of teachers and their pastoral concern for individuals, with the worship and music of the College chapel as further unifiers. In his *Idea of a University* published in 1852 John Henry Newman stressed the importance and value of a university as a community with all its members given over to the pursuit of knowledge. He wrote: 'It is the community that makes the university quite literally an Alma Mater, knowing her children one by one, not a foundry, or a mint, or a treadmill.' If I may borrow two expressions used by the Bishop of Durham in his scintillating lecture in 1986 on the *Purpose of a University*, I would claim for the Faculty of Theology at King's the qualities of both 'creative edge' and 'conviviality'.

During this period an initiative sponsored by the Council of the College raised an endowment for a new Chair in the field of moral and social theology. The Chair was named after Frederick Denison Maurice, as a belated tribute to an eminent Victorian and teacher here who fell victim to a virus known as *odium theologicum*. Professor Gordon Dustan, appointed the first holder in 1966, among much else pioneered a continuing inter-faculty seminar of lawyers, medics and theologians to examine new problems in medical ethics arising out of new knowledge and new skills.

Another important development was the creation of a Department of Religious Studies in the Faculty of Arts by the enterprise of Professor H.D. Lewis, then Professor of the History and Philosophy of Religion. This development is now incorported in a joint Faculty of Theology and Religious Studies organised in three Departments: Biblical Studies; Christian Doctrine and History; the History and Philosophy of Religion. The student is offered various combinations leading either to the Degree of B.D. or to that of B.A. Judging by publications emanating from the present team of teachers, by academic results in examinations and the flourishing of the audiences from other faculties for the weekly voluntary lectures in theology for the A.K.C., the long King's College tradition of exploring religious truth and its theological expression continues with excitement, rigour and commitment.

In 1968 a completely unexpected approach was made to the Senate which was to bring into the University Faculty of Theology a unique access of theological strength. The Rector of Heythrop College in North Oxfordshire wrote to the Principal of the University, Sir Douglas Logan, in January 1969 formally requesting on behalf of his College, recognition as a non-grant-receiving School of Divinity of the University of London. Discussions preliminary to this formal request had already taken place with interested parties and a warmly supportive letter was sent from King's to the Senate House over the signatures of Profesor H.D. Lewis and Professor E.L. Mascall as former and current Deans of the College

Faculty.

Heythrop is an institution with a long and distinctive tradition within the Latin Church of the West. Its origins are to be found in Louvain in 1615, in Liège in 1624, followed by a move to England in 1794 during the wars which followed the French Revolution. In 1926 the two houses of study, one philosophical, one theological, operating within the English Province of the Society of Jesus, were brought together in the village of Heythrop near Chipping Norton. The move to a modern collegiate building in Cavendish Square was achieved in 1970. With its splendid library and impressive staff of teachers the College quickly adjusted to its new situation and introduced fresh ideas and nuances concerning theological education. Their attractive prospectus sets out their courses for university first degrees, for higher degrees in theology and philosophy, together with courses tailored to meet the needs of a variety of students for a Postgraduate Diploma in Pastoral Theology with the recent innovation of an Institute of Spirituality. Nothing could better illustrate the excellent co-operative relationship between King's and Heythrop than the recent appointment to the Frederick Denison Maurice Professorship of Moral and Social Theology in King's of Dr John Mahoney of Heythrop.

Those who can remember what led to that duel between the Duke of Wellington and Earl of Winchilsea in 1829 will appreciate the irony of this appointment: some of you may even be asking if the Earl's suspicions of the Duke's real intentions to found a college for producing crypto-Jesuits have now been confirmed after 150 years! What this appointment does in fact indicate is that a lot of ecclesiastical water has flowed past Battersea Park and under the bridges of the Thames in this century and a half. Ecumenical openness and confraternity have quietly replaced ecclesiastical exclusiveness in academic circles. We all read and learn from each other's theological investigations and explorations. The theological debate and the spiritual quest cannot fail to be stimulated by these encounters and exchanges.

As I see it, the work of a Faculty of Theology is not an end in itself. Its *raison d'être* is to conserve the ancient wisdom in a modern context, and thereby to sustain for new generations of men and women the possibility of a spirituality that is passionate, intelligent and honest; and to do this for a world that is struggling to find its way through complexities that obscure its credibility and threaten its survival. May *Sancte et Sapienter* continue to flourish in King's College!

8

Engineering

H. Billett

It is perhaps appropriate to begin our journey through the history of engineering in the University of London by considering the bronze plaque on the Gower Street wall of what is now the Civil Engineering Laboratory of University College London. Appropriate, first, because that laboratory was arguably the first in the world to be dedicated to the teaching of engineering. And, second, because that plaque commemorates the high technology of 1808, namely the first passenger railway in the world built by the Cornish engineer, Richard Trevithick, and which used a high pressure (two bar) steam locomotive 'Catch me who Can' to draw a single passenger carriage on metal rails round a circular track about 100 ft in diameter. As my former colleague, the late Harry Marriott, put it, 'At the cost of one shilling per ride Londoners enjoyed the exciting novelty of being rapidly moved in a small circle by steam traction'. Those small circles were centred somewhere between that plaque in Gower Street and Senate House probably at a point not far from University College's new Engineering Building. Perhaps I should pass quickly over the fact that this was also the site of the world's first railway *accident*; a rail broke and the engine overturned!

Again, it is appropriate to start with a railway, however small, because so many of the early teachers of engineering had studied science, but had become practising professional engineers in the growing number of railway workshops springing up in the early 1800s.

The Institution of Civil Engineers had been founded in 1818 ('Civil' meaning simply 'not Military') and on 17 July 1827 the 'Council of the University of London' acted on the Institution's advice by appointing John Millington its first Professor of Engineering. (In fact he was 'Professor of Civil Engineering and the Application of the Principles of Mechanical and Chemical Science to the Arts and Manufactures'). Millington had lectured at the Royal Institution of Mechanics and in 1823 had published a book with familiar chapter headings such as: properties of matter; mechanics; pneumatics; acoustics; hydrostatics; and hydraulics. The 1828 edition included a chapter on the steam engine. There is thus little doubt that the first Chair of Engineering in the U.K. was founded in what is now University College London and that the holder was worthy of the title.

Some of our current problems, politics, university politics and financial stringency, are in no way new. They could change the course of events just as surely in 1828 as in 1986. Thus when the Gower Street version of a University of London applied for a university charter it was claimed that such a charter could only be granted to a *group* of colleges and not to a unitary university. It seems probable that this was simply a contrived public excuse suiting the not-too-private objections of parts of the political, religious and university establishments to the fledgling institution in London. In any event, no charter for a university in London was to be forthcoming for another eight years.

In some ways more important for the new foundation was its total dependence for many years to come on private gifts and fees. Its finances were strained to the limit simply to pay for the new buildings rising on the green fields north-west of the city. For engineering this was crucial. Millington, not unreasonably, asked for an annual guaranteed sum of £400 for himself and his department. The guarantee was not forthcoming and on 26 June 1828 he resigned his chair. He had given some lectures but not to an organised group of engineering students and went off to manage a Mexican silver mine.

During the next thirteen years courses in engineering were given at U.C.L. under the auspices of professors of physics and mathematics such as Ritchie and Sylvester, who regarded engineering science as properly belonging within their disciplines. Such an attitude to engineering studies was not wholly absent among professors of pure science when I joined U.C.L. in 1946; perhaps the wheel has now turned full circle since when I retired in 1980 the head of physics and at least two of his professorial colleagues were engineers.

Meanwhile on the political front the problem of a charter for the University of London was eventually resolved by the founding of a second college, King's College, in 1829 and its opening in 1831, 'for the purpose of maintaining the connection between sound religion and useful learning' in the metropolis. As there were now 'colleges' in the plural and the matter of religion, after the manner of the Church of England, had been dealt with, some of the public objections to the granting of a charter to a University of London had disappeared. Thus in 1836 a charter was granted to 'a group of persons eminent in literature and science' to act as a Board of Examiners under the title 'The University of London'. It was clearly intended to deal with King's and U.C.L. but the terms of the charter were so widely drawn that it could accept any candidates wherever they came from at home or shortly after, abroad.

On charter day University College London was also incorproated under its present title. The situation of King's College remained more complex for some years, but in 1838 the decision was taken to form there a department of Civil Engineering and Mining as applied to Arts and Manufactures. In that October the first thirty-one students were recruited.

The course depended at first on service teaching in mathematics, mechanics, chemistry, physics and geology with in-house teaching of machine drawing, surveying and mineralogy. As at U.C.L. the quality of the service teaching was remarkable – chemistry by Daniell of the Daniell Cell and physics by Charles Wheatstone of the Wheatstone bridge. Incidentally, when Daniell died in 1845 the religious criteria set by King's prevented the appointment of Liebig, a Lutheran, to succeed him. A less spectacular Anglican appointment followed in 1848.

In July 1840 W. Hosking was appointed as Professor of the Arts and Construction in connection with Civil Engineering and Architecture and to Hosking must be accorded the honour of being the first professor of engineering actually to teach students in a genuine department of engineering in London or indeed in the United Kingdom.

Whether prompted by this event or by the death of Sylvester in 1841 U.C.L. was moved in that year to re-establish its chair of engineering, a chair filled by the distinguished railway and civil engineer Charles Vignoles (1793-1875) who gave his first lectures in November 1841. Trained as a military engineer he spent ten years as a state civil engineer in South Carolina before returning in 1826 as chief engineer of the new Liverpool-Manchester railway. In 1836 he invented the flat-bottomed rail for use in permanent way, though in true British tradition it was adopted in almost every other country in the world before its adoption here more than a century later! Sadly, financial stringency, though this time not that of U.C.L., intervened. There was then no limited liability act and in 1843, as a shareholder of the Sheffield, Ashton-under-Lyme and Manchester Railway, Vignoles was faced with what in those days must have been a vast bill of £8,000 as his share of the indebtedness of that railway. While restoring his fortunes he could not devote himself full-time to teaching and he resigned his chair in July 1844, but continued to give some lectures and advice to engineering students until the appointment of Herman Hicks Lewis in 1845. What might have been with Vignoles one can only guess, as he was elected F.R.S. in 1855 and President of the Institution of Civil Engineers in 1870.

This period, from 1844 and culminating in the Great Exhibition of 1851 and its Crystal Palace, is of very special significance for engineering education. Largely due to the patronage of the Prince Consort there was a great upsurge of interest in mechanical engineering. Thus the Institution of Mechanical Engineers received its Charter in January 1847. It held its first meeting on 27 January just after six days before King's College Engineering Society held its first meeting making it by some margin the oldest engineering society in the country. The effects on University

College were dramatic – in February 1847 Eaton Hodgkinson was appointed Professor of Mechanical Engineering, and in the same May, Bennet Woodcroft was appointed Professor of Machinery.

Hodgkinson's work on cast and malleable iron girders may be regarded as making him the originator of the modern I-beam and for this and equally fundamental work on long struts he had received the Royal Medal of the Royal Society and been elected a Fellow in 1840. He had also made the calculations on the strength and deflections of the huge tubular beams in Stephenson's Britannia railway bridge across the Menai Stait. The span of 450 feet was a huge advance on the 140 feet of the Newcastle High Level Bridge. The elegant tall towers were not just decorative but in fact show the designer's caution – they are high enough to permit the use of suspension chains if necessary. Hodgkinson served U.C.L. until his death in 1861 at the age of seventy-two. Like Hodgkinson, Woodcroft had been a pupil of John Dalton in Lancashire, where his inventive interests ranged from calico printing and tappets for looms to variable-pitch propellers. Patents for these and many others had proved so profitable that shortly before his appointment to U.C.L. he moved to London as a consultant. Whilst at U.C.L. he gave evidence on changes he believed necessary in the patent system – a new law embodying his proposals was passed in 1852 and that year he left to become the first Superintendent of Specifications in the new Patent Office. In 1853 he founded the Patent Office Library and in 1857 the Patent Office Museum, whose collections formed a nucleus for the Science Museum.

This flurry of professorial imports at U.C.L. in 1847 may well be seen as the trigger for the promotion to chairs at King's of Bradley and Cowper, two of the practising engineers appointed, along with Tennant the mineralogist, as lecturers before Hosking's arrival. Cowper died in 1852 but Bradley and Tennant retired in 1879.

At the time of the Great Exhibition of 1851, Britain held a clear world lead in manufacture but that lead was being rapidly eroded by the advance of engineering in Europe and America, an advance firmly based on technical education.

The only British chairs of engineering were at King's, U.C.L. and Glasgow but Germany was expanding its Technische Hochschulen, France had its array of Grandes Ecoles and Switzerland the Zurich Polytechnic. However, British products were seen by international juries as deserving most of the prizes at the Exhibition. In a glow of satisfaction at this success the Prince Consort was able in 1853 to press the government to form a Department of Science and Art under the none-too-friendly wing of the Board of Trade. One of its early actions was to provide subsidies for schools which taught the sciences and what we would call 'craft subjects' to a decent level and could demonstrate their success in properly conducted examinations. By 1872, 1,000 schools and some 3,600 pupils were involved in the scheme, though it was criticised as encouraging 'cramming' on syllabuses said to be too theoretical to be of value to industry. Almost by accident a supply of candidates for the emerging courses in higher education was being produced. That some such action was needed was shown when at the 1867 Paris Exhibition British exhibitors could muster only ten of the ninety top prizes on offer.

Lewis resigned his U.C.L. Chair in 1859, having found it necessary to introduce evening lectures to keep up numbers from the ever-growing, well-qualified group of pupil engineers in London. At that time there were, for example, four firms building locomotives in the London area and pupilships and premium apprenticeships were an orthodox route to senior posts in the engineering profession.

William Pole (1814-1900) succeeded Lewis at U.C.L. After a pupilship at Birmingham he came to London to manage a gas works. In 1844 he published a classical work on the Cornish Pumping Engine and, almost more significantly, discovered that he was colour blind. Fifteen years of experimentation in this field alongside his engineering culminated in his 1859 *Proceedings of the Royal Society* paper which led to his F.R.S. He spent the period from 1844-7 teaching in Bombay but the climate did not suit him. He returned to assist in the design of Birkenhead and Portland docks and to join Hodkginson in work on the Britannia Bridge. He opened his own practice in London in 1858 and a year later began eight years in his Chair at U.C.L.

Like so many of his contemporaries his interests were wide. He wrote on the 1844 comet, on musical instruments in the 1851 Exhibition – not unrelated to his work on the motion of fluids in pipes – on iron as a material of construction and on the diamonds in the Imperial State Crown. His book on the theory of whist ran to twenty editions. For the degree of Doctor of Music he wrote a vocal fugue in eight parts which was acclaimed by Wagner and was also responsible later for the original London degree regulations in music. In retirement he became Secretary of the Institution of Civil Engineers at the age of seventy-one and held the post for eleven years.

Pole's return to his practice in 1867 exemplified yet again the fragile nature of the finances of both U.C.L. and King's. He was replaced as Professor of Civil Engineering by the first electrical engineer to hold the post – Henry Fleeming Jenkin, a school friend of Clerk Maxwell and collaborator with Lord Kelvin. Kelvin credits Jenkin with the standardisation of the microfarad and Jenkin with Clerk Maxwell (then at King's) with that of the ohm. His work on the effect of cable capacity in limiting morse transmission speeds in marine cables won him election to the Royal Society. He succeeded in attracting to U.C.L. a large class of engineering students (including incidentally Alexander Graham Bell and Ambrose Fleming) and perhaps unwisely proposed a scheme for 'the extension and better organisation of the Department of Engineering in the College'. The money for this was not forthcoming and after only two years

Jenkin left (1869) to take up a Chair of Engineering in Edinburgh supported by public money. His successor Fuller was appointed 'on the understanding that his Courses of Lectures are to be delivered in the evening'. By 1874 Fuller had in turn left to take the publicly supported Chair of Engineering in Queen's College Belfast. The College's inability as a private institution to compete with those endowed from public funds is recognised in the U.C.L. Annual report in 1874.

The financial state of King's College was likewise precarious and the engineering department there was still very dependent on service teaching from chemistry and physics. Thus in 1868, when Whitworth Scholarhips were introduced, it was the stretching of the College's finances to re-equip its chemistry and physics laboratories that could be credited with the successes achieved in the first batch of awards. An almost final blow arrived when in late 1869 the roof of the refectory facing the river fell in, carrying away the floor below and burying the basement kitchen in ruins. By good fortune this happened in the early morning and nobody was in a building which would have been crowded a few hours later. The College could see no means of meeting the costs of rebuilding and when an appeal to the public failed a start was made by selling the colleges silver. Fortunately, the Clothworkers and Drapers Companies came to the rescue at this time.

Fuller's abrupt departure from U.C.L. was followed, after some delay, by the appointment of Alexander Kennedy in 1874. Kennedy, a Londoner, was educated at the Royal School of Mines and served an apprenticeship in marine engineering before designing compound steam engines in Jarrow. After a period of consultancy in Edinburgh and still only twenty-seven he took up his Chair at U.C.L. In his fifteen years he revolutionised the department and arguably the whole teaching of engineering. He wrote a classic text on the *Mechanics of Machinery* but the unique feature of his work at U.C.L. was his introduction of 'engineering laboratory' teaching linked to the theoretical work. He had built and equipped the first engineering teaching laboratory in the world and his concept of teaching was quickly adopted both here and in America. His fifty-ton tensile testing machine, built by Greenwood and Batty, was a giant of its time and quite remarkably accurate. It was still in use until U.C.L.'s New Engineering Building opened in 1961 and even then was significantly more sensitive than some of the new machines on the market. The first reliable torsion testing machine was built in the workshop and a small compound steam engine he had designed was given to the department. In 1889 he left with Burstall, his assistant, to set up his highly successful consultancy and was subsequently President in turn of both the Institutions of Mechanical and Civil Engineers.

Imperial College – a Beginning

The Kennedy years at U.C.L. saw also the early stages in the birth of Imperial College and pursuing that analogy the London Livery Companies must be considered the mid-wives at the birth. They had already become much involved in the training of apprentices and craftsmen and were helping to found technical institutes around the country. A committee of Masters and Wardens formed in 1872 led, by 1878, to the foundation under the presidency of the Prince of Wales of the City and Guilds of the London Institute for the Advancement of Technical Studies. Its two major objectives were to set up and conduct a range of qualifying examinations in technical subjects and to establish in the capital a Central Institution intended to offer technical education at more advanced level. The examination system at once became a great success and it still is. Finding a home delayed the founding of the Central Institution. The desired site in the City could not be found, so a start was made by developing Finsbury Technical College, just off City Road, where large numbers of students came for day and evening classes. H.E. Armstrong and W.E. Ayrton were appointed to teach chemistry and physics but their more important task was to plan the advanced courses for the new institution.

As to the site, the commissioners of the 1851 Exhibition had purchased eighty-seven acres in South Kensington 'to be used in perpetuity for the purposes of art and science' and the Department of Art and Science had by 1880 moved the major elements of its Royal College of Science (R.C.S.) and Royal School of Mines (R.S.M.) into the same area. John Kykes Donnelly, a Royal Engineer officer on secondment to the Department of Art and Science, was able to persuade the Livery Companies to agree that the new Central Institution should be on a site leased from the commissioners along Exhibition Road alongside the two state institutions. A handsome edifice in red brick, embellished by the emblems of Britain's main industrial cities and by the arms of the city companies, the Waterhouse Building was opened in 1884 by the Prince of Wales, who had laid its foundation stone in 1881. Thus the pieces of the future Imperial College were already falling into place.

Armstrong and Ayrton came over from Finsbury. Unwin, who became the first Dean, was appointed Professor of Civil and Mechanical Engineering and Henrici Professor of Mathematics. All were eminent in their own fields and at £1,000 per annum they were at the time very well paid – Kennedy at U.C.L. was appointed at just £200 p.a. The Guild's entrance examination was set at a level at least equal to London matriculation and thus included languages as well as technical subjects. Although four-year courses were advocated by Armstrong and Ayrton the fairly standard three year course was adopted. All students worked for the diploma of Associateship of the City and Guilds Institute (A.C.G.I.).

They could also sit separate examinations for the London University B.Sc. The new Central Institution could easily accommodate 200 day students but in the first year only six were recruited and only 122 by 1887. But by 1894 there were 208 full-time students and talk of an 'expensive white elephant' was silenced. The reputation of the Central Technical College, as it was now called, grew apace especially in electrical engineering to which Ayrton's department was now dedicated.

The University of London as established in 1836 was an examining body but the two colleges, University and King's, who were its *raison d'être* soon found that the essentially external degree system frustrated essential development of their courses. Although most Central students also took the London B.Sc. examinations they too found the system less than satisfactory.

The separation of teaching from examining and lack of representation of the two founding colleges on the Senate of the university led eventually in the early 1890s to the two old rivals petitioning to be formed into a new university to escape 'the stranglehold of examinations over education'. The battles of the 1830s were resumed and it needed the ministrations of two Royal Commissions to bring forward in 1898 legislation which preserved the University while going some way to meet the aspirations of the colleges. The university was now empowered to admit as Schools of the University such suitable institutions in London as applied. 'Internal' students from these schools were recognised as a separate category and for the first time teachers were represented on the Senate by members of their new Faculties: the Faculties of Arts, Science, Laws, Medicine and Engineering. From the eventual approval of the first statutes in 1900 the three schools in the Faculty of Engineering were University College, King's College and the Central Technical College.

This conjunction was achieved only with difficulty and mainly through the diplomacy of R.B. Haldane, M.P. The Central College, like the other Schools of Engineering, needed a say in the framing of new syllabuses and in the appointment of B.Sc. examiners. They also had a common interest in opening the door to future contributions from public funds (small Treasury grants to universities had begun in 1889). In the event, the Central College played a full part in drawing up the new statutes, the dual system of examinations continued and the University acquired the right of inspection, which continued, nominally on a quinquennial basis, into the 1950s. There is litte doubt that the college's retention of its right to appoint its own professors and the unanimous election of Unwin as the first engineering representative on the Senate finally overcame doubts in the 'Central' as to the wisdom of a link with the University. Perhaps, too, the move of the University administration and examinations staff into the nearby Imperial Institute in 1900 also helped to strengthen understanding.

The problems at King's were mainly concerned with the place of the

Department of Theology and of the religious test for entry to the College. The new Principal of King's, Dr Archibald Robertson, was the ideal man to find a suitable compromise: the religious test was retained for the theologians and for candidates for the A.K.C.L. but abolished for all others. Robertson's diplomatic skills were recognised when he was elected the first Vice Chancellor of the reconstituted University.

Haldane, having piloted the University of London Act 1898 through Parliament and having seen the new Statutes approved, visited Charlottenberg in 1901. He returned filled with the idea of a great centre of excellence for science and engineering in London. Abandoning the original notion of a totally new centre at South Kensington, he proposed that the Central, Royal College of Science and Royal School of Mines should combine to form a new and more powerful school of the University. Amazingly, he persuaded the recently formed Board of Education to hand over R.S.M. and R.C.S. to the new foundation and when the transfer was completed in 1905 they even came with a dowry of £2,000 per annum from the Treasury.

In a sense the City and Guilds Institute proved more of a problem since it was not anxious to pass over its own creation and property, the Central College, to the new organisation. However it was agreed that the City and Guilds College as it was now to be called, should become part of the new Imperial College, (I.C.). The basis of agreement was that City and Guilds College would be responsible for all teaching and research in engineering in I.C. but would relinquish to R.C.S. its teaching in chemistry, physics and maths. The relationship of the old 'Central' to the University was now to apply to the whole of Imperial College. To safeguard these provisions City and Guilds College was to be controlled by a Delegacy which had certain rights of veto over the actions of the governing body of I.C. or even of the University. The charter of Imperial College was eventually sealed in July 1907 and there followed a period of building expansion until the outbreak of war in 1914. This was made possible by Haldane's efforts in collecting nearly £300,000. An imposing new home for R.S.M. was eventually sited east of the Royal College of Music and linked to the new extension of City and Guilds which ran north along Exhibition Road. Completion of this was made possible only by a gift of £87,000 from the Goldsmith's Company – hence the name of the building. Unfortunately, the completion of the new building more or less coincided with the outbreak of war, so it was requisitioned and its first occupants were soldiers.

In parallel with these developments, the cautious moves towards chemical engineering led to undergraduate teaching of some aspects of engineering as applied to the chemical industry in the C. & G. Department of Chemistry. In fact, although a diploma course in 'chemical engineering' was advertised in 1885 the early diplomas were all awarded in chemistry and this situation continued until the Guilds Department of

Chemistry closed in 1912. However, it had always been intended to replace it by a Department of Chemical Technology which started to work under Professor Bone from Leeds who took up the Chair of Chemical Technology in 1912. He was fortunate to be available as he had booked on the fateful voyage of the *Titanic* but had cancelled because a colleague who was to have travelled with him had become ill. The embryo department was intially housed in the R.C.S. Department of Chemistry in two basement rooms with a third room available on Mondays and Fridays.

The End of the Century

Alongside these political manoeuvres on the administrative side engineering numbers were rising steadily at King's and unsteadily at U.C.L. and by the turn of the century both were approaching 100. There also emerged new areas of engineering teaching which are all-too-familiar to us today. Thus, in 1881 Vernon Harcourt, an acknowledged expert in river, canal, dock and water sewage engineering, joined Kennedy at U.C.L. as Professor of Civil Engineering leaving Kennedy to concentrate on his mechanical and electrical work, and in 1885 Ambrose Fleming, a former student, returned to U.C.L. as Professor of Electrical Theory (later Electrical engineering). His early interests were in electrical standards and power transmission – he proposed the formation of a National Standardising Laboratory, a proposal which helped the founding of the National Physical Laboratory. Undoubtedly, he is best known as the inventor of the thermionic valve which, especially as improved by Lee de Forest, made possible the success of the transatlantic radio link. With T.H. Beare, who had been Kennedy's assistant and who returned from Glasgow on his resignation, he was responsbile for the development of new laboratories fronting on to Gower Street by 1893. The civil and mechanical laboratories were then single storey and it is perhaps of interest that the present three storey building south of the new entrance building was constructed by direct labour with B.J. Lloyd-Evans – later himself Kennedy Professor – acting as clerk of works. The original roof was jacked up and the two extra floors built underneath – itself something of an engineering achievement in 1924.

A new development at one college (U.C.L.) seems again to have triggered something similar at another (King's). With Daniell, Wheatstone and Clerk Maxwell, electrical research had clearly been a fruitful field at King's. A gift of £6,000 from Lady Siemens in 1890 allowed the new Siemens Electrical Engineering Laboratory to be built; electrical engineering became a separate department and the brilliant John Hopkinson was appointed to the new chair. Sadly he was killed while climbing in the Alps in 1898 but fortunately he had brought with him to King's Ernest Wilson – 'Freddy' to all and a master of the flute – who was appointed to succeed him and remained until 1930. The combination of

Hopkinson, a theoretician said to break almost anything he touched, with Wilson, who could make almost anything work, was formidable.

Another appointee of 1890 was D.S. Capper, Profesor of Mechanical Engineering until his retirement in 1921. It was Capper who brought electric lighting to the King's laboratories in 1897; to his students and friends he brought much more.

Palace and College in the Mile End Road

During the 1890s decisive steps were taken which led to the emergence of the fourth major college in the Faculty of Engineering, Queen Mary College. Its roots in Alderman Bancroft's endowment, its transformation into the People's Palace in the Mile End Road, and the close association with the Drapers' Company, are fully described in the history of Queen Mary College, G.A. Moss and M.V. Saville, *From Palace to College* (1985). The interesting developments from the engineering point of view were that when, in 1894, the technical schools that were part of the People's Palace complex were reconstituted as the East London Technical College its staff included professors of engineering, physics, and art, who provided courses for University of London degrees; and that the Drapers' Company provided new engineering laboratories and workshops. During the next ten years there was rapid progress towards university level teaching: the first University degrees were awarded, and the professor of engineering (Low), chemistry, and physics, together with the newly appointed college professor of electrical engineering (J.T. MacGregor Morris), became Recognised Teachers of the University of London.

This paved the way for the restyled East London College to apply to become a School of the University of London in 1906. The University Senate welcomed this, recording its view that 'there should be a School of the University in the Faculty of Arts, Science and Engineering within easy reach of the very large population of the East End of London'. Extra facilities were provided by funds from the Drapers' Company and in May 1907 the East London College became the fourth School of the University in engineering for an initial period of three years. Perhaps the most notable technical feature of this 'probationary' period (if such it was) was the establishment in 1909 of an aeronautical laboratory in the theatre basement on the basis of a gift and the commencement of lectures in aeronautics by a distinguished young Old Student A.P. Thurston, later the first Briton to be awarded the D.Sc. in aeronautics.

By 1910 the E.L.C. could justly claim success (ninety-one degrees with twenty-one firsts and higher degrees) and asked the University for permanent recognition as one of its Schools. It was rewarded with an extension of five years before being formally admitted in May 1915 as a School of the University in the Faculties of Arts, Science and Engineering without limitation.

The problems of space and of governance arising from coexistence, on a confined site, with the recreational activities of the Palace were acute. These are fully described in *From Palace to College* but may be exemplified by the matter of the Palace Library. The Palace Committee could not afford to run it and was pleased in 1902 to hand over collection and furnishings to the Borough of Stepney; yet in spite of the College's desperate space shortage the Octagon stood empty until 1909 when it became essentially the Palace games room with tables for billiards, chess, draughts, cards and bagetelle. Not till 1920 did it become the E.L.C. library. Sadly the matter of space had to await the disastrous fire, which destroyed Queen's Hall in February 1931, to permit the first major steps towards solution, and one might say that the fire also burnt away the ties of governance between Palace and College and made possible the application of the College for a charter from which it emerged successfully in 1934 under its new name Queen Mary College.

The First World War and its Aftermath

The period of the 1914-18 war was a traumatic time in the history of the University as in the whole country. Student numbers fell to less than half in each of the colleges, workshops turned mainly to work in support of the war effort and buildings were requisitioned, delaying long-planned developments. In the case of the Goldsmith's extension at I.C., the delay was from 1914 to 1926. On the other hand, Chemical Technology had occupied their 'utilitarian' red brick box in 1914 and with it a 'temporary' hut that lasted until 1948. The postgraduate course continued through the war, and war-oriented fuel research even led to extra staff.

At U.C.L. the Civil and Mechanical Department had continued to lose professors to Scottish Regius chairs, Beare in 1901 and his successor Cormack in 1914. However, in 1907 a Faculty of Engineering had been formally constituted in U.C.L. with Cormack as its first Dean. Cormack's replacement, Coker, a student of R.C.S., Cambridge and Edinburgh, had taken a chair at the City and Guilds College at Finsbury in 1905. There he began his work on photo-elastic methods of stress analysis which he brought to early fruition at U.C.L. during the war in collaboration with the head of Applied Maths, Filon, who was later to become Vice-Chancellor. With Coker from Finsbury came a good deal of extra laboratory equipment. Fleming might ordinarily have retired in 1914 but stayed on through the war with his eventual successor Clinton before retiring in 1926, aged seventy-seven. Thus the departments at U.C.L. enjoyed considerable war-time continuity. Nevertheless, all three colleges, depending as they did very largely on student fees, finished the war in serious financial difficulty. To some extent the post-war surge of ex-service students and the raising of tuition fees to £60 per annum (a level which remained for the next forty years) restored a delicate equilibrium.

I.C., in particular, could not quickly bring into use the Goldsmith extension so that engineering numbers were only some 10 per cent above the 1913 level. U.C.L. and King's both moved briefly to about 50 per cent above their pre-war entry.

U.C.L. benefited from two major memorial benefactions for additional space, Viscount Cowdray and the Hawksley family, which provided new hydraulic laboratories and workshops. By 1926 private donations and grants from the L.C.C. saw the Gower Street building altered to give much needed space. Industry and the Ramsay Memorial appeal funded a new Chair of Chemical Engineering in 1923 with E.C. Williams, later a research director of Shell, as its first holder. The new building for the Department of Chemical Engineering in Gordon Street was the final expansion of space for the Faculty until the opening of the Torrington Place building in 1961.

Although both E.L.C. and I.C. had shown a limited pre-war interest in aeronautics, with a lecturer and wind-tunnel at E.L.C. and some specialist lectures at I.C., it was only the Zaharoff benefaction to the University of London in 1916 which triggered a major move. The chair was offered to I.C. but a classic demonstration of the lingering lack of trust between University and College led to delay and to Zaharoff asking for his money back in 1919. Luckily the panic reaction which this produced was inspired, and led to the appointments of Sir Richard Glazebrook, just retired from N.P.L., and of Leonard Bairstow, a first rate aerodynamicist. The resulting Department of Aerodynamics was initially part of R.C.S. and only became, even nominally, part of City and Guilds College in 1932. The East London College was bitterly disappointed that its own pioneering work in aeronatucs had not been recognised by the offer of the Zaharoff Chair but when Thurston left for the war N.A.V. Piercy took over and remained Head of Department until the 1950s.

Outside the Schools

The University of London legislation of 1898 and the 1900 Statutes had introduced Engineering and Economics as new Faculties in the University and with them the degrees of B.Sc. (Eng.) and B.Sc. (Econ.). The concept emerged of Recognised Teachers who, with the Appointed Teachers, made up the faculties and their subject Boards of Studies. This meant that for the first time the teachers could, as of right, influence syllabuses and examinations of the University. In addition to the Schools of the University there were within the prescribed thirty miles 'Institutions with Recognised Teachers' where well-qualified staff in well-found departments could be 'recognised' and so make their own input to the university. Students in engineering departments with such teachers could enter for the Internal B.Sc. (Eng.) degree whereas others had to enter as external students whose teachers had no direct contact with their colleagues in the University. Taking 1906 as an example: Institutions with Recognised Teachers included Battersea Polytechnic, East London College, Finsbury Technical College, Northampton Polytechnic and South West London Polytechnic. Battersea and Northampton Polytechnics eventually became separate universities (Surrey and City) whilst E.C.L. became Q.M.C. and South West Polytechnic became Chelsea College, both Schools of the University. Throughout the country technical colleges which could meet the University's standards submitted students for the external B.Sc. (Eng.) for which the syllabuses and indeed the examiners emerged from the University Board of Studies. The same applied to students in technical colleges throughout the Empire. There were undoubtedly problems in such a system of remote control, not least the time lag in introducing new ideas in the external syllabuses. However, in the engineering field, as elsewhere, it is my belief that the University can take pride in the opportunities which it provided for thousands of students and for the part it played in helping to bring university or polytechnic status to colleges throughout the United Kingdom and indeed around the globe. Many of the civic universities, all the technological universities and most, if not all, of the modern polytechnics sprang from institutions which orignally presented students for the degrees of this university.

The University also developed schemes of 'Special Relationship' mainly with university colleges at home and abroad in which staff from this university helped to develop existing or new departments. Such departments could make an input to their own syllabuses and also to the examining process. In engineering Southampton and Leicester Universities at home and the Universities of Khartoum and Ibadan in Africa come to mind as examples.

The Statutes of 1900, although they gave some influence to engineers in the schools of the University, came rapidly to be regarded as delaying development of syllabuses to meet new needs and in the case of U.C.L., King's and I.C. to a dual examination system, since each college still awarded its own diplomas or associateships alongside the university degree. Certainly some regarded these qualifications as superior to the degree. These and other problems of administration led to the formation of a government committee which produced the Hilton Young report in 1926. Even though Senate and Convocation voted to reject the report, the government legislated and the University of London Act in the same year imposed Commissioners to draw up the new Statutes. Fortunately, all parties in the university seemed to have learnt a lesson and the subsequent negotiations were reasonably amicable so that new statutes were in force by 1929.

From the point of view of the Faculty of Engineering it was fortunate that I.C., not being incorporated like U.C.L. and King's, could bargain away its right to have the final say in appointing professors and readers in return for the acceptance of its home-based A.C.G.I. examinations in qualifying its students for the B.Sc. (Eng.) degree. Thus the B.Sc. (Eng.) Special examination came into operation for I.C. in 1916 and shortly thereafter for U.C.L., King's and East London College. For many years this was a unique feature of the engineering schools in the University and gave them a flexibility and freedom denied to other faculties.

Quinquennial inspections of engineering departments, both internal and external, on behalf of the University continued until after the formation of the C.N.A.A. (Council for National Academic Awards) in 1964. I believe that these inspections were, in general, much to the advantage of the staff in departments concerned since they had an opportunity to seek advice and help from senior members of the University Faculty of Engineering and could often use the Inspectors' reports to influence their paymasters. The annual coursework displays, first at the Imperial Institute and later in the Gordon Square examination halls, were useful in providing contact, however brief, between university examiners and teachers preparing external candidates. Undoubtedly, there was often criticism in the Schools of the mechanics of the External B.Sc. (Eng.) and perhaps some of us who gave a good deal of time to it could have spent that time more profitably.

Between the Wars

Perhaps the most remarkable feature of the period between 1913 and 1939 was lack of change rather than change. In none of the three 1913 Schools of Engineering was there much change in student numbers once the post-war 1919-23 surge of entrants had passed through. Undoubtedly, the depression of the thirties which hit the engineering industry so hard was partly responsible. The U.G.C. came into being in 1919, but although the flow of public funds to the University *as a whole* increased fairly rapidly, as did funds from charities, the Faculty of Engineering was so badly underfunded that even when space became available it tended not to be properly equipped. Recurrent grants to departments were so low that sometimes equipment that they had been given could not be used. When I joined U.C.L. in 1946 from the comparative luxury of the Royal Aircraft Establishment (R.A.E.) many of the major items in use were over fifty years old and most, apart from those made in the workshops were over thirty years old.

The inter-war period was also one of remarkable stability among senior staff. For example, at City and Guilds Dalby (C. & M.), Dixon (C.) and (E.) each served for more than twenty years as departmental head while Mather (E.) served the College for thirty years. At U.C.L. the Fleming-Clinton duo actually spanned forty-nine years from 1885 while Coker (C. & M.) was head for twenty years. At King's too, Wilson (E.) was head for thirty-three years and Cook (C. & M.) spanned both wars whilst

Macgregor Morris (E.) was head for forty years.

Perhaps the biggest changes, though from a small base, occurred at E.L.C. In 1931 the college occupied one third of the Peoples' Palace site, but when the fire of 24 February destroyed Queen's Hall the College was unscathed. Even its basement accommodation under the Winter Gardens escaped. After elaborate negotiation a new site to the immediate west was found for the new Palace building and the College effectively secured a whole site. By 1934 it had its charter as Queen Mary College, its new Hatton Theatre and new electrical laboratories just about complete. A three phase plan to utilise the rest of the area was ready and a start had been made on converting the old theatre into the High Voltage Laboratory. This came into use in 1937 and made it possible to give a decent home to the aeronautical laboratory. All this meant that over the two wars the largest *proportionate* increase in engineering student numbers occurred at Q.M.C.

The Second World War

Some time before the outbreak of war in 1939 its apparent inevitability led to government plans to evacuate U.C.L. engineering to Swansea, King's to Bristol and Q.M.C. to King's College, Cambridge. I.C. was considered less vulnerable and, in spite of an unexploded bomb in the Guilds, so indeed it proved. Thus, engineering courses continued throughout the war – first with somewhat reduced numbers and later in more concentrated form but with increasing numbers.

The three collaborative enterprises were remarkably successful leading to respect and lasting friendships. G.T.R. Hill, who had succeeded Coker at U.C.L. in 1934 was seconded with a group of U.C.L. staff to form the Air Defence department at R.A.E. at Exeter and H.E.M. Barlow (E.) was seconded to R.A.E. becoming head of the Radio department. John Collins the head of Civil Engineering and several of his staff joined the forces. Thus the U.C.L. contingent at Swansea was led by Clinton's successor Kapp (E.) and Lloyd-Evans (C. & M.) sharing the teaching with local staff. Similarly, the Q.M.C. staff at Cambridge filled gaps in the host departments, especially in aeronautical and electrical engineering.

The King's-Bristol relationship was briefer but more intense since Bristol University suffered more severe bomb damage than King's itself and the King's library lost some 7,000 volumes in their temporary home. The King's staff was relatively complete and they had a separate base in the Merchant Venturers' College where a new course in radio and high frequency technology was introduced in the Electrical Department to meet urgent war-time needs. King's engineers returned to the Strand for the 1943-4 session in conditions of great difficulty. The strains of war had told heavily on the health of Professor Catterson-Smith, head of Electrical Engineering, who died in 1945, and on Professor Lobban, head of Civil

Engineering who retired at the end of that session after a long illness.

Post-War Recovery

Fortunately, I.C. had suffered little war damage and returned rapidly to almost normal operation. Student numbers were about 15 per cent pre-war level. Research had continued throughout the war and the research laboratories were full. Tizard's pre-war expansion plan could make progress once the shortages of materials in a hard-pressed economy permitted. The modest extension of Chemical Enginering began first and was complete by 1950. The Royal School of Needlework was purchased and became the Unwin Building but the much needed building for Aernonautical Engineering was delayed.

Q.M.C. had also escaped serious damage; it had rebuilt extensively after the fire and plans for further development already existed. Perhaps more significantly the new Principal appointed in 1944 ready to plan the return to the College in 1945 was Ifor Evans, a great tactician, planner and fund-raiser. Within a year the need to expand and to expand *west* of the new Palace was identified, with the site of the blitzed St Beret's the only other possibility. By 1946 total student numbers were up 50 per cent on pre-war at about 800 and a planning figure of 2,000 had been pencilled in.

King's College had suffered considerable damage. The most severe was a direct hit in the corner of the quadrangle which cut off part of the main building and left underground laboratories, cloakrooms and the slope leading down to the Embankment in a huge hole thirty feet deep and sixty feet across. In retrospect this may be seen as a blessing in disguise since nobody was hurt and the way was now open to rebuild and extend antiquated engineering laboratories under the south-east corner of the main building with a link to chemical engineering. Planning and rebuilding went on under the watchful eyes of three lively new or newish heads of departments: S.J. Davies (M.), A.D. Ross (C.), and J. Grief (E.).

At U.C.L. on the other hand there had beeen dreadful damage perhaps the most severe at any UK university institution. In the main building fire or blast had destroyed most of the library, the dome and much below including the Physics Department. The 1941 landmine which destroyed the Great Hall and much around it left the ten-year-old Chemical Engineering building a heap of rubble. The Gower Street buildings suffered extensive if superficial damage which left them open to the weather for much of the war. So serious was the damage that in the late 1940s the possibility of moving out of London to a green fields site was earnestly discussed as an alternative to the rebuilding of University College. There was, however, a remote silver lining since bombs had cleared the potential site for the new engineering building that would emerge on Torrington Place some twenty years later. G.T.R. Hill (M.)

was something of a genius: really an aeronautical engineer, he had designed and built a flying wing aircraft, which Roderick Hill, his brother and later Rector of I.C., who was a most gifted intuitive pilot could fly, but which was a handful for most others. He was a man of infinite charm and a flamboyant lecturer. After the war he was deeply involved in running Short Brothers of Belfast. Thus the day to day running of the department and its restoration were left to his deputy and in 1948 his successor, B.J. Lloyd-Evans. He got the Civil and Mechanical Laboratories working again and he it was who, when the government gave the universities first pick of surplus war equipment at a few pence per pound went personally with the college lorry to select the tools, instruments and machines on which the refurbishing of many U.C.L. laboratories and workshops depended for several years. Legend has it that he was adept at driving in over the weighbridge beside the driver and finding a good excuse to leave on foot. If so, then at around fifteen or sixteen stones that was good value! Barlow came back from R.A.E. in 1945 to a second Chair of Electrical Engineering and brought with him his eventual successor Alex Cullen and the whole new field of microwave engineering. John Collins came back as the first independent head of Civil Engineering and as the college's structural consultant and Hart, who went to war as a lecturer in surveying, came back in 1946 to take up a new chair in Photogrammetry and Surveying endowed by manufacturers of aerial survey apparatus and equipped mainly by the War Office and Colonial Office. Initially a part of the Civil Department the group became the fifth independent department in the U.C.L Faculty of Engineering some five years later. In spite of increased student numbers the other three departments somehow found room for Chemical Engineering until the Gordon Street building had been rebuilt and re-equipped in 1948. Research was of course very slow to restart in these overcrowded conditions.

The Golden Days

For all the Engineering Schools of the University the 1950s and 60s must now appear as a time of almost unfettered progress, though the problems of underfunding which have arisen so acutely in the 1980s emerged from time to time.

There was a firm belief in 1950 that this country required a major increase in scientific and engineering education and all four Schools responded with offers to increase student numbers if more space and resources could be made available. The government's response through the U.G.C. was to indicate an interest in a major expansion to 3,000 students at I.C. by 1962 and to reserve the island site at South Kensington for use by the College. Planning was complicated by the need to build, demolish and build in a way that always left the College fully operational. In the event Aeronautics and Chemical Engineering each occupied their two extensions in 1957 and 1966. The first stage of Mechanical Engineering became available in 1959 so that the old Waterhouse building could come down in 1962 to permit the completion of the Civil, Mechanical and Electrical buildings in 1965. The Computer Unit formed in that year grew and computer studies permeated the undergraduate teaching in all departments. By 1970 the Unit had become the Department of Computing joining Mathematics and Meteorology in the new Huxley Building in 1975. This saw the effective end of I.C.'s academic building programme planned in 1953.

At Q.M.C. the way to the west and to expansion was opened when, under Ifor Evans' prompting, the College acquired ninety-nine year leases first on the block west of the Palace to Bancroft Road and then by 1951 the two blocks beyond. And then in 1953 the Palace itself, unable to find a role in post-war conditions, came on to the market. A grant from the U.G.C. permitted its purchase and immediately the College had extra space and its planned new hall. Stage one of the new engineering buildings came into use in 1958 and the U.G.C. had accepted Q.M.C.'s offer to raise its total numbers to 1,500 if the building for stage two engineering, physics and chemistry could be completed. By 1962 the whole Bancroft Road complex was in use leaving the old buildings for redevelopment.

At last the four departments were properly housed. In 1960, in a development which has since acquired more than its original significance, an industrial site in Marshgate Lane was leased from the local authority to house a Department of Nuclear Engineering and, in particular, its reactor and to provide for large scale industry-related projects. The new complex was ready in 1966.

Ifor Evans, having launched the post-war expansion at Q.M.C. became Provost of U.C.L. in 1957, just in time to tell the U.G.C. that engineering could double its size at U.C.L. if a building making maximum use of the Torrington Place-Gower Street corner site could be built. When the U.G.C. failed to respond urgently he organised an approach to industry which rapidly raised enough financial support for half of the new building. Thus prompted, the U.G.C. matched this and promised equipment grants. The New Engineering Building, designed to be extremely flexible in use, was occupied in two stages in 1961 mainly by electrical and mechanical engineering, and in 1964 by chemical engineering and the rest of mechanical engineering. The old Gower Street buildings were converted to provide for civil engineering and for photogrammetry and surveying. Both were able at least to expand teaching and research, especially in research directly related to industry.

Subsequently it has proved possible to add two floors to the new building, both funded by industry, for occupation by electrical and electronic engineering. Space has also been found to house biochemical engineering, a new discipline derived from the joint efforts of chemical engineering and biochemistry.

The post war restoration of the King's engineering laboratories was largely complete by 1952 and it was clear that further major expanson could only be achieved on a new site. The old Doulton building across the river, and long a landmark for travellers approaching Waterloo Station, became available in 1961 and plans were made with U.G.C. approval for conversion to provide for 300 extra engineering and science students. But, to the intense disappointment of the whole College, the Treasury declined to make available the extra funds required.

Fortunately, development of the new Strand frontage and the acquisition and conversion of neighbouring properties has permitted useful expansion of engineering. For example, the new Macadam Building in Surrey Street provided new civil engineering laboratories. The merger with Chelsea College has provided strength in the electrical and electronic field. In mechanical engineering too, there has been 'structured collaboration' with U.C.L. to exploit the complementary strengths of the two departments. However, the King's School of Engineering is now the smallest of the four in the University Faculty, even though the King's merger with Queen Elizabeth and Chelsea Colleges forms the largest single unit in the University.

The Robbins and Saunders Reports

The Robbins Committee in Higher Education reported in 1963 and recommended a staged increase in student numbers which would involve London tripling its numbers by 1980. (In London actual internal numbers just about doubled.) Robbins saw London University as a cumbersome giant with some 25,000 internal and 28,000 external students. He saw the elaborate relationship between university-sized colleges and the central university as causing 'problems and inconveniences that call for investigation and remedy' and went on to say that if the University 'cannot satisfactorily and speedily resolve these difficulties for themselves we recommend that they should be the subject of independent enquiry'. For those who still remembered the Hilton Young Report urgent internal action was vital; when the consensus view turned out to be that the Federal University was worth preserving it was obvious that the structual modifications necessary for its preservation must be sorted out. Sir Owen Saunders then head of mechanical engineering at I.C. and chairman of the Academic Council chaired the committee charged to come up with solutions and the fact that R.E.D. Bishop, his opposite number at U.C.L., was another member, perhaps makes it less of a coincidence that the degree of autonomy on syllabuses and control of examining enjoyed by the Faculty of Engineering since 1926 was recommended for the whole University. In addition, the rules on recognition of teachers were liberalised and all teachers became members of Boards of Studies. The old Boards of Faculty became Advisory Boards.

As Dean I was chairman of the last of the former and the first of the latter and frankly I hardly noticed the difference except that, as a Dean who was not at the time an elected member of Senate, I attended Academic Council meetings by invitation. In addition Schools were given more freedom to introduce 'taught masters' degrees with the M.Phil as the research degree. These 'Saunders Reforms' were in place by 1966 and very much matched the mood of the schools of engineering. Course-unit degrees were considered at some length in the Faculty of Engineering but while the engineers *thought* about them the Faculty of Science adopted them with enthusiasm, enshrining odd-sized units. The University also attempted to change the nature of its senior management structure within the constraints of the existing University of London Act. Opposition made this impossible and led to the setting up of yet another independent committee under Lord Murray. I shall say no more on this as the direct outcome was in my view of little consequence to this Faculty.

Developments, 1966-85

The way in which the new course-unit degree regulations were framed, and the insistence that they must apply uniformly to all faculties and to all colleges involved, were seen by some, myself included, as an attempt to claw back to the central University some of the autonomy granted to the Schools by the Saunders reforms. It was not, therefore, until the 1970s that first Q.M.C. and subsequently King's and U.C.L. engineers felt that the advantages of flexibility could be grasped without serious disadvantages due to centralisation. In engineering, of course, the criteria in unit terms for the award of B.Sc. (Eng.) degrees had to be carefully prescribed to avoid problems with professional recognition. Certainly at Q.M.C. the system permitted a smooth transition to the four year B.Eng. degree involving industry which emerged from the 'Dainton' proposals of 1977. However, I.C. introduced these courses equally smoothly without a course-unit structure.

This trend to the involvement of industry and broadening of the curriculum was an important feature of several new courses. One outstanding example of industrial cooperation in sponsorship, project work and industrial training is the 'Total Technology' course in mechanical engineering introduced by Sir Hugh Ford in 1974.

Another example is the close collaboration between engineering departments at U.C.L. with the Royal Corps of Naval Constructors (R.C.N.C.) in providing a course leading after four years of integrated study and training to the B.Sc. (Eng.) and a further year to the M.Sc. (Eng.) in naval architecture and more recently marine engineering. The R.C.N.C. not only arranged industrial training and marine experience for their own sponsored students and others but seconded well-qualified members of the Corps to the College teaching staff, usually for three to five years. The senior corps member has always proved acceptable to the University as Professor of Naval Architecture. It was intended from the start that this collaboration should lead to related research and Professor R.E.D. Bishop envisaged developments into the field of offshore engineering. In the event these have been the basis of the joint I.C./ U.C.L. venture. This has involved the civil departments at I.C. and U.C.L. and U.C.L.'s Mechanical Engineering department in the formation of S.E.R.C.'s London Centre for Marine Technology with Bernard Neal (I.C.) as its first coordinator. There has been funding for new, comprehensively equipped laboratories and also a new M.Sc. (Eng.) course in offshore engineering.

At I.C. industrially based courses already mentioned have led from quite small beginnings within the mechanical engineering department in the field of management studies to a new Department of Management Science and more recently to a Department of Social and Economic Studies in the City and Guilds College. But perhaps I should not have breathed a word of this since these two departments fall within the purview of the Faculty of Economics.

Another interesting development, made possible by the Q.M.C. laboratories in Marshgate Lane has been the growth of the Electromagnetics Group of the Electrical department from its initial work on microwave antennae. And as so often happens with this sort of advanced work there has been feed-back into the undergraduate work with the opening of the Advanced Telecommunications Laboratory, based on joint U.G.C. and industrial funding, in which British Telecom has a special interest. Another sign of the times is the 1982 wind tunnel in the Aeronautical department at I.C. specifically designed for testing road vehicles and funded by Honda of Japan. There is a two-way flow and our engineering departments, along with their teaching and research, provide valuable services for industry and indeed for the community at large. For many years these services were on a small scale and were paid for, if at all, on an even smaller scale. More recently, financial stringency has had a remarkable effect in demonstrating that our engineering departments can help themselves and their Colleges to earn their way out of some of their troubles either by the provision of professional services or, indeed, by marketing their ideas and their products. All four Schools now have properly constituted units to organise work producing a multi-million pound income. Fortunately, our good example has been followed with more or less enthusiasm by our colleagues in other faculties either working in their own specialist fields or in multi-disciplinary projects. Engineering is often said to be undervalued by society, in status and rewards; but within the University it is rightly appreciated, and not solely for this ability to earn income from business and industry.

9

Music

Brian Trowell

There is no mention of music that I have been able to discover in the early history of University College,[1] where the idea of the University began, though its first professor of German, Ludwig von Mühlenfels, was a good friend of Mendelssohn. Perhaps the college's utilitarian atmosphere worked against what was then, in its highest form, an élitist art. The college does not seem to have offered music, theoretical or practical, as a subject in the evening classes on general topics that it arranged, for outsiders as well as for its own students, in the second half of the nineteenth century. As the college's financial circumstances and social life became more secure, however, we do learn of a Musical Society flourishing, if briefly, from 1871-6. Later, a Musical Director was appointed and since the late 1960s a remarkable series of semi-professional opera performances has developed.

In the early years of King's College – the Anglican counterblast to University College – things were very different. There was a chapel with regular services, and there were to be ordinands who would need some knowledge of church music. But the College was short of funds, and for some years no musician was engaged to direct the music. They simply hired a barrel-organ, which must have had a pretty limited repertory, and presumably needed only an unskilled hand to turn it. In 1835 though the College scraped up enough money to ask the barrel-organ's owner, a Mr Bryceson, to replace it with a 'finger-organ', with four stops and what Hearnshaw's history of King's College calls a 'Venetian shell front';[2] this we may safely interpret as a Venetian swell, of the louvred variety not the tidal, for making a crescendo or diminuendo. The organ was to cost £110, and for economy's sake it was to be build in the same case that had housed

---

[1] See H. Hale Bellot, *University College London, 1826-1926* (1929).

[2] F.J.C. Hearnshaw, *The Centenary History of King's College, London, 1828-1928* (1929), on which my account is largely based; certain material, especially for the period after 1928, is taken from Gordon Huelin, *King's College, London, 1828-1978* (1978).

the barrel-organ. As it turned out though, a medical student named Terry happened to have a spare organ, presumably a small chamber instrument, which he donated to his grateful college. The first organist was appointed on 13 November of that same year, 1835: Henry Bevington, doubtless connected to the family of that name who ran a London firm of organ-builders. A larger organ was acquired in 1848. In 1852 W.H. Monk was employed as director of the Choir, and two years later he took over as organist as well. In 1864, when the chapel was enlarged and beautified, he undertook, with some help, to raise funds for a still larger and better organ.

Monk was a learned musician.[3] He was to edit the music of *Hymns Ancient and Modern* (1861). He lectured on music at the London Institution and elsewhere. He became a professor at the National Training School for Music in 1876: this was the body which gave the impetus for the founding of the Royal College of Music. He edited much music for *The Parish Choir* series (from no. 40), produced a hymnbook for the Church of Scotland, and himself composed hymns. Other London colleges with chapels also instituted organist-choirmasters; at Royal Holloway College Dr Emily Daymond served as the first Director of Music (1887-99) and later became a member of the Board of Studies in Music.[4]

Some of Monk's earliest work, producing popular editions of vocal music, was undertaken in collaboration with another important Victorian musician, John Pike Hullah, who was associated with him at King's College.[5] Hullah had been Professor of Vocal Science there since 1844, retiring thirty years later in 1874. He was evidently responsible for general teaching in music and singing, much of it no doubt extra-curricular work for evening classes, but he also offered individual tuition and some classes for ordinands. Hullah was responsible for introducing into England Wilhem's method for training musically illiterate singers, a movement which created the market for John Curwen's later development of Tonic

---

[3] See the entries under his name in *Grove's Dictionary of Music and Musicians*, 5th ed. (1954), by Eric Bolm, and *The New Grove* (1980), ed. Stanley Sadie. Dr Bernarr Rainbow, whose long, valuable and unremunerated service as an 'Other Person' on the University's Board of Studies in Music deserves to be recorded here, pointed out to me after my lecture that I had omitted to mention Monk's debt to William Dyce. He would have met Dyce at King's, where the latter became Professor of the Theory of Fine Art in 1840. Dyce was a learned student of church music and plainsong, helped found the Motett Society in 1841, and published a sumptuous edition of John Merbecke's *Book of Common Prayer Noted* (1550) in 1843. Dr Rainbow has established that Monk became organist at King's as early as 1847, and that the Council instituted choral exhibitioners to sing a daily choral service in 1849; even in 1842 Edward Rimbault had noted in *The Musical World*, xvii, p. 375, that the service at King's was 'far superior' to that at Westminster Abbey or St Paul's; Bernarr Rainbow, *The Choral Revival in the Anglican Church 1839-1872* (1970), pp. 79ff., 220f., 310f.

[4] See M.J. Powell (ed.), *The Royal Holloway College, 1887-1937* (1937).

[5] See the editions of *Grove* cited in footnote 3 above.

Sol-fa; it has been estimated that between 1840 and 1860 some 25,000 choral singers and choirmasters passed through Hullah's classes at Exeter Hall and St Martin's Hall, which was specially built for him by friends and supporters. He was indefatigable in promoting music in schools and in March 1872 became Inspector of Training Schools for the United Kingdom. He was also a serious musical historian – a rare bird in mid-Victorian England – and he put his musical discoveries into practice (a happy characteristic of English musical historians). In the first four months of 1847 he conducted four historical concerts illustrating chronologically the rise and progress of English vocal music. His *History of Modern Music* (1862) and his book *The Third or Transition Period of Musical History* (1865) were developed from courses of lectures give at the Royal Institution of Great Britain. His God was Handel, whom he likened to 'an oak spreading all over English music'; he contrasted him suspiciously with Bach, who, he thought, addressed only the learned, asking 'but is Bach the Handel, even, of Germany?' His good work and academic knowledge were recognised by the award of an Hon. LL.D. of Edinburgh in 1876, and in the following year he was made a member of the Society of Santa Cecilia in Rome and of the Musical Academy of Florence.

One wonders whether Monk and Hullah gave William Schwenk Gilbert or Thomas Hardy a taste for music: the former studied at King's from 1853 to 1857, and the latter attended evening classes there in 1859-60. And one wonders whether the Wilhem method involved whistling: when the Prince Imperial, Napoleon III's son, came to King's College in 1871-2 to attend lectures in physics, his French tutor was disagreeably impressed on their first visit because the corridors were:

> filled with students who whistled incessantly. As in France I had never heard whistling except from the lower orders I had some doubts as to the young gentleman's designs. But almost immediately I became convinced that they were whistling for their own pleasure. 'It's not a school', said the prince to me, 'it's a nest of blackbirds' – but, just to be sure, the prince never entered into conversation with any of them.

This is an unusal glimpse of a college usually thought of as grave and sombre, dominated by ecclesiastics in subfusc. But King's College certainly had its lighter side. It is not I think generally known that Charles Wheatstone, the famous and inventive Professor of Experimental Philosophy at King's College from 1834 to 1875, ran a family business on the side in Conduit Street, manufacturing musical instruments. His latest biographer grandly lists his intellectual accomplishments: 'He discovered the principle of stereoscopy; he used his encyclopedic knowledge of the literature to spread scientific ideas; he designed ingenious electromechanical devices and pioneered precise electrical measurements'; and, he adds, 'he invented the concertina'.[6] Nearer our own time, another distinguished professor, S.W. Wooldridge, founded and ran a Gilbert and Sullivan Society which assumed a life of its own outside the college: it is said that he was remembered less for his geography lectures than for his impersonation of the Mikado. A more professional figure, perhaps, was the indigent refugee Russian who in the First World War, 'while receiving free medical tuition from the college, free books (from a special Jewish fund) and free meals (from a fund provided by the college staff), was found to be making a quite respectable income as a member of the Russian Ballet, in which his duties were on some days so engrossing as to allow him no time to come to college at all except for food'.

It was in King's that the first teaching Faculty of Music was eventually to be founded in 1964/5. There must have been a serious climate of opinion about music in the college at that time for it to engage in such a space-consuming and expensive innovation. As early as 1919 the College, aware no doubt of its distinguished musical servants in former times, had very nearly founded a Chair of Ecclesiastical Music; but funds proved insufficient. One of the chairs that *was* founded, though, was that of Ecclesiastical Art: it was occupied by Percy Dearmer, who made up for the failure to endow a musical chair by giving general lectures on music; he was also of course one of the trimvirate who edited the popular but thoroughly scholarly *Oxford Book of Carols* in 1928; his collaborators were Ralph Vaughan Williams and Martin Shaw. With the same pair, he had earlier edited *Songs of Praise* (1925). Another King's ecclesiastic who apparently had strong and serious musical interests was the theologian Professor H.J. White, who came to the College in 1905 and was interested enough to join the University's Faculty of Music in 1911 – the only University member – though he did not stay long.

The tuition of music and the giving of general lectures spread quite early on into other London institutions, particularly those associated with the education of women. In 1848, the ubiquitous Hullah founded the music class at the new Queen's College in Harley Street (which did not, however, develop into an institution of higher education).[7] In the following year, with four other King's teachers, he was seconded to Bedford College, then in Baker Street, as professor of vocal music, continuing until 1878;[8] from 1856 he took over the harmony teaching too, from no less a personage than the composer William Sterndale Bennett (who had also taught the pianoforte pupils from 1849 to 1855). Hullah was succeeded in both capacities by his King's colleague W.H. Monk, and Monk, in 1882, by Walter Parratt. 'Vocal music' probably meant a small

[6] Huelin, *King's College*, 13, citing B. Bowers, *Sir Charles Wheatstone* (1975).
[7] See Elaine Kaye, *A History of Queen's College, London, 1848-1972* (1972).
[8] See Dame Margaret J. Tuke, *A History of Bedford College for Women, 1849-1937* (1939).

choir of eight or so voices, for it was a class that ran alongside another on 'singing' – the latter no doubt comprising individual lessons. Other piano teachers were John Jay, Madam Alma Haas, the German wife of the Professor of Sanskrit at University College, and a Miss Harrison; Mrs Alexander Kaye Butterworth, mother of the composer George Butterworth, taught singing.

It is evident that Hullah was generally trusted by all his Bedford colleagues, not just the musicians, since his was one of three names suggested as professorial representatives on the Standing Committee of Professors proposed for a new college constitution in 1868. His young lady students provided the music and recitations for the Principals' weekly tea-cum-entertainments: the Misses Bostock and Thomas no doubt kept a careful ear on their progress, while profiting from their performing abilities.

When the university decided to admit women to higher education in 1878, King's College for Women was founded (later Queen Elizabeth College and now reintegrated with its parent institution).[9] Money was raised in 1883 and 1886 by mounting an ambitious play by the Professor of Classics at King's College, Dr Warr, called *Tales from Troy*. It was performed both in Greek and English. The scenery was designed by Sir E. Poynter, Walter Crane, Henry Halliday and Lord Leighton. The music was by Walter Parratt, Otto Goldschmidt and others. The actor-manager George Alexander seems to have produced, and among the distinguished cast were Mr and Mrs Beerbohm Tree, Mrs Andrew Lang, Jane Harrison, J.K. Stephen, Lionel Tennyson and Rennell Rodd. A sum of no less than £650 was raised. W.E. Gladstone came; Ruskin presented George Alexander with a superbly-bound Shakespeare; Professor Warr mock-modestly observed later on that the event 'for a whole season put my name on a level with Homer's'. After this, in the 1890s, music promised to become a strong feature in the College. Madame Haas taught piano here also, and her fellow recitalist Mrs Hutchinson looked after the singing; piano tuition was also given by Mr Dykes (not John Bacchus Dykes but his son, a less purple and passionate composer). This musical interest, however, faded after a time.

It was not only well-to-do young ladies who needed music. The choral movement started by Hullah in the 1840s had its roots in and owed its success to a growing body of avid amateur musicians. We find them signing up for the singing-classes that became so important in the early years of George Birkbeck's London Mechanics' Institute, found in 1823.[10] The *London Mechanics' Register* tells us that from its earliest years 'lectures and illustrations were regularly given on music'. *The London Saturday*

---

[9] See Neville Marsh, *The History of Queen Elizabeth College: One Hundred Years of University Education in Kensington* (1986).

[10] See C. Delisle Burns, *A Short History of Birkbeck College* (1924).

Journal for June 1839 informs us that an extra subscription was required for the classes in vocal and instrumental music, who gave occasional concerts in the theatre. By now, however, two-thirds of the clientèle were not working men but attorney's clerks, hungry for culture. The classes were only elementary, for this was before the Education Act of 1870 had placed music firmly in the school curriculum. In 1857, Dr Lyon Playfair (who invented the word-square cypher) was asked to report on the work of the Institute. He was not impressed. Learning took second place after enjoyment:

> the classes are cumbrous and inefficient . . . the teachers of most . . . are unpaid . . . Each class is . . . a little independent republic, appointing its own teacher, and electing a secretary for its especial management . . . The members appear to relish amusement more than instruction . . . The lectures . . . are as disjointed as one usually finds them at such places: the course for the present quarter is:

> The Atlantic and Ocean Telegraph
> A Gossiping Concert
> Christmas Books of Charles Dickens
> A Second Peep at Scotland
> A Broad Stare at Ireland
> Characters in Imaginative Literature
> The Romance of Biography
> Concert by the Vocal Music Class
> On the Apparent Contradictions of Chemistry
> Gems of Scottish Song
> On Explosive Compounds
> Entertainment by the Elocution Class

There were classes in music, vocal and instrumental, and in six other subjects. But music must have accounted for well over half the students, who numbered 700 in all, for 'elementary vocal music' alone accounted for 340 of them. It was not surprising therefore that Dr Playfair advocated radical changes.[11]

This popular appetite for music eventually led to the founding of the Guildhall School of Music, which was at first intended for amateurs. In some ways it is a pity that the University did not manage to find a way of building its higher musical instruction on this broad foundation, rather than trying to construct its degrees from top downwards. The more ambitious provision drove out the less. One effect of the much higher status that Birkbeck achieved from 1920 onwards was the dropping of

---

[11] Negley Harte's *The University of London, 1836-1986: an Illustrated History* (1986), to which I owe a great debt, states on p. 146 that in 1877 there were no fewer than 950 students in the music classes, as against 29 in the class preparing for the University's matriculation exam.

music as a taught subject, and the same seems to have happened at Bedford College. Musicians, of course, were thought to be strange people with peculiar, almost mystical abilities, hard to tie down to an academic syllabus. They were subject to eccentric bursts of emotion, as an old Birkbeck student recalled in 1922, looking back some decades in a letter to the *Sunday Times*. He was amazed that the silent reading of a score could produce an effect as violent as hearing the music performed:

It was in the old days of the Birkbeck Literary and Scientific Institution, and its then shabby home in the rear of a certain bank of blessed memory. I was in the reading-room, and among others seated near was the old Professor of Music attached to the Institution – I forget his name – and he had before him the printed score or part of some composition in which he appeared engrossed. I was about to leave, but before I could reach the door he hastily rose and fled past me down the staircase. I followed at my leisure and, as I neared the bottom, was pained to observe our old friend in the obscurity of a passage which many may remember as leading to the theatre. Here, in the darkest corner, he had taken refuge to hide the emotion with which, as I passed, his whole frame seemed shaken.

The professor's name, it seems, was John Henken. He seems otherwise unknown to fame, and I fear he was not one of those chosen to pronounce upon the idea of instituting degrees in music, first mooted in the university as early as 1849. Ten 'distinguished members of the musical profession' petitioned Senate for music degrees similar to those at Oxford and Cambridge.[12] The University did nothing immediately, beyond remembering to ensure that its Charter of 1858 empowered it to grant degrees in music. The matter was raised again by Convocation in 1862-3, and a committee was formed to draft proposals for a B.Mus. These were then circulated to 'all the leading musicians whose addresses could be found'. James Turle and others replied – quite rightly – that the Oxford and Cambridge degrees were poor models. They required no residence, let alone matriculation or Responsions or 'Little-go'; and although Ouseley at Oxford and Sterndale Bennett at Cambridge had recently set up an element of formal examination in music to go with the submitted exercise, very few candidates had yet taken it and the degrees tested little save academic composition. George Macfarren objected to 'craft' degrees: 'all the reasons that prevail against conferring degrees in painting . . . prevail equally in regard to music', he said. (He changed his tune when he became Professor of Music at Cambridge.) John Hullah, on the other hand, insisted characteristically on the practical element: candidates 'should be called upon . . . to exhibit their skill in vocal or instrumental

[12] For this account of the early attempts to institute degrees in music I am much indebted to Professor Ian Spink's article '100 Years of the B.Mus.', University of London *Bulletin* no. 43 (Oct. 1977), p. 6f.

performance'. Sir F.A. Gore Ouseley, who was even then reforming the Oxford Faculty, thought optimistically that the degree 'would stimulate many dabblers in music to the mastery of the science and art.' Cipriani Potter, ex-Principal of the Royal Academy of Music, and sadly experienced in trying to combat the then common illiteracy of even good young performers, doubted whether many musicians would be able to pass the matriculation exam. The University was indeed daunted by the difficulty of finding candidates of sufficient general culture to offer Latin and two other foreign languages, English, history, geography and mathematics, with either natural philosophy or chemistry: once again, nothing was done.

In 1822-3 the foundation of the Royal Academy of Music had at first raised hopes that it would be possible to provide a decent general education for performing musicians.[13] The Academy's first principal, William Crotch, was a learned man as well as a composer and executant, and a noted lecturer on the history of musical forms and styles. His *Specimens*, a historically chosen collection of examples of music, are still a useful 'quarry' today.[14] The Academy's Prospectus of 1822 engages that the young musicians shall at least 'study their own and the Italian languages, writing and arithmetic', and an early timetable shows at least four or five hours set aside for this purpose. Almost immediately, though, it was resolved 'to reduce Italian (and dancing) for those not destined to the stage or singing'. Financial exigency imposed still further cuts: 'some of the subordinate branches of education (especially those not appertaining to music) were lopped off, but this was too slight a relief'. This made something of a mockery out of Lord Burghersh's original plan that 'the education should be general, and not restricted to particular departments of the science and practice of music', and that the Royal Academy 'must be considered as a place offering general instruction to all those who seek it.' The same difficulty was to crop up later on, as we shall see, at the Royal College of Music; and it is still a familiar problem today. It is musical expertise, and competitive expertise at that, which really counts in a college of music; talent might appear in a low and then quite uneducated class of society, and the time for professional training was short. What is more, the growth of large orchestras now required larger numbers of rank-and-file musicians; the new music of Berlioz or Wagner demanded a higher level of performing skills, and among these was the ability to play ever more difficult music at first sight. Such fluency came only with long practice, yet it was vital to the precarious existence of a free-lance instrumentalist. Students and teachers both knew that in a limited period of training the reading of musical notation must take precedence over the reading of English prose and poetry. Superior education and the

---

[13] F. Corder, *A History of the Royal Academy of Music* (1922).
[14] *Specimens of Various Styles of Music* (*c.* 1808-1815).

acquisition of social graces were necessary only for those who would perform in the salons of the wealthy: solo singers, higher-class pianists and similar virtuosos.

But the 1870s ushered in the revolutionary Education Act, which placed sight-singing and music on the national curriculum; and the simultaneous revival in Anglican church music, coupled with a growing belief in self-betterment and a determination to do something to improve social conditions – all these factors were brought to bear on the question of musical education by one man of remarkable vision and energy.

This was the Revd. Dr. Henry George Bonavia Hunt, the founder and first Warden of Trinity College of Music. He had studied at Kings' College and Christ Church, Oxford, though I must own with shame that neither of the two otherwise excellent histories of King's College mentions him; nor does the *D.N.B.*[15] Trained for both the Church and the Law (at the Temple), he took the Oxford B.Mus. in 1876 and the Dublin D.Mus. in 1887. Ordained in 1878, he held several London curacies, finishing up as vicar of St Paul's, Kilburn, where he founded Kilburn Grammar School; he was an ardent choralist, composed music, and wrote a *Concise History of Music* that reached nineteen editions;[16] he was a Fellow the Royal Society of Edinburgh and for many years edited *Cassell's Family Magazine* and another called *The Quiver*.

Trinity College grew out of the interests of the London Church Choral Association and Church Choral Society, and the discussions that Hunt engaged in with various concerned Anglican organists: Sir John Goss, E.J. Hopkins of the Temple Church, George Elvey of St George's Chapel, Windsor, George Garrett of St John's College, Cambridge, and Henry Smart. Its first President was the Heather Professor at Oxford, Sir F.A. Gore Ouseley. The college was to teach music, perform music and test the musical abilities of students who were all to be male members of the Church of England. Many other distinguished Anglican organists lent their efforts and goodwill, men who had already come together in 1864 to found the College of Organists (though this was and remains purely an examining body and did not teach). In 1875 Hunt's college was incorporated as Trinity College, London; within two years the restriction to male Anglicans was dropped and the college and its examinations were thrown open to all, 'without restriction of sex or creed'.

Unlike the Royal Academy of Music, Trinity College developed a series of public examinations on a national scale, with dozens of local centres; these were seen as a means of educating both leaders of taste and a broad constituency of performers for them to lead. The initiative seems all the

---

[15] My account of him is drawn from Harold Rutland, *Trinity College of Music: The First Hundred Years* (1972).

[16] A modest little 200-page handbook, first published in 1877, its sixteenth edition, 'revised to date', appeared in 1902.

more remarkable when we consider that there were as yet no school examinations in music and no means of training and assessing school music-teachers. At the same time, again unlike the Royal Academy, Trinity College established as part of its central teaching and examinations a general arts training for teachers and choirmasters in its academic department; the arts subjects had to be passed before a candidate, however musical, could qualify as a licentiate. In 1921 Sir Wilfred Collet, by then Governor of British Guiana, wrote a letter describing his early training at Trinity College several decades before. 'Many young men attended', he wrote, 'to fill up gaps in their musical education. Trinity College was the only institution requiring educational qualifications as a preliminary to the grant of diplomas. At the same time it provided teachers with an Arts course. For while the L.T.C.L. of Trinity College had a prestige over the B.Mus. of Oxford or Cambridge, as holders of the latter might be devoid of any but the most primitive education.'[17]

The college had brought this complete arts course into existence by 1879, with forty-one professors and lecturers (there was even a Physiological School for the study of the vocal and aural organs, associated with the Central London Throat and Ear Hospital). It had three halls of residence and a lively social life. In 1881 the subject of its Gold Medal Essay prize, instituted the year before, was 'The importance of General Culture to the Musician'. By then its Honorary Fellows included the poet Tennyson, the painter Lord Leighton and the historian J.A. Froude, and in 1887 the poet Browning joined them. The College proved extremely successful and prosperous and ran its affairs – until recently – without any public subvention, deriving almost all its income from examination fees. It evoked jealousy. Doubts were raised about the validity of its legal constitution and the qualifications of its teachers and administrators. These were easily quelled, but the College girded its loins and created a Senate of forty-six to protect itself, including five M.P.s and four lawyers.

This was the college whose Council, in February 1876, petitioned the Senate of London University to reconsider the question of instituting degrees in music, on the grounds that the general improvement in education ought now to produce a sizeable number of adequately qualified candidates. The sixty signatories included Bonavia Hunt, the composer Sir Julius Benedict, the conductor Sir Michael Costa, the organists Sir John Goss, Sir George Elvey and Frederick Bridge, and Arthur Sullivan. A Senate sub-committee now pronounced itself in favour of degrees in music, stressing in its report the particular role that Trinity College had played in reopening the discussion, 'a body which has been

[17] Rutland, *Trinity College*, p. 14.

formed to promote musical education on the basis of general culture'.[18]

Draft proposals for the degrees of B.Mus. and D.Mus. were drawn up by William Pole, Professor of Civil Engineering at University College, in consultation with the Professors of Music at Oxford, Cambridge and Dublin. (Pole had an Oxford D .Mus.; he composed, and was for thirty years organist at St Mark's, North Audley Street.)

The details of the B.Mus. were published in 1877. The general impression was that the syllabus was too demanding. The matriculation requirements were as stiff as ever. After that came an exclusively theoretical 'First B.Mus.' examination, with a good deal of acoustical theory and a paper on the general history of music, 'so far as it relates to the growth of musical forms and rules' – in other words, musical history was seen purely as a history of the development of musical style and theory. The 'Second B.Mus.' examination, taken a year later, covered the notes themselves: harmony, counterpoint, instrumentation, with composition as an approved exercise, and further technical history, tested through set works. A D.Mus. was to follow later, with 'further on the same lines'. This was intended to be a 'higher distinction than the certificate of any purely professional body', needing 'evidence of general culture as well as of special proficiencies'.

As might have been foreseen (and no doubt was foreseen by the Oxbridge advisers), the syllabus proved too like those of Oxford and Cambridge, but harder, since it added the problems of matriculation and acoustics. Few candidates attempted it, and fewer passed. In one sense this was to be expected: since the University was at that time purely an examining body, a degree-granting mechanism validating the results of the teaching done by the constituent colleges, a higher failure rate was nothing unusual. In the 1860s nearly half of all candidates for all degrees failed. Of eight candidates who attempted the first part of the B.Mus. in 1877, five passed, three with first and two with second class honours. It took three more years – not one – before any of them passed the second B.Mus. to gain the degree. Our first Bachelors graduated in 1880, W.H. Hunt and H. Moore. In 1885 Hunt and another man, A.H. Walker, passed the higher hurdle of D.Mus. One wonders where they came from and where they were taught. At least Walker, I suspect, was a 'Trinity man'; he had a Cambridge B.A. and was thirty when he took his D.Mus. He became a lecturer and examiner in Acoustics at Trinity College, so his hard work in that area was not wasted; he also became Tutor in Music at the University's Correspondence College, was a teacher of pianoforte and composition, and lived at 62 Enmore Road, South Norwood, S.E. We know this because he achieved the distinction of being included in John Warriner's *National Portrait Gallery of British Musicians* (*c.* 1896).

A sampling at five-yearly intervals reveals how little sought-after and

[18] *Ibid.*, p. 15.

how difficult the B.Mus. was.[19] In 1885, one candidate attempted it and failed. In 1890 only one of five candidates passed. In 1895 four tried: none succeeded. In 1900 two out of three satisfied the examiners. This two-thirds pass rate was better than the general pass rate for all London University Bachelor's degrees, for in the same year only 472 candidates passed out of 890.

Dissatisfaction with the structure of the university had been growing, however, throughout this period. Irresistible voices, led by University College and King's College, were clamouring for a teaching university, with funds for lectures, a real professoriate, and examinations harnessed closely to the courses taught. Two Royal Commissions considered the problems, in 1888-9 and 1892-4. The so-called Gresham report of 1894, on the proposals for a teaching university, proved to offer exciting possiblities for music. In February 1893, the six commissioners, headed by the Earl Cowper, took evidence from (in the following order): the Royal College of Music, represented by its Director Sir George Grove, and Lord Charles Bruce for the governing body; the Royal Academy of Music, represented by its Principal, Alexander Mackenzie, with Thomas Threlfall for its governors; and Trinity College, represented by Bonavia Hunt, recently retired as Warden, and Dr Edmund H. Turpin, the new Warden.[20]

The long sessions comprised some 600 questions and answers, and the minutes of evidence, taken down verbatim, occupy twenty-four closely-printed folio pages. It is a fascinating document, enormously revealing about the aims and methods of the three institutions concerned, about their uneasy relationship to each other and the minds and personalities of the principal speakers. It deserves to be reprinted in full as a most important source of information about the philosophy and methods of musical education in this country; yet I have never seen any reference to it in any book or article concerned with the development of musical studies in Britain, and its existence has evidently remained quite unknown to subsequent historians of the three institutions concerned. Grove and Mackenzie were very guarded and sometimes disingenuous in their replies to the extremely shrewd questioning of the commissioners, which came mainly from Earl Cowper. The Academy had had only ten years to accustom itself to the existence of a powerful rival in the very well-endowed and well-connected Royal College, and was still concerned about its own inefficiency and relative poverty. Both the Academy and the College must have been alarmed at the fact that Trinity College was to give evidence on an equal footing with themselves. The new Guildhall School of Music, headed by Joseph Barnby, was also a possible threat and, though it was not asked to give evidence, would be recommended for

---

[19] Figures are taken from Harte, *University of London*, p. 139.
[20] *Report of the Commissioners Appointed to Consider the Draft Charter for the Proposed Gresham University in London* (1894); see pp. xlvii, 975-99.

inclusion in the University with the others. Both the Royal schools wished to preserve their independence at all costs.

Grove, though a great lover of music and a musical lexicographer and editor, was not a professional musician but an engineer; he was by now in poor health, and sometimes floundered or veered off the point when the questioning grew technical or explored too precisely his College's possible future relationship with the University. It would appear from his and Lord Bruce's replies, and indeed from some of Mackenzie's and Threlfall's for the Academy, that they had never seriously discussed what the purpose of the Commission was, that they had no idea what the University was, or what a Faculty of Music or a degree in music might do – although the Royal College's charter actually empowered it to grant its own degrees. Grove, a strictly practical man, disliked the whole notion of degrees in music; 'They are mainly theoretical,' he said; asked if they are of much advantage, he replied: 'the world seems to consider them to be of advantage, or so many people would not apply for them; but I have never been able to see the advantage.' Cowper: 'You do not yourself, as a practical man, see much good in them?' – 'No, I do not indeed; probably from ignorance.' Yet he saw that a *new* type of degree, drawn up by a Faculty made up of professors from the colleges of music, might be practical as well as theoretical. If an entirely practical degree were proposed, one feels he would have been interested: 'why should you not give a man a degree for being an accomplished performer?' – 'Those who get degrees at present are not often really accomplished. They write exercises in eight parts, and their exercises are often put on a shelf and never heard of afterwards. The great musicians as a rule have not gone in for degrees . . . I have always looked upon these degrees rather with astonishment.'

He became confused and escaped into lexicography when the question of musical learning and science was discussed, being much more at home with 'rules' than with 'sciences'. A long and irrelevant disquisition on early English music contains the totally erroneous statement that 'our English madrigals were as much sung in Italy then as Italian madrigals were sung here'. The British upper middle class is excoriated at one moment for its alleged indifference to music and at the next for spending vast sums on importing foreign music. But these are side-issues. His other really interesting replies relate to the general culture of the musician: however one may encourage a performer's cultural education, not much can be done by syllabus and legislation, Grove thought, except in a few unusual cases – though singers need some polishing. There is not time, and technical education must start at too early an age. No test of literacy is asked of students on entry to the college and general culture, though advantageous to a leader of taste, a composer or conductor, can be insisted on only at scholarship level – that is, for the solo virtuoso.

The Royal College offered lessons in general knowledge from a schoolmaster two evenings a week. Grove gave an extraordinary answer to the question, 'I suppose for singers at all events the knowledge of foreign languages is very material?' – 'As far as the sound goes . . . At the strong recommendation of Madam Jenny Lind Goldschmidt, who was our first chief professor of singing, we have an Italian class, but though instituted for pronounciation, grammar is too much taught at it. German and French we have not yet tried. I am afraid of overworking the children. They sometimes break down as it is.'

When Cowper asked Grove why a University should not give a *diploma* in practical music without the arts trimmings, just as it might offer instruction toward specialised practical engineering diplomas, Grove, himself an engineer (but not university-trained), simply could not grasp the question or the opportunity offered; he drifted away from the point and rambled off into irrelevance about the totally absorbing nature of music. But why need he have worried? The University appeared to have no money, and no additional financial resources were on offer. The new and wealthy young College's line was to wait and see, to exploit what little advantage might be gained from any association with the University; with patrons such as the Prince of Wales, why fear Earl Cowper?

Mackenzie's evidence for the Academy was also rambling, though he was evidently a most likeable man. It is similar to Grove's in failing to engage with many of the questions, but Mackenzie seems to have been much more aware of the problem of providing a true and broader higher education for the Academy's students, and the Academy seems to have been better at coaxing them into it. What he appeared most to fear, underneath his actual words, was a re-opening of the old question of an amalgamation with the College. Himself a D.Mus., he knew what a university was, and at one moment offered suggestions for making degrees more practical, a process which Edinburgh University was apparently proposing to institute: 'I see there that the Musical Bachelor and also the Doctor of Music will be compelled to undergo an examination on some instrument. That is the first case I have heard of. I was rather surprised, and I have hardly taken it in, but I saw that as being quite a step in a new direction. I think that some such test is really necessary. The present examinations are entirely based on the scientific side of music, and really give no clue to what a man's innate talent is . . .' A few questions later, however, he affected to despise the musical degree in principle: 'Many of us do not see the necessity of the thing, but it exists, and I am afraid it will never be rubbed out probably. It is considered absolutely necessary for a cathedral organist to have a degree.'

And indeed the attitudes and techniques of the London degrees, which did not change much after all this until the 1960s, were to continue for a long time to inhabit a curiously artificial sound-world, increasingly divorced from the real concerns both of contemporary music, and of scholarly developments in historical, theoretical and analytical thinking.

Bonavia Hunt's evidence was quite different; it reveals real and compelling intellectual command and an unshakeable belief in the importance of general culture to the practising musician. I have no time and no need to go into his vision in detail over again; but Trinity College would greatly have liked to form the closest possible association with the University, whether as a School or through a Faculty and Board of Studies comprising recognised teachers from its own and other institutions. Hunt rattled off very impressively the University matriculation exemptions that Trinity College accepted as equivalents to its own academic courses, pointing out that a great many of his candidates for licentiateship were already graduates of the universities. As many as seventy licentiates out of 160 were graduates. What he was after was the cultivated leader of musical taste, the new and intellectual kind of musician represented by the German Klesmer in George Eliot's recent *Daniel Deronda*.[21] He rammed home the necessity for a residential London degree, pointing to the great, indeed unique, advantages offered by the musical life and general culture of a great metropolis, and asked 'once and for all that the Faculty of Music should be made a real living thing'. He would have welcomed a professoriate validated by the University. He saw the social as well as the educational advantage of his students being able to mix with those of other disciplines. He deplored the low regard in which existing university music degrees were held, though Trinity College had prepared many B.Mus. and D.Mus. candidates for Oxford and Cambridge, and he saw the opportunity for change and new vigour; he even predicted postgraduate developments. He had nothing to fear from university control, or from serving on a faculty with teachers from the Royal Academy and Royal College. Why, he even approved of the Guildhall School of Music, and would have liked them in the scheme as well! It was plainly the testimony of this very far-seeing, clear-thinking and thoroughly modern-minded man that persuaded the Commissioners to a view of the University's role in developing musical studies that proved far too optimistic, given the seniority and influential patronage of the institutions that they were dealing with. They recommended at first that not only the Royal Academy, Royal College and Trinity College, but also the Guildhall School, should actually become Schools of the University; but the two former were not prepared to do so 'except upon conditions which it was not within the power of the Commissioners to accept'. The

---

[21] Julius Klesmer, however, gains social acceptance precisely because he is not English. Well paid as a pianist and composer, he lives like an honoured guest in a wealthy household; no native English musician could have aspired to such a status. A 'felicitous combination of the German, the Sclave, and the Semite', his genius forces only a reluctant admiration from one astonished gentleman: 'What extreme guys those artistic fellows usually are!' Though no 'gentleman', Klesmer is nevertheless eventually permitted to marry an heiress. The contrast with the poor man Elgar's slow climb to social acceptance could not be more striking.

music colleges were therefore left outside the University, as were also, in law (and for similar reasons), the Inns of Court. Nevertheless, a Faculty Board of Music and a Board of Studies were created.

The effect of this on the music degrees was slight, and Hunt himself would not, I think, have suggested anything very different for the historical and technical syllabus: my enthusiasm for his attitude stems not from his musical ideas but from his evident openness, receptivity and readiness to envisage a structure capable of rapid development. The new Faculty Board met for the first time on Friday 12 October 1900.[22] It consisted of Sir Hubert Parry for the Royal College, Charles Villiers Stanford for the Royal Academy, Sir Walter Parratt (who had once taught in the University), Dr E.M. Turpin for Trinity College and Mr J. Higgs, also from Trinity, as Secretary; he was later elected Dean. Parry was to be the Senator for the Faculty, along with J.W. Sidebotham, a Trinity man, as member for Convocation; Sidebotham was not on the Faculty, but in 1900 he was a prime mover of an Act in Parliament to regulate music-teaching and teacher-training. With such powerful representation of Oxbridge and the senior music colleges in Parry and Stanford, and with the Trinity representatives in a minority, it is perhaps not surprising that the Board of Studies proved so unwilling to open up the music degrees for potential new developments. Music continued to be organised entirely by representatives from the Institutions having Recognised Teachers, so that there was hardly ever a purely university figure involved in the Faculty's deliberations.

The degrees were reviewed and slightly altered; but the Report of the Board of Studies in Music of 7 June 1901 desired little change and was evidently concerned to damp down all consideration of reform and to avoid interference from the University. Nothing in the syllabus and teaching was to be spelled out in any great detail, and the three teaching institutions were to rule supreme and alone, with no separate university provision for music whatever. Acoustics were to be removed from the B.Mus. syllabus, perhaps put into the matriculation requirements and even there with an alternative; the subject has proved, says the Board, 'purely fallacious'. The scheme for the musical part of the exam remained much as it was, but now provided a steady progression through the intermediate examination to the final B.Mus. in all areas of music and a little history and analysis. Harmony, counterpoint and 'free composition' each required an hour's study a week; history and analysis only twenty minutes each, to be certified by the candidate's institution. The exercise was to be an independently-composed piece lasting from twenty to forty minutes; it must be written for voices with string accompaniment, using

---

[22] The following account of the Faculty of Music since 1900 derives from the minutes of the Faculty (Oct. 1900-Oct. 1927; Oct 1946-present) and of the Board of Studies in Music (since Jan. 1901), preserved in the University Library.

real five-part vocal counterpoint with examples of imitation, canon and fugue, and 'must be a good composition from a musical point of view'. No mention was made of the standards by which the musical offerings were to be judged, but one may deduce from the theoretical publications of future teachers and examiners, such as C.W. Pearce and Percy Buck, that the norm was the language of purely academic harmony and counterpoint, not founded, except as a distant memory, on any actual musical style. (It was in fact a debasement of the teaching of Fux, who had codified the ancient heritage of Palestrina's church style and interpreted it in the eighteenth century for the new age of florid and instrumental counterpoint.) The D.Mus. simply carried the same notions to a more complex level. The maintenance and defence of this tradition continued to be the principal concern of the Faculty and Board of Studies for over sixty years; music failed to share in the extraordinary growth of the University, or to gain extra resources, or to develop significant research teaching.

One suspects, however, that Trinity College was not content. In 1902, in honour of the recent coronation and in commemoration of its own thirtieth anniversary, Trinity graduates subscribed £5,000 to endow a part-time Professorship in Music, the King Edward VII Chair, whose first holder was Sir Frederick Bridge, organist of Westminter Abbey. The Professor gave a few lectures and took part in the deliberations of the Faculty Board (which were on occasion cancelled because inquorate, as indeed was one meeting of the Board of Studies, which had to reduce its quorum from six to four). The Professor had no special status, and indeed was not appointed for life but came up for annual re-election, though a three-year term was recommended. He was not empowered, let alone required, to act as an examiner for degrees (there were only two examiners); and though this step was recommended by the Board of Studies in 1904, in answer to a question from the University, the minutes of 1910, 1917 and 1925 show that the change had still not been implemented. Trinity continued, nevertheless, to improve the status of university studies and to increase the number of students. As there were no University or School scholarships for music students, Trinity College provided funds for no less than eighteen three-year scholarships offered for open competition to matriculated students in the universities of Oxford, Durham and London, to enable them to prepare for the B.Mus., with tuition and all examination and other fees paid. This valuable facility was eventually dropped when funds ran out.

The Board of Studies continued on its path of masterly inactivity. When in 1909 the University asked if there should be more professorships and readerships in music, created by conferment of title, the Board replied that they thought it 'inadvisable to confer the title of Professor of Music on any individual', and actually refused to appoint the necessary Faculty Board of Advisors. None of the Faculty's 'Recognised Teachers' received a salary, of course, or any money for administration or research: only their teaching was paid for, at an hourly rate. Examiners were paid per capita. We should certainly acknowledge how much money the University saved, over many decades, by its reliance on these teachers.

In answer to a request, also in 1909, for provision of resources for the teaching of music, the Board replied that 'inasmuch as the teaching of music is in the hands of the institutions whose teachers are 'recognised' by the University, the responsibility of providing adequately for that teaching rests with those institutions, and it is unnecessary for the University to make any special arrangements in connection with the subject'. Another chance missed. Trinity's scholarships were perhaps in part intended as an initiative towards provision of this kind.

In 1919 the Board of Studies in History wanted to add to the B.A. Pass degree a special subject in the History and Appreciation of Music: a laudable attempt to spread an interest in music, and to capitalise on an existing one, in a university where none of the constituent schools contained music teachers or students. The Board of Studies at first felt moved to approve it, simply adding the word 'critical' to 'appreciation of music'; but a year later the Board proposed substituting harmony, counterpoint and fugue for this special paper, though the King Edward Professor spoke up, I am happy to say, for the retention of history.

Some good things were done. The Board vetted the proposals for a General School Examination in music in 1922, and two years later set up a sub-committee to produce an optional matriculation paper in music that would be equivalent to it, thus easing the matriculation process for candidates who were well-prepared. When 'Advanced Lectures' were proposed in 1924, the historian Sir Henry Hadow was invited to speak on 'English Composers of the Tudor Period', the first of a long procession of such notables.

In 1924 Sir Frederick Bridge, the first King Edward Professor, died; and the University took the chance of reviewing the 'possibilities which exist for the work of the King Edward Professor'. The Faculty cautiously decided that, 'although the need for a Report did not arise, it was desirable that evidence should be given to the committee on matters concerning the position of music in the University'. Dr E.F. Horner and the Dean, then Stewart Macpherson, were asked to give evidence but, curiously, only in their capacity as 'individual members' of the Faculty. In the event Dr Horner went to South America, so nothing was done. Dr Percy Buck, meanwhile, had been smartly appointed as Bridge's successor in the Chair, thus avoiding any prior review of the Professor's duties; he was asked to make a report with the Dean. They sent in a memorandum in 1926 pointing out that the King Edward Professor had no powers beyond his ex officio membership of the Board of Studies, not even, yet, to act as an examiner and concern himself with standards. The alteration of this state of affairs was however:

presumably a domestic matter, and there appears to be a likelihood that in the near future the Professor will be in a position to exercise an influence over, and assume a responsibility for, the degree examinations. Should this occur he will be able to get in touch with all students preparing for musical degrees and to help them by courses of lectures, by advice in individual cases, by planning courses of work, extensive or intensive, and by broadening opinion and outlook.

His task in helping the cause of practical music is, in the University of London, one of considerable difficulty. The component colleges and affiliated institutions are of a very varied character and differ widely in educational aims, in social character, and in geographical position. These institutions have, for the most part, musical societies of their own, and prefer (as is natural) to preserve their identities rather than to merge them into a representative university body. The King Edward Professor has already taken steps to get together a round-table conference of all these units, with a view to finding out whether any feeling of loyalty and duty to the University as a whole exists or can be created. If any such spirit is found, or can be aroused, it should not prove impossible to enlist the sympathy of the great London schools of music – which are themselves definitely connected with the University – and lay the foundations of a great deal of mutual help and goodwill, and possibly of a more ambitious future. If such a procedure commends itself to the higher authorities it should not be difficult to make some progress in this half of the work of the Professor of Music.

Here was the prospect of action at last. Senate was so interested that it offered to call a special meeting, but this the Board declined.

Frederick Bridge had attempted university concerts; Trinity College orchestra had played at Presentation Day ceremonies. In 1923 Bridge had even composed a University anthem on a text from *Ecclesiasticus* chosen by Rudyard Kipling; but it had not caught on. The main fruit of Buck's consultations was the production of *The University of London Song Book* published in 1927; this contains a hundred unison community songs, fluently arranged by Buck (though he turns the lute part of Morley's 'It was a lover and his lass' into modern academic counterpoint). The songs had been chosen by balloting the many choirs in the University's colleges, following an initiative from the famous historian Sir Bernard Pares, of King's College and the School of Slavonic and East European Studies, who wrote the preface. The book also gives the music of the London University Song, commissioned by Senate in 1925: it has words by John Drinkwater (whose father was a Trinity man) and music by John Ireland, a Royal College teacher. The song is not listed in the John Ireland Trust's *Catalogue of Works* (1968), nor in *The New Grove*; it too failed to establish itself, perhaps because of its metrical irregularity (more apparent than real). It takes very much after Parry's *Jerusalem*, and is reproduced on p. 202.

In general these laudable hopes of developing the corporate musical life of the University came to nothing, because they lacked any social basis in

University Song

JOHN DRINKWATER.
By permission of the University of London.

JOHN IRELAND.*
Used by permission.*

beat. O London maids, and London men, Bring

(Without 8ves) *(8ves)*

in the gold-en age a - gain.

(*Men*) 3 Life calls us, and we bid farewell
To this the latest of our springs,
But on our travels we will tell
How fellowship of gentle things
Is kept for ever where they dwell,
Who know the song that England sings.
O London maids, and London men,
Bring in the golden age again.

(*Women*) 2 In no seclusion pastur'd round,
As where the Cam and Isis flow,
Our cloister'd learning have we found
Where loud the tides of traffic go.
Our nightingales have been the sound
Of London bells from Fleet to Bow:
O London maids, and London men,
Bring in the golden age again.

(*All*) 4 In field or market-place or mill,
Beneath a dear or alien sun,
We'll build a generation still,
Of faith and honour here begun,
That sires of the old English will
Shall know their own and cry—well done!
O London maids, O London men,
Bring in the golden age again.

residential collegiate life. The King Edward Professor remained a person with no resources behind him and little influence. The B.Mus. and D.Mus. drifted yet further from reality, and in their existing form became less and less necessary, because better degrees in music, based on residential courses, burgeoned in other universities. After the Second World War and the great post-Robbins expansion in university provision, the position became much more acute, and after three more King Edward Professors had served their terms – the organist Sir Stanley Marchant, George Oldroyd, who wrote a valuable book on fugue, and the very distinguished composer Herbert Howells, who retired in 1961 – the time was ripe for a new initiative.

In its report on Development Policy for the Quinquennium, 1962-67, the Board of Studies in Music made the long overdue but epoch-making recommendation that the time had come to establish a full-time Chair and Department of Music, with lectureships, preferably placed somewhere in the Central Precinct, though in the closest association with a School. The University was delighted to act, added to the endowment of the King Edward Chair and moved it, now as a full-time professorship, with proposals for a Faculty of Music, to King's College. But who would fill the Chair?

What follows is recent and in some quarters still painful history, and – though it is in the end a record of proud success – I shall not dwell on it at length. The King Edward Chair was offered to Robert Thurston Dart, the Professor of Music in the University of Cambridge. He had been unable to reform the Cambridge syllabus as he had wished, and in 1965 he gratefully accepted the chance to set up a faculty in London on new lines. His proposals were radical, and there was no avoiding a clash with the interests and teaching qualifications of the Recognised Teachers at the Colleges of Music. He put forward a scheme for the B.Mus. which greatly reduced the emphasis on vocational training and opened out the subject to a wide range of intellectual, critical and historical enquiry. There were to be compulsory papers, 'such as will quicken the perceptions, stretch the mind, and temper the judgement', in the history of instruments (not restricted to European instruments, nor to the last 500 years), twentieth-century music (including jazz, avant-garde music, folksong and electro-acoustic developments), and a choice from five fifty-year periods of musical history. Two optional subjects, from among the following, were designed to place music in the context of the intellectual, literary, artistic, religious and social life of its time, or to make possible the study of ethnomusicology: music and theatre (including opera, ballet, musical comedy, masque, film and television); music and poetry (principally solo song); music and science (including acoustics of concert halls, studios, musical acoustics and 'noise' – Dart was a leading member of the Noise Abatement Society); music and education (methods of teaching music, for the professional and amateur, from Guido d'Arezzo to Kódaly and Orff);

music and religion; music and European society (area studies: Britain, France, Slav countries, German-speaking lands, Italy, Iberia or Medieval Europe); non-European music (two areas from China and Japan, India and S.E. Asia, Africa, Middle East, N. and S. America); music in London since 1800 ('In England, as in France, the history of its music is to a large extent identical with the history of the capital city's musical activities and organisations'); and one traditional subject, composition. To make room for all this Dart reduced the technical musical exercises of the B.Mus. to two terms' work in the first year, and an optional Finals paper in composition. He put up a sign above the entrance to his King's College Faculty which read 'Abandon counterpoint all ye who enter here': many teachers and gradutes, outraged by his reforms, no doubt drew the Dantean conclusion that his sign, beautifully copied on parchment, indicated the entrance to some musicological Hell. The laconic minutes of the Board of Studies must conceal some extraordinarily angry discussions; the sniping continued in letters printed in the *Musical Times* of 1966, admirably answered by Dr Paul Steinitz of Goldsmiths' College and Dr Anthony Milner of King's College. The old D.Mus. – horror of horrors – was abolished and brought into line with the other higher doctorates as a degree for the senior composer whose position had been critically established, like that of a scholar, by published (and publicly performed) work; a musicologist might also submit scholarly publications for it. Dr Milner was the first new London D.Mus. of this kind.

Many members of the Board resigned, for Dart had reduced their voting strength by adding to it several new university members; some of these possessed scholarly musical or tangentially musical interests, but some did not. Imposing figures were enlisted such as Professors Ernst Gombrich (history of art), Kevin Nash (civil engineering), N.C. Scott (phonetics), R.P. Winnington Ingram (classics and ancient Greek music), and Dr D.P. Walker (intellectual and musical history) together with Dr J.R. Marr (Indian music) and other distinguished ethnomusicologists from the School of Oriental and African Studies. The music colleges, now out-voted, found that a syllabus was to be imposed on them, for many areas of which they had no teachers. They tried to set up their own degree or continue the old one alongside the new; when defeated, they very nearly left the University's orbit altogether. But wiser counsels prevailed – thanks largely to the efforts of the composer Dr Bernard Stevens at the Royal College of Music and Dr Arthur Pritchard at the Royal Academy of Music: they and others were prepared to give the new ideas a chance. Dart offered to teach Music College students at King's for certain subjects; he added musical performance and interpretation as a B.Mus. option particularly suitable for them; and he made strenuous attempts, though unsuccessfully, to obtain new lectureships from the University which might be shared between the music colleges.

Dart did not give way on the much smaller allocation of time to harmony and counterpoint studies in the B.Mus., and based them on the imitation of real musical styles, not on the old academic language. After his death, however, experience suggested that he had gone too far, and more space was found for such work: many music graduates, after all, do enter the profession as practitioners. Dart also set out an ambitious programme for Master's Degrees, and his advent created a tremendous impetus in higher research which his successors Howard Mayer Brown and myself have been delighted to build on.[23] The B.Mus. proved a most attractive degree, and within a few years London could boast the largest and most varied collection of music students in the country. Dart encouraged the registration of internal music students at Goldsmiths' College, starting in 1965; in 1970 Royal Holloway College founded what has also become a large and successful department under Professor Ian Spink. He also persuaded Dr W.H. Swinburne to enter students as externals for the London degree from the fine school of music at the North East Essex Technical College in Colchester. All this unremitting effort cost Dart dear, and in 1971 he died of cancer at the early age of forty-nine.

The present world-renowned excellence of London in music studies, particularly in research, is sufficiently known, and need not form part of my theme. What is not sufficiently known is how slender the resources have been, in terms of both finance and space, with which it has been achieved. Our University began to feel the pinch almost as soon as Dart arrived on the scene in the mid 1960s, and the screw has been so tightened since then that the music colleges too now face a period of considerable difficulty over teaching resources, and this when their teachers have at last achieved salaried status. Dart was promised an Institute of Advanced Musical Studies, which he intended should not only foster its own members' and students' researches, but act as a clearing-house and a co-ordinating and facilitating body for the work of other important centres of musical research in the University, such as the School of Oriental and African Studies, the Warburg Institute, Chelsea College (now united with King's College) and the Institute of Education; in spite of the presence on their staff of researchers excellent in music, these institutions could not

[23] The remarkable success of musicological and related research in the University of London may be measured by the following figures for research dissertations and shorter studies (excluding musical compositions) completed during the quinquennium 1976-80, compiled from the Royal Musical Association's 'Register of Theses on Music in Britain and Ireland' (R.M.A. *Research Chronicle* 15 (1979), compiled by Nick Sandon, pp. 38-116, with Supplements 1 (*ibid.* 16, (1980) p. 110-134) and 2 *ibid.* 17 (1981), pp. 110-134), both by Sandon; and 3 (*ibid.* 18 (1982), pp. 85-118), compiled by Ian Bartlett). Special studies, etc., for Master's degrees: London, 102; thirty-three other British and Irish universities, ninety-five (an average of three each). M.Phil. and doctoral dissertations: London, thirty-eight; Oxford, twenty-six; Cambridge twenty-three; thirty-seven others, 126 (an average of 3.5 each).

then teach in the Faculty of Music. This need perceived by Dart continues. To cite only one example, there is no mechanism for co-ordinating interdisciplinary research into the psycho-physiology of musical performance and practice, particularly of singing, although this would best be undertaken in London, where one might achieve a team drawn from a variety of institutions, involving established singers and teachers in the colleges of music, anatomists, radiologists, psychologists, phoneticians, educationists, and electrical engineers. Many important national musical institutions active in the metropolis lack homes of their own, such as the Royal Musical Association – the learned society for musical studies – and the Plainsong and Mediaeval Music Society; or they live in accommodation of uncertain tenure – such as the British Music Information Centre or the English Folk Dance and Song Society and its successor body, which it seems can no longer afford to run Cecil Sharp House. At present the Institute of Advanced Musical Studies barely exists; it can make occasional small grants in aid of publication, and has provided a valuable forum in its colloquia at King's College for distinguished foreign musicologists to meet their British counterparts. London University has achieved so much with its music, and at so little expense compared with other subjects, that it must now be prepared to place its advocacy, in the absence of money which it does not possess, behind the raising of funds for the preservation and development of its excellence in music and musicology. In celebrating the past 150 years, it is our duty to plan wisely for the next.

10

The Social Sciences

O.R. McGregor

This sesquicentenary is not the occasion for dispassionate historical assessment. From me, an old student of the London School of Economics, it calls rather for filial though candid respect allied with diffidence, and this is the spirit in which I shall approach the task assigned to me in this series of lectures, commissioned by the University, to survey the growth and achievements of its several faculties. Happily, a lecturer in the LSE has no need to argue whether the social sciences are possible or desirable or useful or to be valued as good in themselves. As memories are short, I shall devote much of my time to the more distant than to the recent past in what cannot be other than an impressionistic retrospect.

In 1900, the five-year old L.S.E. was admitted as a School of the reconstituted University of London. The first university degree in this country devoted to the social sciences was the B.Sc. (Econ.), introduced a year later. These subjects were drawn together within a new Faculty of the University too narrowly designated, even at the beginning, as Economics and Political Science. But in fact the Faculty, whatever its title, has always been the L.S.E. and, for internal students in the social sciences, the School is the University of London. Certainly, a small number of other Schools has played a part in the development of some subjects though, in the field as a whole, it has never been other than a marginal part. Indeed, this generalisation goes far beyond our own university because in many of the social sciences L.S.E. has also been the chief influence, especially as the supplier of teachers, throughout the Kingdom during most of this century.

In the early nineteenth century, London was the only major European capital without a university. England had Oxford and Cambridge; both were expensive and socially exclusive, and both restricted admissions to members of the established church. Before that time, the sciences developed in Scotland's four universities had made an essential contribution to the industrial revolution in England. Further, the astonishing and still unexplained vigour of the Enlightenment in Scotland had embraced the study of society as well as of nature though such lesser but highly original contemporaries of Hume and Smith as Hutcheson, Kames, Monboddo, Robertson, Ferguson and Millar have only recently begun to receive the scholarly attention which their importance in the history of social thought merits.

No wonder, then, that young men from the dissenting wealthier, commercial and industrial families and from the old and new centres of population, made an educational pilgrimage to the Scottish universities. No wonder either that Edinburgh became the strongest of the influences upon the group of papists, Jews, protestant dissenters and agnostic Benthamities who, under the leadership of Brougham, founded an alternative university in London.[1] In the spirit of the age, they set it up as a joint stock company offering £100 shares at 4 per cent interest to the general public.

That first University of London survived for ten years, by which time the market was valuing the stock at £23. Its title then changed to University College when a new Charter was sealed. This established a body to be known as the University of London, empowered to grant degrees, after examinations, in Arts, Laws and Medicine, to male candidates who had completed a course at University College, King's College or such other institution subsequently approved by the Government for the purpose. This requirement was removed by the Charter of 1858 which opened the non-medical examinations to all matriculated comers. By the mid-century, some thirty colleges had been approved; twenty years later London became the first university in Britain to admit women on equal terms to all its degrees.

In the nineteenth century, British universities were not nurseries for the social sciences. Many of the great names worked outside them. In London, with all its advantages, University and King's Colleges failed even to establish a school of political economy, although they both attracted some talented economists from time to time – Cairnes and Jevons at University College and Edgeworth and Cunningham at King's. H.S. Foxwell, the sixth holder of the Chair at University College, was appointed in 1881 and remained until 1927. He has an assured place in the history of the University not only as an economist and a very long serving part-time teacher at L.S.E. but chiefly as the bibliomaniac who assembled after 1875 the library of 40,000 books and pamphlets on economics and economic thought which the Goldsmiths' Company bought in 1901 for

---

[1] Among the secondary sources, H. Hale Bellot, *University College London, 1826-1926* (1929), F.G. Brook, *The University of London, 1820-1860, with special reference to its Influence on the Development of Higher Education* (Ph.D. London, 1958), and the commissioned sesquicentennial history of Negley Harte, *The University of London, 1836-1986* (1986) are particularly valuable.

£10,000 and gave subequently to the University. This happy event for the University was precipitated by Foxwell's having to raise money urgently when he decided to marry in 1898. With remarkable generosity, the Company also made grants of an additional £4,000 to enable him to make further acquisitions to complete the collection and to bind the pamphlets. Thus, one of the three outstanding collections of economic literature in the world is now housed in Senate House Library in a room also donated by the Goldsmiths' Company. The indefatigable Foxwell went on collecting until his death in 1936 to the great advantage of Harvard which obtained what is now the Kress Library from him.[2]

In an article of 1896 on 'The Organisation of Economic Teaching in London', published in the University Extension Journal, Sidney Webb examined the 'quite infinitesimal amount of opportunities for serious study of economics and political questions . . . At University and King's College, Professors Foxwell and Cunningham were squandering their very great powers on tiny handfuls of students'. When lectures at the Birkbeck Institution, the City of London College and the Institute of Bankers, the sporadic University Extension courses, were taken into consideration, 'we have . . . exhausted the whole provision made in 1894-95 for the instruction in Economics for five millions of people'.[3] It was no better elsewhere, and other social sciences were only just beginning to make the acquaintance of universities. However, such deficiences in the universities were in part remedied by the University Extension Movement which began in 1872 and has been unduly neglected in accounts of the period. The London Society for the Extension of University Teaching, a voluntary body, managed by a Council under the presidency of Goschen and advised on academic matters by a joint Board representing the Universities of Oxford, Cambridge and London, was set up in 1876.

[2] The sad story of the forced sale of Foxwell's two main collections is told by his daughter, Audrey G.D. Foxwell, and J.M. Keynes in *The Kress Library of Business and Economics, Publication Number 1* (1939), pp. 3-30 and pp. 31-8. Harvard's luck with Foxwell's second collection of more than 20,000 volumes, picked up from the disposals of country house libraries after 1918, resulted from the insistence of his bankers in 1929 that he should repay his overdraft. Thus, the Harvard Business School acquired for £4,000 the second outstanding collection put together by this remarkable bibliophile. J.M. Keynes recalled that 'He came to regard it almost as a moral fault to miss a desirable purchase. I remember his advice to me . . . "I have often regretted *not* buying a book . . . but I have *never* regretted buying one." He had no rules of prudence for rationing his purchases. This unrestricted ardour involved him in considerable embarrassments and anxiety. Foxwell had but small means, and never held a well-paid appointment; I doubt if his income reached £1,000 a year at any time. It is extraordinary that he should have managed to carry on as one of the largest-scale book collectors in the world.' (*ibid.*, p. 32).

[3] Quoted J.H. Burrows, 'The Teaching of Economics in the Early Days of the University Extension Movement in London, 1876-1902' in *History of Economic Thought Newsletter* (Spring 1978) no. 20.

Extension courses in economics were taught by lecturers of the highest calibre over the years, they included F.Y. Edgeworth, James Bonar, H.H. Asquith, Foxwell, J.A. Hobson[4] and, most successful of them all, Philip Wicksteed, Unitarian minister and disciple of Jevons, whose *Commonsense of Political Economy*, published in 1910, was on my required reading list as a first year student in the University of Aberdeen in 1938. Extension lecturers were better paid than the holders of Chairs. Jevons never earned more than £70 a year at University College where, on the Edinburgh model, he was given a proportion of the fees received from his students.[5] Wicksteed commanded £5 a lecture and probably earned £500 a year, around £22,000 in today's money, from that source. Extension lectures often attracted very large audiences. In the autumn term of 1879, Foxwell had one hundred students in the Hampstead Centre; in the session 1894/5, Armitage-Smith, the Principal of Birkbeck Institute from 1896 to 1918, lectured to a total of more than four hundred students in four courses on different economic subjects in the City and in Poplar. In the session 1901/2, Extension lecturers in London had more than 15,000 paying students in fifty-nine centres. University Extension courses in the social sciences achieved a golden age in the years before the First World War when their conduct was in the hands of people like Graham Wallas, Gilbert Slater, A.C. Haddon and Edward Westermarck, all associated with the early years of L.S.E.[6] Indeed, student audiences there during the first session were described by Graham Wallas as 'mainly of the type to which I had become accustomed in the University Extension Movement – a few ambitious young civil servants and teachers, and a few women of leisure interested in the subject or engaged in public work'.[7]

The story of the foundation of L.S.E. by the Webbs has been told so often and so well that repetition is unnecessary. What must be emphasised is the spirit and outlook in which Sidney Webb reared his child. In a letter in 1903 to the Vice-Chancellor of the University, he wrote of himself as 'a person of decided views, Radical and Socialist, and that I wanted the

---

[4] Mr Burrows exposes, *ibid.*, the fiction first contained in Hobson's autobiography, *Confessions of an Economic Heretic* (1938) of a 'refusal of the London Extension Board [*sic*] to allow me to offer courses of political economy' (p. 30) and repeated by R.H. Tawney in the *Dictionary of National Biography, 1931-1940*. In fact, Hobson applied for recognition as Lecturer in Economics in 1888 and was turned down. He applied again early in 1893; his name was added to the list and he taught courses from 1894 onwards.

[5] *Letters and Journals of W. Stanley Jevons* (edited by his wife) (1886), p. 420.

[6] I have taken this information about the history of the University Extension Movement from the indispensable study of John Burrows, *Adult University Education in London: A Century of Achievement* (1976), especially pp. 1-44, and from his article, *op. cit.*, on 'The Teaching of Economics in the Early Days of the University Extension Movement in London'.

[7] Quoted F.A. von Hayek, 'The London School of Economics', 1895-1945', *Economica*, new ser. XIII (1946), p. 8.

policy that I believed in to prevail. But that I was also a profound believer in Knowledge and Science and Truth. I thought that we were suffering much from lack of research in social matters, and I wanted to promote it. I believed that research and new discoveries would prove some, at any rate, of my views of policy to be right, but that, if they proved the contrary, I should count it all the more gain to have prevented error, and should cheerfully abandon my policy'.[8] Commenting on the first appointments of staff, Professor F.A. von Hayek observed that 'politics entered no more than through Webb's conviction that a careful study of the facts ought to lead most sensible people to socialism; but he took care to select the staff from all shades of political opinion, more anxious to bring promising men under the influence of the new institution than to have it dominated by any one kind of outlook'.[9] Sidney Webb behaved in accordance with that conviction throughout his connection with the School which lasted for more than fifty years.

At the beginning, eleven members of staff were appointed, all of them part-timers. They included William Cunningham, A.L. Bowley, Halford Mackinder, Graham Wallas and the ubiquitous Foxwell. 285 students entered in the first session, there were over 400 five years later and more than 2,000 on the eve of the First World War. By then the number of staff had also increased dramatically; some had been recruited from among a remarkably gifted group of holders of research studentships. C.K. Hobson joined in 1909, Hugh Dalton and Eileen Power in 1913, and Theodore Gregory and Bronislaw Malinowski in 1914. The increase in staff and student numbers demonstrated the predicted demand for training in the social sciences which, even in 1905, went much wider than economics and political science. In this period, wrote Beveridge, the School was 'a place of evening study and of part-time teachers. Those who came to learn were for the most part already in employment. Most of their teachers were men already occupied elsewhere, giving evening lectures as a by-product of other interests. Only in this way could the School, with its ludicrously small financial resources, have obtained, as it did obtain, men of the high distinction it needed'.[10]

A memorandum in the name of L.S.E. and the Board of Studies in Economics and Political Science, submitted by the Chairman of the Board, Sidney Webb, to the Haldane Commission on University Education in London in 1909, clearly delineated how the School perceived the new undergraduates for whom it was going to provide:

---

[8] Quoted Janet Beveridge, *An Epic of Clare Market* (1960), pp. 49-50.

[9] Beveridge, *Clare Market*, p. 5.

[10] W.H. Beveridge, *Introduction*, p. x, to the *Register, 1895-1932, of the London Schools of Economics and Political Science* (1934).

Being *as regards its undergraduate class*, essentially a University for the sons and daughters of households of limited means and strenuous lives, it cannot, like Oxford and Cambridge, set itself to skim from the surface of society the topmost layer of rich men's sons and scholarship winners. Widely organised and adequately endowed, it must dive deep down through every stratum of its ten or fifteen million of constituents, selecting by the tests of parental or other selection of a career, personal ambition and endurance, talent and 'grit', for membership of all the brain-working professions and for scientific research, every capable recruit that London rears. Hence it must stand ready to enrol in its undergraduate ranks not hundreds a year, but thousands . . . we can see that (an) effective London University might number 20,000.[11]

The memorandum went on to emphasise that teaching undergraduates came second only to the duty to advance knowledge. In the first place:

The most obvious and imperative duty of a rightly organised and adequately endowed London University is to become the foremost postgraduate centre of the intellectual world . . . With a highly specialised staff . . . in each faculty, the London University would attract, not one or two here and there, but a continuous stream of the ablest and most enterprising of young graduates from the colonies and the United States, from every university of Europpe and the Far East. In the provision of facilites for this highest grade of students the Senate of the new London University has an opportunity of combining a sane and patriotic Imperialism with the largest-minded Internationalism.[12]

Secondly, the University would provide special opportunities for Londoners wishing to pursue post-graduate work:

Here London makes possible a postgraduate life unattainable in the more leisurely cloistered homes of University culture. Exactly because the London University is set down in the very midst of warehouses and offices, monotonous squares and mean streets, the poor and talented graduate, living inexpensively at his own home, or already gaining his livelihood, can, as a day or evening student, pursue his little bit of original research . . . The very combination of two such distinct classes of postgraduate students – the one bringing the training and experience of alien universtities, the other contributing the intimate knowledge of the actual processes of bank or factory, government department or merchants's office – constitutes in itself an extraordinarily stimulating intellectual atmosphere for the advanced student.[13]

Demobilisation in 1919 precipitated an avalanche of students whose

---

[11] *Appendix to the First Report of the Commissioners on University Education in London*, 1910, Cd. 5166, XXIII, 643, Q. 396, para 11. Ital. in original.

[12] *Ibid.*, paras 18 and 20.

[13] *Ibid.*, para 20.

numbers throughout the inter-war years fluctuated between 2,800 and 3,000, but the character of the student body changed decisively. At the beginning of this period, one-third were taking full courses for a degree or some other qualification and two-thirds were occasional students paying for courses on an *ad hoc* basis. In 1937, the proportions had been reversed; by then, two-thirds of the students were registered for full-time courses. This group maintained an unaltered division between the two-thirds who were day students, with one woman to three men, and the remainder, overwhelmingly men, who came to the School in the evenings and went on to take a degree. The international appeal and reputation of the School can be measured by the increase of two and a half times in overseas students who numbered over 700 at the end of the thirties. Finally, there was the steep rise in the number of higher degree students from thirty-two in the first post-war session to 293 just before the next war began. From what he called 'these cheering changes', William Beveridge, the Director from 1919 to 1937, concluded:

First, it shows how right Sidney Webb had been, when as Chairman of the Technical Education Board (of the L.C.C.) in 1893, he had made it a condition of giving money to the School or any other teaching institution that the institution should provide for evening study. Second, it means that the School buildings, from 1919-37, were occupied more fully than any other place of study probably than can be found anywhere in the world.[14]

Sidney Webb had been right about nearly everything connected with the establishment and growth of the School, which stands as the real memorial of his greatness. He always acted on his belief that 'it is a condition of progress that we allow freedom for error',[15] and it is sad that elderly socialists, for whom the light has failed, should nowadays heap blame upon the Webbs for their own disenchantment and disappointments. The students of the 1920s and 30s were taught in an institution which was quickly establishing an international reputation in its fields of study. The first *Calendar* of the School listed courses in economics, statistics, geography, law, economic history, and political science. Admission to all or any of the lectures and classes and entitlement to all the privileges of membership of the School cost £3 a year and compared very favourably with the charges for Extension lectures. An impressive list, it may be thought, for a new institution. Even so, the range of subjects offered widened rapidly during the directorship of Beveridge. At the same time, newly appointed full-time staff greatly strengthened economics so that the Department bred Nobel Prizewinners, made law a

[14] W.H. Beveridge, *The London School of Economics and its Problems* (1960), pp. 52-3.
[15] *Appendix to First Report of the Commissioners on University Education in London, op. cit.*, Q. 651.

major department and established anthropology and sociology, economic history, statistics, political science and geography as important disciplines. The study of international relations was present at the beginning in the person of Goldsworthy Lowes Dickinson and acquired the status of a Chair with the appointment of Philip Noel Baker.

The regime of the Beveridge years brought new achievements but new strains and conflicts. More students, more staff, and more subjects meant more buildings. From the first conception of the idea of the School, Sidney Webb had it in mind to establish a research library. This was formally opened at the end of 1896. When it moved to Clare Market in 1902,[16] there were forty-eight reader places, by 1933 these had increased to 550. A great library is a heavy consumer of space, and for more than ninety years the School has been a giant compelled to live on a site fit only for a dwarf. What easement there has been in recent years stems particularly from the labours of Lionel Robbins in raising the millions needed for the new Library. From its foundation, L.S.E. has been no stranger to the begging bowl. Sir Ernest Cassel set up an Educational Trust from which in 1920 a large endowment went to funding professorships and readerships. Early in his period of office, Beveridge tapped the resources of the Rockefeller Trust. The Trust became closely connected with the work of the School and its massive grants were first used to establish Chairs in International Law and Anthropology.

The Rockefeller beneficence lay behind two of the well-known, fierce conflicts which engaged the School under Beveridge. He was anxious to pursue his own strongly held views on the nature of the social sciences by exploring the border land between natural and social science. He told the trustees that:

> To complete the circle of social sciences a third group of studies is required, dealing with the natural bases of economics and politics, with the human material and with its physical environment, and forming a bridge between the natural and the social sciences.[17]

He envisaged that this territory would be colonised in the first instance by anthropology and social biology. He already had social anthropology so he pressed social biology on his colleagues. It needed 'a man of biological training to learn economics and politics,' to 'apply himself to economic and social problems' and to develop links with other areas of research.[18] Beveridge's programme had secured general support in the School when it was adopted in 1927, but enthusiasm waned after he chose

---

[16] From 1903 the Goldsmiths' Library was housed at the Imperial Institute, South Kensington; it moved to the new Senate House in 1937.

[17] Beveridge, *The L.S.E. and its problems*, p. 88.

[18] *Ibid.*, p. 89.

Lancelot Hogben who came to the Chair in 1930. One difficulty was that Hogben was a wayward colleague though a brilliant biologist. Another arose because he made enemies of Lionel Robbins and the theoretical economists as well as getting on the wrong side of Harold Laski and the political scientists by expressing contempt for the intellectual procedures and academic interests of both. 'The trouble was', wrote Hogben to Beatrice Webb, 'that the Left Wingers were just as dialectical as the Right, and the few who . . . were sympathetic to realistic research (as opposed to tautological necromancy and belles-lettres) were not in powerful positions . . . But if what is called social science is what is done at the L.S.E., thank Heavens I am still a biologist.'[19] Accordingly, what Beveridge described as 'a wedding of natural and economic science' was never consummated and he found himself isolated and facing the hostility of most of his colleagues. His attempt, as many thought of it, to impose his own theory of the natural bases of the social sciences upon the School soured his last years as Director. Hogben's laboratory was closed to the relief, so it is said, of the many unscientific social scientists who could not abide the stench and cries of the animals. The next Director, Alexander Carr-Saunders, a biologist by early training and occupation, declared that the experiment had been a mistake. He took the lead in establishing demography as a discipline in the School under the celebrated scholarship of David Glass.[20]

Another strain arose from the frequent and outspoken political commentaries, expressed in no impartial manner, of Harold Laski, the Professor of Political Science who had been at the School since 1920, becoming a well-known public figure, and, as Beveridge put it, 'deepening our red colour in many eyes.' Laski became, too, it should never be forgotten, a teacher loved deeply by his students to whom he gave affection as he received it. Nevertheless, he would have been a problem to any institution seeking to become a strong, unified and unequivocal School of the very conservative University of London. He was an even greater problem to those trying to raise money to promote teaching and research in the social sciences at L.S.E. At the time, there was a growing student unrest, natural enough with a new war visibly shaping in the years ahead. In that atmosphere, the political commitments and adventurous or infelicitous or tactless phrases of Harold Laski, in Moscow or elsewhere, were thought by conservatively minded people to be dangerous to the School's future, predjudicing the inflow of funds for expansion. It

[19] Quoted José Harris, *William Beveridge. A Biography* (Oxford, 1977), p. 290.
[20] Bertrand Russell, Karl Popper and David Glass have been the only teachers at L.S.E. to become Fellows of both the British Academy and the Royal Society. David Glass had been a student of the School; as far as I know, only one other, Margaret Gowing, originally an economic historian and from 1973 to 1986 Professor of the History of Science in the University of Oxford, achieved these two honours when she became a Fellow of the Royal Society in 1988.

was said, for example, that the City declined to subscribe to appeals for an enlargement of the Commerce Department because of the School's reputation for socialism reinforced by Laski's obtrusive political doctrines and associations. Fortunately, he would not and could not be silenced although the University tried hard to keep him quiet.[21]

In 1904 Sidney Webb obtained money from the railway companies to establish a Railway Department. In 1910, he experienced similar discrimination on political grounds because he supported the demand of railway workers for higher wages, and Lord George Hamilton, on behalf of the railway companies, demanded successfully that Webb should cease to be Chairman of the Governors at the School as the price of maintaining funds for the Railway Department. Selflessly, he stood down. A conflict between the means of securing private money for the social sciences and the right of teachers to speak their minds, publicly as well as in the lecture theatre, is sometimes inescapable. There can be no solution to the strains set up by such a conflict save the practice of good sense and tolerance on everybody's part. These virtues are often in short supply in universities and experience suggests that the more dependent an institution for the social sciences becomes on private money, and, under some governments, on public, the more essential it is that teachers who have demonstrated their academic competence should be irremovable by governing bodies or colleagues who dislike their academic or political opinions or wish to reduce provision for teaching and research in their subjects. There is no other way to balance the power attaching to the vital contribution which academic money raisers make to their institutions and the freedom of expression without which universities perish.

Beyond doubt, the remarkable feature of those turbulent years was the School's assured take-off into intellectual growth. In less than half a century, it had come to dominate the development of the social sciences in Britain.

I now turn to the work of the University of London in teaching the social sciences to adult students, a significant but too often forgotten part of its story in which the Faculty of Economics played a vital role. The University took over responsibility for Extension Lectures and their 15,000 students in 1900. That system had worked well in late-Victorian days for middle class students, with a vocational bent, who could afford the fees. But the Workers Education Association had to be founded in 1903 to give working-class people access to democratically organised

---

[21] The Hogben and Laski episodes are very well and fairly presented by José Harris, *Beveridge*, chs. 11 and 12. Of the accounts by members of the staff who lived through the Beveridge years, by far the most judicious, informative and entertaining is that of Lord Chorley, 'Beveridge and the L.S.E.' in *L.S.E. The Magazine of the London School of Economics and Political Science*, pt. 1, no. 44 (1972), pt. 2, no. 45 (1973).

liberal education to the end that they might employ more effectively such political and economic power as they had been able to grasp. By the mid-1920s, the Association, the universities and the Board of Education had established settled working relationships for the provision of adult classes.

The central medium of teaching was, and has remained, the University Tutorial class which followed the University Extension class by imposing upon students an obligation of serious systematic study and regular written work. It comprised not more than thirty students, meeting regularly for twenty-four weeks for each of three years, with provision for a fourth year of advanced work, under a tutor appointed by a university. The tutor was paid by the university and three-quarters of the fee was reimbursed by the Board of Education under arrangements devised by Sir Robert Morant. Such classes could be testing for tutor and students alike.

G.D.H. Cole had been the staff tutor responsible for arranging such classes in London. After he was appointed Reader in Economics at Oxford, the Extra-Mural Department was reorganised. Two committees were established under an Extension and Tutorial Classes Council, the one to oversee extension work, the other to be responsible for tutorial classes. In this way, the two sides of the University's provision for adult education were institutionalised. Barbara Wootton was appointed Director of Studies for tutorial classes in 1928; she was, in effect, the academic head of that side of the work which extended also to running Saturday and Summer Schools. As many of the classes would be organised by the W.E.A. the University had to work closely and sympathetically with that body. At this time, the subjects studied in tutorial classes were chiefly economics, widely and empirically interpreted, and economic history. Of the sixty-eight tutorial classes of the session 1937/8 in London, two-thirds were in the social sciences and had enrolled over 750 students. In addition, some 500 students attended eight university Extension Courses for the diploma in economics and social science and a similar number was going to other Extension Lectures on economics, economic history, demography, social philosophy and the like. The University was carrying all told almost 2,000 extra-mural students in the social sciences, and for lecturers it relied heavily on internal teachers, mainly from L.S.E.

For many working-class people seeking to make a reality of democracy, the adult class offered the only means of acquiring the training and knowledge without which the power to change society could not be extracted from the electoral system in local and central government. For such folk, the tutorial class was a finishing school where they learnt to apply their minds very often in the first instance to the economic and social history of the Industrial Revolution. It was for such audiences that historians like R.H. Tawney, G.D.H. Cole, H.L. Beales and Henry Hamilton occasionally wrote and frequently taught. Of the economic historians at the School, Tawney, Beales and F.J. Fisher were committed to adult education and took a hand in shaping a tutorial class interpretation of economic and social history just as there had been a Whig interpretation of political history. Thirty years ago Professor F.A. von Hayek saw this as one of the steps on the road to serfdom. He pointed with truth and without exaggeration to the creation of 'a socialist interpretation of history which has governed political thinking for the last two or three generations and which consists mainly of a particular view of economic history . . almost universally accepted as the basis for the estimate of the existing economic order.'[22] Hayek blamed the accounts of the social consequences of the Industrial Revolution which were embodied in this interpretation of economic history for what he described as 'the widespread emotional aversion to capitalism.'[23]

It is not fanciful to attribute a significant political influence to those then engaged in adult education. In the years before the Second World War, they helped to give the Labour Party historical letters of credit, a framework for its programme of social reforms, and faith in the future possibilities of social amelioration. The social development of industrialism came to be thought of as an inevitable evolution towards a welfare society. In schools and universities the 'socialist interpretation of economic history', which troubled Hayek, went almost unchallenged. A good deal of it, and of the accompanying economics, passed into the education of citizen soldiers during the Second World War. One of the University's staff tutors in London in the 1930s, W.E. (later Sir William) Williams, became head of the Army Bureau of Current Affairs which adopted the procedures and outlook of university adult education. In the history and content of that form of education lies more than a small part of the explanation of political developments in the aftermath of that war.

Thirty years later, the character of economic and social history had changed; in the School, the mantle of Tawney passed to Richard Titmuss. But it was sociology, not social administration, which replaced economic history as a main enthusiam of adult students in the social sciences. The Extra-Mural Department catered for this in 1953 by establishing a four year Diploma in Sociology with written examinations. It attracted very large numbers of students at its peak in the late 1960s and early 1970s, when between 200 and 250 candidates each year persevered to obtain diplomas. Then, fewer than 100 internal students sat for the first degree in sociology. Internal teachers of the University helped in many ways to make the diploma possible. They advised upon and drafted syllabuses and they served as examiners. They were recruited and organised by John Burrows whose dedicated labours in Senate House sustained the Diploma for more than thirty years. The Diploma ended in 1989 when the heart had gone out of sociology in adult classes.

----

[22] F.A. Hayek, ed., *Capitalism and the Historians* (1954), p. 7.
[23] *Ibid.*, p. 10.

I have emphasised the work of the Extra-Mural Department in order to show that the teaching of the social sciences by the University of London has gone far beyond its internal schools. I emphasise, too, that for the whole of this century, internal teachers, and that mostly means the staff of L.S.E., have shouldered considerable obligations for a very large number of adult students drawn from the London area.

One consequence of the nineteenth-century inheritance from an examining university has been the generosity which London showed towards emergent universities at home as well as overseas. There is more than rhetoric in the description of London as a mother of universities. The first brood were the younger civic universities of Reading, Nottingham, Southampton, Hull, Exeter and Leicester which were founded as university colleges before and after the First World War. Reading received university status in 1926 but all the others had to wait until shortly after the Second World War. So, for a long period, they all took London External Degrees. In the social sciences, therefore, they worked largely to London syllabuses; they all had to meet London standards, and their work bore the thumb print of L.S.E.

As a result of the *Report*[24] in 1945 of the Asquith Commission 'to consider the principles which should guide the promotion of higher education, learning and research and the development of universities in the Colonies and to explore means whereby universities . . . in the United Kingdom may be able to cooperate with institutions of Higher Education in the Colonies . . .', the University of London undertook to nurture new colonial universities as it had looked after the English university colleges. The Director of the L.S.E., Alexander Carr-Saunders, was a member of the Asquith Commission, and himself took the lead in setting up the Special Committee of the Senate on Higher Education in the Colonies. The Senate Committee guided the development of the university colleges in East Africa, Sudan, Central Africa, Nigeria, the Gold Coast and the West Indies. Carr-Saunders also organised the help of all the United Kingdom universities, through an Inter-University Council, for the six university colleges and universities of Malta, Hong Kong and Malaya. He was Chairman in 1947 of the Commission that led to the creation of the University of Malaya in 1953, and of the Commission on Higher Education for Africans in Central Africa from which came the foundation of the multi-racial University College of Rhodesia and Nyasaland.

For internal teachers of the University of London in most Faculties, these developments imposed obligations of advising on syllabuses, assisting teachers in the new institutions and conducting examinations on the London model.

The first of the Colleges in Special Relation, Gordon Memorial College in Khartoum, was established in 1946, the last to withdraw on becoming

---

[24] *On Higher Education in the Colonies*, Cmd. 6647, 1945.

an independent university was the University College of Rhodesia in 1971.[25] Meanwhile, the ordinary external Degree of the University continued. Unhappily, the University is a very uncertain statistician and there are no even approximately reliable statistics of the numbers of candidates for examinations from different places for the various external examinations. Nevertheless, there is no doubt that a very heavy weight of examining both for the indigenous and overseas external candidates fell upon those responsible for the B.Sc. (Econ.) and sociology degrees. Without reliable statistics about the B.Sc. (Econ.) degree, my own memory as chairman of the internal and external Boards of Examiners in Sociology for sixteen years will permit one point to be made about the situation of internal teachers. After a long experience of examining for external overseas candidates, the Board of Studies in Sociology fought a battle with the University to withdraw the external degree. The Board won because the failure rate of the degree was over 90 per cent. The Board did, however, agree to provide a degree for candidates who had received systematic teaching in an educational institution. In its naivety, the Board had failed to foresee the binary system at home, and ended up having to deal with almost 1,000 external candidates in 1971. This meant that a relatively small group of internal teachers became responsible for a very large examination and for supervising a horde of assistant examiners who were not internal teachers. Naturally, teachers in the many polytechnics submitting candidates demanded to meet internal teachers in order to discuss syllabuses, teaching methods and problems arising from the examinations. I do not doubt that the external system had many virtues; it also imposed intolerable burdens upon internal teachers on whose shoulders landed the real costs of the system to the disadvantage of their internal students. Before the University revives or extends the external examinations, it is to be hoped that past experience will be examined from the point of view of those who will have to provide the academic services.

For the whole of this century, the social sciences in the University of London have been concentrated in one powerful institution. The gains from this development are too obvious to be worth listing. On the other hand, in a university as big as London, there have been losses as well. Whole generations of students of, say, medicine, architecture, or engineering have never made the acquaintance of such of the social sciences as may be relevant to their work. What has been missed can be illustrated from developments in the Law Department at L.S.E. and in the establishment of a Social Research Unit, specialising in the Sociology of Medicine, in the Sociology Department at Bedford College.

[25] The best guide to this history is the exhaustive study of Bruce Pattison, *Special Relations. The University of London and New Universities Overseas, 1947-1970* (1984).

Beveridge had been trained as a lawyer and his very first step for widening the intellectual scope of the School was to strengthen that Department. In 1920 he brought in H.C. Gutteridge and, three years later, Edward Jenks; he later brought Theodore Plucknett, one of the most distinguished of legal historians, back from Harvard. Sir Otto Kahn-Freund, 'looking back at the history of legal studies in this country in the course of the last three-quarters of a century', was:

> Persuaded that the L.S.E. played a pioneering role in the development of the new subjects and that it did so especially at three periods of its existence: the first was at the beginning in the 1890s and the first decade of this century, the second was immediately after the First World War and the third was . . . after the Second World War. The first two of these three crucial periods saw the evolution of commerical law, industrial or labour law, and administrative law, and after 1945 the L.S.E. set the pace for the others by developing family law and the law of taxation.[26]

Sir Otto found the explanation for these innovations 'in the organisation and scope of activities of the L.S.E. which are . . . decisive. The symbiosis in the L.S.E. of law and . . . the other social sciences is an important element. More important even is the symbiosis of the lawyers, the economists, sociologists, political scientists, and others. Here, and I am now for a moment speaking personally against a background of memory going back for many decades, it is the subjective factor which counts . . . (in) an atmosphere in which one's assumptions as a lawyer were unconsciously questioned by the spontaneous attitudes of one's colleagues, perhaps it was mutual.'[27]

The experience of medicine has been similar. Although medical sociology has a long history without and within this University, only in the last twenty years has the subject found its way into the medical curriculum. Margot Jefferys became Professor of Medical Sociology at Bedford College in 1968, the year in which the Todd Commission on Medical Education recommended such teaching for medical students. Under her persuasive advocacy, the Medical Faculty of the University introduced medical sociology as a compulsory subject in the second M.B. in 1972. At that stage, medical sociologists were appointed to teach in the twelve Medical Schools and their work was co-ordinated by a Special Advisory Committee on Sociology as Applied to Medicine which advised the Academic Advisory Board in Medicine. In this way, the social sciences were introduced into medical education, their legitimacy recognised and their influence upon the practice of clinical medicine established. The formal introduction of sociology into the medical

---

[26] 'The Legal Framework of Society' in William A. Robson, ed., *Man and the Social Sciences* (1972), p. 206.
[27] *Ibid.*, p. 204.

curriculum which, Professor Jefferys observes, 'by the 1980s had taken place in most of the medical schools of the United Kingdom', was a radical innovation. 'Compared with most of the other new subjects it involves a break away from the traditional preparation for medicine based exclusively on the detailed study of parts of the biological organism . . . Its focus is not on the human individual *per se*: it is on the two-way relationships between the individual and society. Sociology as applied to medicine is concerned specifically with those aspects of the relationship which influence the experiences of health and illness in individuals and the response to them of others – relatives, doctors, nurses, administrators and governments.'[28]

A similar commentary could be made in such other fields as industrial and educational sociology and social psychiatry to which this University has made important contributions. The conclusion is that today, if the social sciences are to teach practitioners, policy makers and politicians to avoid errors, to question assumptions, and to limit the areas of ignorance in which choice must be made, teaching, at least specialised teaching for those going into the professions, will have to be more widely spread than it now is within a university as big as London.

When reflecting on the approaching centenary of LSE and on the great expansion of teaching and research in the social sciences which it will mark, we might be wise not to dismiss out of hand Shelley's belief in his *A Defence of Poetry* of 1821, that

> We have more moral, political and historical wisdom, than we know how to reduce into practice; we have more scientific and economical knowledge than can be accommodated to the just distribution of the produce which it multiplies. The poetry, in these systems of thought, is concealed by the accumulation of facts and calculating processes. There is no want of knowledge respecting what is wisest and best in morals, government, and political economy, or at least what is wiser and better than what men now practise and endure . . . We want the creative faculty to imagine that which we know; we want the generous impulse to act that which we imagine; we want the poetry of life: our calculations have outrun conception; we have eaten more than we can digest.[29]

[28] Margot Jefferys, 'Foreword', pp. ix-x, to D.L. Patrick and C. Scambler, eds., *Sociology as Applied to Medicine* (2nd ed., 1986).
[29] Harry Buxton Forman (ed.), *The Works of Percy Bysshe Shelley* (1880), Seventh Volume Prose III, pp. 134-135.

11

Education

Sir William Taylor

In his article on the London Day Training College published in the *Education Libraries Bulletin* in 1958, Richard Goodings comments:

> It is surely significant that though logically one would expect a book about the training of teachers to deal primarily with the evolution of an idea or group of ideas, this is never the case and histories of teacher training tend to be written almost exclusively in terms of institutions.[1]

The broader and more various the range of ideas that have entered into the study of education and the initial and post-experience training of educators, the harder it has become to generalise about the process in terms other than structural and institutional. As Richard Peters put it in the first number of the *London Educational Review*:

> The trouble about educational studies, which, in part, explains the traditional hostility of universities towards them is that, logically speaking, they are a mess and necessarily a mess. By this I mean that they are concerned with problems which cannot be tackled, like mathematical problems or problems in physics, by reliance on just one way of thinking.[2]

Given the way in which the specialisms and sub-specialisms that contribute to the study of education have developed and proliferated, it is today virtually impossible for any one individual to speak or write usefully about the field in terms of its prevailing ideas, concepts and theories. Such an enterprise requires a multi-disciplinary team and a book rather than a single chapter. Hence the temptation to stick to structures and institutions, to narrate how the London Day Training College of 1902 became the Institute of Education of 1932 and the federal, post-McNair,

---

[1] Richard Goodings, 'The London Day Training College,' *Education Libraries Bulleting*, 2 (1958), p. 5.
[2] Richard S. Peters, 'The Role and Responsibilities of the University in Teacher Education', *London Educational Review*, 1 (1972), pp.

'Central activity' Institute of 1948, and together with the Departments of Education at King's and Chelsea and Goldsmiths', played a part in the post-Robbins establishment of a distinct University Faculty in 1967; to recount the story of the setting up of the Area Training Organisations, the expansion of initial training in the 'sixties, the reorganisation and diversification of the 'seventies; to describe the increasing range of educational research for which the Schools of the University, the Institute and Goldsmiths' became responsible, the withdrawal of the University from its validating responsibilities and the impact of new arrangements for the accreditation of initial training and the support of INSET.

It is a story of no little importance within the history of post-war education. We are fortunate that large parts of it up to 1972 have already been so well told by Dr. Willis Dixon in his recently published History of the Institute.[3] In what follows I shall discuss some of the more recent of these events, especially insofar as they relate to the interaction between teaching and research in education in the University of London and the development of the study and practice of education.

Task and Response

Much has been written about the institutions within which the study of education is pursued and a certain amount (although not enough) on how ideas and concepts and theories about education have been organised into courses and programmes of study. Much less is in print about the processes by means of which individual academics or group of academics go about the business of exerting influence on thought and practice in education – or for that matter, on many other professional domains.

In general terms, the prescription is easily enough stated. The primary functions of universities are teaching and research. Those responsible have to have something interesting and worthwhile to enquire into and to talk about, based on extensive knowledge of the literature and practice of their respective specialisms. Their papers need to appear in high-status and widely read journals. And they have to attract students who are either already in positions of responsibility or who can be expected in due course to assume them.

For a very few individuals and teams, this can be all that is needed to attract attention. Graduates and the media will ensure that the world beats a path to one's door. But most academics have to try harder. Their efforts are likely to include:

1. Active participation in conferences and symposia organised by other institutions and academic organisations; initially a matter of responding

[3] C. Willis Dixon, *The Institute: a Personal Account of the History of the University of London Institute of Education, 1932-1972* (1986).

to calls for papers, later of being responsive to requests to speak, to appear on panels and to Chair sessions.

2. Willingness to apply ones ideas to specific fields of educational activity and to the solution of contemporary educational problems, through publication, presentation and, when opportunity offers, consultation. By this means contact can be made with policy makers and practitioners and the relevance and usefulness of one's contribution established.

3. Developing among the members of teaching and research teams an approach to disciplinary and professional problems recognisable within and beyond the profession as consistent and coherent (although this nearly always makes the work of the group look more homogeneous than its own members feel it to be).

4. Encouraging a climate in which the ideas expressed by members of the group are regularly exposed to critical comment and evaluation.

5. Retaining active contact with former students through disciplinary associations, bulletins, meetings and correspondence.

6. Acquiring status in the international disciplinary or professional network by attending overseas conferences and meetings, maintaining regular correspondence and exchanging papers with academics and practitioners in other systems.

7. Attracting and responding positively to requests to serve on the committees and councils of disciplinary and professional bodies at home and abroad, as well as on official and unofficial committees and working groups concerned with public policy.

8. Playing sufficient part in the political and administrative life of the parent institution to ensure that the academic and resource claims of the group are respected and as far as possible met, without giving up so much time to administration and internal politics as to threaten the effectiveness of teaching and scholarly productivity.

9. Demonstrating enough interest in interdisciplinary effort and enquiry to secure a positive response from colleagues, without losing disciplinary focus or appearing to make judgements in fields where no special competence can be claimed.

10. Avoiding commitment to political or policy positions which the judgements of the day identify as 'extreme' or irrational, or being taken up by groups identified with such positions.

11. Offering attractive facilities and contacts for scholars from other universities and systems for shorter or longer periods, and welcoming academic visitors.

12. Accepting examining responsibilities in other universities.

13. Disseminating regular reports on the activities of the group, in a form likely to be read rather than consigned immediately to file or waste paper basket.

All obvious enough, although you do not have to be a member of a U.G.C. sub-committee engaged in evaluating research performance to know that there are variations in the extent to which these requirements for the exercise of influence are met.

For a department or institution to exert influence on professional practice, quality is obviously of first importance. Size also matters. It is by no means impossible for individual scholars, without a departmental base, or very small groups of two or three like-minded people, to make their mark; but it is difficult. As far as education is concerned, in respect of both quality and size, London has long had the edge.

Early Years

For three-quarters of a century the work of this university in the study and teaching of education went on very successfully without benefit of a faculty organisation. In the words of the Report of the 1967 Joint Planning Committee for the B.Ed. degree:

> The Faculty of Education has been instituted in the first place so that the Colleges of Education forming the London Institute may provide courses for the degree of Bachelor of Education and in due course for higher degrees.[4]

It causes no surprise to anyone who has worked in London, and who thus has no expectation of logic in such arrangements, that the faculty possessed no Board (these functions being discharged by the Board of Educational Studies) and that the sole formal duty (there are many onerous informal ones) of its duly appointed Dean is to present to the Chancellor at the Albert Hall those upon whom degrees of the university have already been conferred.

The history of education in London University starts much earlier than 1967. It might have begun as long ago as 1837. A year earlier, a course of lectures on education had been given in Gower St. by the Rev. James Bryce, Principal of the Belfast Academy. Then a Mr J.H. Morgan published what Hale Bellott[5] calls 'a rather confused proposal' to establish a professorship of education, and even offered some money in support. In 1841, Lord Brougham, whose earlier proposal to a Select Committee of the House of Commons that four Normal Schools be established in London, Exeter, Lancaster and York had led to the first parliamentary grant, of £10,000, being put aside for the education of teachers, wanted to found a Chair at University College, but failed to secure the concurrence of the existing professors.[6] So nothing came of either proposal.

It was not until the final decade of the century that the University

---

[4] Minute 829 of the University of London Academic Council (AC/8/18/1/4 dated 29 November 1967).

[5] H. Hale Bellot, *University College London, 1826-1926* (1929).

[6] H.C. Dent, *The Training of Teachers in England and Wales* (1975), p. 11.

entered formally into the business of professional training for teaching. But the fifty years from 1840 to 1890 were not without importance as far as its contribution to the work of the elementary and secondary schools was concerned. Many of those who obtained London degrees subsequently found careers in secondary teaching. Certificated teachers benefited from opportunities after 1858 to take external degrees. Both University College and King's College had 'lower departments', which still flourish as independent foundations in Hampstead and Wimbledon (University College School and King's College School,
Margaret Bryant points out that:

> King's, like London University, in its early period was more of a secondary school than a college of university standing, reminding us not only that adolescence was then an ambiguous and imperfectly defined stage of development, but of continuing difficulties in drawing boundaries between secondary and tertiary education. [King's] 'general course of study' designed for youths admitted at the age of sixteen constituted it as a kind of sixth-form college for the London area . . .[7]

In view of the importance later to attach to issues of state inspection, it is of some interest that in the 1870s the university itself decided to 'undertake the Examination and Inspection from time to time of any schools, other than primary, which may apply for such Examination or Inspection, provided that the cost to be incurred be paid when an application is made.' The Senate Minutes for 28 February and 26 April 1878 go on to say:

> There is a large and increasing number of schools, either bound by their legal constitution, or impelled by their teachers' desire of standing well with the public, to undergo annually the examination and criticism of some external authority, but unable at present to obtain the assistance of this kind which they require, and which the University is well fitted to supply.

The Examiner's reports would be wide-ranging:

> The Examiner will report . . on the work of each class; on the proficiency attained in respect of each subject of instruction; and on the methods, discipline, and general conditions of the School. His report will in the first instance be submitted to the Senate, by whom a copy will be communicated to the Governing body or to the Head Master or Mistress.

The first attempt to introduce a degree in Education was made in the same year, when the Senate received a letter from the College of Preceptors

[7] Margaret E. Bryant, *The London Experience of Secondary Education* (1986), p. 198. See also J. Springhall, *Coming of Age: Adolescence in Britain, 1860-1960* (Dublin, 1986).

urging 'the institution of a distinctive educational degree' which would assist in 'the recognition of the claims of Education to rank on a par with the other learned professions to which it is in no way inferior, either in the knowledge necessary for its successful pursuit, or in its importance to the community'.[8]

The College's request was unsuccessful, but further proposals were made in the following year by Miss Buss on behalf of the headmistresses and by Mr Fitch. In 1881 the University agreed to recommendations from a Committee to set up an examination in 'Theory and Practice of Teaching' which would be called a Teachers' Diploma.

The Day Training Colleges

In 1888 the Cross Commission proposed that in order to improve both the quantity and quality of elementary teachers, the universities should be drawn into their preparation, at that time the province of the forty-three residential training colleges supported by voluntary bodies (thirty of them by the Church of England) all but eight of which imposed religious tests. The proposal was somewhat tentative as far as the majority of the Commission's members were concerned, although more strongly supported by a minority. The Commission had been concerned about the moral dangers of training teachers outside the controlling atmosphere of a residential environment: 'Do you not find', they asked Dr Morrison [of the Free Church Normal School in Glasgow]:

'that the system of having the students, male and female, outside the college is attended with any moral danger?'. Their misgivings on hearing that men and women students left the college at the same time was only partially allayed by his assurance that they did so by different doors.[9]

Perhaps the Commission would have been happier with the arrangements for undergraduates that applied in the 1860s in Gower Street. Classes for women 'met and separated at the half-hours, that the men might be safely occupied at their coming and going, and the women were admitted by a side door to avoid the risks of crossing the quadrangle'.[10]

Schedule 116 of the Code of 1890 invited university institutions to apply for recognition as 'Day Training Colleges'. In June of that year King's College Council 'fully approved of the action of the Principal, in lodging an application for such status and before the year was out J.W. Adamson

[8] University of London, *Senate Minutes*, 26 April 1878.
[9] Richard Goodings, unpublished MS, p. 4.
[10] Bellot, quoted by Harold Silver and S.J. Teague (eds), *Chelsea College: a History* (1977), p. 19.

had been appointed as 'normal master' to run the new Department. Within five years the College had proposed, although initially without success, to start a department to train teachers for secondary schools.[11]

In the meantime, University College had in October 1891 opened its own Day Training Department.[12] It did not prosper. There were too few well qualified candidates. Its able first head, William Mitchell, resigned to become Professor of Philosophy and English Literature at Adelaide (where he was subsequently Vice-Chancellor and Chancellor). In 1894 its remaining students were transferred to the Strand.[13]

One other existing college of the University involved itself directly in teacher training during this period (although Birkbeck College had a close association with the London School Board's Graystoke Place Training College.) The Training Department at Bedford College, set up in 1892, had with Maria Grey College, the Cambridge Training College for Women and the centre attached to the Mary Datchelor School been one of the earliest centres for training women for secondary teaching.[14] The initial success of this work was in marked contrast to the relative failure of efforts to involve intending schoolmasters. In Bryant's words, 'It is hardly too strong a claim that the idea of a profession of secondary teaching was established by women'.[15]

By the beginning of the First World War there were sixty students in the Bedford Training Department. Its head was a Reader in Education in the University. In 1920 it was renamed the Department of Education. Yet two years later it was closed.

As Thomas has made clear in his valuable history of the Department,[16] one of the factors in its demise was the policy of the London County Council in concentrating graduate training in the London Day Training College, set up in Clare Market in 1902 on the recommendaton of its Technical Education Board to ameliorate a serious shortage of teachers in the capital. Bedford College had been as unhappy about proposals to introduce teacher training at the East London College (now Queen Mary College) as it was doubtful about the:

assumption of the London County Council that the London Day Training College is *the* University Education Department in London. . . . we beg respectfully to submit to the University that in the opinion of the Council of Bedford College it is essential to the national interest that centres other than

[11] F.J.C. Hearnshaw, *The Centenary History of King's College* (1929), p. 368.

[12] J.B. Thomas, 'University College London, and the Training of Teachers', *History of Education Society Bulletin*, 37 (1986).

[13] J.W. Adamson, 'The Department of Education' in Hearnshaw, *The Centenary History*.

[14] M.J. Tuke, *A History of Bedford College for Women, 1849-1937* (1939), p. 260.

[15] Bryant, *The London Experience*, p. 352.

[16] J.B. Thomas, 'Teacher Training at Bedford College, London, 1891-1922', *Durham/Newcastle Research Review*, 10:50 (1984), pp. 59-64.

the London Day Training College should be recognised as Departments of Education in the University of London, and that of these centres Bedford College claims the right to be placed among the most important. (Senate Minute 25 Feb. 1920)

In the event no Department of Education was set up at the East London College or in any other School of the University, and after Bedford closed its Department in 1922 and until Chelsea College became a School forty-five years later, King's remained the only Education Department within the University apart from the London Day Training College/London Institute.

The commemorative booklet published by the London County Council on the occasion of the Day College's removal in 1907 to new premises in Southampton Row (later to be used by the Central School of Arts and Crafts and now part of a consortium of Art institutes that the I.L.E.A. (calls and labels) The London Institute) records that the total output of teachers from all the existing training colleges in 1902 was only some 3,150. The London School Board alone needed 900.

Then as now, significant innovations in teacher education tended to be driven by shortage or surplus rather than by broader educational considerations. Goodings describes the position at the turn of the century as follows:

The shortage of teachers in London, long critical, had, by 1900, become desperate. The number required in that year was more than double the total output of the training colleges in the area. Among the women teachers in London over half were untrained and of those the majority possessed no attested qualifications for the work other than willingness to confess themselves women over eighteen years of age who could display satisfactory proof of vaccination. A teacher in this category was currently known as an Article 68.[17]

From the beginning, the University was a partner of the L.C.C. in the College's work. An administrative relationship was required to secure recognition by the Board of Education of suitability to train third-year students. But as Goodings records, it was personal links that really counted. The first Principal of the College, John Adams, was also appointed a Professor of the University. In the next year, the Master and Mistress of Method (Percy Nunn and Margaret Punnett) became Recognised Teachers.

The work of the Day Training College was initially of two main kinds. Students worked for degrees in arts and sciences in Colleges of the University and followed concurrent professional courses. And graduates were enrolled for the Teachers' Diploma of the University, predecessor to

[17] R. Goodings, (n.d.), unpublished MS.

the present Post-Graduate Certificate.

Lest we believe that the idea of a federal Institute of Education originated with the McNair Report of 1944, based on the post-1926 Joint Board arrangements, it is salutary to be reminded that in January 1905[18] the L.C.C.'s sub-committee on the Training of Teachers received a memorandum from its educational adviser, Dr William Garnett, which proposed that the Authority's need for teachers should be met by adding to the output of the London Day, the Graystoke College, and the Goldsmiths' Institute, that of four or five new colleges to be set up on the outskirts of London, which would form a system with the Principal of the London Day as its Director.

Goldsmiths' and Chelsea

The University had also taken a hand in the supply of teachers for the metropolis; in particular by the Academic Council's recommendation that the Goldsmiths' Institute, gifted unconditionally to it by the Goldsmiths' Company in 1904, should be used a training college for 400 students (later increased to 500) and for providing day and evening classes up to intermediate and degree levels and as a School of Art.[19] Few of the many thousands of excellent teachers that Goldsmiths' has sent out into the schools with London awards over the last eighty years have been aware that for practically the whole of that period the financial and constitutional relations between the College and the University have been a source of anxiety to both parties.

Finally, as far as institutional involvement is concerned, the existence of the external degree system facilitated the development of the London Polytechnics, many students of which took university courses, and which also provided post-certification study for teachers. Before the turn of the century the Principal of South-Western Polytechnic, later to be Chelsea College, was running 'research classes' in scientific subjects for school teachers, and the Polytechnic's early concern for the reform of science teaching was to be reflected in the College's leadership in science curriculum developments in the 1960s.

The scheme of study for the training course at Goldsmiths' had been drawn up by the University's Board of Studies in Pedagogy. The Board had been established following acceptance by the Commissioners responsible for the new statutes of a recommendation from a conference representing University College, King's, Bedford and the College of Preceptors, which had also proposed the introduction of a one-year course

---

[18] I.J. Hayward, 'The London County Council and the Training of Teachers, 1902-52' in *Studies and Impressions* (1952).

[19] A.E. Dean, 'Fifty Years of Growth' in D. Dymond, *The Forge, the History of Goldsmiths' College, 1905-1955* (1955).

of post-graduate training.[20] It was not until 1934 that the Board of Studies was renamed 'Education'. Sadly, its records appear to have been lost.

Education as a Field of Study

As Dent has commented, one of the major effects of the setting up of university based day training colleges was to give the study of education academic status.[21] Such study was of relatively recent origin in this country. In the book that Gordon identifies as the 'first textbook in the subject' the Revd R.H. Quick,[22] after restating Arnold's aphorism that: 'It is clear that in whatever it is our duty to act, these matters also it is our duty to study' goes on to say that:

> All study of this kind, however, is very much impeded by want of books. 'Good books are in German', says Professor Seeley. I have found that on the history of Education, not only good books but all books are in German, or some other foreign language.[23]

Until the later years of the century, the aspiring student of education was limited to not much more than editions of classical works of education theory and a number of handbooks of school management.[24]

The staff appointed to the new day training colleges, and some of those taking part in the better residential establishments, soon began to contribute to the literature of educational study from their own reading and experience – not only texts to be used as the basis of courses, but works of scholarship in the history and philosophy of education and in educational psychology. Students did not always immediately appreciate being taught in what later was to be spoken of as 'the atmosphere of research' but with mature reflection were ready to concede its value. Sir Ronald Gould, who for many years led the largest of our teachers' unions, wrote in his autobiography of his early experiences at Westminster College:

> The first lecture I attended ... was entitled 'The Psychology of the Unconscious'. As I was not quite eighteen, had never heard of psychology, could not even spell it correctly, and laboured under the delusion that 'unconscious' meant being knocked silly, I did not find this easy to follow. But

[20] Adamson, 'Department of Education', p. 512.
[21] Dent, *Training of Teachers*, p. 33.
[22] Peter Gordon, *The Study of Education: a Collection of Inaugural Lectures*, I (1980), p. ix.
[23] R.H. Quick, *Essays on Educational Reformers* (Cincinnati, 1887).
[24] A list of such texts can be found in D. Hamilton, 'A Note on Masters of Method and the Pedagogy of Nineteenth Century Schooling' in *History of Education Society Bulletin*, 29 (1982), p. 13. For additional references see J.B. Thomas, 'A Note on Masters of Method in the Universities of England and Wales' in *History of Education Society Bulletin*, 30 (1982), p. 27.

we had a remarkable staff of scholars and teachers, and despite this confusing start I was happy in my work and actually became particularly successful in psychology and the theory of education.[25]

The structure of the concurrent and the post-graduate initial training courses at the London Day and at King's was established early in their history as falling into four parts.

The first was the principles of education, which included elements of philosophy, logic, ethics, psychology and history applied to the processes of learning and teaching in schools.

Second was the 'practical development of the scientific principles and included the methods of teaching particular subjects'; generally speaking those which the candidate was studying or had studied in his or her degree course.

Third, for the aspiring elementary teachers, came work in subjects of the elementary curriculum such as nature study, P.E., music and manual instruction which was not included in their degree courses, and in which the College staff had thus to provide courses in content as well as methods.

Fourth, for both groups, came teaching practice.

These four elements, often categorised as Education, general and special method, curriculum subjects and school experience, remained mainstays of the initial training programme for many years. In 1962 the Chairman of the Board of Studies in Education was to write to the Dean of the Faculty of Arts that the Board 'has been conscious for several years that the Regulations for the Postgraduate Certificate in Education needed rather drastic revision and modification. Apart from minor alterations, these Regulations have now been in force for about forty years'.[26]

Without in any way wishing to diminish the importance of the changes that took place then, and those which have occurred since, the overall structure of initial training courses is still today very similar to that of the early years of the century. Balance, sequence and timing have been modified on many occasions. The content of what is taught within each element has been transformed. But the course is still structured in terms of aspects of Education, methods of teaching the subjects in which a student has specialised at university or polytechnic, other curriculum subjects, and practical teaching in schools. Arguments about how much time should be given to each element, its sequence in the programme and

[25] Ronald Gould, *Chalk up the Memory* (Birmingham, 1976), p. 25.
[26] University of London, Minutes of the Board of Studies in Education, Letter from Professor J.A. Lauwerys, included in Minutes for meeting on 26 November 1962 (AC/8/18/1/31).

relation to other aspects of the course, the choice of content and its organisation and the criteria for the assessment of competence and mastery, continues, as it has often done, to wax furiously in committee chamber, corridor and common room. But it does so within a framework defined not by academic fashion or theoretical conceptions of the teachers' role, but by the enduring realities of life in classrooms. Given that secondary school curricula are still largely subject based, and that children are still organised for learning in classes and schools, could it be otherwise?

The Federal Institute

There is another respect in which continuity between the work of the university and its institutions in teacher education half a century ago and today is apparent – that of scale. In 1931/2, when the L.C.C. handed over the London Day to the University and it formally began its life as the University of London Institute of Education, attendance at the main lecture courses on two mornings a week, which were open to all students in institutions with Recognised Teachers, already totalled 432: 226 from the London Day and the remainder from King's, Goldsmiths', Furzedown, Maria Grey and St Mary's.[27]

As early as 1921 the Senate had proposed that the University might conduct the Teachers' Certificate Examinations for the two-year training colleges in the London area as a body but this had been rejected by the college Principals.[28] The Departmental Committee on the Training of Teachers of 1926 used this London proposal as the basis for their recommendation that throughout the country, colleges should be associated with the universities by means of Joint Boards, which would take over examining responsibility from the Board of Education itself.

It has been suggested that the Committee would have liked to have gone further in bringing universities and colleges together,[29] but in the interests of realism limited themselves to suggesting that colleges might appoint university representatives to their governing bodies and that both could benefit from reciprocal teaching arrangements.

After much complex negotiation, agreement was reached in 1928 to group the colleges with thirteen universities or university colleges (which did not include Oxford and Cambridge, and left the colleges in the eastern counties temporarily in limbo, a problem that was to recur in another form a third of a century later when Cambridge initially declined to award a B.Ed. degree).

[27] Dixon, *The Institute*.
[28] Lance G. Jones, *The Training of Teachers* (Oxford, 1923).
[29] W.R. Niblett, W.R. Humphreys and J.R. Fairhurst, *The University Connection* (Slough, 1975).

The twenty training colleges associated with London were initially linked with University College, King's, King's College of Household Science (later Queen Elizabeth College), Bedford, L.S.E. and Birkbeck. Queen Mary College later linked with Shoreditch College to form a further group, and L.S.E. dropped out when its only college, Avery Hill, moved to another group. The University established a Training College Delegacy to provide general oversight, on which representatives of each of the group committees sat and which reported to Senate.

Within a very few years the Board of Education's 'Reference Committee', set up to monitor operation of the new scheme, was referring to the 'cumbrous London system' and the University was itself showing dissatisfaction with aspects of the examination arrangements. Niblett refers to a Board of Education document headed 'Violently Informal Interview with Representatives of London University'. Fears that the University might withdraw from the scheme were not realised, either at this time or after other meetings that took place during the thirties to resolve problems in relations between the Board, H.M. Inspectorate, the colleges and the universities. The Board resisted calls for an enquiry into teacher training, called for by R.H. Tawney, in *The Manchester Guardian* and by the N.U.T., but the issue was inflamed by the appearance in 1938 of a document entitled 'Suggestions by a Committee of H.M. Inspectors for a revised Scheme of Training in Training Colleges' which advocated a return to the central assessment of examinations and course work.

The War intervened, but in 1942, following the Government's 'Green Book' on post-war educational reform, it was decided to undertake a thorough enquiry into teacher training. Many of the problems in the relations of central government, the Inspectorate, the training institutions and the universities that it fell to Sir Arnold McNair and the ten members of his committee to examine seem very familiar.

The Institute and the New Pattern of Degrees

Willis Dixon's admirable short history stops at 1972. Something needs to be said, therefore, about the events that after 1973 caused an initial flowering in the range of the work of the associated colleges for which the University accepted responsibility and then, before the decade was out, to the end of the federal institute.

The overall 'blueprint for a new B.Ed. degree' (to quote a *T.H.E.S.* headline in May 1974) following the post-James White Paper of 1972, was provided by a working party convened by the U.G.C. and the C.N.A.A. and chaired by Sir Norman Lindop. Building on earlier work undertaken by a Dip.H.E. study group, a three-year programme for the ordinary degree and one of four years for honours was recommended – although some members thought that exceptional students might attain honours in three years.

Of particular relevance to what later happened in London was the group's suggestion that:

> Many institutions will want to provide courses on a unit or modular basis, with a choice of sets or units for different qualifications. This will make it easier for different students to make up different programmes and faciliate entry from other courses. It will also make it easier for students following different courses to take part of their programme together, which we regard as offering educational advantages.
>
> It is, however, essential that any progamme leading to any qualification should be coherent. There is obviously some conflict between the two aims but no doubt various ways of reconciling them will be devised.

Given the- anticipation that many universities would continue to participate in validation alongside the C.N.A.A. it is unsurprising that the group's curricular proposals were in very general form. Students should be 'brought to an understanding of some of the fundamental problems of education and its underlying philosophy'. The so-called 'four disciplines' approach to education studies was espoused.

The 1972 White Paper's proposal for fifteen weeks of practical teaching was accepted. A distinction was made between the subject studies that would need to be followed by intending secondary teachers and by those looking towards careers in the primary school, for whom 'a wider range of subjects' might be more appropriate.

The educational grounds on which modular or course unit degrees can be defended have mainly to do with the differing needs and potential of individual students and the flexibility that units offer in meeting course and programme objectives. It is no criticism of the architects of the new B.Ed. degree that, given the circumstances of the time, logistic and administrative considerations weighed as heavily as the educational in favouring a course unit structure. Course units enabled candidates for a variety of qualifications to be taught together in groups of a viable size, by staff already in post, and in sequence that could be varied from one entry group to another. Students' programmes could be assembled from the available units in whichever way seemed most appropriate to the types of work they would later be called upon to undertake.

London already had the means to hand. The definition of a course unit was taken over from well-established practice in the Science Faculty as 'being one third of the average amount of study which any adequately prepared student can reasonably be expected to complete in a year'. Set out on paper the whole scheme was both simple and logical. There was a strong will on the part of large numbers of people, not only in the Institute, but more widely throughout the university – and not least in Senate House – to make it work. Many of the senior staff of the Institute, both academic and administrative, enjoyed good relations with their counterparts in the

Schools. There were respected university teachers in many disciplines, perhaps most notably in the Sciences, keenly interested in the courses by which future teachers were prepared, and willing to devote time to their upgrading and improvement. Others, less happy about the direction in which developments were going, were nevertheless willing to give the new arrangements a fair wind, or at the very least to play an active role in order to avoid their worst fears being realised.

Some academics were influenced by what they took to be official support for the new B.Ed. Others still saw long term dangers to the universities themselves if the C.N.A.A. acquired by default a monopoly in public sector validation. Academics from the Schools sat on the governing bodies of colleges, and some had been involved in arrangements for the post-Robbins B.Ed. Nor was it irrelevant that many senior members of the university had children who were or had earlier been students of colleges in the federal Institute, and thus acquired either some loyalty to the colleges, or – and as far as a desire to participate was concerned, the effect was the same – a wish to see their academic work thoroughly reformed.

The part played by the 'University connection' in the post-war development of the Institute was also important in providing a driving force, especially the stamp put upon it by Dr Jeffrey and continued by Professor Elvin, for both of whom the federal arrangements were a safeguard of academic and professional freedom against the power of the state exercised through the Ministry of Education and the Inspectorate. The tradition thus established did much to ensure the willingness of Institute staff to endure working days and nights of exceptional length and intensity of effort in setting up the new schemes.

All these factors provided a powerful initial momentum which carried the new arrangements over many of the initial hurdles and difficulties. In the early stages, overt criticism and opposition were not much in evidence. There were no set piece debates, for example, of the kind that had occurred in Senate in 1945 when Dame Lillian Penson had clashed with Dr Jeffrey over the terms on which the University would accept A.T.O. responsibilites.

It was not long, however, before some of the structural weaknesses of the new arrangements began to manifest themselves. Greatly exacerbated by centrally imposed reductions on numbers and finance, these eventually brought into focus the latent doubts that had from the beginning existed in some quarters of the University about the wisdom of direct involvement in the public sector and finally destroyed the necessary basis of internal support for such work.

The main structural impediments to a continued university involvement in validation arose from the very characteristics that had always given the Institute strength in comparison with Education departments in other Universities, namely its relative independence of operation and academic decision making. Until the introduction of the 'old' B.Ed. there had been very little academic integration between the work of the Institute and that of the rest of the University – except, of course, with King's College, Chelsea College and Goldsmiths' through the Board of Studies in Education. The introduction of degree level studies in the colleges in subjects other than Education posed problems of academic control to which in 1967 the creation of a Faculty of Education was seen as the answer. Although university academics in relevant disciplines sat on the committees that controlled subject teaching for the old-style post-Robbins B.Ed., these committees remained part of the Faculty of Education structure.

Beginnings and Endings

The diversified degree programmes to be offered by the colleges, following the 1972 White Paper 'Education: A Framework for Expansion' raised new problems. Whatever the elegance and simplicity of the modular design, subjects offered elsewhere in the University were now to be taught in the colleges not only for a B.Ed. but also for a B.A. and B.Sc. This would require the direct involvement of specialist staff employed not by the Institute but by other Schools of the University, with no established personal or professional relations with the staff in Education.

In unitary universities, the members of the subject departments who helped to establish the new pattern of courses were on the same payroll, and sat on the same academic and faculty boards and committees as their Education colleagues. The independence of the Institute meant that university teachers in subjects other than Education who were involved in the approval and supervision of the new degrees were not members of the academic boards of the institution responsible for the coordination of courses and programmes. Furthermore, there were requests to offer degree programmes in subjects that were not taught elsewhere in the University, such as movement studies and dance. For these it had been necessary to invent a new degree altogether, the Bachelor of Humanities, later shortened to B.H.

All the new two-subject B.A., B.Sc. and B.H. degrees were to be within the Faculty of Education. Academic course control was to be exercised by twenty Joint Subject Committees, made up of one half members of the relevant Boards of Studies and one half Institute nominees. The control of degree programmes was undertaken by four Joint Degree Committees for the B.Ed., B.A., B.Sc., and B.Hum. respectively. At the pinnacle of this structure, which in the nature of academic life soon sprouted numerous ad hoc and specialist groups to cope with particular problems and issues, was a Joint Committee of the Institute and the Academic Council, which reported to the Council of the Institute, to the Academic and Collegiate Councils and thence to Senate. It was within this structure that formal negotiations took place on the introduction and approval of courses for the new degrees, and where some of the underlying structural weaknesses began to show themselves.

The willing cooperation of University Boards of Studies other than Education was crucial to the success of the new arrangements. A few were eager, many were willing, some were sceptical. For some Boards of Studies in Arts, the course unit degree constituted a real problem.

The hopes of the U.G.C./C.N.A.A. working party that 'no doubt' ways would be found to ensure coherence proved difficult to fulfil. A paper submitted to the Joint Committee in January 1975 argued that coherence could be tested in terms of concepts, methodologies, themes, problems, skills and occupational relevance, the last of these being a justification for almost any combination of subjects in the B.Ed. Denis Lawton has subsequently written that in the event the committees responsible for the various degrees had neither the time nor the expertise to make judgements about coherence:

> . . . and the practice grew of looking (briefly) at each programme on a purely *ad hoc* basis. Most programmes were passed unless specific objections on the grounds of incoherence or overlap of material were strongly established. Even if it had been possible to establish clear principles or criteria on such questions as coherence, it would have been extremely difficult to have 'policed' the system. Once again, the ethos of the cafeteria tended to dominate.[30]

To make matters worse, the complications of the new two subject degree programmes and the requirements of professional courses, soon made it necessary to seek approval for half and even quarter units, suggesting a dangerous fragmentation of effort and attention. None of this helped to convince those sceptical of course unit structures, especially on the Arts side, that the new arrangements offered opportunity for a progressive development and deepening of knowledge and understanding over the whole duration of the degree programme.

Another structural problem was the cost in administrative time and resources of servicing the complicated machinery of academic control. The nationally agreed validation fees were insufficient to meet the costs incurred by the university central administration (which had first call) and by the Institute, which by the end of the decade was estimated to be subsidising the process to the tune of £100,000 per annum.

Staff in the Schools of the University began to be anxious about the amount of time they were required to spend in Joint Committee work, including visitations to the colleges and the provision of *ad hoc* advice. Whilst college of education teachers were for the most part assiduous in their attendance at meetings, the demands on the time of university staff with their own students to teach and their own college's affairs to attend

[30] D. Lawton, 'The B.Ed.: a Case Study', *Higher Education Bulletin*, 2 (1982).

to, made it difficult for them to come to all the many meetings that had to be called, fuelling anxieties about lack of proper university control of courses and awards.

A further structural problem arose from the University's system of recognising teachers in associated institutions. Only those college teachers so recognised could play a full part in examining students and in the new structure of awards. Despite changes in the rules that in 1973 added to the existing academic and research requirements the possibility of being recognised as an 'able and valued teacher' of at least seven years standing, and in 1975 separated recognition for undergraduate teaching from that for post-graduates, only a minority of college teachers were able to secure recognition.

It says much for the University and for the colleges that, despite all the actual and incipient difficulties, and thanks to an enormous amount of administrative and committee work, including Board of Studies visits, a total of 480 B.Ed., thirty-six B.A., thirty-four B.Sc. and ninety-five B.H. programmes were approved for 1975 entries. By this time the original estimate of 15,000 candidates for the new London degrees was having to be drastically revised in the light of government decisions on numbers in higher education and the future of the colleges.

At the end of the 'sixties the federal Area Training Organisation had comprised the Institute of Education in Bloomsbury, the Departments of Education at King's, Chelsea and Goldsmiths', and thirty-one constituent colleges. Eleven colleges of the Cambridge Institute had also been temporarily admitted to enable students to take London examinations, since Cambridge did not offer the 'old' B.Ed. (The Cambridge arrangements came to an end with the disappearance of that award.) Over the next eight years, as a consequence of the policy of absorbing the colleges of education into the mainstream of higher education, of reductions in initial teacher training, and of financial exigency, the former constitutent colleges either closed their doors, merged with polytechnics or other post-secondary institutions that validated their courses through C.N.A.A., joined with each other to form new diversified institutions, or transferred their validation to other universities.

The Decision to Withdraw

The University's agreement to the new pattern of diversified degrees had been for a period of five years from 1975. By the time a sub-committee of the Academic Council came to review the position in 1979 there were only three institutions out of the original thirty-one, plus Goldsmiths' that were likely to wish to continue to offer London awards after 1980 (the Roehampton Institute of Higher Education, an amalgamation of four previously free-standing voluntary colleges; St Mary's College,

Strawberry Hill; and the West London Institute of Higher Education, which had been formed from Maria Grey and Borough Road Colleges). The original estimate of 15,000 students had been reduced to 2,450.

Having examined the historical background, the problems that had arisen in maintaining adequate academic control of the new course-unit degrees, and the Reports, some of them very critical, of thirty-one Review Panels set up by Boards of Studies to examine the standards achieved in each subject, the sub-committee discussed four possible courses of action: to continue the existing system of validation through the Institute of Education; to continue only after a drastic overhaul of the machinery of validation; to associate the three remaining institutions with a multi-faculty School or Schools of the University; or to terminate validation as soon as possible after 1980. This last course was the one which the sub-commitee finally recommended.[31]

The debate on the sub-committee's recommendation in the Council of the Institute, many members of which had been closely identified with the federal Institute over a long period before the changes initiated by the 1972 White Paper, was conducted in a sombre mood, lit by occasional flashes of anger at the way in which the University was ending a long and valued association. Some members wanted to carry the argument to the floor of the Senate, where it was believed there would be more support than in the Academic Council for the retention of academic links with the remaining colleges. To others, however, there seemed little point in fighting what had become a hopeless case. To end validation would not mean that King's, Chelsea and the Institute would be cut off from the work of the colleges. By means of advanced studies and research programmes and services for teachers they would continue to relate to the teacher education institutions in the region, including those that validated their courses through the C.N.A.A.

In a way not unknown in academic committees, the Council tea-break was utilised to draw up a statement which would satisfy those who wished to make their protest but would avoid dividing the Senate. This was duly agreed and included in the report of the Council to Senate on 12 December 1979, which also had before it the Academic Council's recommendation. No proposal to defer was made. There was little debate and no division. The federal Institute passed away quietly.

In this 150th anniversary year the University has examined the last few students registered for its awards in the former colleges of education. Those who feared that a large number of other universities would follow London in withdrawing from validation were proved wrong. Two of the three remaining London colleges linked with the University of Surrey (a

---

[31] *Report* of the Academic Council Sub-Committee on the Review of Courses at Colleges Associated with the Institute of Education, University of London *Senate Minutes*, 12 December 1979.

new venture on its part). In the country as a whole there were still in 1986 thirteen universities validating initial teacher education courses in public sector institutions. Many of them also cover B.A. and B.Sc. programmes and courses for other awards. There is a flourishing Conference of Validating Universities. It has recently been proposed that a number of smaller colleges should forge links of a new type with their neighbouring universities, whereby the latter take responsibility for a substantial part of B.Ed. students' subject studies. There are few signs of the feared C.N.A.A. monopoly. And even those who were anxious that the end of validation might see the University of London moving away from its traditional openness to a more enclosed, restrictive stance, have to consider the implications of the recent revival of the External system and the University's willing participation in discussions of credit transfer.

Both in respect of the Joint Board arrangements after 1928, and the federal Institute for the thirty years from 1945, the University of London led the way in establishing closer relations between initial teacher education and the universities, with profound effects on the status of the colleges, the development of the three year course, opportunities for staff actively to engage in curriculum development, the growth of advanced studies in education, the bringing of research and scholarship to bear on problems of the classroom, and, not least, the quality of each annual intake to the teaching profession. The University also played an important part in placing the control of teacher education on a broader base than that which had existed prior to 1928, and which, but for the willingness of the universities, led by London, to acept a modified version of McNair's 'Scheme A', might have returned in the early post-war period.

Departments and Disciplines

The belief seems to exist in some quarters that the organisation of educational studies into specialised areas of enquiry is a product of the early 'sixties. As far as the Colleges of Education were concerned that may well have been the case. The 1964 Conference organised by H.M.I. in Hull to which Richard Peters and Basil Bernstein made important contributions is regarded as a watershed. But specialisation in the study of education in London began much earlier, especially at the Institute.

In the early days, departments were identified mainly in terms of the subjects of the school curriculum or as catering for particular groups of students. Thus the Colonial Department was established in 1927, and a Department of Child Development in 1933. Within the heading of 'General Theory' there were by the mid 'thirties distinct courses in principles of education, educational psychology, history of education, comparative education, and the English educational system. History, administration and comparative education were all King's College specialities. By an agreement between King's and the London Day Training College in the mid 'twenties, King's staff contributed importantly to the Institute's teaching, especially at advanced levels.

In the initial training course for graduates as it was organised by the mid 'thirties, principles of education, teaching methods, psychology and hygiene, the English educational system and practical teaching were compulsory elements. In addition, students could choose either history of education, or comparative education or further educational psychology.

The second Chair to be founded at the London Day Training College, initially on a part-time basis, had been in psychology; its first occupant was Cyril Burt:

> His eight years at the London Day were in some respects the peak of Burt's career, He was at the height of his powers; he was in an environment that suited him admirably; his practical and academic duties were nicely balanced . . . But the most important feature of the college for Burt was the high status occupied by psychology . . . the groundwork had been laid by John Adams, Percy Nunn and Margaret Punnett . . . what Burt did was to bring psychology to life.[32]

Referring to the recent criticism of aspects of Burt's work, Hearnshaw goes on to say that during his time at the College:

> Burt may perhaps have been over confident, and prone to play to the gallery, but there was no taint of duplicity. No fair assessment of Burt's work and personality is possible unless this phase of his career is given its due weight.[33]

If the psychometric tradition pioneered by Burt, which as numerous authors have since shown was a major influence on pre-war and post-war official thinking about the organisation of primary and secondary education,[34] was to some extent continued by his successors, it was also from research at the Institute that came the greater understanding of the limitation of test validity and reliability which speeded the movement away from eleven-plus selection.

As the Institute's work in psychology broadened in scope during the post-war period, and the National Foundation for Educational Research, the precursor of which had been located at the Institute in 1938 with the help of Carnegie money, developed its testing activities, diversification into sub-specialities such as educational handicap, reading research and

[32] L.S. Hearnshaw, *Cyril Burt, Psychologist* (1979).

[33] *Ibid.*, p. 44. See also C.M. Fleming and J.A. Lauwerys, 'Advanced Studies and Research' in *Studies and Impressions*.

[34] R. Lowe, 'Eugenics and Education: a Note on the Origins of the Intelligence Testing Movement in England', *Educational Studies*, 6 (1980). Brian Simon, *Intelligence, Psychology and Education* (1971).

longitudinal studies replaced the early psychometric focus.

Initially created in 1933 to provide a base for the work of Susan Issacs, whose work at the Malting House School in Cambridge and whose writings on children were much admired by Percy Nunn, Child Development retained a separate existence from psychology until recent times, the two departments only coming together on the appointment in 1973 of a head (Professor W.D. Wall, formerly Dean of the Institute) who had not only been Director of the N.F.E.R., but who had published widely on child and adolescent development.

The department's original purpose was to train experienced teachers who would then become lecturers in infant methods and nursery school practice.[35] It represented a very different tradition from that of the Institute's psychologists, drawing heavily on the work of Freud and Dewey and providing an alternative research path to that being pursued elsewhere by Piaget.[36] Susan Issacs' involvement with the New Education Fellowship, in which over the years many London staff have been active, and her contribution to official studies (notably the 1933 Hadow Report on Infant and Nursery Schools), coupled with the work of her students, gave her ideas great influence on the development of the education of the young child, and in that sphere are still powerfully felt today.[37]

The process by which 'principles of education' and 'theory of education' were redefined and contributed to by specialist staff and departments, rather than defined as a single course (and the responsibility in the early days of a single individual) was accelerated by the appointment in 1947 of the first Professor in Philosophy of Education, Louis Arnaud Reid, whose last book was published in 1986 and who was still active in the Institute in the months prior to his recent death at the age of ninety-one.[38]

It was during the rapid growth of the 'sixties that the Institute began, through Richard Peters and his colleagues, to exert its formidable influence on the development of philosophy of education on an international as well as a national front, now often referred to as the 'London Line'.[39]

---

[35] Dorothy M. Gardner, 'Studies in Child Development', in *Studies and Impressions*.

[36] Margaret Roberts, 'A Celebration of the Centenary of the Birth of Susan Issacs', *International Journal of Early Childhood*, 17 (1985).

[37] The archive of the New Education Fellowship is now lodged in the Institute of Education Library.

[38] L.A. Reid, *Ways of Understanding* (1986).

[39] See David Aspin, 'The Philosophy of Education' in L. Cohen, L. Mannion and J. Thomas, *Educational Research in Great Britain, 1970-1980* (Slough, 1982), Robert Dearden, 'Philosophy of Education, 1952-1982' in *British Journal of Educational Studies*, XXXI (1983), and Frank Dunlop, review of L.A. Reid, *Ways of Understanding* in *Journal of the Philosophy of Education* (1986).

Sociology of Education in London owes it origin to the pre-war contribution that Karl Mannheim, then on the staff of the L.S.E., made to teaching at the Institute. He and Fred Clarke were both active in a Christian discussion group known as 'The Moot', which also numbered T.S. Eliott, A.D. Lindsay, Walter Moberly, Walter Oakeshott and Geoffrey Vickers among its members.[40] Mannheim transferred from L.S.E. to the Institute as Professor of the Sociology of Education in 1946, but died the following year.[41] Professor W.O. Lester Smith held the Chair from 1949 to 1953, and was succeeded as head of department by Jean Floud, who followed the same path as Mannheim in transferring from L.S.E. In collaboration with her former colleagues and students, she contributed signficantly to empirical sociological studies in several aspects of education.

Once again, however, it was the expansion of the 'sixties that provided the opportunity for the Institute to extend its influence in this field, and for the new head of department, Basil Bernstein, to establish a strongly funded research base and to recruit staff who would themselves do much to extend the subject into colleges and departments of education within and beyond the federal Institute itself.

In sociology of education London has not only exerted major influence on the development of an educational specialism but it has been able to support theoretical work of great importance, not only to education, but to the parent discipline itself.

The Colonial Department, initially founded to offer courses of training to those about to teach and administer in the British Empire, has since, in reflection of the changing world without, gone through three more name changes (Department of Education in Tropical Areas, then Department of Education in Developing Countries, and today, following a merger with the Department of Comparative Education, Department of International and Comparative Education). Its activities have done much over the years to ensure that not only are the Institute's name and activities known in every continent, but that many of the men and women who today hold senior educational appointments in Anglophone Africa, in the old Commonwealth and in many other countries are its graduates or associates. This is something to which many other Departments of the Institute, which has from the beginning had a large proportion of overseas students among its full-time degree candidates, and the Departments at King's, Chelsea and Goldsmiths', have also made a prominent contribution.

In this respect it is also opportune to remember that the Scheme of Special Relations, by means of which African Universities were able in

---

[40] The Moot archive is also held in the Institute of Education Library.

[41] C. Loader, *The Intellectual Development of Karl Mannheim: Culture, Politics and Planning* (Cambridge, 1986).

their fledgling years to teach for London awards,[42] and the External Degree system, which is still flourishing, have been important sources of qualified teachers and senior staff in both developing and developed countries.[43]

The many connections that from the earliest days Institute and King's College departments and academics had with educationists and institutions overseas, and the large numbers of foreign visitors who passed through London, had always given the University's work in Education an important international and comparative flavour. In 1943 the Faculty Board in Arts and the Academic Council, on recommendation from the Institute, gave high priority to an appointment to a Chair of Comparative Education. King's had provided the lead for such work, initially by Nicholas Hans and Winthrop Young, who used the Year Book of Education, first published in 1932 and edited by Eustace Percy, as a vehicle to drive the subject forward. The first occupant of the Chair when it was established in 1947 was Joseph Lauwerys, originally appointed to the Institute as a scientist, but who had developed increasingly strong international interests during the 'thirties and the war years.

The first Doctorate in Comparative Education was awarded in 1948 (to William Connell). Work in comparative education at King's under Edmund King developed along lines distinct from and complementary to those of the Institute, where Brian Holmes did much to focus attention on the importance of the comparative study of policy making and the methodology of the subject.

History of education was one of the earliest distinct elements of educational study in courses of initial teacher training, partly no doubt due to the historical interest of some of the pioneers in the field, such as Adams at the Day Training College and J.W. Adamson at King's. With its established Chair in History of Education, it was King's that led the way in developing this aspect of the study of education in London. Cooperation between the Institute and King's, especially in advanced courses and research supervision, has always been a feature of London's work in this subject, but has been affected (although perhaps less than elsewhere) by the relative decline in the place of history of education as a distinct element in initial teacher education, popular though it remains with first degree and research candidates.[44]

Curriculum and Foundations

In its submission prepared in connection with the 1965 U.G.C visit, the Division of Humanities reminded the Institute of a problem that had never been far below the surface of its academic organisation:

[42] Bruce Pattison, *Special Relations* (1984).

[43] Dixon, *The Institute*, pp. 28, 57.

[44] Richard Aldrich, 'History of Education at the Crossroads', *The Historian*, 11 (1986).

It has been stated at various times that the structure of the Institute should, by policy, be one of 'vertical segments' and not 'layers' i.e., it should be an organisation primarily of departments operating both at initial training and advanced level. If departments concerned with schools and students continue to be neglected, while those not directly so concerned are further enlarged, the Institute will have to renounce this policy altogether, and this would result, in our view, in a serious dimunition of the contribution it can make to education.

There are overtones here of the familiar divisions of interest between 'Foundations' and 'subject' departments in University Schools of Education in the United States or in English and Welsh Colleges of Education, There are also important differences, arising from the wholly graduate status of the student body at the Institute, King's and Chelsea, and, from the earliest days – higher degrees were offered from 1916 – the involvement in advanced work of many of those originally appointed because of their 'curriculum' interests.

If over the years through its work in the psychology, philosophy, sociology, history and administration of education, the University has made highly significant contributions to the way in which we think about educational policy and practice, it has been equally influential in the content, pedagogy and modes of assessment of the various subjects that feature in the school curriculum. The way in which Jimmy Britten, Nancy Martin and Harold Rosen influenced the teaching of English was only one example of how Institute, King's and Chelsea staff partnered the professionals in developing new curricula, new methods of teaching and new approaches to assessment. During the 'seventies the University was able to establish Chairs or to appoint personal professorships in such fields as science education, mathematics education, English education, music education, geography education, in English for speakers of other languages and in curriculum studies. Many of these titles remain unique within the British university system.

Given the growing importance of science in the school curriculum, it is unsurprising that each of the London institutions concerned with the study of education offered both initial and post-experience courses in this field. The most striking developments since the establishment of the Faculty were at Chelsea College, where the Centre for Science Education was set up in 1967 under the leadership of Kevin Keohane. The Centre's initial location – in a former cigarette factory in Pulton Place – was hardly consistent with the pioneering M.Ed. in health education which, along with awards in science and mathematics education, represented a new departure for London; a move was soon made to Bridges Place – another factory, but with a better resonance, as it had formerly been used for manufacturing electronic devices.

The Chelsea Centre soon established a reputation not only for pioneering Master's courses but also for curriculum research in many areas of science and mathematics education, and attracted large research grants. With the coming into existence of the new King's College (K.Q.C.), the former King's Department and the Chelsea Centre have become the K.Q.C. Centre for Educational Studies, which with some thirty-eight staff, is now located at 552 King's Road, the former home of the College of St Mark, which in around 1830 was the second teacher training institution to be set up in this country.

The University has also had a leading part in developing the overall study of the school curriculum. In specific curriculum fields such as art and design, economics, media studies, religious education, social studies and modern languages, the University also has departments and groups actively engaged in teaching at both initial and advanced levels and in research. It has been able to initiate important work in multi-cultural education, in statistics and computing, in curriculum analysis and in cross curricula studies of primary and secondary education, the sixteen to nineteen age group, and further and higher education. Indeed, in looking at the range of courses, departments and units that now feature in the Institute's, K.Q.C.'s and Goldsmiths' prospectuses, it is difficult to find any aspect of contemporary educational provision or any issue of contemporary educational debate that is not provided for by someone, somewhere.

The perceptiveness, professionalism, knowledge, dedication and commitment of the many hundreds of staff who have over the years served the University in this field have been a necessary but not a sufficient condition for the influence that London has exerted. Such efforts have been given focus and direction by the ideas generated and disseminated by a much smaller number of people, most of them past and present appointed teachers of the University.

Emerson says somewhere that there is no history, only biography. And it is impossible to look at the history of the study of Education in the University of London without being struck by the importance of the contribution of outstanding men and women who have over the years offered the intellectual and institutional leadership that has given the Institute, King's, Chelsea and Goldsmiths' their distinctive place in the consciousness of the educated teacher.

In these democratic times, when many departments and units have non-professorial heads and the emphasis is on the team rather than the individual, it is well to remind ourselves that it is on the ability of a university to identify, to attract and to hold those who can make a distinctive contribution in the realm of ideas that the future excellence and reputation of its work in Education, as in other fields, depends.

Unity and Diversity

Questions about how intellectual effort is differentiated and integrated are among the most important to be asked and answered in organising studies in a particular field of enquiry. The answers that emerge are reflected in the designations and activities of, and relationships between, the faculties, schools, departments, centres, areas, units and other groups through which intellectual effort is organised, and in ongoing arguments about the distribution of resources, 'rationalisation', 'restructuring' and all the other processes of academic change.

The popular assumption of academic conservatism usually fails to distinguish between rates of change in structure, in process and in content. Although such changes are obviously related, they do not move in accordance with similar timetables. In any field in which active research is underway, the content of courses and programmes, at all levels, is continuously modified by increments of knowledge and understanding and irregular paradigm shifts. Academic processes – pedagogy, curriculum, assessment – usually change more slowly. What matters is that they be open to revision in the light of validated changes in knowledge and altered external conditions.

On the whole, institutional structures are resistant to change, serving to protect settlements of past conflicts of interest and providing a more or less ordered framework within which current differences can be resolved. Many centuries-old organisationsal features of the ancient universities remain firmly in place, despite the revolutions that have occurred in what is taught and researched upon in these institutions. On the other side, the sweeping structural changes that took place in the organisation of initial teacher preparation in the 'seventies were not accompanied by any very fundamental modification in course content and academic process.

At each stage of the development of educational studies in London, concern has been expressed about lack of integration, the dangers of fragmentation, and the need for some kind of synthesis. Over the years many ways have been tried to bring staff in different specialisms closer together and to focus the formidable academic talent of the Institute and the constitutent departments upon the solution of educational problems. Inter-disciplinary seminars; the two-subject Master's degree; joint inter-departmental supervision of research students; the staff residential weekend; 'centres' that draw upon staff from several departments; both piecemeal and radical departmental reorganisation, are all illustrative of such effort. Valuable as these have been, there are educators both within and beyond London who regard the continuing separation of departments and units as a problem and regret the lack of coordinated research programmes, the small amount of inter-citation between disciplines, and the absence of a single unifying concept of teacher professionalism, such as they believe exist in the training of, for example, doctors and lawyers.

The work of any complex organisation is facilitated by the existence of shared purposes and symbols. But it is a mistake to look for a high level of integration in bodies as oriented to research and advanced studies as the Institute and the Centre for Educational Studies at the 'new' King's College. Insofar as medical parallels are appropriate, a great deal of the fundamental research carried out in medical schools and research units is the province not of doctors but of physicists, chemists, biologists, biochemists, biotechnologists, electronics specialists and others whose training is other than in medicine.

In any event, the degree of fragmentation that exists in educational studies in London may have been exaggerated. There are few single-discipline departments among the fifteen into which the Institute has over the past few years reorganised itself. Much of the funded research currently being undertaken requires inputs from more than one area of educational study. The more or less sharp distinction between those departments whose work focussed mainly on subjects taught in schools, and those concerned mainly with advanced studies and research in the so-called foundations, has with the appointment of Professors and the growth of research in the former curriculum subjects become very much less clear.

To borrow structuralist terminology, some aspects of the 'reality' of the study of Education may indeed be functions of its internal textual practice, conducted within a discourse largely disassociated from the power relations inherent in the life of other educational systems and institutions. But the relative autonomy that such disassociation confers enables a language to be provided in which possibilities for change can be explored in ways unthinkable within more tightly integrated and ideologically more coherent systems. Hence, of course, the attacks of totalitarians of both left and right on what they see as the pernicious influence of universities on education – and the need for this and other universities to foster and maintain the scope and quality of the work they do in this sphere.

Towards 2036

Fifteen years ago there was a great deal of gloom in the air about the future of teacher education in general and teacher education in the universities in particular. Some aspects of the James Report and the subsequent government White Paper had not been well received by teacher educators. The difficulties encountered within the university in establishing a new pattern of validated awards against a background of rapid institutional change in the colleges made it difficult to be sanguine about the future.

Yet these developments had little real impact on the majority of those teaching and undertaking research within King's, Chelsea and the Institute of Education. With the financial restrictions imposed on universities from the mid 'seventies there were fewer new appointments. Some vacancies were left unfilled and staff student ratios worsened. But post-graduate initial training numbers were largely maintained. P.G.C.E. courses for primary teachers were initiated. The range of post-experience and advanced courses increased. Overseas student recruitment, hit by the impact of full-cost fees, was through the efforts of staff soon quite restored; in this as in so many other respects, the University's international status and long standing professional connections have stood it in good stead. Research income continued to increase. The expenditure of the Institute from research grants and contracts as a percentage of total expenditure is comparable to that of some science-oriented institutions. The K.Q.C. Centre's five year average is higher than that of any other single department in the College. London University alone accounts for some 30 per cent of all the money spent by English and Welsh universities on educational research, and getting on for 40 per cent of all university postgraduates in Education are registered here. And, not least, the Institute is likely to be the first institution within the University to receive its own Royal Charter in the post sesquicentennial period.

There can be no certainty that any educational institution will still have its present size, shape and pattern of organisation fifty, fifteen or, such is the nature of the revolution into which we have been backing recently, even five years ahead. What is certain is that education in all its forms will remain a major and indeed increasingly important activity of societies at all stages of their development, that institutions will be needed that educate and train men and women for such service, and that curiosity and uncertainty about the nature of what it is we are about when we set out to educate will still need to be satisfied by means of research and enquiry. There is no doubt, therefore, about the continuing importance of the work that this University undertakes under the auspices of its Faculty of Education. Few universities in the world, and none in Britain, can claim to have played such a significant part in the development and dissemination of educational ideas and practices as London University.

Index

Abbreviations used in the index (except those given in full in the index entries themselves)

B.Ed.	Bachelor of Education	L.S.E.	London School of Economics [and Political
H.M.S.	Hospital Medical School		Science]
I.C.	Imperial College	Q.M.C.	Queen Mary College
K.C.	King's College	U.C.H.	University College Hospital
K.Q.C.	King's, Queen Elizabeth	U.C.H.M.S.	University College Hospital Medical School
	and Chelsea [College]	U.C.L.	University College London